THE
AUDACITY
OF
INEZ
BURNS

STEPHEN G. BLOOM

Regan Arts.

NEW YORK

Regan Arts.

New York, NY

The names Corinne Patchen, Anna Thompson, and Señor Ortega have been substituted for real names. All other persons described herein are identified by their true full names, except where only nicknames are used. Various encounters and conversations have been re-created for the sake of clarity, insight, and continuity. Observations have been drawn from a variety of sources, including interviews, historic records, directories, family correspondence, genealogical materials, newspapers, census data, government archives, as well as public and private documents.

First Regan Arts hardcover edition, February 2018.

Library of Congress Control Number: 2017937181

ISBN 978-1-68245-009-3

Cover design by Richard Ljoenes
Interior design by Nancy Singer

Image credits, which constitute and extension of this copyright page, appear on page 427.

Printed in the United States of America

10 9 8 7 6 5 4 3 2 1

Endpapers: San Francisco in ruins following the earthquake and fire of 1906.

This page: The sun shining through clouds on the San Francisco Bay, prior to the construction of the Golden Gate Bridge, ca. 1902.

FOR IRIS

CONTENTS

AUTHOR'S NOTE

Once upon a time, I was a reporter who had the good fortune to be assigned to San Francisco as a correspondent for an out-of-town newspaper. As such, it fell upon me to cover breaking news, but between earthquakes, grisly crimes, and internecine city politics, most of my dispatches fortunately were accounts of how the city's culture, geography, and commerce affected the seven million people who called the Bay Area their home. It was sort of a glamorous job, and I fancied myself as a man-about-town, writing nuanced stories urbane readers would want to devour every morning.

Despite a dream job that had its origins when I hitchhiked cross-country to San Francisco and stayed there for college and much of my professional career, by 1992 I was looking to leave the daily grind of newspaper work. My love affair with San Francisco continued to blossom, but writing about it for a newspaper had not. Most reporters of my generation shared a similar complaint. There was less room to tell stories that mattered—dispatches that in fifty years would be viewed as prescient enough to have marked a pivotal social trend. As newspaper graphics got more colorful, the stories turned more black and white. Dispatches that got the best play were short, upbeat, and zippy. Even back then.

So when a friend suggested that I contact a woman who had "some weird kind of story" about her grandmother, I jumped at the opportunity. Reporters get tips like that all the time, and I was eager to see what my friend's friend was offering.

On a Tuesday morning, I met Caroline Carlisle at a Richmond District coffee shop and what she told me got my attention instantly. It was the story of her grandmother, Inez Burns, a San Francisco abortionist who lived from 1886 to 1976.

Inez had bribed scores of public officials and cops to stay in business, performed tens of thousands of illegal abortions on rich and poor alike, and had become the worst-kept secret not just in San Francisco but throughout California. Inez, Caroline told me, lived a dazzling, risqué life and played it out to the fullest, becoming one of the wealthiest self-made women in California. Inez met her match in a young and opportunistic district attorney by the name of Edmund G. (Pat) Brown, who would eventually become governor, and if kismet had swung his way, president of the United States. Inez and Pat became lifelong foils, cat and mouse. Or mouse and cat. Depending on who was taunting whom and when the taunting took place.

I knew Inez's story wasn't for a newspaper. Journalism is about the here and now, and this was a saga about a sliver of untold history. Still, it seemed like a forgotten story of how an extraordinary woman and a singular city commingled. Inez's rags-to-riches life paralleled the trajectory of California. Her exploits were a metaphor of post–World War II and the race for America to become what it is today. I was instantly hooked.

But when I pitched the story to book agents and editors, I got eye rolls: Who'd want to read about an abortionist, even one who hobnobbed with the rich and famous? Too risky, too contentious. The less revealed about Inez, the better, they told me.

No one encouraged me to plumb Inez's scandalous life. They waved aside her story as though it were a foul odor defiling the air. "Let sleeping dogs lie" was an expression I heard not just a few times. "Stop your research," others offered more emphatically. "No good shall come of this." What exactly were they scared of? I put Inez's story on hold, one more in a long string of leads that reporters wish they could write but never get to.

Until I found myself writing a feature about a boomlet in San Francisco real estate development along the waterfront.

That's when I happened to call Corinne Patchen, a smart San Francisco native and gadfly in her mid-sixties. Corinne had the uncanny ability to put anything contemporary into context and leaven it with just the right amount of wisdom and insight. Corinne gave me the astute quotes I was looking for to finish my story, I thought, with a small degree of eloquence.

After I finished the interview with Corinne, I thought to bring up the name Inez Burns. Corinne had a steel-trap memory. That's why I had called her in the first place. She could recall lines from obscure books and plays she'd read twenty-five years earlier. Corinne was always popping in and out of scores of different-tiered

San Francisco social circles. She knew everyone who'd ever been anybody and had the gossipy stories to prove it. She also was just about the right age to have known Inez—or, at least, to have known about her.

"Does the name Inez Burns ring a bell?" I asked tentatively.

Chatty Corinne paused, a pause that seemed to last forever.

Then she dropped the phone. From my end, I heard the landline's receiver skittering across the floor.

"Corinne, are you still there?"

After several seconds, Corinne followed the accordion cord to the phone and picked it up.

"Oh my," she said in a barely audible voice. "I haven't thought about Mrs. Burns in more than forty years."

I wasn't sure where this was going, but I noticed a ridge of goose bumps popping up on my forearms.

Corinne took a deep breath and began her story slowly and precisely.

In 1946, Corinne and a soldier met at a USO dance on Mission Street and took an immediate liking to each other. He was to ship out in a week, and over the next five days they spent as much time together as the soldier's training schedule allowed. On his last night in San Francisco, they ate dinner at Flor d'Italia. They split a bottle of Chianti, and after their meal, drank two espressos and shared a cannoli. Perhaps they had too much wine, perhaps they didn't. Corinne and the soldier returned to her studio apartment on Russian Hill, where the soldier spent the night. Six weeks later, Corinne discovered she was pregnant.

Corinne did not seek to contact the soldier. Theirs had been no more than a weeklong fling. Corinne had her whole life ahead of her. Marriage to any man, much less a soldier she hardly knew, was the last thing on her mind.

A family friend who was a North Beach attorney in San Francisco directed Corinne to Inez Burns. "Talk to her. She'll help you. If that's what you want."

"I remember going to her Guerrero Street house and sitting in the front room, a beautiful, elegant room," Corinne told me as though recalling a vivid dream from long ago. "And I remember meeting Inez, a pleasant, kind woman, who sat down in the parlor with me.

"The first thing she asked was, 'Do you want this baby?'

"Yes!" Corinne recalled blurting out without a moment's hesitation.

Inez smiled and then paused. "Well, dear, then you don't belong here," she said.

"She took me by the hand and showed me the door. And that was the last I ever saw of Mrs. Burns."

Today, Corinne's only son is seventy-one, and he has no idea he almost was never born.

There was a moment of silence between Corinne and me, each of us registering the magnitude of my inquiry. Then Corinne asked anxiously, "You won't be using my name, will you?"

Before I could answer, she added, "Please, please don't use my name in anything you write about this. *Please.*"

I assured her I wouldn't, a promise I've kept for twenty-five years, and why I've used a pseudonym here, one of two in this book.

"In San Francisco then, we looked out for each other," Corinne said. "We protected each other. There was nothing sinister about Inez. She was like your grandmother." We talked some more and I thanked Corinne.

I hung up and promptly wrote my story on land development for the newspaper. But the conversation shook me, as I'm sure it shook Corinne. Her comments piqued my interest once again in Inez Burns. The agents and editors who had told me to drop my fascination had to be wrong.

Delving into Inez's life and times, I discovered that she had performed a staggering fifty thousand abortions over a forty-year period. Neither a doctor nor nurse, she was known for her clean, hygienic and sterile clinic on lower Fillmore Street, performing abortions on as many as twenty women a day. From Inez's years as a young unmarried mother toiling in a Pittsburgh pickle factory to her starring role as a national fixer for women "in trouble," she was an outrageous, larger-than-life figure, a kind of combination of Wallis Simpson, Mae West, Margaret Sanger, and Coco Chanel.

Was Inez a prescient, indefatigable advocate for women—or an opportunistic femme fatale hustler?

It took almost a quarter of a century to answer that question. Inez became a siren that never stopped calling me.

Several years ago, I set out to find Corinne again, and I was heartened to discover that she was still alive at ninety-three. Corinne and her only son now lived together, and it was he who answered the phone when I called. After exchanging pleasantries, he handed the phone to his mother. Corinne's speech had grown labored and halting over the intervening years. We lamented all the time that had passed. "Where'd it all go?" Corinne asked wistfully.

When I brought up Inez Burns once again, Corinne paused as she had during our last conversation. A tantalizing ten seconds elapsed without a response. This time, Corinne didn't drop the phone but said she'd have to think about the name. This time, she said, nothing came to mind.

Whether Corinne was concealing a memory in deference to her son, or whether her once-keen recollection had now grown foggy, is something I'll never know for sure. I certainly felt mighty intrusive, inquiring about the woman who had almost terminated Corinne's pregnancy, when her son was within shouting distance of her. We chatted some more, wished each other well, and said goodbye.

Between my first and last conversation with Corinne, I've spent tens of thousands of hours accessing court records, government documents, and newspaper archives, along with interviewing the precious few still alive who knew Inez. Her story has stayed with me as few others have. Descending into Inez's checkered life became a detective story that matched anything Dashiell Hammett ever could have written. Just when I thought I knew all there was, another curiosity tempted me to go deeper.

Inez is a dark and jagged puzzle piece of lost Americana. History seeks to understand heroes and villains, but it has little interest in those in between. Almost all traces of Inez Burns today have been obliterated, as though she never existed. Like the sea, which seeks to cover everything in its wake, time has removed any remnants of Inez's impact. Newspaper clippings about her are yellowed, in the process of disintegrating into dust. Today Inez is a nonperson.

But if, as actress Tallulah Bankhead once observed, "it's the good girls who keep the diaries; the bad ones never have the time,"[1] then Inez's story was one that screamed to be told.

Pierce-Arrow luxury car, 1936.

PINKY, BOOTSIE, and FATS

Whenever Inez and Joe Burns threw a party at their sprawling eight-hundred-acre ranch in the Santa Cruz Mountains, it was an event to remember. Scoring an invitation to one of her gala soirees might not have meant you were on society's A-list, but it did mean you had a rakish value to the richest abortionist in California and her ex-politician husband. This particular bash was supposed to have been a celebration of Inez's acquittal from abortion charges, not the hung jury that she got. At least, Inez hadn't been convicted, so that was something worth celebrating. And who knew what would happen at the next trial—or even if there was going to be a next trial.

So why not? Inez and Joe never needed an excuse to throw a party.

Burns Ranch was a Great Gatsby–like compound with servants, cooks, horse groomers, and trainers. Located forty miles south of San Francisco, near Kingston Creek in La Honda, a rugged outpost along State Route 84, the ranch was several hairpin turns down the blacktop from the Log Cabin School for Boys and a raucous bar by the name of Apple Jacks. Burns Ranch was a boarding and training facility for thoroughbreds, including a gelding by the name of Sun Portland, who had just won big at Santa Anita, Del Mar, Belmont, and Bay Meadows.

At the ranch that evening in May 1946, Inez had invited the usual complement of cops, physicians, attorneys, Hollywood entertainers, and not just a few well-dressed, well-coiffed call girls. Inez's old friends, Mabel Malotte, a popular San Francisco madam, and Nelly Gaffney, the owner of a couture women's clothing store on Post Street, were there, as were Inez's courtroom defendants, Mabel Spaulding, Myrtle

Ramsey, Musette Briggs, and Joe Hoff. Inez's oversize lawyer, Walter McGovern, came with his three chins, as did crooked private investigator Pop Aureguy with his thin, wormy lips and a few wispy threads that went for hair. Inez's three-hundred-pound aide-de-camp, Fats Selmi, a kind of consigliere for issues large and small, wandered through the crowd to make sure no one was having *too* good a time. A harried and toothless cook by the name of Bootsie grilled rib eyes and corn on the cob on the stone patio behind the main house, while the "Latin Lowdown on Swing," Joaquin Garay, strolled among the guests, serenading any señorita or señora who smiled at him. Joaquin's big break had come in Frank Capra's 1934 hit movie, *It Happened One Night,* starring Clark Gable and Claudette Colbert, when he sang "The Man on the Flying Trapeze."

Everyone seemed to be having a grand time, eating but mostly drinking, sitting at linen-covered tables spread out on the rolling lawn. The burnt-orange sun had set and a swath of moist fog was beginning to roll in from the Pacific. By now, men on the terrace were pulling out Montecristo Especiales, and puffs of flames lit up their faces as trails of gray smoke rose, curled, and disappeared into the evening air.

The headliner that evening was a young comedian named Pinky Lee, who would soon have everyone in stitches. Pinky hadn't made it big yet. Television would usher him into millions of American living rooms, but that wouldn't be until the mid-1950s. At the time, Pinky was still a burlesque comic with impeccable timing and a bawdy sense of humor.

Pinky came up with a skit that had everybody laughing hysterically, even those who weren't in their cups already. Men were slapping their knees and women held their hands to their chests as though it would help them breathe through their side-splitting laughter. Pinky wore a silly polka-dot jacket, cutoff tie, and short baggy pants. He was singing an impromptu ditty about San Francisco district attorney Pat Brown, Inez's nemesis:

There once was a rat named Pat,
This cat by the name of Brown.
Who wore a hat he thought was his crown.
With a bat he sicced his man Lynch
Only to learn that it wouldn't be a cinch
To take down Inez, our lovable wench.

The crowd roared, clapping and hooting, and then joined in with a chorus of what would become Pinky's trademark: *Oooooh! You make me so mad!* The stanzas soon got raunchier and raunchier, but no one expected less.

Inez was there to throw the dice.
But Pat got his carrot stuck in a vice
With Inez there to give his manhood a slice,
Only to find there was nothing much to suffice.[1]

By the fifth round, Pinky had everybody rolling on the lawn, laughing uproariously under the flickering lights strung like in a Tuscany vineyard.

Comedian Pinky Lee, who rose to fame with his children's television program in the 1950s, was a frequent entertainer at the Burns Ranch.

Inez stood with Joe, both of them gazing out at the multitude of their friends, spread in a semicircle on this magnificent estate. It was as much a time to commemorate Inez's success as to mark whatever lay around the corner. As Pinky played to the crowd, which was all his by now, Inez smiled and nodded. These were her intimates and supporters. Her people. Not the twelve strangers deciding her fate. What did *they* know? Would a judge really send a sixty-year-old woman to prison?

Inez felt a chill and buttoned up the soft yellow cashmere sweater she had draped over her shoulders.

Ever since she was eighteen, Inez had been an unsung savior to women, an invisible hand mending marriages, families, and reputations. All the while, she'd been the keeper of fifty thousand secrets. From incest and adultery to mothers with too many mouths to feed, Inez had fixed the consequences of ill-advised romances that never should have been. Industrialists sent their mistresses to her, politicians directed their "secretaries" her way, Hollywood moguls steered leggy starlets to her clinic, madams brought in girls in trouble, and, oh yes, every once in a while a nun pressed the buzzer to Inez's front door. Just because you wore a black-and-white habit didn't mean you weren't like everyone else. "Natural desires" was how Inez put it. Everyone has them, you know.

Mothers, daughters, sisters, wives. Every woman. Contrary to any salacious notion about who might find herself in an abortion clinic, the majority of Inez's patients were neither rich nor famous, single nor promiscuous. Most were married. Many were women whose husbands didn't have a clue that their wives were pregnant, and never would. Even if Inez wasn't officially recommended by the San Francisco Chamber of Commerce, she was endorsed by nearly everyone in town. She was a public utility, only a lot more reliable.

Why wasn't in Inez's lexicon. That was none of her business. She didn't get in this line of work to counsel women. In an era when women had few rights, Inez gave them the most basic.

Word circulated, as it always does, when what you do, you do exceedingly well and your particular skill is highly specialized, in demand, and illegal. Women came from around the corner and across the nation. Whether they arrived in San Francisco by bus, automobile, train, ferry, or plane, they'd discreetly ask other women, sometimes strangers on the street, "Know where that Burns woman lives?"

Through an underground woman-to-woman network, they'd end up at one place—327 Fillmore Street, just south of San Francisco's lively Jewish district, filled with butchers, bakeries, markets, synagogues, theaters, and kosher restaurants.

At the time, the prevailing standard in San Francisco and other American cities when it came to abortion was that if the woman undergoing the procedure didn't die, the police looked the other way. Let the abortionists do what they do, as long as no woman gets killed or maimed in the process. A necessary evil with two mandatory components: the services had to be safe and discreet.

The fact was that just about every city in America had someone like Inez. Thousands of abortionists were spread far and wide in every region of the nation. They seldom were physicians, but in their medical specialty, women trusted them more than they trusted doctors. The difference between Inez and other abortion providers was that she was among the best and most experienced anywhere.

Why *shouldn't* she be proud of what she did for a living? She didn't have anything to be ashamed of. At the San Francisco Opera season opening, she had sashayed down the opera house's red carpet, wearing an ostrich-feather hat, couture gown, sable stole, all accented by diamonds and pearls. Inez had not only been one of the most beautiful women in San Francisco, she was also among the most notorious.

If the blushing bluenoses at the opera hadn't been patients of Inez at one time, then they knew women who had. Everyone in San Francisco did. Inez was San Francisco's worst-kept secret.

She earned so much from performing so many abortions that she didn't know what to do with it all, so she spent freely and frequently. She converted much of her profits into real estate, often purchased under aliases. In the process, she became a real estate mogul, collecting homes in and out of San Francisco the way philatelists collect stamps.

Any cash that didn't go toward real estate went to custom-designed clothes and jewelry, meals at the city's best restaurants, antiques, and cars. The hundreds of thousands of dollars left over found its way bundled into thick wads tied with red rubber bands, hidden for safekeeping inside banisters, wall compartments, hems of drapes, and under the basement floor of the elegant Mission District home she shared with Joe.

Through it all, Inez was an unapologetic libertine. Society's stodgy rules were for other people. Why miss out on all the fun? She'd embarrass a sailor before *and* after she slept with him. All the while as Inez helped women, protecting them from the toxic clutches of predatory men, she was picking and choosing suitors for herself, whether for an evening or a month, whether she was married or not. She had the moxie to steal beaus from her own teenage granddaughter, Caroline, under the guise of offering the young men tutorials. "Forget Caroline. I want you for myself!" Inez would announce, pulling a young caller upstairs.

Vain to a fault, Inez underwent two ghoulish body-modification surgeries to accentuate her showstopper figure, subscribing to the benefits of cosmetic surgery before the two words were ever uttered together.

It was around that time when a young and aggressive district attorney by the name of Edmund G. (Pat) Brown decided Inez could do him some good. Pat needed someone to help spread his name far and wide, so why not pick Inez? Family values always sold well, and assailing the state's No. 1 abortionist would surely pay off with votes.

With hoopla and fanfare, Pat convened grand juries, hired zealous prosecutors, and platooned legions of cops to raid her clinic as often as necessary. That's what ambition does to a politician who wants to go places, and Pat wanted to go as far as the people would allow him, maybe further.

A young man in a hurry. Inez had known plenty like him. Bastards who wanted to use her. What men do to women all the time. Wham, bam, not even a thank-you-ma'am.

In the evenings, when the raft of her patients had left, Inez would draw a chamomile and rose hips bath in the big claw-foot porcelain tub on the second floor of her Guerrero Street palace, and depending on her mood and the day it had been, she'd shake her head and laugh. That was the only thing to do.

Could a woman really trust any man? Could *she* ever trust any man? Four husbands, if you counted the first and fourth ones, whom she never married. The first, George Washington Merritt, abandoned her in Pittsburgh, of all places. A charmer who swept her off her feet and dropped her with a thud while she was clutching two babies. The second, Billy Brown, a lazy sea captain whom Inez took care of for good. Best not to dwell on Billy. The third, continental four-flusher Charlie Granelli, what a disaster he'd been, robbing her blind. As though he could get away with raiding her chest of treasures. And finally, Joe, good ol' Joe, the handsomest of them all.

Men are men and Pat Brown wasn't any different. Just hungrier. He and his posse declared they knew what was best for women, even though it was men just like them who had gotten women into the predicaments that had prompted all the anguished trips to Inez's clinic in the first place. Pat and his deputies screamed that women bore one hundred percent of the brunt of any pregnancy. The last time Inez checked, though, weren't men fifty percent responsible? If there hadn't been such a never-ending demand for her services, then why was there always a queue of women waiting for her every morning even before she unlocked the front door?

Not that Pat Brown ever worried about that. He was there to enforce the laws, by God, and if making a name for himself happened along the way, then who could blame righteous Pat for just doing his job?

Collateral damage? Newton's third law of motion: for every action, there is an equal and opposite reaction. But that wasn't Pat's worry.

Putting Inez out of business meant it'd be more difficult for women to get what they would anyway, often at a terrible risk. Inez's ready-made clinic kept women from attempting abortions on themselves using needles, crochet hooks, coat hangers, bleach, and scores of other deadly homespun remedies. Over the years, Inez had attended to untold numbers of panicked women who had thought to commit suicide while attempting to conceal a swelling stomach.

Pat might be able to put Inez in prison, but one thing he could never take away was her magic touch. Like clockwork, one after another. Line 'em up.

Bootsie and Fats were busy pouring silver fizzes all around. A toast.

Joe lifted his glass and everyone followed.

"Here, here," Joe said, smiling broadly, as was his way. "To my wife, the Queen of San Francisco."

Everyone clinked glasses and cheered. Inez smiled and nodded, as though she was royalty. "Down the hatch!" she said, followed by more applause.

As the evening wound down, Caroline's job was to be the coat-check girl. She retrieved the men's long wool coats and the women's jackets and stoles. Tipsy Dr. Long Shot, who had known Inez forever, reached into his wallet and with fanfare gave Caroline a twenty-dollar tip, suggesting she "go buy an ice cream cone and have a lick on me."

"Thank you, sir!" ten-year-old Caroline said, stuffing the bill in a little crochet purse she carried around and had slung over her right shoulder.

As the last of the guests woozily made their way to their cars, turning on their headlights in the gray fog, Inez stood at the oversize, hand-carved oak door to the rambling redwood house, Joe's arm around her waist. It was one of the last times Caroline saw her grandmother and Joe so happy.

PART I
DREAMS

San Franciscans at the beach with Cliff House in the background, ca. 1902.

A Jewish balloon man sells his wares on the edge of Chinatown, ca. 1896–1906.

ONE

MISFORTUNE IN THE
PROMISED LAND

Inez's spectacular saga actually began thirty-eight years before she was born when an itinerant carpenter by the name of James W. Marshall discovered in 1848 glinting flakes in the cascading waters of Sutter's Mill, midway between Sacramento and Lake Tahoe. That auspicious find led to what became known as the California gold rush. San Francisco, the port city down the road, became infused with more capital more quickly than any other city in American history. From 1847 to 1870, San Francisco's population climbed from five hundred to one hundred and fifty thousand. By 1890, it had soared to three hundred thousand, making San Francisco the eighth largest city in the United States. In a little more than forty years, the number of people who lived in compact San Francisco had surged nearly sixty thousand percent. Wells Fargo moved its headquarters lock, stock, and barrel from New York City to San Francisco just to handle the avalanche.[1]

Like anyplace that spews instant wealth, whether from gold, silver, diamonds, emeralds, rubies, or oil, the men who seek to extract precious resources from the earth always have a vision of striking it not just big but *huge*. San Francisco epitomized this notion in spades, and conspicuous consumption became a virtue, making this a boomtown like no other. The city turned into a schizophrenic destination of competing halves: twenty-four-hour adult entertainment versus cultural and epicurean mecca. San Francisco was a confluence of violence, debauchery, *and* refinement.

While thugs roamed the streets and vigilantes took justice into their own hands, bulging tycoons and hourglass-figured mistresses consorted; cigar-champing moguls bought and sold vast swaths of real estate, some underwater, some above; wealthy whalers set up shop at Point Lobos on the lookout for blubbery cetaceans; and eccentric millionaires, fixated on being remembered forever, planted outlandish extravaganzas onto the city's perpendicular landscape. Into that peculiar mix toss in an assortment of bon vivants, adventurers, dreamers, con men, risk takers, go-getters, religious wackos, bohemians, and freeloaders. All were optimists seeking to cash in on the windfall of the American West's mother lode of riches.

After six months in the dusty Sierra Nevada foothills, thrill seekers far from home became hell-bent on partaking in an outrageously good time, and San Francisco was their personal pleasure palace. Wide-eyed forty-niners (so named because of the year 1849) traveled to the Bay City with cash scorching holes in their pockets. Among the best ways to lose it all was a high-stakes card game called faro, also known as Bucking the Tiger, played in every saloon in town.

For those with resources still intact after shills rigged the tables, ravenous demand was met by a cornucopia of goods and services. In the process, San Francisco became a wholly separate American enclave—a spirited, anything-goes city that sold everything imaginable. About the only thing temperate about the city was its weather. Grizzly prospectors who lived in hot ravines and gullies were bowled over by what the breathtaking beautiful city by the bay offered. Carnivals, circuses, breweries, saloons, restaurants, hotels, opium dens, cigar parlors, and houses of prostitution lined San Francisco streets to provide men with whatever they could imagine and more, in a gung ho market financed by a gold fountain that gushed cash.

The most populated district was San Francisco's Barbary Coast, a rowdy nine-block quarter bisected by Pacific Avenue, which went from the water's edge at horseshoe-shaped Buena Vista Cove to Portsmouth Square, and from Montgomery to Stockton Streets. The district derived its name from the Barbary Coast of North Africa, where pirates, sailors, pimps, slave traders, extortionists, and other lowlifes transacted business. As in Africa, it was recommended that visitors to San

Panoramic view of San Francisco, ca. 1851.

Francisco's Barbary Coast take firm hold of their wallets and not let go. Such advice was seldom followed. Wallets were frequently emptied, and not infrequently their owners found themselves subsequently drugged or beaten, only to awaken in a clipper ship's hull sailing through the Golden Gate toward China, hence the transitive verb *shanghai*. The Barbary Coast was a dangerous place, made that way by gangs from New York's Five Points neighborhood who called themselves the Hounds, followed by an equally lawless contingent of crooks and convicts from Down Under who took the name the Sydney Ducks.

Among those partaking in the lawless revelry was a young man who arrived as Samuel Clemens and left two years later as Mark Twain. Twain found San Francisco "the most cordial and sociable city in the Union," and while he settled there to further his journalism career, like everyone else, he also made the trek in hopes of making a financial killing. Twain owned a portfolio of temperamental stocks in the Comstock silver mines. His career as a reporter fared as well as the volatile promissory notes he held, and after Twain was fired from the *San Francisco Daily Morning Call*, he headed to a place called Jackass Hill in Tuolumne County, and three months later sold a story about a feller in nearby Calaveras County named Jim Smiley and his pet frog who could jump prodigious lengths. The account made Twain an overnight sensation.[2]

Twain was among the tens of thousands who flocked to San Francisco, but it wasn't just Americans who came in throngs to the Golden Gate to realize their dreams. Men from around the globe converged on San Francisco, transforming the city into a mélange of cultures. French, Chinese, Mexicans, Japanese, Italians, Irish, Swiss, Scots, Germans, and Brits all commingled on sandy hillocks, muddy alleys, and newly paved streets in what had become an international city. Each brought his own culture, clothing, cuisine, customs, and conversation.

In the beginning, few women joined this westward-ho mania sweeping America. "There was such a dearth of females in the San Francisco of gold-rush days that a woman was almost as rare a sight as an elephant, while a child was an even rarer spectacle," wrote Herbert Asbury in his 1933 classic, *The Barbary Coast*. "It is doubtful if the so-called fair sex ever before received such adulation and homage anywhere in the United States; even prostitutes, ordinarily scorned and ostracized by their honest and respectable customers, were treated with an exaggerated deference. Men stood for hours watching the few children at play; and whenever a woman appeared on the street, business was practically suspended. She was followed through the town by an adoring crowd, while self-appointed committees marched ahead to clear the way to protect her from the too boisterous salutations of the emotional miners."[3]

Another city observer, James R. Smith, wrote there were "no wives, no mothers, no one to cook dinner. The men in the gold fields didn't have time to cook and likely didn't know how."[4] Or as Robert O'Brien, a columnist for the *San Francisco Chronicle*, kindly put it: "Most of the women who arrived were hardly the home-cooking type."[5]

San Francisco grew into an increasingly cosmopolitan place. Its port became the busiest on the Pacific Coast, its financial district labeled the Wall Street of the West. Dozens of foreign consulates began opening. Rincon Hill and South Park, between Third Street and the Bay, became fashionable neighborhoods for the nouveau riche.[6] Opera came to town, as did theater, dance, and spirited lectures, rolled out in opulent palaces, such as the Grand and Tivoli opera houses, the Alcazar, Alhambra, Baldwin, Bush Street, California, Central, Chinese, Columbia, Fisher's, Majestic, Morosco, Olympia, Orpheum, Republic, Valencia, and Wigwam theaters.

Some of the most sophisticated restaurants in America opened, including the pricey Poodle Dog, Maison Dorée, Maison Riche, Marchand's, and the Grill at the Palace Hotel. In these vaunted establishments, diners vied to be seen (or not, depending on who their dining companion was). Food was viewed differently from almost anywhere else in America, where meals were fuel for sustenance, slopped on a plate to be gobbled down. Meals in San Francisco had been elevated to an art form. Sophisticated diners began eating for the newfound sensation of the pleasure of the palate. In the process, the affluent didn't eat to live; they lived to eat. As often is the case, such a cultural transformation trickled down from the elites to a burgeoning middle class, and then to other American cities, making for the early beginnings of California cuisine.

While all of these newly arrived San Franciscans surely lived in the United States, many, particularly those able to keep some money in their pockets, fancied themselves separate and apart—brash, smart, often flamboyant, closer to habitués of Paris or Vienna than denizens of stodgy American cities like Boston or Philadelphia, places San Franciscans dismissed as parochial and provincial. The city of vertiginous hills and swaddling fog certainly didn't look American and at times didn't behave American. At its entrepreneurial core, San Francisco had morphed into a glamorous, diverse, and enlightened version of a wholly different America sprinting toward the twentieth century.

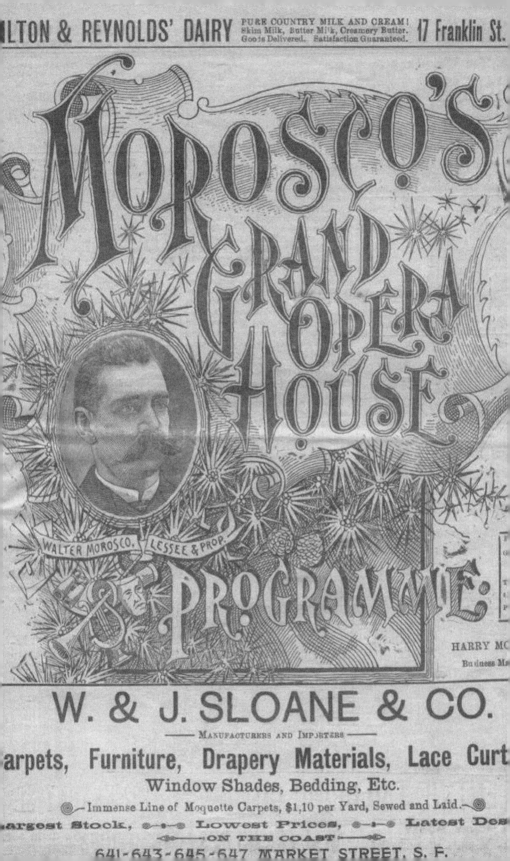

MOROSCO'S GRAND OPERA HOUSE

WALTER MOROSCO, LESSEE & PROP.

PROGRAMME

HARRY MO...
Business Ma...

It was in this promised land, still celebrating the twin bounties of gold and then silver, that Inez Ingenthron was born on September 5, 1886. Although family lore put Inez as a Philadelphia native, the truth is that Inez was born in San Francisco, not in a hospital, but in a rear tenement, south of the city's dividing line, Market Street, in an area known as South of the Slot (*slot*, because streetcars moved up and down the city's main thoroughfare along a metal rail). South of the Slot was San Francisco's equivalent to New York's Hell's Kitchen. In this neighborhood of warehouses, factories, flats, and wooden frame houses, ethnic gangs controlled each and every block, facing off when a rival gang member made the egregious mistake of setting foot on the wrong corner.

Like nearly all children born in San Francisco in that dawning era just thirty-six years after California joined the union, Inez was the product of parents who were newcomers, recent arrivals to America hell-bent on partaking in the bonanza the Golden Gate telegraphed to the rest of the world. Getting to San Francisco was an arduous journey for anyone, but especially for European immigrants. California represented the second leg of an impossibly long, ambitious, and treacherous trip. Once immigrants crossed the Atlantic, another uncertain expedition awaited them: three thousand more miles overland across the expanse of a foreign nation, marked by great prairies, expansive rivers and lakes, and treacherous mountains. Immigrating to the New World from Europe usually meant sailing to New York, although immigrant ships also headed for cities such as Baltimore, Boston, Philadelphia, New Orleans, and Quebec. Sailing directly to San Francisco, traversing the Panama Isthmus or going around the Cape Horn, wasn't a ready option for poor Europeans at the time.

Inez's father, Friedrich Ingenthron, was born in June 1853 in Traunstein, in southern Bavaria, Germany, thirty miles west of Salzburg, Austria. Friedrich was the youngest son of Dominic and Katherine Renjer Ingenthron; the couple had four other children: Barbara, Jacob, Catherine, and Joseph. Two months after Friedrich's birth, Katherine hemorrhaged to death. With five mouths to feed, Dominic promptly found another wife, Magdalena Hock, nine years his junior. In spring, the newly reconstituted Ingenthron family set sail for America, trading all that was secure and comfortable for the wild unknown. With them, they packed a pioneer spirit, a heady dose of confidence that whatever might lie around the bend must be better than what they knew for certain was straight ahead.

Cover of a Morosco's Grand Opera House program, 1895.

The Ingenthrons left Europe from Le Havre, France, with five hundred and eighteen other emigrants aboard the ship *Hemisphere*. In cramped and odoriferous steerage, the seven Ingenthrons, including eleven-month-old Friedrich, made the Atlantic crossing in nine days. All but forty-one of the passengers registered their citizenship as German. Every adult on board listed his or her profession as a farmer, another way to say landless day laborer. The *Hemisphere*'s captain was John G. Pray, a surname that suited the trepidation shared by the ship's masses huddled inside the vessel's hull.[7]

Armed with John Shea's *Englisch-Amerikanisches Handbuch für Auswanderer und Reisende,* an American-English pronunciation guide, the German-speaking Ingenthrons arrived in New York City on May 8, 1854. The family was herded through Castle Garden, the first immigration station established in the United States, predating Ellis Island by four decades.[8]

New York proved to be a transitory home for the Ingenthrons. Within two years, the family moved a thousand miles inland to the American heartland, settling in Petersburg, Indiana, the western dot of an isosceles triangle with vertices at Cincinnati and Lexington, Kentucky. Dominic Ingenthron chose southwest Indiana to engage in the artisanal profession of cigar making—rolling the aromatic, broad tobacco leaves found in abundance in the region. Son Friedrich was to follow in the same calling. At the time, the anesthetizing practice of cigar smoking, as well as tobacco chewing, was wildly popular throughout the United States, a habit promulgated by soldiers in the Civil War.

At a Saturday evening church social, Friedrich chatted up a dark-haired local girl, Alice Belle Cross, the middle daughter of seven children born to brickmaker William Cross and his wife, Mary. When Alice was fifteen, William had died, and Mary pushed Alice to find a husband, making for one less child to drain the family's limited resources. In 1873, Alice and Friedrich married in Lawrenceburg, Indiana, a mercantile port along the Ohio River. Both were twenty years old. The couple's first child, Nettie, was born a year later, followed by Harry in 1877.

Alice and Friedrich, who by now had Americanized his Germanic name and was known as Frederick, along with children Nettie and Harry, moved three hundred miles north to teeming Chicago, where Frederick secured work as a cigar maker. There, the couple had another son, Walter. The five Ingenthrons squeezed into a tiny

Madam Blache Oulif's French Millinery on the northwest
corner of Grant Avenue and O'Farrell Street, ca. 1881.

apartment at 571 Fourteenth Street in a working-class neighborhood that today is adjacent to Grant Park.

If not for personal reasons, moving to Chicago made economic sense. Cigars were king and a ready market awaited Frederick there. One of the largest suppliers in the nation was Grommes & Ullrich, an importer of Cuban cigars, located at 174–76 Madison Street; Chicago boasted hundreds of other cigar makers, including titans Sprague, Warner; Franklin MacVeagh; Best, Russell & Co.; and Sutter Bros. In addition to firms readily hiring tobacco rollers, there was a familial reason for the Ingenthrons to relocate. Frederick's oldest brother, Jacob, had established himself as a mover and shaker in the rising city on the shores of Lake Michigan. Frederick adored his prosperous big brother and relished the prospect of a reunion.[9]

Jacob was a joiner. He'd been elected Noble Grand Arch of the United Ancient Order of Druids, a fraternal order founded in London a century earlier; he was elected secretary to two progressive international organizations, German-American Democracy and the Anti-British Alliance League. Without any formal training, he hung out a shingle as an attorney, taking on an assortment of clients, and throwing himself headfirst into the rowdy world of Cook County politics. In 1900, Jacob was elected a delegate to the Democratic National Convention held in Indianapolis, and supported the party's presidential nominee, populist William Jennings Bryan. That same year Jacob Ingenthron was named Chicago city prosecutor.[10]

One immigrant's meteoric rise into the political world of America's fourth-largest city didn't necessarily mean his brother would follow suit. Frederick Ingenthron's skills weren't oratory or cerebral but manual, and for a man of his skills and resources, the attraction of San Francisco's economic windfall was too great a draw. An experienced tobacco roller with a ready market on the West Coast, Frederick would have a job for life. Or so he thought.

In a city as flush with money as San Francisco was, men who were men showed their wealth in direct proportion to the length, girth, and quality of the cigars they stuck in their mouths. The demand for premium cigars was so great that there were more smokers than high-quality cigars available. In the wake of the gold rush, journeymen cigar makers had abandoned their workbenches to head for the Sierra Nevada foothills, where they could make more money panning for gold than rolling tobacco. Chinese immigrants promptly filled the labor void, and by 1870, eighty percent of the cigars rolled west of the Rockies were made by Chinese laborers working in sweatshops for rock-bottom wages. In San Francisco, there were thirty thousand Chinese nationals, and more were arriving on ships streaming through the Golden Gate every week. The ethnic tilt produced a backlash of virulent racism, as seen in the federal Chinese Exclusion Act in 1862, which set a moratorium on Chinese immigration for ten years, at a time when every other nationality was setting out for America daily. Vigilantes burned down Chinese laundries, and arson became an almost daily occurrence in San Francisco's Chinatown.[11]

No matter their quality, cigars produced by Chinese workers were viewed as inferior. A white man who put his lips to a cigar touched by Chinese hands was considered a traitor to his race. As a result, the Cigar Makers Union organized in San Francisco with the mandate to replace Chinese laborers with white rollers. To do this, manufacturers needed experienced white cigar makers. But there was such a scarcity that union representatives had to travel east to Chicago and New York to entice journeyman rollers to San Francisco with the promise of employment. As a bonus to relocate, white cigar makers were offered train passage west.

It was an offer impossible to refuse. To celebrate the move west, Frederick cast off his last German vestige, announcing to one and all his intention to be called Fred once he arrived in San Francisco. As a send-off, Jacob gave his younger brother the munificent gift of twenty Liberty Head five-dollar gold coins to establish Frederick's family in San Francisco. Jacob ordered the shiny coins directly from the San Francisco Mint as a way to welcome the reinvented Fred and his family.

In the late fall of 1885, two scions of the Ingenthron family parted at Chicago's newly opened General Union Passenger Depot, at the corner of Madison and Canal Streets. Together, Jacob and Frederick had nine children, all of whom they brought to the station on a cold but sunny November morning. The two brothers stiffly shook hands, then, realizing the formality of such a stilted encounter, embraced. Frederick's wife, Alice, tearfully bade farewell to Lette, Jacob's wife. The children played blind-man's bluff in the boarding area, hiding behind wooden benches till they heard a high-pitched whistle and a blue-uniformed conductor with a matching hat, shout, "All aboard!" As Frederick and his family stepped onto the Overland Flyer, there was too much gaiety and excitement in the air to comprehend the gravity of the two families' imminent division. That was the last any of them would see one another again.

The Ingenthrons traveled to Council Bluffs, Iowa, then took the Union Pacific to Ogden, Utah, followed by the Southern Pacific to Reno, Sacramento, and finally to the western terminus at Oakland Mole, before ferrying across the Bay to wondrous San Francisco. The family stayed in a series of rooming houses on the

A view looking west on California Street from Sansome Street, ca. 1905.

waterfront, then found permanent housing at 235½ Perry Street, South of the Slot, where Inez was born and spent her first six years.

As promised, Fred Ingenthron secured employment in 1888 at Louis Wertheimer & Co., 115 Front Street, one of the largest cigar manufacturers in San Francisco. Two years later, the city directory showed Fred working for H. Plagemann & Co., at 212–20 Sansome Street, another prominent cigar maker. Both manufacturers took pride in boasting they hired only white men as cigar makers. Cigar boxes from the "White Cigar Makers," as the manufacturers proudly called themselves, contained this advisory: "The cigars contained in this box are made by skilled labor,

A mother and child carry New Year's presents in Chinatown, ca. 1896–1906.

A union label of the Cigar Makers' Association of the Pacific Coast asserting that the cigars were made exclusively by white men.

Patrons linger outside the Joss
House, or temple, in Chinatown, ca.
1896–1906.

under the control of white men." Being white allowed Fred to earn twice what Chinese cigar makers made, twelve dollars a week versus six.[12]

While expensive cigars may have been representative of San Francisco's ascendant wealth, the cigar industry's capitalization missed a critical correction. The Cigar Makers' International Union failed in its efforts to exclude Chinese laborers from the industry, and the lower-priced cigars triumphed. Smokers chose to pay less for stogies no matter whose hands they were rolled by. With an abundance of Chinese cigar makers, the disparity of labor costs made white rollers cost-prohibitive and they were soon priced out of the workplace.[13] Cigar making belonged to the Chinese.

Unemployed in a distant and expensive city, Fred Ingenthron took to spending more and more time in neighborhood saloons South of the Slot. Jobs were difficult to find, at least that's what Fred told Alice, and Inez's father began to pass more and more of his days drinking steins of steam beers, *steams*, as they were called. As men proceeded farther south, the neighborhoods got dicier, the taverns rougher. Most taprooms had cuspidors as a convenience for patrons, but in the saloons Fred frequented, patrons spit on the floor, and on occasion at each other. Fred often fell asleep drunk, slumped on a stool, head pitched forward on the bar.

Alice wouldn't see her husband for days, and when he finally did show up at the family's walk-up, he was alternatively angry and sullen. Any warmth Alice once had for her husband had disappeared. To the four Ingenthron children, their father was to be avoided, particularly when he was on a bender. By now, Alice knew how to defend herself, and any match between the two strongly favored Alice, who wasn't shy about throwing punches. One night, Alice threw Fred out of the apartment, pushing him down the flat's steep flight of rickety wooden steps. If Fred already hadn't felt defeated, he endured the disgrace of getting beaten up by his wife. He soon found himself in a squalid flophouse near what was known as Butchertown, a district of slaughterhouses and tanneries, where gambling on cockfights and exactly how many rats men could stomp and kill were popular pastimes. Abattoir workers threw habitués intestines, brains, tongues, and hearts that they'd fight over and then cook at open-pit fires in China Basin. The twenty Liberty Heads Jacob had given Fred to herald a new life in San Francisco were long gone.

At the age of thirty-nine, Fred Ingenthron died of either consumption or acute alcoholism. No one seemed to care enough to find out which. A worker from the city morgue visited the family flat to inform Alice of her husband's death and asked whether she'd come downtown to identify the body, a request she declined.[14]

Inez's sister, Nettie Ingenthron.

Unable to afford the walk-up, the family moved to 444 Fifth Street, then hop-scotched to flats at 1165 and 1346 Howard Street, and finally to 221 Elsie Street in a faraway and inaccessible district with muddy, unpaved hilly streets, filled mostly with working-class Irish families. The rents in Bernal Heights were a fraction of other neighborhoods in the city.[15] Alice, Inez, and Nettie slept in one bed, and Walter and Harry in another. Alice advertised for tenants to make ends meet, and as long as they took an occasional bath, they could sleep anywhere they wanted, which sometimes meant with Nettie and Inez. Meanwhile, Alice and Nettie, who had become an honors student at Rincon Grammar School,[16] became seamstresses and dressmakers with a fourth-hand Singer sewing machine that broke down more than it worked. Harry was a numbers runner, spiriting bets to and from cigar stores along Courtland Avenue. Walter took a streetcar to work for a South of the Slot blacksmith, tending carriage horses. The Ingenthrons' meal of the day was potatoes. If Harry or Walter passed by Butchertown early enough to scavenge a scrap, the potatoes would be ac-companied by an animal organ neither Nettie nor Inez wanted to identify.

The Music Pavillion at Golden Gate Park, ca. 1902.

As for Inez, the baby of the family, she got the brunt of the family's misfortune. Alice, at forty, had turned into a bitter widow. When precocious, russet-haired Inez would seek attention, climbing onto her mother's lap, she'd be greeted with a swift slap of the back of Alice's callused hand, with the warning "Stay away from me, you little brat!"

Inez started at Franklin Grammar School on Eighth Street, between Harrison and Bryant Streets, but when the family moved to Bernal Heights, Alice didn't bother to enroll Inez in school, a luxury Alice said the family couldn't afford. During evenings, Alice used to rail at Inez and Nettie about how to ensure any semblance of fairness or equality with a man, none of whom she trusted. "Don't ever fight with 'em with an open hand," Alice would counsel her daughters. "Go after 'em with your fists, so they know you mean business."[17]

Visitors to Golden Gate park look out on the conservatory greenhouses, ca. 1897.

Meanwhile, Nettie had met a stenographer by the name of Edwin Conhem Haw-kins, and the two married on July 18, 1894, when Nettie was twenty. But after a whirl-wind courtship, the newlyweds fought constantly. Money was one issue, mother-in-law Alice another. Edwin had quit his job as a stenographer and fancied himself an artist.[18] One particularly tempestuous evening, Hawkins left the couple's flat only to return with a wagon and a pair of friends. The three men carted off all of the couple's posses-sions, including the matrimonial bed and kitchen stove. A nasty divorce subsequently played out on the third floor of San Francisco superior court in Department Five. Edwin charged that his wife was a "weak woman and entirely controlled and domi-nated by the stronger mind of her mother," whom he labeled as a "designing person"; Superior Court Judge John Hunt Jr. granted Nettie a dissolution of marriage decree.[19]

The Sutro Baths, ca. 1898.

At twenty-two, Nettie was a scorned woman. So was adolescent Inez by association. Both girls knew that Edwin Hawkins had been right in his assessment of
Alice, whose response to her daughter's divorce was "Haven't met a man I could trust
further than I could throw 'im."

Nettie dusted herself off as well as she could. She merited two notices on the society
pages of San Francisco newspapers. The *San Francisco Call* reported Nettie went to the
thirty-third annual gala banquet of the Caledonian Club, held at the Scottish Hall, at
117 Larkin Street, with four hundred other guests who danced the night away five days

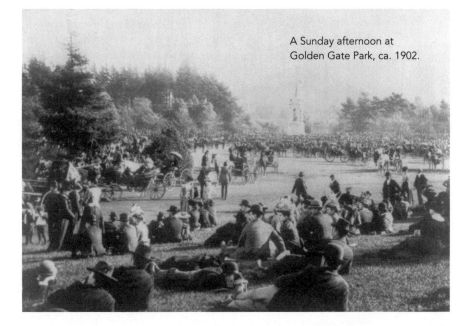

A Sunday afternoon at
Golden Gate Park, ca. 1902.

before Christmas.[20] Six weeks later, Nettie wangled another invitation to society king
Ned Greenway's First Friday Cotillion, held at the Assembly Hall, 320 Post Street.[21]

One positive element of Nettie's divorce was that she could now better care for
Inez. The two girls rode the streetcar to the just-opened Golden Gate Park to marvel
at the assortment of exotic trees chosen and planted by a man named McLaren. There
was a preponderance of pines, cypresses, and strange saplings called eucalyptus, whose
seeds had come all the way from Australia. Eucalypti emitted a pungent, tangy aroma
the sisters had never smelled before, and they grew to enjoy sitting in an arboreal grove
near Stanyan Street. Nettie and Inez would then catch the Ocean Shore Railroad, which
dropped them off in front of another new and magnificent city attraction, the Sutro
Baths, with its seven resplendent pools. The sisters would perambulate inside the huge
glass structure, perched on forested cliffs overlooking the Golden Gate. Nettie and Inez
never swam. Instead, they promenaded with fans in hand, smiling coyly at admirers, even
though Inez was barely a teenager. Nettie was pretty but compared to her sister—well,
there was no comparison.

In any free time, Inez took to reading, a skill she had taught herself. She had to
keep books she'd borrowed hidden from her mother. Reading was a waste of time,
frittering away your life when you ought to be working, and if you weren't working,
then you ought to be cleaning, washing, dusting, sewing. "What's it gonna do for you

'cept fill your head with dreams," Alice raged. Any book found in the house would be tossed into the rubbish.

On a Monday afternoon in early March, Inez planned to meet one of her girl-friends, a girl with high cheekbones and dark eyes by the name of Anna Thompson, at Westerfeld's, a bakery downtown on Market and Sixth Streets. Anna and Inez bought six sugar-sprinkled cinnamon and clove cookies called *pfeffernüsse*, their favorites.

Anna brought her five-year-old niece, Mabel, to the bakery with her. Mabel's fa-ther had gone out to the corner store for a cigar one evening and never came back; that left Anna to care for her niece while Mabel's mother, Gladys, worked as a laundress at Peerless Laundry on Eighth Street downtown. With dark-haired Mabel sitting at a table, alternately playing with a rag "Brownie" doll and making a mess eating one of the powdery cookies, Anna had news to share with Inez. The Palace Hotel was hiring.

"*Really?*" was all Inez could say breathlessly. "Doing what?"

The opening was for manicurists in the hotel barbershop, Anna said, a profes-sion about which neither girl knew anything. That job didn't interest the girls, but working in the Palace did.

The new Palace Hotel on Market and New Montgomery Streets was the most refined hostelry not just in San Francisco but in all of America. The brainchild of William Chapman Ralston, who wanted to build a hotel as worthy of San Francisco as it would be of its name, the Palace was spectacular. Six years earlier, Ralston had built the twenty-four-hundred-seat California Theatre on Bush Street with instruc-tions to his architect to "find out the biggest theater in the world and make this one ten feet bigger." When finished, for opening night Ralston chose Edward Bulwer Lytton's five-act play, *Money*,[22] as sure a sign of resplendent San Francisco as any.

However opulent the California Theatre was, it paled in comparison with the Palace, a source of civic pride even among jaded city dwellers who thought they had seen it all. Bells and whistles rang throughout. The Palace dazzled with a seven-story courtyard into which horse-drawn carriages dropped off guests on a circular marble driveway. The courtyard was surrounded by seven hundred fifty-five rooms. Under-girding the building were twenty miles of gas lines, six miles of sewer drains, and twenty-eight miles of water pipes. In each room, there were vitreous water closets manufactured by china makers from Staffordshire, England. Private artesian wells pumped twenty-eight thousand gallons an hour through the hotel. Five elevators (called "rising rooms") with redwood paneling and red-velvet cushioned benches in-side sped guests to their floors. The dining room was illuminated by chandeliers with thousands of crystal prisms. Dishes were Haviland from Limoges, France; Irish linens came from Belfast, then known as "Linenopolis"; blankets were woven at Ralston's own Mission Woolen Mills; tables, dressers, beds, and chairs had been assembled in the Eastlake style from Ralston's West Coast Furniture Company; rugs, carpets, draperies, canopies, and window shades came from W. & J. Sloane in New York; the silver was handcrafted by E. H. H. Smith Silver in Bridgeport, Connecticut. Hand-painted murals of clipper ships, the *Golden Gate*, *Lake Tahoe*, and *Yosemite*, adorned the first-floor walls. Each floor had a corps of black servants who waited on guests hand and foot.

"Ralston had planned the Palace as a symbol of San Francisco's coming of age," is how historians Oscar Lewis and Carroll D. Hall put it, "to mark the closing of one era and the beginning of another, the end of the transition from mining camp and raw boom town to established city."[23]

And Inez and Anna would be smack in the middle of it all. Little Mabel would soon be old enough to go to school, and that would free Anna to work at the Palace.

At the time, wealthy men, not women, got their nails cut, polished, and buffed in barbershops. Holding a fine cigar with ragged cuticles and unlacquered nails just wouldn't do in San Francisco society. Think of the men they'd meet, Inez suggested. Both girls giggled.

What other job allowed a woman to sit so close to a man who wasn't her husband? And in public? Other than prostitution, what other job allowed strangers of the opposite sex to touch? The girls were breathless with anticipation.

Working at the Palace would be an opportunity to rub elbows with men Inez had only stolen glances at from afar, moneyed men she'd never have reason to associate with. On Tuesday, Inez and Anna planned to present themselves at the barbershop.

But just before Monday dinner, Anna came by the Ingenthron flat on Elsie Street. She told Inez that her parents had forbidden her to take the job. No good Catholic girl worked as a manicurist, even if it was at the Palace. With Mabel in school, Anna would have to find work, perhaps at Peerless or Westerfeld's, her parents suggested. For her part, Inez hadn't bothered to tell Alice where she planned to go the next morning. She already knew what the answer would be.

"They seemed awfully set on me not working there, especially my father," Anna said, lifting her shoulders into a shrug. "You go tomorrow, Inez. I'll be rootin' for you."

The next day, Inez put on her only lace dress, grabbed a modest brimmed hat of Nettie's, took the streetcar downtown, and strode right into the magnificent Palace.

She could feel herself ogling the glass ceiling, the open grand parlor, and the well-dressed guests with their array of matching leather luggage piled sky high.

Inez had walked into a fantasy spun out of one of her books—until a bellboy walked up to her and said that all job applicants had to enter through the Jessie Street side of the hotel.

"Next time, when ya start, dose are da rules, miss," the boy, no more than sixteen, told Inez before winking at her.

Inez got herself to the barbershop and talked to the woman in charge of the manicure girls, who looked Inez up and down.

"She look all right to you, Vernon?"

A thin, bald man with a red face, dressed in a white smock, glanced Inez's way. "Sure do," he said, nodding at Inez in an amiable way. "We'd be glad to have you work in the shop, ma'am," he said.

The stout woman who introduced herself as Myrtle, perhaps ten years older than Inez, pronounced that Inez could come back the next morning to start, even after Inez had confessed that she'd never given a manicure in her life. "Oh, that don't make no difference," Myrtle said. "You know how to smile, doncha?"

The court of the Palace Hotel, 1895.

TWO

THE WONDERFUL WIZARDESS
OF THE PALACE HOTEL

Myrtle had been right. Learning to attend to the cuticles of rich men was easy. Within two months, seventeen-year-old Inez had mastered the delicate art of the manicure. There were certain tasks at which she wasn't yet proficient, but Inez, or Iney as they called her in the barbershop, seemed to be able to handle nearly anything that came her way.

She looked forward to leaving the cramped Bernal Heights flat she shared with her mother, sister, brothers, and the revolving door of rough-and-tumble pensioners. Every morning when she walked past the swirling red, white, and blue barbershop pole, Inez entered a wholly distinct world.

The four barbers, Vernon, Henry, Virgil, and Dewey, went about their appointed tasks on the other side of a vitrine in full view of everyone passing by—their every movement on display. Sometimes it was a shave, other times a haircut, often it was both. Inez liked the routine, sights, and smells: the unfurling of the starched white cape; the stiff collar affixed around each man's prickly neck; the steaming-hot Turkish towels draped, curled, and wrapped atop each customer's face with just the tip of a red nose peeking out; the constant whoosh of scissors *snip, snip, snipping*. When the barbers honed their ivory-handled straight razors against the smooth thick leather strop, Inez grew to anticipate the *swacking* sound, as she did the smell of the hot-shave lather and the lime-green elixir the barbers slapped on the men's faces that made them wince. As a kind of grand denouement, the barbers would sprinkle talcum powder from a metal can on the men's necks, whisked away by a soft horsehair brush, which had the effect of creating for a second or two a snowy wonderland. Vernon and Virgil worked fast, speaking only when asked a question. Henry and Dewey were the talkers, volubly holding forth about everything from the weather, sports, politics, and the latest opening in town.

Inez wore the uniform the Palace supplied her: an elongated flared dress with a hem that came to the floor, accentuated by a high, tight waist, and a collar that covered the bottom half of her neck. Inez softened the ensemble with a coral cameo Nettie had given her or by wearing a rose she made from strips of red silk she curled and then pressed into a blossom. Both complemented her thick, long hair, which a smitten client one day pronounced was "Titian-colored," a reference to the sixteenth-century Venetian painter Tiziano Vecellio. Titian painted young women, often courtesans, voluptuous and seminude, with rich, dark-red hair.[1] Inez had no idea who Titian was or what he painted, but she took the comparison as a compliment.

Two walls of the shop were covered with mirrors, and more than once Inez caught men staring at her reflection. She knew never to look back, of course. That would be inappropriate, so she'd gaze downward, half smiling, at the veined marble floor. Sometimes, Inez felt customers' eyes boring into her from their perches in the high barber chairs. As she commenced a manicure, some men would curl their fingers into a bowl of soapy water and never say a word. With their other hand, some men could fold a newspaper into quarter sections and read every article on every page, word for word, it seemed. Sometimes, they'd talk to the barbers about the news while Inez would listen and nod amiably. For the most part, these men seemed timid, almost afraid of her.

Myrtle's initial counsel to Inez proved to be spot-on. The job of the manicurist, Inez soon discovered, was the art of smiling, lending a sympathetic ear to whatever the man was talking about, whether it was the latest sporting event or political matchup. Inez was a quick study, whether the subject at hand was the Big Game between Stanford and Cal or the Big Four monopoly. But she knew never to express an opinion. She deferred to the barbers for that, and usually they demurred.

In addition to being swallowed up by the testosterone-saturated culture of the barbershop, there was another reason for Inez's taciturn manner: She hadn't gone beyond the sixth grade. Inez had little understanding of business, politics, sports, or culture, at least at this point in her life she didn't. She couldn't very well engage these men in the issues of the day. About the only statement she could make was her captivating feminine presence.

In the meantime, Inez set out to improve herself. She had boosted her reading skills and elocution enough so that her speech, she hoped, wouldn't betray her origins. She picked up a book at the public library that everyone was reading at the time, a bizarre story of a girl from Kansas who'd been whisked away by a tornado to a magical land of witches and talking animals. It was a fanciful tale called *The Wonderful Wizard of Oz*. Inez related to Dorothy Gale and took to reading the book aloud to herself, softly, as she rode the streetcar to work every morning. She didn't dare leave the L. Frank Baum volume in the house, lest her mother find it and toss it in the garbage.

By all accounts, as a manicurist at the city's swankiest hotel, Inez had elevated herself from a penurious girl destined to marry a neighborhood boy, have a brood of children, struggle to feed them, get smacked on more than several occasions, and then die of an undetermined disease by age fifty. Instead, Inez was hobnobbing with some of the richest men in California. These were men of means and merit. By the turn of the century, San Francisco had become second only to New York in the value of its domestic and foreign trade. Railroad tycoons Charles Crocker, Leland Stanford, Collis Huntington, and Mark Hopkins had all died by this time, but Inez had regulars who had done business with each of them. These men didn't live South of the Slot but instead had built majestic homes on the newly developed hills north of Market called Russian and Nob.

Inez could tell that Joey, the bellboy who had winked at her that first day in the Palace, was interested in her, but he was no more than a bellboy. Pleasant and amiable, but why would Inez want to return the favor when there were so many rich, learned, and connected men all around her? This was the golden age of San Francisco, brighter and better than the brawling years of the gold rush. Inez sensed greater opportunities, even for her.

As an employee, Inez wasn't allowed to ride the redwood-paneled rising rooms, and even if she could afford the famous Grill Room, she wasn't permitted to eat there. But she had heard about the delicacies offered therein. A man by the name of Ernest Arbogast was the chef and had turned into one of the nation's arbiters of high cuisine. At least, that's what several of Inez's clients had told her. Arbogast served unconventional and exotic meals that included frog legs, oysters, duck, pheasant, quail, and a sweet tender meat that came from a shellfish called abalone.

Anyone who was anyone chose to stay at the Palace, and Inez found herself stealing glances at the most notable as they made their way through the lobby. Wealthy families stayed for weeks on end, often as a prelude to boarding ocean liners bound for Europe around the horn, or across the Pacific to the Orient. One day, as Inez walked on New Montgomery Street to the employees' entrance, she found herself face-to-face with John D. Rockefeller himself, the industrialist said to be the wealthiest man in America. She was so nervous she felt faint, forgetting for a moment to breathe. Inez had seen Mr. Rockefeller's picture in the newspaper, and at first she couldn't believe that the very same man was striding her way at the center of a phalanx of assistants, valets, accountants, bookkeepers, and guards who had exited the hotel's rear door to avoid the growing knot of reporters crowding the lobby. Behind Rockefeller and his entourage was a diminutive, homely woman at the center of her own bevy, whom Inez assumed to be Mrs. Rockefeller. The Rockefeller retinue had taken over the entire sixth floor at the Palace, and the scuttlebutt among hotel employees was that Mr. Rockefeller's personal physician was among the convoy, attending to a disease that had rid his boss of every strand of hair! Now on Jessie Street, Inez couldn't take her eyes off Mr. Rockefeller. He was carrying a bowler hat in his right hand presently to cover his head, but when she looked at him closely, she noticed he was wearing a full wig, and one that very much looked like a wig. A man as rich as Mr. Rockefeller, Inez mused, and he had a disease all the money in the world couldn't cure.

Rockefeller wasn't the only celebrity Inez saw at the Palace. One day she looked out the barbershop vitrine to see a real prince, dressed in the spanking-white military regalia of his country, with a resplendent sash diagonally spanning his chest, accented by a battalion of glimmering gold medals. He was striding through the main hallway as though he was about to seize control of a neighboring nation. Dewey said the man was Rama V, the crown prince of Siam, who had passed through the portals of the Golden Gate the day before on his own royal steamer.

The Palace was also the temporary home for opera singers, musicians, dancers, and actors imported to perform for wealthy San Franciscans eager to get their dose of culture. The list included such megawatt stars as Sarah Bernhardt, Emma Nevada, Adelina Patti, Frederick Warde, Trixie Friganza, Anna Held, Eugenie Pappenheim, Loie Fuller, Lillie Langtry, Sibyl Sanderson, and Ellen Terry. Just catching a glimpse of any one of these celebrities made Inez go weak at the knees, but of all of them, it was tiny Emma Nevada who struck Inez as the greatest. Known as the Sagebrush

Linnet, Miss Nevada slayed all of San Francisco with her rendition of "Listen to the Mockingbird," a ballad of a grief-stricken man who hears a mockingbird warble above the grave of his dead fiancée.[2] Many in the audience at the Grand Opera House were so moved by her performance that they lost their composure and openly wept. The next day, Miss Nevada visited the Palace's barbershop, the only female customer ever to set foot in the shop, at least since Inez had started. Miss Nevada promptly instructed Virgil to give her a trim. While he was "lowering her ears," as Virgil put it with a smile, Inez had the honor of attending to Miss Nevada's nails, which had nary a cuticle.

There also were regulars who showed up at the Palace barbershop, including San Francisco mayor Eugene Schmitz, a former conductor of the Columbia Theatre orchestra, and Abraham Ruef, an attorney with a thick black triangle of a mustache that made his upper lip impenetrable. Both would talk in sotto voce whispers through steaming towels covering their faces. Henry and Vernon had their hands full trying to shave the men's sandpaper beards smooth while they carried on their hushed conversation. Neither ever had his hands manicured, but Inez was fascinated nonetheless. They seemed polar opposites. Handsome Gene had watery blue eyes, a full head of wavy hair, and a ready smile. Ruef had an angular face and slits for eyes that gave Inez the willies. Henry once whispered that Ruef was what was called a "political boss." Inez wasn't sure what that meant exactly, but on several occasions, she saw the mayor slipping into the pocket of Ruef's morning coat a bulging envelope. Inez glanced over at Myrtle, who lowered her eyes, telegraphing that Inez might want to do the same.

Another regular at the barbershop was a horseman by the name of Dan Mc-Carty, though everyone called him "White Hat" due to the fuzzy white beaver hat he always wore with the exception of when he got a haircut. White Hat showed up daily at the Palace, where he picked up his mail and had a kind of personal office in the lobby. White Hat boasted that he owned more horses than anyone else in the world. The *San Francisco Call*'s racing reporter Freddie Green recorded that White Hat had "won and lost more than a million dollars on the racetracks of the country, and was known from Maine to California." White Hat's biggest claim to fame was winning a hundred thousand dollars in the American Derby at Washington Park in Chicago back in 1887 with a fifty-to-one shot. He proudly confided to Inez

Actress Anna Held, seen here ca. 1900, was one of the many stars Inez encountered at the Palace Hotel.

that he'd been arrested fifty-seven times for racing his horses on the streets of San Francisco. He also had a habit of never tying them up, so when police found a horse roaming the city, they knew whom it belonged to.[3]

For their part, most of the men who frequented the barbershop dressed in cutaway morning suits or frock coats (known as Prince Alberts), waistcoats, high-collared shirts, bowlers, silk top hats, stovepipes, and slouch and plug hats. The bottom halves of their faces were often covered with beards or mustaches waxed and curled. Almost all were married, legally at least. Many had "arrangements," Inez was to learn. They appeared in public with their wives, they raised their children with their wives, they went to the theater, opera, and church with their wives, but in private they squired around young women, escorting them to restaurants with screened-off upstairs dining rooms. Inez had heard about such places, restaurants with exquisite food, endless bottles of French wines, and expectations for dessert.

Inez observed married men who checked into the Palace with women who

Abe Ruef (center) receives whispered news from one of his attorneys, ca. 1907.

weren't their wives, as well as married women who consorted with men who weren't their husbands. Occasionally, women checked in together, saying they were sisters, and the front-desk clerks hardly raised an eyebrow. Plenty of women weren't who they said they were, angling to impress men who, truth be known, weren't anywhere near who they represented themselves to be, either.

After a year on the job, Inez grew bold enough to try an experiment. She began by softly stroking her clients' hands under the guise that she was massaging them. It became a discreet dance of flirtation; the men could make whatever they wanted of her manipulations. She also took to positioning herself beside the men, occasionally brushing up against their knees and forearms, by accident of course. She was a third the age of many of these men, and taking nothing away from their wives, she was not only fresh and buxom but also radiant. What man wouldn't enjoy savoring such proximity with such a young and engaging woman, even if it led to nothing more than a bigger tip for her?

"The Vander Weyde Light"

Mrs. Langtry as Cleopatra

U. S. Copyright, 1891.

182 Regent St. W.

Actress Lillie Langtry as Cleopatra, ca. 1891.

Whatever it was that she was doing, Inez began building a clientele of besotted gentlemen who'd ask for her by name. Regulars told their business associates about the winsome manicurist at the Palace, and they too became clients. They were pleased to pay a dollar for the thirty-minute pleasure of holding Inez's hand as she softened, repaired, filed, and polished their nails.

It meant that for the first time in her life, Inez was able to save money of her own. One day she splurged and actually bought L. Frank Baum's next book, *The Marvelous Land of Oz*, an extravagance she realized, but nonetheless a treat she devoured. With her mounting savings, Inez also bought several stiff corsets, the woman's undergarment that was all the rage, which sharply pulled in her naturally cinched waist and accentuated her curves. Each morning, Inez took to having Nettie lace the corset so tightly that it occasionally rendered her light-headed. The bodice actually made Inez sound breathy.[4]

Soon, the real reason legions of men frequented the barbershop wasn't as much to get their hair or whiskers shorn as it was to socialize with the comely manicurist with long chestnut-colored hair. These men might have been among the most influential in San Francisco, but in Inez's hands, they were putty. Floating down the main

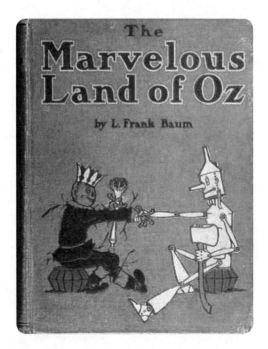

hallway at the Palace, she'd toss her tresses over her girlish shoulders and arch her back, tilting her head just so as she pursed her full lips.

Who is that woman?

Men smiled, craning their necks to get a view; women seethed, shaking their heads.

Inez had become a melding of confidence, beauty, smarts, and sexuality during an era when women weren't given to flaunting much except subservience. Emboldened, Inez created a signature to go with her manicure. To mark the end of a session, she'd stand, then instruct the men to wrap their hands around her waist, its circumference no more than twenty-one inches. The ploy was twofold: to allow the men a sanctioned way to touch her and to show off her tiny, pinioned waistline. She'd lift her chin, her thick hair cascading the length of her back, and as the men would put their hands on either side of her waist, she'd giggle as though she'd just been tickled.

No one knows whether Inez provided more than manicures, but she certainly took in an awful lot of tips and, on occasion, pocketed more than cash. Regulars regaled her with gifts of necklaces, brooches, cameos, and earrings. She took care not to wear any of them to work. If other men thought she was someone else's favorite, there'd be no more trinkets, she knew.

Without a formal education, setting her sights on becoming a schoolteacher, nurse, or bookkeeper wasn't in the cards for enterprising Inez. She knew that being a manicurist was hardly a path to financial security. The best she could hope for was to secure a job as a clerk at a downtown department store or working with her friend Anna Thompson, who had found employment at Westerfeld's Bakery. But in either employ, Inez wouldn't earn nearly as much as she was making now.

Her prospects for marriage? San Francisco gentlemen picked wives from similarly suited well-to-do families. If a single woman sought to earn any substantial income on her own, she'd have to offer a necessary and vital service, and she'd have to do it better than anyone else. And what could that possibly be for a respectable young woman?

The answer came one morning when a man with a receding hairline and full beard came striding into the Palace barbershop, inquiring which of the manicurists could take him at this very moment. The man was a physician and needed a girl to minister to his hands. Inez smiled and began. The new client was Eugene West, a man of great notoriety in San Francisco.

THREE

WAYWARD GIRLS AND
LECHEROUS ROGUES

Everyone has a past, but Eugene West's was particularly colorful. Some might call it sordid, even gruesome. But that would be if you didn't trust Dr. West and what he did for a living. It was all a matter of perspective.

Eugene Francis West was born in Mount Vernon, Iowa, in 1852, which made him fifty-two on the day he walked into the Palace barbershop and met eighteen-year-old Inez Ingenthron. He was old enough to be her grandfather. Dr. West was five feet, ten inches tall, and weighed one hundred eighty-five pounds. He was a solid-looking man, with a large head, aquiline nose, and deeply set, striking blue eyes. He was handsome in an odd, distinguished sort of way.

Dr. West was as likely a candidate as any to sweep Inez off her feet. During the ensuing manicure, he asked *her* questions. He listened to *her*. It was he who nodded and smiled when the two talked. While Inez was ostensibly holding his hand as she buffed and lacquered his fingernails, it really was he who was holding hers. Dr. West had turned the tables on Inez.

The second time Dr. West showed up at the Palace barbershop was two days after their first meeting, and following that, Dr. West returned the next day and again the day after. No man needed a manicure that often. By the fifth time they saw each other, Inez was pouring her heart out to him. On his next visit, Dr. West brought with him a piece of jewelry, a small gold heart, which he pressed into Inez's hand. No inscription, just a simple locket to commemorate their budding romance.

Myrtle shook her head at the dalliance. She had seen plenty of manicure girls get seduced by wealthy men with silver tongues that promised the moon. The girls were conquests and nothing more. Inez would be neither the first nor the last. Dewey and the other barbers stayed out of it. Perhaps their reticence stemmed from the fact that they belonged to the fraternity of men. Or perhaps it was because they had gone through this with other clients and manicure girls, and there was just no point in saying anything. In this particular case, maybe it was because of what they knew about Dr. West.

To Inez, that Dr. West was married was beside the point. Cinderella might be some girls' fantasy, but it wasn't Inez's. She was a realist, and Dr. West was a catch, not just because he was generous with gifts—and soon the pleasure trips he took Inez on—but because he was generous of spirit. He also was an educated man who had been to college no less. There was something else about him. He knew women. He understood them. He was charming and chivalrous, solicitous and courtly. He actually bowed before Inez. He kissed her hand. He held her chair and opened any door she was about to enter.

Two or three days a week, after her shift ended at the Palace, Inez would meet Dr. West at Lotta's Fountain. The gilded fountain, given to the city by beloved actress Lotta Crabtree, had become a San Francisco landmark. Locals called it "Cape Horn" because it stood in a vortex of blustery crosscurrents. Lotta's Fountain was *the* place to meet, and Inez felt a part of the city's hustle and bustle while waiting expectantly for her Dr. West to appear, his long legs propelling him like a windup toy motoring around the corner of Geary and Kearny onto Market Street.

All the men Inez had met at the Palace had money, and few would have been reticent about spending it on such an appealing young woman. But Dr. West and Inez were especially simpatico. He was more than willing to show Inez a side of San Francisco that she'd only dreamt about—extravagant restaurants such as the Hoffman House on Pacific, Marchand's on Geary and Stockton, Techau's on Mason, Zinkand's on Market, Bergez on Pine, and, of course, the Poodle Dog on Mason and Eddy. Once at Jack's on Sacramento, Dr. West introduced Inez to owner Edouard Blanquie! Unmarried women weren't welcomed in the main dining rooms at these restaurants, and Inez and Dr. West dined in the private, curtained rooms off to the side or upstairs. At Tadich & Dumaraz on Leidesdorff, Inez drank champagne for the first time. Dr. West spared no expense, ordering a bottle with a label that read

Edouard Blanquie, owner of Jack's Restaurant, ca. 1896.

Moët & Chandon. The bubbly gave Inez a light-headed sensation that wasn't unpleasant.[1]

Inez was flying high, an impressionable young woman dining among the most powerful men in San Francisco. What difference did it make if people looked twice at her and her gentleman caller, the two of them, hand in hand, dashing to make the rounds at the city's most coveted nightspots? Dr. West never mentioned his wife, and Inez had no reason to bring her up. Why would she?

Dr. West followed a daily routine. Every morning at eleven, he'd close his medical offices at 318 Kearny Street for two hours. Then he'd pay a visit to Dr. Ferdinand Bazan's Russian and Turkish Baths three blocks away at 415 Sutter Street. There were apocryphal stories about the therapeutic waters curing everything from asthma to epilepsy. The baths occupied a three-story brick building, with the men's baths on the first floor and the women's on the second.[2]

Dr. West was a graduate of a curious medical school in Los Angeles called the California Eclectic Medical College. The Eclectics' approach to healing was based on herbal and botanical remedies; they rejected much of mainstream medicine, including coming-of-age research on germ-generated disease.[3] The college graduated its first class six years before Dr. West was to receive his license to practice medicine in 1889, and when he returned to the Bay Area, he opened an office on Turk Street between Taylor and Jones Streets.[4] Dr. West's business card read: "Eugene F. West, Accoucheur, Physician and Surgeon." *Accoucher* is the French word for the act of giving birth, and *accoucheur* is a medical specialist in labor and delivery. That, though, was a convenient cover. In reality, Dr. West was one of San Francisco's most prominent abortionists.

Ten years before he had the pleasure of first meeting Inez, Dr. West had been the suspect in a murder the *San Francisco Call* labeled "one of the most sensational and mysterious crimes in the criminal history of California." For a city as well acquainted with misdeeds as San Francisco, that was a particularly telling characterization.

As best as can be determined, these are the facts:

Ada Regent Gilmour was a thirty-year-old milliner from Colusa, California, a gold-mining town one hundred twenty-five miles northeast of San Francisco. Known as Addie and the identical twin sister of Emma, Miss Gilmour became pregnant (she'd been "wronged" and needed to "hide her shame," she told a friend), so she came to anonymous San Francisco, adopted an alias, Alice Gould, checked into a rooming house on Front Street, and made her way to Dr. West's office. Miss Gilmour couldn't bear to face her mother pregnant and unmarried, so she paid fifty dollars to "get herself out of trouble."[5] Addie recuperated at Dr. West's office for several days after which no one ever saw her alive again.

Within a week, a dismembered woman's head was found near Lime Point in the fishing village of Sausalito on the northern side of the Golden Gate. The head was inside a screen-and-wire netting, tied to a pier piling. If that wasn't macabre enough, in the Alameda mud flats in the East Bay, a boy named Stephenson discovered a woman's foot, jaggedly severed at the ankle, while he was chasing frogs. More remains were found by two other boys, Lloyd Hughes and Eddie Menges, in a five-gallon oil-can near Oakland's Peralta Street Wharf, which contained two hands, a pair of thighs, calves, arms, and intestines. At the bottom of the drum, police found an alligator-skin purse, two buttons, and assorted hatpins, all belonging to Miss Gilmour. An examination of the skull showed that the skin had been removed, ostensibly to prevent facial identification. The ears had been sheared off the head, and both eyeballs had been removed. Miss Gilmour's dentist, Dr. Richard Stewart, identified the skull as belonging to his former patient upon matching four incisor teeth he had recently filled. Police did not elaborate on how they matched the severed foot to Miss Gilmour, which fish in the bay had partially consumed.

DR. WEST ARRESTED.

Damaging Admission by the Physician.

FLIGHT FROM HIS OFFICE.

A Young Woman Also Taken Into Custody.

THE CRIME CLEARLY TRACED.

Claims of the Police That They Have Sufficient Evidence to Secure Conviction.

On August 20 last Miss Ada Regent Gilmour, a milliner of Colusa, arrived in this city presumably on business connected with her store at home. On September 2 Miss Gilmour disappeared from her room at the Esmer House, leaving no trace whatever behind her.

On the 14th inst., twelve days later, a woman's head was found inclosed in a loose wire netting and anchored in the bay not far from Sausalito, which was subsequently identified as that of the missing girl. At nearly the same time parts of the body of a woman were washed ashore on the flats near Oakland.

On Tuesday, both in the afternoon, Dr. Eugene F. West of 132 Turk street suddenly dropped out of sight, and was not to be found until he was arrested by detectives at 535 Turk street about 6 o'clock last evening. A few moments later Annie Staley, alias Johnson, an assistant of Dr. West, was arrested at her room in the Golden West Hotel.

These are the main facts, and form the framework about which the detectives and police are weaving the thread of a story which has seldom been equaled in the annals of crime, and which, if substantiated by evidence, which Chief Crowley says he has in abundance, would merit a punish-

Dr. Eugene F. West.

ment more severe than the limitations of modern justice will permit.

An arrest warrant for murder was issued for Dr. West, and a subsequent manhunt led police to a home on Turk Street, just as Dr. West was about to sit down for dinner. As a courtesy, detectives allowed Dr. West to finish his meal before he was remanded to the city jail. When word circulated that Miss Gilmour's accused murderer was behind bars, five hundred men and women converged on Broadway between Kearny and DuPont Streets, craning their necks to get a glimpse of the suspect inside. The man was no ordinary thug, but a popular and trusted physician. The vigilante crowd looked like a lynch mob, something San Francisco had plenty of experience with.

Interviewed in his cell, Dr. West told a reporter, "I suppose sentiment is going strong against me outside. The feeling is all one way, no doubt, because the people hear only one side of the story. But there's two sides to every story."

At his arraignment at Old City Hall, in police courtroom No. 2 before Judge Charles T. Conlan, Dr. West was described as "debonair," a man "at peace with the world and all mankind and nodded smilingly to a number of acquaintances whom he recognized among the crowd of spectators. . . . The prisoner gazed cautiously about the dingy courtroom or complacently stroked his brown beard as he smiled up at the Judge. Either the defendant is entirely careless of public sentiment or opinion or else he is really confident that he will be able to prove himself innocent of the awful crime with which he is charged."

Dr. West's most pressing matter at the moment was securing legal counsel, and he chose a well-connected attorney, J. N. E. Wilson. Escorted by detectives, Dr. West went to the People's Home Savings Bank on the first floor of the Flood Building on Market Street,

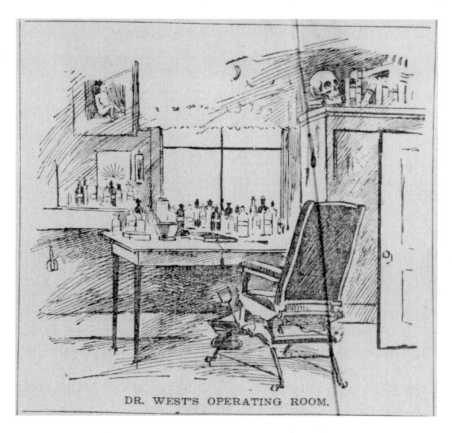

DR. WEST'S OPERATING ROOM.

where he kept the sizable amount of fifteen thousand dollars, along with several gold ingots stashed in a safe-deposit box. Dr. West gave his attorney a retainer of two thousand dollars and said he was prepared to pay three thousand more.

Dr. West was among scores of physicians, nurses, and lesser-trained personnel who routinely practiced abortions in San Francisco. So many women were desperate and insistent that these practitioners perform the illegal procedure on them that they often wouldn't leave until they received what they came for. The classified sections of the San Francisco newspapers were full of providers advertising their services, using transparent code. Dr. West's daily newspaper ad, for instance, read:

> Ladies' old reliable specialist for many years: all cases successfully treated; I am the most reliable specialist for you to consult: my services are recommended by thousands: my reputation world-renown; fees low.[6]

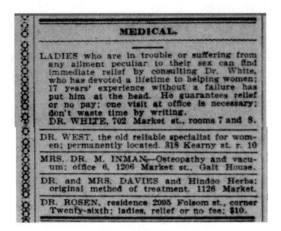

Even before the Addie Gilmour case, Dr. West had been involved in other incidents of abortions that had resulted in deaths. Two months earlier, a woman had died under suspicious circumstances, and Dr. West had signed her death certificate. The official cause of death was pelvic peritonitis, but an autopsy revealed the patient had a week earlier undergone an abortion.[7]

As his trial began in the fall of 1893, one of his patients, twenty-year-old May Howard testified that the day following Miss Gilmour's death, Dr. West had asked her to manufacture a scenario of seeing Addie on a San Francisco–Oakland ferry and, during an ensuing conversation, that Addie confessed to Miss Howard she was despondent and contemplating suicide. Miss Howard testified that Dr. West had coached her to say that Addie bolted downstairs on the ferry and suddenly disappeared, presumably jumping into the bay.

A jury convicted Dr. West of murder, but the California Supreme Court overturned that decision because of an arcane legal technicality. A new trial got under way in late 1895, and in this proceeding, Dr. West was not charged with murder, but with performing an illegal surgery—an abortion. He admitted that he ministered to Addie Gilmour, but maintained that it was only after she had already received a botched abortion. Dr. West testified that Miss Gilmour had refused to disclose who had operated on her; he speculated that she might have tried to abort the fetus herself.

The defense portrayed Dr. West not as an abortion provider, but as a physician who was an exceptionally skilled healer. When Dr. West took the stand, he testified about an encounter he had with John Gilmour, Addie's father, who had traveled to

San Francisco desperate to find his daughter. Mr. Gilmour had pleaded with Dr. West: "If she is in a disreputable house, tell me where she is. If she is sick, take me to her. If she is dead, show me where she is buried." Dr. West testified that he told the grief-stricken father that Addie had died and that he had turned her body over to medical students.

As in most murder trials, there were many versions of what exactly led to Miss Gilmour's death; perhaps the most credible belonged to a twenty-four-year-old medical student by the name of D. B. Plymire, who said that a despondent Addie confided in him that she was pregnant and "did not dare face her mother" and "was determined to have something done." She had a trunk filled with her belongings shipped to Dr. West's office, and the day after the procedure, she had a high fever. The next time D. B. Plymire came by Dr. West's office to visit Miss Gilmour, she and her trunk had disappeared.

An unnamed reporter covering the trial for the *San Francisco Chronicle* talked to ferry agents who, following Miss Gilmour's death, recalled seeing a man who resembled Dr. West cross the bay several times, always at night, and each time with a series of packages or valises. The man took the ferry to Tiburon, Oakland, and Alameda, the agents recalled, where he dropped the containers overboard. The reporter suggested that Miss Gilmour's pregnancy likely was the result of an ill-fated romance with a married family friend from Colusa.

The judge reminded the jury that the crime for which Dr. West was being tried was not murder, but performing an illegal operation. The issue wasn't whether Dr. West had dissected or sold Addie Gilmour's cadaver or whether he had killed her and dumped her into the bay. The judge told the jurors that if Addie had visited Dr. West after an abortion had been performed and Dr. West's role had been to attend to her medical needs, then it was his professional duty to do so.

The jurors filed out of the courtroom at three fifteen the day after Christmas, never a good time for the prosecution. Those polled in the courtroom, though, said they believed the jury wouldn't be out long and that a guilty verdict would surely be rendered, considering the multitude of evidence pointing to Dr. West's culpability.

Within fifty minutes, the jurors returned. Those in the courtroom noticed Dr. West's neck glistened with perspiration. He and attorney J. N. E. Wilson stood and turned right to hear the foreman announce the jury's verdict:

"*Not guilty!*"

The judge banged his gavel to silence those in the gallery, which did little.

DR. WEST ACQUITTED

Of the Charge of Murdering Addie Gilmour Late Testimony

SAN FRANCISCO, Dec. 26.—In the trial of Dr. West for the murder of Addie Gilmour, today, Dr. West took the stand in his own behalf and testified that a criminal operation on the girl had been performed by some one before she came to him. The girl had been sent to him by Dr. W. A. Harvey. The witness said he had given the girl's body to Dr. A. S. Tuchler for dissecting purposes, and Tuchler had afterwards said he had cut up the body and thrown it into the bay.

The jury returned a verdict of not guilty. Now that Dr. West has been acquitted, Dr. Tuchler, to whom West gave the body of Addie Gilmore, partially corroborates the story. Tuchler says that West called on him at midnight and asked his assistance in dissecting the body of a young woman. He declined, but offered to take the head, which West gave to him. He wrapped it in wire gauze and put it in the water off Lime point, where it was found, in order that the action of the salt water might remove the flesh. When asked why he had not come forward and testified to this at the trial, Tuchler said he considered it none of his business. Before West was acquitted Tuchler denied all connection with the case, and said he would go on the stand and deny it.

Dr. Harvey, who West says sent the girl to him, still denies that he had anything to do with it.

Mr. Wilson cupped Dr. West's elbow, and the two made their way out of the courtroom and through the crowds. Dr. West was a free man.

Despite his acquittal, considering the ghoulish testimony against him, one might think that after two scandalous trials, Dr. West's reputation in San Francisco would have been ruined, and that if he intended to continue practicing his illegal specialty, he would have moved and set up a practice in another city, preferably far away.

But San Francisco being San Francisco, Dr. West's practice didn't seem to have been affected in the least. If anything, his business increased. A week later, Dr. West's waiting room was filled with even more pregnant women than before his run-in with the law and Addie Gilmour. Even though abortion had been outlawed throughout the United States, starting in Connecticut in 1821, in California in 1872, and in all states by 1880,[8] San Franciscans didn't seem very outraged that Dr. West and scores of providers continued to perform thousands of abortions on demand every year.

A myth promulgated by newspapers, magazines, and novels of the day was that women who went to abortion clinics were young, unmarried, and promiscuous.

"Wayward girls" is how they were often described. The narrative portrayed went something like this: God-fearing and naive girls, plied with liquor or drugs by lecherous rogues, were seduced, ravaged, and abandoned, often turning to prostitution as a last resort before dying an ignominious death.

Incidents such as these surely happened. But the majority of any abortion provider's patients were mothers already with several children. Economics dictated most abortions; couples or women alone didn't have enough money to feed, clothe, and raise an extra child. At the turn of the century, more and more unmarried women had moved to big cities like San Francisco to seek jobs, living apart from their families, often rooming in female-only boardinghouses. Some of these women undoubtedly became pregnant outside the institution of marriage. Occasionally, such women showed up at an abortion provider's door, but hardly as often as married women. Instead, single pregnant women were usually channeled to homes for unwed mothers; these facilities were common throughout the United States, and especially so in San Francisco.

The Pacific Rescue Home for Erring Women, founded in 1888, was one such facility, and in its first three years, it cared for one hundred ninety pregnant women who gave up newborns for adoption. With support from New York millionaire Charles N. Crittenton, it was renamed the Florence Crittenton Home shortly after its opening. Organizations that catered to unwed pregnant women with lodging, food, and guidance were generally structured along religious lines, with San Francisco's Crittenton Home and the Beulah Rescue Home, run by the Salvation Army, among the largest. In the Bay Area, there were many smaller private facilities, including a lodging called Dr. Funke's Maternity Clinic in Alameda.[9]

Such temporary housing and support was not designed for married women, who had few options should they find themselves with an unwanted pregnancy and chose to go full-term and place the newborn up for adoption. The church did little except counsel married women to submit to their husbands' carnal desires and, if they found themselves pregnant, bear yet another child, swelling the size of their family. Clergy seldom discussed economics and children. In many households, women feared for their safety if their husbands discovered they were pregnant; beatings weren't uncommon. For many, abortion served as a couple's only means of birth control. That's why Dr. West and others who practiced abortion became so financially well-off.

It's unclear what Inez knew about Dr. West when the two began their dalliance. Surely the barbers at the Palace would have known about the lurid trials involving Dr. West. If Inez had heard about Addie Gilmour, one wonders whether she would

A window exhibit at the Florence Crittenton Home, 1914.

have proceeded so quickly. Perhaps Dr. West's history of helping women out of their predicaments made him all the more attractive to Inez. That, and all the money he was spending, wining and dining her. It was during a late-evening dinner at swank Delmonico's in May when Dr. West came clean. Holding her hand at a candlelight dinner, he told Inez that he did just one thing in his medical practice: terminate pregnancies. The way Dr. West described his calling to Inez was that he helped women in need. Inez seemed surprised, but that might have just been the reaction she figured that Dr. West was hoping for.

In polite company, there were many ways to describe his services. The word *abortion* had harsh connotations, and few people used the term openly. Handling female problems was one way to describe it. Suppressing or relieving female irregularities was another. Dozens of euphemisms abounded: relief for women in trouble; ladies' help; female issues positively and quickly resolved; remedies of irregularity; suppression of sickness; osteopathy and vacuum; or, simply, women fixed up.[10]

The way police and prosecutors officially saw it, Dr. West was performing a felony criminal act.[11] California Penal Code Section 274 read:

> Every person who provides, supplies, or administers to any woman, or procures any woman, or procures any woman to take any medicine, drug or substance, or uses or employs any instrument or other means whatever, with intent thereby to procure the miscarriage of such woman, unless the same is necessary to preserve her life, is punishable by imprisonment in the state prison for not less than two nor more than five years.[12]

The onus of the law fell on abortion providers, not the women who sought or received abortions. But in practice, few abortion providers ever were arrested, particularly in a city as unchaste as San Francisco. Seldom did abortionists end up in prison for performing what was generally considered nothing more than a necessary evil. If an abortionist was ever tried in court, a conviction was exceedingly difficult to obtain. Testimony from patients was usually needed, and few women would go public with the admission that they had had an abortion. The demand for abortionists' services was so great anyway that officials almost always chose to look the other way. There was no collective will to shut abortion providers down. Dr. West and other abortionists—competent or not—had little to worry about, as long as patients didn't die and providers continued to operate discreetly.

In addition, there were bundles of money to be made by keeping abortion alive. San Francisco mayor Eugene Schmitz and political boss Abe Ruef, the same men Inez had seen at the Palace barbershop, routinely took bribes to ensure that dozens of abortionists could operate with impunity. Schmitz and Ruef had their hands in practically everything illegal that went on in the city, not just the abortion business. In reality, bribes from abortion providers to police and city officials were normal and expected. It was the way business was conducted. There were great sums of money to be made by everyone, except, of course, the women who received the abortions. As Inez grew savvier and more sophisticated, she would find that out firsthand.

FOUR

MEN WITH
RESOURCES

Almost a decade after the Gilmour trial, after performing thousands more abortions, Dr. West found himself reclining on a couch next to his mistress, Inez. They were sipping champagne in a private upstairs dining room at Delmonico's, enjoying a newly discovered delicacy that originated in the ovaries of Pacific white sturgeon and was called caviar. While dabbing the tiny black roe pearls on petite crackers, Dr. West posed a proposition to Inez: He needed a trusted employee, a receptionist, someone to welcome and put women at ease, but he also needed an assistant at his side in the operating room. Dr. West's wife, the former Annie Staley, who had worked part-time in her husband's employ had recently turned to painting Chinese murals. Whatever Inez was earning at the Palace, Dr. West would double.

There was no question that Inez would accept the offer. The manicurist job had served its purpose, and that was to get out of her mother's clutches and to meet men like Eugene West. By getting hired at the Palace, Inez had already climbed a half dozen rungs of an impossibly steep ladder. If she could get into Dr. West's operating room, she'd climb higher. She'd learn a trade, possibly become a nurse. Inez knew the position wouldn't snare her a husband, but she had never gone out with Dr. West to get married. What she sought was something more substantial: an opportunity to be independent. Emotions like love and affection didn't enter into Inez's life equation. She was from too poor a family. She needed every break she could entice her way.

Inez had to grab hold of the slippery brass ring the first time it went around, because in her circles, it seldom went around at all. In that sense, Alice Ingenthron, Inez's overbearing mother, and Fred, her alcoholic father, had taught her well.

On a chilly December evening in 1904, just before her shift at the Palace ended, Inez told Myrtle that she'd be quitting the barbershop to work full-time for Dr. West.

"Don't think he'll ever marry you, Iney," Myrtle said, shaking her head. "He's like all the others. He'll treat you fine until he gets tired of you, and then he'll find another girl, and you'll be out on that pretty fanny of yours. And by then, I'll have another girl and I won't be able to hire you back. You sure you wanna leave? You sure it's the best for you, honey?"

Enterprising Inez wanted to make something of herself, and to do that she had to get out of the barbershop. It had served her purposes. Surely Myrtle could understand that. But Inez stopped short in explaining her motives for quitting. Myrtle had a job, but was she successful? Hardly, Inez thought. The last thing Inez wanted was to end up running a manicure concession in a barbershop, even as swanky as the one in the Palace.

Dewey and Virgil, the two barbers Inez had gotten to know the best, wished her well. They'd miss her, and so would her customers, they told her.

Just as she was saying her goodbyes, Dewey, a pale string bean with a wife and five children, asked Inez a rather peculiar favor.

"Would you let me do it?"

Inez looked puzzled.

"You know, Iney. What you do."

Inez tilted her head and understood. "Why, of course, Dewey," she said, flipping her mane of Titian hair over her shoulder, then standing directly in front of him, perfectly still.

Dewey placed both hands around Inez's corseted waist and interlocked his bony fingers. She giggled as she always did on such occasions, and everyone—Myrtle, Vernon, Henry, Virgil, even Dewey—laughed.

"Thank you, ma'am," Dewey said, embarrassed, quickly turning around to the marble counter, busying himself rearranging a display of celluloid combs, the latest innovation in personal grooming.

Inez showed up for work the next day at Dr. West's office, at 318 Kearny Street. She started in the front office, as agreed, welcoming women at the door, offering them tea, politely yet firmly arranging for payment for Dr. West's services, which ran the hefty fee of fifty dollars. If after an examination the woman was judged to be past two months, the fee increased to seventy-five dollars. Dr. West instructed Inez to be stern on the issue of money. There would be no negotiation. No partial payments. Sobbing would not sway Inez or Dr. West. It was all or nothing.

Dr. West instructed Inez to take down the names of each and every patient, along with her address, and record it in a leather-bound book. This was more than book-keeping. It was insurance. This was Dr. West's way of ensuring that if he ever were arrested, he'd have collateral information to use as a bargaining chip. To go public with names of women who had had abortions at his hands was a powerful tool Dr. West could someday wield. He'd rather not, but at least he'd have the ammunition. Women always could have given Inez aliases, but considering the agitated state almost all were in, as well as the surroundings of a medical office, that seldom happened.

All of Dr. West's patients were white and middle or upper middle class. This was because finding an abortionist was almost always accomplished through a network of like-minded women of the same socioeconomic level. Whispered word of mouth led patients to Dr. West, which had the effect of excluding Chinese, Mexicans, or black women. His fees, too, limited who came to his office. In almost all cases, they amounted to more than a month's salary for any woman. Why so much? Because Dr. West could get it. There was a built-in premium for engaging in an illegal practice that carried such a high demand.

In fact, Inez soon realized that women would pay almost anything for Dr. West's services. By the time they gathered up enough nerve to show up at his office, with their internal clock ticking louder and louder each day, Dr. West's fees were the least of their worries. His patients were equal parts forlorn and grateful. Almost all looked at their medical condition as a personal affliction they could absolutely no longer bear. Some seemed relieved to pay the doctor his exorbitant fee, as though it was an assurance that Dr. West was highly regarded and expert in his field.

While complications could arise, the procedure was straightforward, particu-larly for an experienced provider like Dr. West. The chief risk was infection. The discovery and implementation of sulfa drugs, penicillin, and antibiotics, which work to stabilize infection, was decades away; experienced and competent abortionists during this era knew they had to be vigilant in maintaining a sterile and hygienic environment. That was paramount for the well-being of patients, as well as the lon-gevity of any abortionist's business.

Just as she had hoped, within three months, Inez had elevated herself from receptionist to full-time medical assistant. Annie Staley West occasionally came by the office and was decidedly cool to Inez. Mrs. West had learned to turn a blind eye to her husband's flirtations. After all, she was Mrs. West. It was she, not Inez, who shared the couple's grand Russian Hill home with Dr. West. It was Annie, who got to stroll arm in arm with Dr. West into the grand foyer of the Tivoli Opera House, among throngs of other wealthy couples out for the evening.

At nineteen, Inez was on her own. She had moved out of her family's Bernal Heights flat into a women's rooming house at 324 Bush Street called the Elmer House. Inez and Nettie tried to meet once a week at Westerfeld's downtown, but Inez took care not to talk about Dr. West. Like Myrtle at the barbershop, Nettie didn't approve of Inez's liaison with Dr. West, and she'd disapprove more if she knew that he was paying Inez's rent, a salary, along with spending money that Inez used to buy hats and an occasional dress for herself. Inez had come a long way.

After six months on the job, standing next to Dr. West in his operating room with an anesthetized patient lying in front of them, Inez came to the realization that the procedure Dr. West was about to perform, she could learn too. More than learn—master. Inez didn't need to go to medical or nursing school. She was a quick study. Why wouldn't she be able to do what Dr. West did? Why couldn't she earn the kind of money Dr. West earned?

Dr. West seemed to take a certain professional pride in the number of patients he could perform procedures on in a single day, working quickly, one woman after the other. On particularly busy days, he'd often attend to two women on adjoining operating tables simultaneously. Some days he performed as many as fifteen abortions. The speed with which he worked might also have had to do with something else Inez was to discover about Dr. West. Before an operation, he'd often snort a powdery substance Inez soon learned was cocaine. Such a practice wasn't unusual at the time, particularly for physicians. Cocaine was touted as a fashionable and inexpensive curative, a pick-me-up tonic. Legal and readily available to everyone without a prescription, the drug was particularly accessible to physicians, dentists, and pharmacists, and many became enthusiasts. Inez noticed that Dr. West would become chatty, energetic, and even amorous with some of his patients after he inhaled the powder. It wasn't until 1911 that California joined forty-five other states in restricting recreational cocaine and other such substances, but that was six years away. Even then, many physicians indulged in the drug for purely personal pleasure.[1]

Under the influence, Dr. West worked rapidly and that occasionally led to mistakes. He'd get sloppy while operating, Inez noticed. If you were a strong woman, you'd do fine in his hands. But if you came in sickly, it might take longer to recover. Some women got infections. Some got sick. Some weren't able to bounce back from the procedure for weeks.

Why work for a man when I can work for myself, Inez thought. And, perhaps even more forward-thinking for the time, why should a pregnant woman go to a man for an abortion when a skilled woman could provide the same service better? Once they paid, once he completed the procedure, Dr. West was finished. On to another girl, another patient, another admirer desperate for his services. Dr. West seemed to crave the adulation he got from the women he attended to.

Inez made a promise to herself. Take what she could from this man. Learn what she could. Profit from his knowledge and experience. Figure out the business. Then, if she could amass enough savings, she'd open her own clinic for women run by a woman.[2]

One late afternoon, as Inez was making her way back to the Elmer House from the clinic, a tall, full-chested man with an elaborate waxed mustache buttonholed her in the street.

"Inez?" he asked as she was turning the windy corner at Montgomery, so gusty she had to hold on to her hat so it didn't fly off her head.

"You look wonderful," the man said.

Inez was accustomed to strangers accosting her. It happened all the time. San Francisco was full of hustlers. They said they were "lost" and needed directions, or they wanted to know the time. Occasionally, they'd pay her a compliment, but some men had the most asinine way of flattering a young lady. "I just wanted to see if the front was as good as the back" was a popular pickup line. Some of these men were pickpockets and purse snatchers. You had to be careful.

But there was something familiar with this man. Had he been one of her customers at the barbershop?

Inez realized that the man had lived in a walk-up around the corner from the Ingenthrons[3] when she, Alice, Nettie, Walter, and Harry shared the tiny flat at 1346 Howard Street, between Ninth and Tenth Streets. She recalled that he was married, and that he and his wife, Mary, had a young son. George Washington Merritt was the man's name, which he said with a certain pomp and flourish.

Under the guise of "talking about the old neighborhood," Inez consented to meet him next Tuesday. "Won't your wife be joining us?" Inez asked. She was used to men like him.

"Mary and I have gone our separate ways."[4]

Well, at least he's single. Or so he said. But what could this George Washington Merritt, with his serpentine moustache and thick brush of hair, do for her?

Dr. West would soon be onto another girl, another acquisition. That was no surprise. Her apprenticeship with Dr. West had taught Inez more than a profession. It had taught her about herself. She didn't mind being escorted, pampered, even ogled at by men with resources. Inez had thoroughly enjoyed the life Dr. West had shown her. Perhaps this George Washington Merritt might well serve as a replacement for Dr. West. A kind of suitor in the wings.

Inez met Mr. Merritt for a cup of coffee, and like most men she encountered, he spun an elaborate yarn. They always had stories, these men. He was born in Baltimore and had worked, it seemed, everywhere. In Pittsburgh, Washington, Brooklyn, and now San Francisco. He said he had worked for the railroad, sold medical tonics out of the back of a horse-drawn truck, and fancied himself a budding playwright.[5] Mr. Merritt wasn't as old as Dr. West; he volunteered that he was thirty-seven, still almost twice Inez's age. He said people called him "the General," and he seemed to have some money. That, at least, sounded promising.

"Where can I take you to show you what you deserve?" George Washington Merritt asked Inez in the kind of grand way that should have sent her running.

"The Palace," she replied automatically.

"Then the Palace it is," Mr. Merritt declared triumphantly.

That Tuesday, they'd go to the Palace Grill.

It'd been ten months since she'd last been inside the Palace Hotel. It felt odd to walk into the main entrance on New Montgomery instead of the employees' portico around the corner. Inez thought of herself as an imposter, and Joey, the squeaky clean bellboy, noticed her right away.

"Iney, it's you!" he piped up.

The two exchanged pleasantries, and Inez introduced him to Mr. Merritt. "Pleasure to meet ya, sir," Joey said.

As Mr. Merritt escorted Inez arm in arm through the lobby, White Hat was corralling a man with a drooping belly into a discussion about his latest filly. A covey of reporters milling around the reception area was hoping to pick up an item or two about anyone famous staying upstairs.

As Inez and George Washington Merritt walked past the swirling barbershop's pole, Inez glanced inside. At once, she saw a new girl dressed in a manicurist's uniform. Myrtle and Vernon, Virgil, Dewey and Henry all were going about their business, the after-work trade, with four men in the high leather chairs. Two were getting haircuts, one had a hot towel covering his face, and the other had a beard of shaving cream that looked like whisks of meringue. Inez thought she even could hear Henry running his straight razor up and down the thick leather strop.

But that's not what Inez was staring at. The girl, the manicurist at his side, she looked tawdry and, just as bad, brassy. She was leaning way too close in to the man whose hand she was cradling. And was talking!

Inez couldn't breathe for a second or two. She had seen all she needed. This new girl who didn't want to be poor any longer, doing everything she could to vault from the barbershop to somewhere else, and Inez had a good idea where that would be.

Inez tightened her grasp on George Washington Merritt's arm, and the two strode into the Palace Grill, where that evening they ate like railroad barons. Where Mr. Merritt got the money to pay for the magnificent dinner wasn't Inez's concern. He had a way about himself, a man of presence that commanded respect. For dessert, he ordered a bottle of champagne and strawberries Romanoff, which they fed each other.

FIVE

MONEY SOAP, ITALIAN POTION NO. 12, AND THE BRAZILIAN BELEZA

Throwing caution to the wind, Inez started what began as a fling with George Washington Merritt, who turned out to be forty-two, not thirty-seven. Mr. Merritt was a large, handsome, and, at times, boisterous man who got what he wanted. He was a determined salesman who wouldn't take no for an answer. He had a ready smile and striking, mahogany-colored eyes with a dreamy, faraway look, which might have presaged prodigious accomplishments or that Mr. Merritt was an irredeemable ne'er-do-well. Inez had her own thoughts about which.

While certainly not of the same social class as Dr. West, Mr. Merritt had the same gift of gab. Wherever he went, he made friends. He seemed to know everyone. As far as Inez could tell, he and his wife had been granted a divorce in February 1904.[1] For however long Inez and his romance would last, marriage wasn't in the mix, at least for her it wasn't. Inez had seen the ravages marriage wreaked on her parents, and when she considered Dr. West and her customers at the Palace, marriage was just a license to philander. If you were a man, that is. For Inez, the older and wealthier the man, the more grateful he'd be for her company and the more he'd have to spend on her. To Inez, Mr. Merritt would be a way to amuse herself, to continue seeing the city lights, and what was wrong with that?

George Washington Merritt.

At Dr. West's clinic, Inez was on her way to becoming as proficient an abortionist as Dr. West. Occasionally he'd step back during a procedure and motion Inez to take over, just to see how effortlessly, expertly, and quickly his protégée worked. Dr. West confided that Inez was a better student than Annie, his wife, had been. "You've got the touch," he'd tell Inez, a compliment she cherished. Dr. West might have been exaggerating for his own purposes, but Inez chose to think he was sincere in this regard.

His clinic was as busy as it had ever been, and the city was booming once again. Huge quantities of gold were said to have been discovered in Alaska's Yukon region, and San Francisco was the embarkation port to access the auric find. The goldfields were said to rival California's bonanza of '49, and that beckoned tens of thousands of miners every month to the wilds of the Alaska frontier. At the same time, the Spanish-American War had begun, and thousands of military recruits from across the United States were convoying to the San Francisco Bay Area to be trained and shipped out to the Philippines and Guam, both Spanish possessions.

Once again, men poured into San Francisco, wowed by the city's geography, climate, and mix of European-style civility and bawdy excess. Of the hundreds of burgeoning brothels in town, none could compete with the famed Hotel Nymphia, on Pacific near Stockton Street, a three-story sex factory built in 1899 with one hundred fifty cubicles on each floor, each with a smiling nude woman inside looking for company. Police nixed the owners' first choice for the bagnio's name, which they wanted to call Hotel Nymphomaniac.[2]

The renewed influx of men transformed San Francisco's bustling port into a never-ending flotilla of ships, both military and mercantile, further connecting the West Coast with the rest of the world. Outside of New York, no other port was busier; in the process, San Francisco became the fourth largest city in America. A runaway economy and an abundance of men fueled spending Everyone seemingly prospered. And as economists and statisticians are wont to say, when spending booms, pregnancies soar.

With Mr. Merritt taking over Dr. West's role as Inez's paramour, Inez became more independent and self-sufficient. She had received a crash course in San Francisco high life from Dr. West, and it was now her time to illuminate for G. W. Merritt all that San Francisco had to offer. As long as he was paying for the lessons, Inez had no problem tutoring him. The arrangement seemed to suit Mr. Merritt and, curiously, Dr. West, who was able to keep his proficient assistant, as well as press on to new conquests. Dr. West didn't mind in the least.

As was his habit, Dr. West continued sniffing cocaine while displaying effusive attention to his most captivating patients. He seemed to consider Inez as more a colleague than a lover, and as long as Inez kept straight in her mind why she was in Dr. West's office—to learn a profession—she was fine with this turn of affection.

Sometime near the first of the year in 1906, Inez began to experience something she'd never felt before. On a Wednesday morning, she awoke in a cold sweat, and without a moment's notice, she vomited. Over the coming weeks, she felt exhausted. No one needed to tell Inez she was pregnant.

How she had managed to get in such a state was beyond her. She had taken all the precautions of the day—insisting that her partner use a condom and, as an extra barrier, inserting a small round sponge soaked in quinine sulfate before engaging in sex. As far as Inez could figure, the father had to be G. W. Merritt. At least, she *thought* the father had to be G. W. Merritt. Inez had started seeing him in October and they became intimate shortly thereafter. She had stopped sleeping with Dr. West in September, by her recollection. But the truth was there had been other men, discreet affairs, some men

from the Palace, others she had met when she and Nettie had gone out to social events. It went without saying that Inez had kept these liaisons from both G.W. and Dr. West.

When she could no longer conceal her pregnancy, Inez informed G.W. For what it was worth, his reaction was heartening. Mr. Merritt was proud of the fact that a man his age had sired what undoubtedly would be a child as beautiful and as smart as its young mother. He unabashedly hoped it would be a boy; Inez shrugged her shoulders to that last bit of whimsy.

All this, of course, was dependent on Inez's choosing to go full-term and have the baby. When she mulled over her options, there really were only two: have an abortion or move to the Florence Crittenton Home or any of the other homes for unwed mothers. The latter was out of the question. Inez wasn't about to live with a bunch of pregnant girls, get lectured on the evils of premarital sex, and then give away the baby to strangers. That left getting an abortion.

Evening rush hour at the Ferry Building, September 1912.

By her own estimate, the baby would be due sometime at the beginning of August. Inez's belly was growing. She could feel her body changing. She was beginning to have difficulty fitting into her clothes, which were tight over her slender, cinched waist.

Inez continued working at Dr. West's clinic, but her bouts of vomiting betrayed her condition, and when asked point-blank one day whether she was pregnant, Inez could hardly conceal the fact any longer. Dr. West proposed terminating her pregnancy without cost, perhaps a self-serving offer considering her growing importance in his clinic. But it was a proposition Inez politely declined.

For the time being, she told the doctor she intended to go full-term, not give the baby up for adoption, and that she'd raise it with G. W. Merritt.

Though his practice was never to second-guess his patients' decisions, Dr. West had his doubts. But that would be Inez's business, not his. Dr. West knew, though, that employing a pregnant woman in an abortion clinic would appear somehow wholly unseemly, and he suggested that Inez take a temporary leave from the clinic, even though that would necessitate a replacement. Ever prepared, Dr. West was in the midst of a romance with a young woman he'd met on the ferry coming back from Sausalito to San Francisco, and she seemed to be just the kind of assistant he could train. Not coincidentally, Inez noticed in Dr. West's desk drawer several gold heart lockets in a box from a Market Street jewelry store.

When informed of her decision, the doctor saw no reason to continue paying Inez's rent at the Elmer House. Dr. West assured Inez that she'd be welcomed back whenever she wanted to return. There'd always be a place for her, he promised.

There is no record of G. W. Merritt and Inez Ingenthron ever marrying; the San Francisco newspapers carried each and every notice of vital statistics, which included births, marriages, divorces, and deaths, along with all filed real estate transactions, so it's unlikely the two tied the knot, at least in the Bay Area. After her public dalliance with Dr. West, it's unlikely too that Inez, who by this time could be labeled a bohemian and an iconoclast, cared one way or the other.

On her last day of employment with Dr. West, Inez did something she'd never done before, an action foreign to Inez's character. Dr. West kept in a glass cabinet several sets of medical instruments—forceps, speculums, dilators, curettes, and wire catheters. He maintained a travel kit of seventeen German-made stainless steel instruments, should he ever pay a visit to a patient's home. Several were as long as eighteen inches, others as stout as five inches. They fit in the pockets of a canvas satchel, a sort of apron that rolled up and tied with a sash.

With a fleeting pang of guilt, Inez opened the cabinet and lifted the cloth carrying case and medical instruments inside. As a second thought, she stuffed in her
purse two brown-tinted bottles: one containing quinine pills, the other chloroform.
The pills would be a salve against most infection, the anesthetic liquid—well,
who knew when that would come in handy. What good would all that she had
learned be if she didn't have the tools to practice her newly acquired trade?

Perhaps she stole the instruments in the event she decided to use them on herself.
Or to instruct someone she trusted to use them on her. Did she really want a baby, despite G. W. Merritt's assurances of support? Did she really want to become a mother?

When Inez confided all this to her sister, Nettie first told her to separate herself
from Mr. Merritt immediately. Nettie had met him on one occasion, and once had
been enough. Nettie had made her own mistake with a dreamer and had paid the
price for it. As for the pregnancy, Nettie advised Inez to go back to Dr. West and ask
him to do what he did for all his patients. "Do what you ought to do, and you know
what that is," Nettie told Inez, who nodded and said she'd think about both.

"Well, you better think quickly!" Nettie replied, shaking her head, not believing
her smart little sister had gotten into such a mess.

With Inez out of Dr. West's clinic, G.W. proposed that Inez go into business with
him. Merritt could come up with a dozen surefire ways to become rich, but executing
any one of them was usually too much work, the devil always being in the details. His
latest was selling medicinal tonics, ointments, soaps, and potions out of the back of a
wagon he parked South of the Slot, moving from neighborhood to neighborhood, one
street at a time. He'd park his horse-drawn wagon on a corner near a farmers' market,
where he'd hawk his concoctions, which ranged from elixirs that guaranteed pretty
much everything—from making intractable bowels move smoothly to curing "total and
complete insanity," as well as a host of maladies in between, including heartburn, headaches, hair loss, menstrual cramps, flat feet, ulcers, and hemorrhoids. Specific creams
made breasts either larger or smaller, and the multitude of liniments he sold made
penises larger. The trick was in the packaging, G.W. had discovered. He hired the premier printing firm in the city, Mutual Label & Lithographic, which produced tricolor
boxes and labels that heralded cures to the most skeptical of buyers. G.W. mixed all
the potions himself in the corner of a cluttered livery on Harrison near Seventh Street.

He touted that all his products were extracted from exotic, rare plants found
in the depths of the Brazilian Amazon, available in limited supply and exclusively
through him. G.W. advertised that he was the sole US distributor of everything he

sold. He maintained that he had acquired the botanicals on expeditions to Manaus during which he had been taken captive by a tribe of savage Indians, and after escaping, swimming through piranha-infested waters, he had smuggled the seeds back to California, where he had cultivated them into thriving plants and trees.

One of G.W.'s best sellers was a magical soap that, if the buyer bathed in it twice a day, would bring riches (and very dry skin) to the bather. The bar carried the straightforward name Money Soap. G.W. sold medicinal rubs that guaranteed love, pregnancy, and marriage. He also stocked ointments that assured bad luck—health reversals, divorces, or crushing unrelenting headaches. He sold a viscous liquid that when applied to a mother-in-law's soles, presumably while asleep, was guaranteed to make her go mad. These particular products smelled horrible and, for obvious reasons, were stocked under the counter, available only on referral from a trusted customer. All told, G.W. had more than one hundred fifty medicines for ailments, desires, and vendettas. When the potions were combined, the number of offerings was greater than ten thousand. If you wished for your homely daughter to meet a suitable man who had financial resources and was handsome but courting another woman, there was an assortment to choose from, and for a fee, Merritt would compound them into a single remedy. Customers were assured success or would receive a full refund.

Now on the road with G.W., Inez proved to be a silver-tongued barker herself, extolling the virtues of every elixir, which in reality were made from camphor, rubbing alcohol, cod liver oil, fragrance, and vegetable dye. Anything botanical came from the fields of Marin County, north of the Golden Gate, and included sprinklings of hyssop, sage, or marjoram G.W. pulverized himself with a mortar and pestle in the Harrison Street livery. Would-be customers jostled each other, often standing ten rows deep around the wagon, craning to get a glimpse of Inez, dressed as a gypsy in a peasant dress with a scarf over her head, and a foreign-sounding accent spouting from her lips. Ever the showman, G.W. would introduce Inez to one and all as the Brazilian Beleza.

Inez was to make an important and lucrative innovation to the itinerant enterprise of which she and G.W. were presumed partners. Inez insisted that G.W. carry an assortment of feminine and "personal" items, which included a variety of contraceptives. These were not placebos, but the real thing and were the only items in G.W.'s wagon that actually worked.

Inez's employ in Dr. West's clinic had taught her not to be shy when it came to issues of such intimate nature, and as the Brazilian Beleza, Inez sold condoms to both men and women, which went under names such as "safes," "skins," "protectors," "capotes," and "caps." Each was different in size, material, and cost. Inez wasn't the least reticent about showing what the differences were by demonstrating them on a carrot or a cucumber (depending on whether her audience was primarily female or male) kept under the counter. Although they might have blushed, women in particular were fascinated by both the demonstration and the family-planning impact such materials might have on their lives. Women could engage in intercourse and not be burdened with pregnancy. What a concept!

If they used any birth control beyond the rhythm method, most couples didn't choose condoms, which at the time were considered disreputable, for use in brothels with prostitutes who might carry disease. Men complained about the lack of sensation using them. Their effectiveness was wholly in the hands of men too. Realizing this, Inez sold a host of feminine contraceptives, which included "sponge balls" and "Mediterranean toilet sponges." These were cervical barriers soaked in compounds such as chloride of soda, carbolic acid, boric acid, tannic acid, and glycerin. Inez also offered an assortment of douches, pessaries, and herbal pills that contained aloe, hellebore, savin, tansy, and rue.[3] These were to induce abortions; sometimes they worked, most of the time they didn't. Once word got around about the Brazilian Beleza, customers would line up at an appointed corner even before Inez and G.W. arrived for the day.

Inez also convinced G.W. to create another product for sale, and this proved to be the most popular of everything the couple sold. It was a green-tinted bottle of plain olive oil but packaged as Italian Lotion No. 12, under a lithographic sticker of a raven-haired woman in what appeared to be the throes of something very intense, either an orgasm or a bowel movement. Women swore by the oil's efficacy. It made intercourse painless and, for many, actually enjoyable.

G.W. naturally assumed the role as inventor of all these amazing tinctures and achieved greater status as a chemist, botanist, and world explorer than he ever had as "the General." All were secretly compounded and all carried unique patents issued by the US Office of Patents in Washington, DC. Or so Dr. Merritt swore.[4]

Through it all, the question Inez continued to grapple with daily was how to resolve her own personal dilemma: a pregnancy that in several months would produce a child. Perhaps she'd keep the baby. On some days, she fancied herself primed to become a mother; on other days, when common sense returned, Inez woke up dead set against giving birth. G. W. Merritt was part showman, conman, huckster—but hardly a father. How he could have afforded the Palace Grill for their first date was beyond Inez. If she chose to terminate the pregnancy, she needed to decide now. The window to safely abort was drawing to a close. By her own reckoning, she was going on three months. It was now or never.

SIX

THE EARTH MOVES

On Tuesday, April 17, Enrico Caruso made his San Francisco debut in Georges Bizet's *Carmen* at the Grand Opera House on Mission between Third and Fourth Streets. It was the second night of the opera season and followed Karl Goldmark's extravaganza *Queen of Sheba*, which San Francisco critics had mercilessly panned. Goldmark's production was one of wretched excess, with scores of slaves, harem girls, and anguished lovers flitting on and off the stage. The great Caruso was what all of San Francisco had been waiting for. Caruso was as big as opera got in San Francisco or anywhere else. To showcase the great Caruso, the Conried Metropolitan Opera Company of New York had sent its entire company of two hundred thirty cast members three thousand miles west, along with eight specially outfitted train coaches to carry tons of scenery and a multitude of costumes.

At soirees atop Nob and Russian Hills that evening, gossip was the only commodity more in demand than Baccarat flutes topped with bubbling Dom Pérignon. Since the story of *Carmen* takes place in Seville, the craze among society women that evening was to wear anything and everything Spanish. Mrs. James Flood sparkled in black lace, a tiara, choker, and corsage of diamonds; Mrs. Frederick Kohl turned heads in a lace-and-silk gown, and a two-inch-wide pearl dog collar fastened with a large diamond clasp; Mrs. Evan S. Pillsbury debuted a white lace gown highlighted with pale blue chiffon, diamonds, and pearls; Mrs. Edward Barron wore a lavender gown and a daring see-through lace vest; Mrs. Frank A. Deering dropped jaws in a purple pompadour gown with flounces of white lace; stunning Miss Jennie

Famed opera singer Enrico Caruso, February 1906.

Dunphy took the cake with a sheer lace gown the color of shrimp.[1] By eight that evening, three thousand of the city's wealthiest benefactors had descended on the opera house. The anticipation in the lobby was positively eléctric.

Caruso's debut didn't disappoint. The audience's first "bravo" erupted ten minutes into the first act, and by the time the curtain rang down after Caruso's thundering wail, *"Ah! Carmen! Ma Carmen adorée!"* the audience wouldn't stop roaring, "Caruso, Caruso, Caruso!" Patrons wouldn't let the singer leave the stage, throwing bouquet after bouquet of roses, wisteria, and carnations at him. He had to duck for his own safety. The standing ovation was the longest in the opera house's history.[2]

After the satiated crowds made their way home that night, Caruso was fidgety, pacing as he waited for reviews from the next day's early-edition newspapers. Only after Joey, Inez's bellboy friend at the Palace, rushed the papers up to Caruso's fifth-floor suite, would the opera sensation relax. The critics were tepid when it came to Olive Fremstad, the diva mezzo-soprano who played opposite him as Carmen, but they couldn't heap enough praise on Caruso. The *San Francisco Chronicle*'s headline trumpeted, "Caruso Superb in the Role of Don Jose." Critic Peter Robertson raved, "Caruso has the kind of tone that rings in the ears long after it is heard and seems to echo in memory at recall."[3] *San Francisco Call* critic Blanche Partington hailed Caruso as a "magician," who "made one forget that it was only an opera. The excitement was simply sizzling as he dashed open the doors of the arena with his knife and dared Carmen to enter. And that is the way he sang it all, as no one else in the world can sing."[4] The *Call*'s society columnist, Laura Bride Powers, described the exultant audience's reaction: "The thrill, the throb, the quiver—without which grand opera becomes a mere recital—was in the air last night. And it got into your blood. . . . Last night—Ah! It was sublime!"[5]

Triumphant, Caruso descended in one of the Palace's plush elevators and poked his head outside the hotel's east portico for a breath of fresh air. The early-morning air was still and warm. Odd, he thought. Upon leaving New York, friends had told him San Francisco weather in April would be brisk and breezy. Bring an overcoat, they advised.

Caruso shrugged his shoulders and took the rising room back upstairs. The elevator operator wished him a restful night.

Some two hours later, Inez was sleeping soundly in her third-floor room at the Elmer House, three blocks north. She had intended to awaken early that morning; Inez and G.W. were to take the wagon of wondrous medicinals to a market across from Mission Delores Park. The Irish, who primarily lived in the neighborhood, were enthusiastic buyers of G.W.'s potions and salves, as well as of Inez's cache of feminine products. Whenever the Brazilian Beleza appeared in the Mission, it was an event with crowds fanning around the cart. Perhaps with the day's receipts, Inez and G.W. could celebrate by going out to dinner and the theater. *The Show Girl* was playing at the Tivoli, and it was something Inez thought she might like.

Inez was awakened before the first rays of dawn. If she wasn't mistaken, she felt her bed shaking. Curious, she thought. Her first reaction was that the vibration must have been coming from Harriet in the room atop hers. A large, buxom German girl, Harriet often engaged in robust lovemaking and, if Inez had to guess, made pocket money from entertaining guests overnight.

Within seconds, though, the shaking turned to rocking and banging, so raucous that no way could it have originated from any girl and her gentleman friend, no matter what activity they were engaged in. Inez's bed was actually bouncing up and down. Then it suddenly lurched across the oak floorboards. Inez could feel surging, wavelike motions coming from beneath the Elmer House, which seemed to be twisting and turning the building at its very foundation. She heard stretching sounds of nails and timbers pulling apart. Inez instinctively put her hand on her stomach. The Elmer House was about to collapse, taking everyone with it.

As the world soon discovered, at 5:12 on this Wednesday morning, April 18, a massive earthquake ground together two tectonic plates ten miles beneath the earth's surface. One plate was the Pacific, the other the North American. The longest fault line in the world was an eight-hundred-mile ancient rift that ran from Cape Mendocino in Humboldt County to the Salton Sea in Imperial County. There wasn't just one earthquake that day, but twenty-seven separate temblors along the same California fissure. The quake's epicenter was two miles northwest of the Golden Gate, creating convulsions that lasted forty-eight seconds. But to Inez, they seemed to last a lifetime.

Built entirely of wood, the Elmer House was the kind of building most susceptible to collapse during such a catastrophic event. Within seconds, Inez heard one of the walls in the hallway buckle. She knew she had to get out immediately. She hurriedly put on a dress, not having the time to button up the front, and instinctively grabbed the canvas satchel of medical instruments and the bottles of quinine and chloroform she'd lifted from Dr. West's clinic. She grabbed a hat she'd purchased that Monday, a straw leghorn with flowers and ribbons, and raced like the dickens downstairs.

Women were bolting out the front door helter-skelter onto Bush Street, some wearing nothing but nightgowns and knickerbockers. Many held their hands outward at chest level as though a robber was holding them up; others, terrified, ran with their hands covering their mouths that emitted nary a sound. Some women carried armfuls of belongings, but most were too panicked to do anything but run as though they'd seen the devil. A lug of a man, his pants down to his ankles, joined the stampede, but tripped and rolled into the gutter as a herd of women galloped past him. Maybe Harriett had been entertaining, after all.

Just a mile west and north, stolid masonry mansions that twelve hours earlier had been the sites of festive galas were now swaying and convulsing. Inside the great Flood mansion on California Street, the prisms of chandeliers tingled in a crescendo

Fire engulfs San Francisco after the earthquake, April 1906.

COPYRIGHTED 1906,
BY A L MURD

The destruction of Nob Hill
and the Fairmont Hotel with
Chinatown in the foreground,
April 1906.

and crashed to the floor. City Hall on Fulton Street, which was the largest building west of Chicago when it was built ten years earlier, collapsed. Ninety-five percent of the chimneys throughout San Francisco crumbled to the ground. Buildings, grotesquely out of plumb, sunk three stories into the earth. Sidewalks bulged and buckled. The metal slot along Market Street zigzagged.

Survivors make their way up the hill on California Street, April 1906.

Structures built on landfill—"made ground" created from garbage, wood debris, sand, and soil, even wreckage of old sailing vessels—-suffered the most since the quake's spasmodic movements transferred faster through landfill than through bedrock. Seventy thousand residents lived in homes built on such shaky ground. The rippling motion brought down row after row of buildings, speeding west to east through the city.

City Hall in ruins after the earthquake, April 1906.

If the disaster had been confined to an earthquake, the damage would have been substantial, the fatalities high, but San Francisco would likely have healed over the course of several years. However, the city didn't just crumble; it burned.

Fires accounted for the vast majority of fatalities, estimated at four hundred seventy-eight, as the official toll put it in 1906, but in reality more than three thousand residents perished in the quake and ensuing conflagration.[6] The combination leveled five hundred city blocks and thirty thousand buildings.

For some, San Francisco had it coming. The city was Sodom and Gomorrah rolled into one. San Francisco was the home to eighteen hundred forty saloons.[7] Not only did prostitution and gambling reign unabated, but San Francisco also had the highest per capita murder rate in America. That San Francisco had also become the default destination for thousands of women every year seeking abortions only confirmed that the city was a crucible of moral decay. Religious zealots had long railed that God would punish the sybarites and swallow the city of sin.

Broken gas lines, shorted electrical wires, and overturned wood-burning stoves were initially the main culprits that spread the flames. But when the city's water supply failed, there was nothing with which to fight the out-of-control fires, and blazes advanced maniacally. City reservoirs still held supplies of water, but without a way to distribute it, fires hopscotched from block to block. The first district to go was the oldest, South of Market, where Inez had grown up. By afternoon, the Palace Hotel's private water wells had been exhausted, and the great building was engulfed. Fires leaped across Mission Street, then Minna and Jessie Streets, and breached the city's main broad thoroughfare, Market Street. By evening, the entire downtown was engulfed. Smoke rose two miles, resembling a dark volcanic plume.

In a daze, Inez staggered to Market Street toward the Palace. A brigade of uniformed employees was manning a fire line, transporting Palace guests' suitcases and trunks out the front door.

"Iney, ya all right?" came a young man's voice from the line.

It was Joey. Without waiting for an answer, he volunteered, "Ya best leave downtown. It ain't safe. These buildings could come down any minute. Git as far away as ya can, Iney!" Picking up a steamer trunk and passing it to another Palace employee down the line, Joey said, "Ya git yourself to the park, that's where they're makin' a camp."

Word had spread that soldiers were setting up a tent city at Golden Gate Park. Smaller refugee camps were supposedly going up in the Western Addition, Mission Dolores Park, and the Presidio. People were said to be converging on the Southern Pacific Railroad yards and the sandy dunes of Ocean Beach.

Everything Inez owned was gone with the exception of the apron of instruments, the tinted medical bottles, the dress she was wearing, and her once-chic straw hat, now blackened, atop her head. After the initial shock and dismay, people turned sullen and uncomprehending. Inez could see it in their eyes. Nature had violated a sacred trust: the ground, the foundation upon which all was based, had moved without warning. Inez saw an elderly woman holding an umbrella in one hand and a parrot in a cage in another. Residents wandered in the center of streets for safety's sake, but also because it seemed to signal the inverse of order. Inez passed men in pajamas and top hats, women in bloomers with ermine stoles wrapped around uncontrollably shivering shoulders.[8] People walked in a trance. James Hopper, a reporter for the *San Francisco Call*, characterized the miasma, "When the roar of crumbling buildings was over, and only a brick fell here and there, this silence continued, and it was an awful thing." The streets, Hopper wrote, "were full of people, half-clad, disheveled, but silent, as if suddenly they had become speechless idiots. . . . All of them had a

A fire truck works to put out a block smoldering buildings, April 1906.

singular hurt expression—not of physical pain, but rather of injured sensibilities, as if some trusted friend had wronged them."⁹

For three days, corps of firefighters and soldiers took to dynamiting buildings to create breaks in the fire line. With no water left to extinguish flames, the rationale was that by taking away fuel, the fires would burn themselves out. But sparks from the dynamited buildings ignited more structures, creating a chain reaction. As the fire brigade went from block to block with explosives, a trumpeter would announce that yet another building would be set ablaze or dynamited. Those who wouldn't leave risked being shot to death.

Looters roamed the city. Grocery stores and butcher shops were the first to be overrun. Tillmann & Bendel, a wholesaler on Battery Street, was robbed of thousands of boxes of cigars. To curtail disorder, soldiers went from saloon to saloon, smashing barrels and bottles of liquor.¹⁰ By early afternoon, a shaken San Francisco mayor Eugene Schmitz declared a state of emergency and authorized officers "to kill any and all persons found engaged in Looting or in the Commission of Any Other Crime."¹¹

Through the dust and particles swirling in the air, Inez looked up at Delmonico's, the mirrored and gilt restaurant that she and Dr. West had frequented. The third floor had sunk into O'Farrell Street. Under buildings on either side of the street, victims lay trapped. Bodies were slumped on streets and sidewalks. Inez saw a rat nibbling a dead man's finger.

The fires continued unabated, aided by strong breezes from the Bay. Inez's hat

doubled as a mask, protecting her from the heat and smoke. She had no idea whether Nettie, the rest of her family, or G. W. Merritt were alive.

As Inez approached Van Ness Avenue, she saw six horses harnessed in a carriage, their eyes large and terrified, foam oozing from steaming nostrils. Suddenly, the sky ignited with fire—another structure had gone up in flames—and at that instant the horses bucked and broke free. A soldier took out a pistol and shot three horses point-blank between their eyes. Inez screamed—for the horses, for herself, and for the only city she had known now destroyed.

By now, Enrico Caruso had run the several blocks from the Palace northwest to Union Square with his valet Martino somehow lugging the opera star's heavy trunks. The singer lay down in the center of the grassy plaza, fearful that the buildings around the square would come tumbling down; this way he might save himself. Handing twenty-dollar bills to strangers, Martino found a driver to take the two of them to the Ferry Building, where police initially barred them from boarding a ferry, but upon recognizing the opera star, they allowed Caruso and Martino to make their way to Oakland and eventually onto a train bound for New York, where they arrived six days later.[12]

Inez joined a human convoy moving inexorably west toward Golden Gate Park, where within forty-eight hours, soldiers and national guardsmen had set up the beginnings of a tent city. On her third day at the park, Inez found Nettie and her mother, Alice. Brothers Harry and Walter were yet to be found. Inez presumed they had died.

On the fourth day, she ran into G. W. Merritt. They were so happy to see each

Survivors taking refuge in a tent city in Jefferson Square, April 1906.

A food line at an American Red Cross relief station, April 1906.

other that they hugged and kissed, and neither dared to let go of the other for a full ten minutes. All of G.W.'s botanicals, the hundreds of salves, ointments, soaps, and herbal remedies, along with his wagon, had gone up in flames. That evening the two moved into an army tent on the broad slope of Sharon Meadow on the east side of the park.

Forty thousand displaced persons found their way to the park that week. Twice-daily food lines wound around the park's meadows. The refugee camps became self-contained cities; the proximity of humanity, along with the collective sense of loss and longing, naturally made for hundreds of romances and marriages.[13] While not a trained nurse, Inez had plenty of experience from her days at Dr. West's clinic, and she volunteered as a medical technician, attending to women. While ministering to their needs, Inez found a charred deck of tarot cards and read fortunes to huddled groups of desolate women.

It was sometime during the third week, while in a soup line in the panhandle to the park, that Inez ran into her old friend Anna Thompson, the girl who had told Inez about the job at the Palace. She was with Mabel, Anna's niece, who by now was

A family cooks on the street amidst the destruction, April 1906.

Two women sort through the
rubble following the earthquake
and fire, April 1906.

nine. The trio was elated to be reunited once again. Anna knew about Inez's job at the Palace but had no idea about Dr. West, her apprenticeship in his clinic, or her involvement with G. W. Merritt.

Anna looked especially weary, starkly pale with gray circles under her eyes. Outside the trauma of the earthquake, given Inez's vocational experience, she instantly knew why. Anna had slept with a man two months ago, and she was vomiting every morning.

Could Inez help? It was more a plea than a question.

"I'm in the same way," Inez volunteered. "But I'm going to keep the baby."

Inez shocked herself with her own words. It was the first time she had articulated what she'd been considering. With destruction everywhere, to destroy what was growing inside her somehow seemed wrong. By now, Inez also was at a point of no return, almost three months. Raising a child required resources and commitment, though, and the thought returned to her: Was G. W. Merritt the man she wanted to do it with?

"I can't," Anna replied. "I ain't got a fella. And I'm as sick as a dog. I ain't the motherin' kind, anyways. Can ya help me, Inez? *Please.*"

Inez saw and heard in Anna the same desperation that she had grown to expect in the women who had made the trip to Dr. West's clinic. Inez told Anna that if she was willing, she'd perform the procedure. It wouldn't be easy, but there was no other choice in the aftermath of the earthquake. She'd follow everything Dr. West had taught her.

The following afternoon, Inez batted her eyelashes at a soldier, who procured two cast iron pots to boil water, as well as two blankets. She gathered twigs and kindling and lit a small fire. The fire would allow Inez to sterilize the stainless steel tools she'd pinched from Dr. West, as well as to heat a calming herbal tea mixture of chamomile and rose hips.

Amid a grove of peeling eucalyptus trees that emitted a clean, medicinal smell, Inez draped one of the woolen blankets over Anna, who by now was shivering. She instructed her to drink two consecutive straight shots from a bottle of R. B. Blair Whiskey, which G.W. had pilfered from an overrun bar on Stanyan Street. That ought to calm her; at the least, it'd stop her from trembling. Next, Inez poured the tea into an earthenware cup. Calmer now, Inez took Anna's hand and laid her atop the other blanket. Inez doused a handkerchief with chloroform and gently covered Anna's nose, which made her woozy. From the apron of instruments, Inez picked up a speculum, then inserted a dilator, followed by a catheter, which in turn induced labor. Inez inserted a steamed rag to stem bleeding. By now, Mabel had returned to comfort Anna and crawled under the blanket with her. When Anna awoke, she was still groggy but understood what had happened. Inez gave her a dozen quinine pills and told her to take two every four hours.

In a matter of four weeks at the park, Inez performed six more abortions. One was on an unmarried woman, the rest on married women who had children. Inez disposed of the remains in oil drums that were set ablaze at night for light and warmth. For these half dozen women, this was no time to bring a child into the world. Everything was collapsing around them. The last thing they could afford was to feed and clothe a baby.

During the evenings, Inez continued reading tarot cards to women who didn't know who had perished and who was alive, as well as to women who had found out who had died and chose not to believe it. Women gathered, forming a tight circle, as Inez turned over the creased, oversize cards indicating the moon, stars, sun, magician, the fool, the empress. A gasp erupted when Inez flipped onto the ground the hanged man, star, or emperor. When the card of death materialized, several women burst into inconsolable tears.

With San Francisco smoldering and Inez choosing not to do anything about her own pregnancy, G. W. Merritt in the fifth week of their stay at Golden Gate Park made a bold proposal: Why not leave all that had befallen San Francisco and travel to where he had family, clear across the country, in Pittsburgh?

Would she at least consider it? he asked Inez.

Her first reaction was that G.W. must be crazy. Move with a man who was a con artist, and not a very good one at that?

But she thought more. Why *not* start anew? With a child. Her own.

It was a turning point for Inez. By performing the abortions on these desperate women, Inez realized what she was capable of doing with her own hands and brains. She had performed a necessary service for these women, who were so thankful that they demanded to pay Inez, even though she asked for nothing. One woman gave Inez twenty dollars, another a rose-colored cameo she took from a chain around her neck. Inez had a skill. She wouldn't ever again have to hawk ointments. She once again realized that women who didn't want to stay pregnant would do *anything* to rid their bodies of what was growing inside. And once word circulated in the park of Inez's services, women were making a beeline her way. Inez had seen the fortune Dr. West had amassed. Once life returned to normal, couldn't Inez do the same?

When San Francisco repairs itself, she'd come back, with her own child, with or without G. W. Merritt. But now, besides Nettie, what did Inez have in this city of ruin?

Maybe Pittsburgh would turn into her Emerald City?

SEVEN

PICKLED IN PITTSBURGH

The earthquake had changed everything and everyone, including Inez. Demand to leave San Francisco to points east was sky-high. The Ferry Building at the foot of Market Street, built as a replica of the Moorish Giralda Tower in Seville, Spain, had been damaged but didn't topple; packed ferries left from there every thirty minutes to connect with trains departing from Oakland, making for the largest mass evacuation in American history.[1] San Francisco's population at the time was four hundred sixty thousand, and half of them—a quarter of a million—were homeless. The city was in such upheaval that officials urged everyone who could to vacate immediately.

Inez had no place to live and no way to make a living, other than perform abortions in the most primitive of settings. Inez didn't know what had happened to Dr. West; he very well could have perished. The Elmer House was in rubble, and even if she and G.W. could resurrect their truckload of miracle medicinals, customers were without money to buy them. When G.W. proposed leaving, Inez looked at the offer as a last-ditch opportunity. The farthest she'd ever been from the city was seventy miles north on a Sunday outing she and G.W. had taken to St. Helena in Napa County. From a new home in the faraway state with an impossibly long name, she could start over. Whatever was to happen between her and G. W. Merritt, Inez would at least be with a child of her own.

This improbable adventure on her own Yellow Brick Road played to Inez's sense of risk-taking, even though she knew Nettie would say that she was absolutely mad. The entire Ingenthron family had survived the quake, and for the moment, all were reconstituted in the Army's refugee camp in Golden Gate Park. The raging fires had been halted at Twentieth and Dolores Streets in the Mission; the Ingenthron house in Bernal Heights had been spared, but soldiers had ordered the evacuation of the neighborhood until each home could be inspected.

When Inez told Nettie about her plans, Nettie was as straightforward as Inez feared she'd be. Her opinion of G. W. Merritt hadn't changed—he was a straight-away "con man." Inez countered that if she didn't go to Pittsburgh, there was no way he would support a child two thousand miles away back in San Francisco. G.W. had fully accepted his role as the father, Inez countered, and with that came financial obligations. All Nettie could do was shake her head and bite her tongue.

"What will you do with yourself?" Nettie asked tepidly. "Will you get married?"

Inez replied that marriage to G.W. was out of the question. She didn't care about marrying G.W. or about having a child out of wedlock.

Nettie raised her eyebrows. She couldn't help herself.

"Do you love Mr. Merritt?"

"I wouldn't say so," Inez replied. "No."

"Then what are you doing with him?" Nettie asked, losing patience. "Why the hell would you be going to Pittsburgh with a man you don't love?"

Inez had never put much stock in the romantic notion of love. This much Nettie already knew. From what Inez had seen and experienced, love was a kind of social contract that either party could break at any time. Did love truly exist? Inez didn't think so. Men and women needed each other for financial and physical reasons, but because of love? Inez doubted it. For the women in lace and chiffon and the men in top hats and tails, marriage was a financial transaction—no less, no more. For the rest, marriage was two people who could barely put up with each other. It's what happened when a neighborhood girl got pregnant and the boy who knocked her up got strong-armed into marrying her.

For these girls, Inez knew, abortion wasn't much of an option. It cost too much, for one. Dr. West didn't cater to Inez's contemporaries. And any medical procedure, as practiced on South of the Slot girls, was risky. Pregnant girls were lucky they didn't die at the hands of the butchers who preyed on them. The abortionists who targeted Inez's old neighborhood had little understanding of hygiene and sterility. Given these options, most of the girls who got pregnant carried to full-term, either living with or marrying the men who impregnated them, or checking into a home like the Crittenton House and giving the baby up for adoption.

It was up to women to take charge of their lives, however impossible that was. That's what Inez's mother had done and taught Inez, whether by design or default. For women to survive in the real world, they needed to gird themselves against men. If they didn't do it for themselves, who else was going to do it for them?

So much for love and marriage.

That evening with the orange-streaked sky above them, Inez and Nettie talked about these and other matters of intimate sororal substance. In Nettie's mind, Inez was incorrigible. Going out with wealthy married men or with men just because she fancied them, accepting gifts from men who wanted nothing more than to bed her, renting a room with bevy of like-minded girls. And that wasn't the worst of it. Inez had actually worked for that Dr. West, performing "medical procedures"—well, Nettie couldn't even say the word. What kind of girl does that? Nettie surely understood the condition that necessitated such intervention and why a girl would submit to such an operation. That was one thing. But to perform the surgery? That Inez herself had actually operated on pregnant women in Golden Gate Park was beyond the pale. Her little sister was impossible.

And how she talked! About there being no reason to marry, about love being a fraud. Nettie didn't know what to do with Inez. It was just like her to reject the most basic beliefs that everyone lived by. Then there was the issue of the tarot cards and telling fortunes. And dressing like a gypsy, demonstrating condoms on vegetables for everyone to see. Would it ever end?

Inez didn't need a lecture. She told Nettie she'd be leaving San Francisco with Mr. Merritt by the end of the week. If her adventure didn't work out, Inez promised she'd return "lickety-split, I swear to it." Either way, she said, hoping for a smile, Nettie would be an aunt by the end of August, and that was cause for celebration, wasn't it?

Given the circumstances, Nettie was as cheerful as she could be. The two women hugged, and when they separated, Nettie explained that she wouldn't be seeing Inez and Mr. Merritt off at the Ferry Building. Too much commotion and tumult, so many people saying goodbye to their relatives and friends that they might get separated. The real reason, of course, was that Nettie couldn't bear to see Inez leave. Nettie feared she'd never see her sister again.

The trip on the Southern Pacific Railroad was a wild and woolly journey over five days and two thousand eight hundred miles. Filled to capacity with not just passengers but stacks of suitcases and possessions salvaged from the ravages of the quake and fire, the fetid third-class cars were emotional caravans of American refugees. Families cried and prayed, sang, some spoke in tongues, as the chugging trains steamed eastward across the American countryside.

Such emotional, cramped circumstances served another group well—swindlers. Passengers had to be constantly vigilant. If they fell asleep, they were targets for pickpockets and thieves. Bandits were so adept that even awake travelers found themselves fleeced of their wallets and valises. If that wasn't enough, a never-ending queue of men in straws or bowlers hawked land, or something called "land futures"—whatever they were.

Before leaving San Francisco, G.W. had been able to buy from tents pitched in front of Eagle Pharmacy and Broyer Grocers on Mission Street a supply of herbal pills, pessaries, douches, and Mediterranean toilet sponges, along with a ten-gallon tin of olive oil, so that on the second day of their travels, between Reno and Salt Lake City, Inez, not as the Brazilian Beleza, but as herself, could mount an impromptu sales presentation for two dozen ladies. Inez made a whopping thirty-seven dollars, which G.W. promptly snatched, so he could buy into a round of faro.

If card playing wasn't a man's métier, he could gamble on pretty much anything else, including numbers, baseball games, even a pool on the exact time, down to the second, when the locomotive's nose would pull into train depots along the way. Some of the pots were as large as three hundred dollars.

No transcontinental train trip would be complete without a cluster of brazen women, financing their passage east by slipping into first-class sleeping berths with gentlemen, some accompanied by wives and families, some not. While the wives were fanning themselves to keep from fainting in the heat, these women, some of them younger than Inez, managed to meet men in the dining, parlor, or drinking car simply by smiling. Any man of means was suitable for such a conquest. A quick wink, a discreet nod, or a perfumed handkerchief dropped at just the right moment was the cue. Enterprising women could get all the way to the East Coast with enough money for a new start.

G.W. and Inez arrived in Pittsburgh in six days, and soon thereafter, they found an upstairs room in a house at 800 Center Street, off North Chestnut Street, in the tiny borough of Avalon on the banks of the Ohio River. The rent was fourteen dollars a month.[2] Barely settled, G.W. quickly involved himself in a variety of ventures, cooking up business schemes, meeting would-be benefactors, and once again compounding medicinals in the house's basement. He was seldom around; he had work "to consolidate" is how he explained his frequent absences to Inez. No fool, Inez figured the consolidation was another woman.

Inez's pregnancy came with no complications. She was healthy and felt well during the last trimester, and at ten forty p.m. on August 12, 1906, she gave birth to a boy, who predictably got named George Washington Merritt Jr. A local physician, A. H. Elliott, attended the delivery, which took place at the home in Avalon. On the birth certificate, for unknown reasons, Inez chose not to use her real name and instead opted to call herself Inez L. Wilson.[3]

Six weeks after the birth, Inez discovered something about her common-law husband that was even more unsettling than his suspected womanizing. G. W. Merritt had been keeping a whopper of a secret.

Inez knew that G.W. had married and divorced in San Francisco, and had a son there by the name of Edwin. What Inez didn't know was that in 1902, Merritt had met a fourteen-year-old girl in Pittsburgh by the name of Sarah Ann, who had given birth to a baby boy by the name of Les Washington Merritt that same year.

But there was more.

Sarah Ann and the boy were living just blocks away from Inez, G.W., and George Jr.

Without knowing about each other, Inez and Sarah Ann had both become G.W.'s mistresses and both had given birth to his children. G.W.'s desire to bring Inez from San Francisco to Pittsburgh had been his way of installing Inez and his soon-to-be-born child in close proximity to Merritt's *other* mistress, nineteen-year-old Sarah Ann, the mother of another one of his children.[4] While G. W. Merritt was married to neither Inez nor Sarah Ann, it sure seemed as though he was a bigamist, if not in the eyes of the law, then in the eyes of anyone who wasn't blind.

One year after George Jr. was born, G.W. had another child with Sarah Ann. That child, a daughter, was named Elizabeth.

When Inez discovered what was going on under her nose, G.W. tried to convince her that she should become friends with Sarah Ann rather than pack up and leave. G.W. had the idea that his two common-law wives should become friends. Not surprisingly, Inez didn't want to have anything to do with Sarah Ann. As for G.W., she could barely look at him. But whether out of economic necessity or some other form of coercion, physical or mental, Inez stayed with G.W.

Between his revived cart of snake oils and get-rich schemes that went bust, G.W. wasn't bringing home a dime. Nettie had been right. G.W. was a four-flusher, always on the verge of winning the big hand but folding before hauling in the jackpot. Inez couldn't sit by and wait for G.W. to be dealt aces, and even with them, she'd have to split any winnings with Sarah Ann. Or not. Inez needed to get a job to support herself and her baby, whom she affectionately called Georgie. She had to depend on herself. If Inez couldn't find work, she and Georgie would be on the poor man's diet of potatoes and scraps of barely recognizable meat, a replay of her own life as a child. With no resources, Inez's dream of opening up her own medical clinic had gone up in smoke. She tried to get work as an assistant to a physician in the same line of work, but no one would hire a girl from out of town.

H. J. Heinz's giant pickle factory, the largest in the world, was located in Allegheny City, just east of Avalon, and sometime in 1907, Inez secured work at the plant. But what was she to do with little Georgie while she worked? Despite a raging mutual antipathy, Inez and Sarah Ann struck a deal: G.W.'s other mistress would care for Georgie, as long as Inez chipped in for expenses.

Heinz hired exclusively women to work in its huge pickle building. At each shift, one hundred women toiled in an enormous room, eight women side by side at a long table, each wearing a striped frock with a long apron and matching white hat, packing pickles in clear glass jars with wooden paddles, taking care so that the pickles formed an exacting geometric pattern. The job required no small degree of dexterity. Inez had to hold in one hand a grooved wooden paddle while with her other hand she inserted pickles in the precise order patterned after a model jar that sat high on a kind of pickle throne for workers to follow. A single sliver of a red pepper was placed inside the jar in the hope of drawing shoppers' attention. Rubber gloves hadn't been invented yet, so to ensure cleanliness, Heinz employees were given weekly manicures.[5] The last thing Inez wanted was to do was to cut and burnish ladies' fingernails, so she kept her mouth shut, even though she knew something about giving manicures.

At the time, H. J. Heinz was the capitalist wunderkind of food processing. The new north side plant had an auditorium, roof garden, dining rooms, and a library constructed for the benefit of employees.[6] While the work was painstaking and monotonous, Heinz paid the highest of all canneries in the area: seven dollars a week.[7]

However much her salary was, Inez hated the dreary, monochromatic Pittsburgh winters. For months, there wouldn't be a ray of sunshine, just a blanket of frigid gray that smothered everything. That was something Inez had never experienced. Fog and rain, yes, but never snow, ice, sleet, and a dreary sky that never yielded to blue. Inez took to lining her shoes with cardboard to keep her feet warm.[8] Then when July rolled around came the oppressive, raging summer heat. It was as though someone had propped open the door to a giant furnace. The blast of sweltering heat made Inez wilt, extracting any life left in her. She was utterly disconsolate.

Life got worse when Inez discovered she was allergic to mosquitoes, which left her with patches of blotchy welts all over her legs and arms. San Francisco was too temperate to welcome such infernal winged buggers. But in Pittsburgh, they feasted on Inez's blanched skin with frenzied delight.

Then there was the matter of the stink of the pickles. H.J. Heinz packed three kinds: fancy sweet, dill, and sour-spiced. Each carried its own distinct odor. The pickle building was outfitted with a wall of windows, which during the summers helped circulate the vinegar-and-garlic smell out of the plant; during the winters, whirling fans dissipated the pungent odor. But the plant still reeked. Women couldn't rid themselves of the stench, and not just in their clothing. It was as though the fetor had a way of getting absorbed into their bodies through some kind of indirect osmosis. Women carried the stink for as long as they worked at Heinz; some would say for the rest of their lives. The only way to mask the odor, Inez learned from a coworker, was to squeeze fresh lemons over her hands, face, and body as soon as she got home every night. That neutralized the smell, until she returned to the plant the next day.

While she hated the work, the money allowed Inez to move from Avalon to another borough, Ben Avon, less than a mile away, to a flat in a new house at 112 Watt Avenue, with a view of the Ohio River and Neville Island.[9] Whether out of familiarity or necessity, she made up with G. W. Merritt, in effect sharing him with Sarah Ann, who continued to look after Georgie while Inez carried on at the pickle plant.

If Inez was already despondent, she found herself more so when the telltale signs of pregnancy revealed themselves once again. Whether G.W. was the father was something only Inez knew for sure, but no one suspected any differently, and six months later, Inez gave birth to another child, a son named Robert Edward Lee Merritt, whom she called Bobby.[10] For a woman who had once made her living through family planning through abortion or contraceptives, Inez had been either exceedingly fertile or reckless. Surely, there were skilled abortion providers in Pittsburgh, but Inez chose not to seek any of them out. Perhaps she thought Georgie would prosper with a sibling. Perhaps G.W. forbade her from terminating the pregnancy; perhaps he said he'd reward Inez monetarily if she bore him another child. How could bright Inez have been so clueless? For his part, G.W. was an unrepentant baby maker. All told, he fathered eight children with three women, and in all likelihood, there were more children and more women.

Inez continued at the pickle plant through the end of 1908. While Sarah Ann cared for Inez's two young sons, as well as her own children, Sarah Ann and Inez continued to look at each other as mortal enemies. They hardly talked. G.W. found himself as a go-between, splitting his time between the two women.

In May of 1909, G.W. applied to the state of Pennsylvania to incorporate himself with four partners to form a business called Merritt Manufacturing Company whose purpose was "the manufacture and marketing of preparations for the hair, scalp and face and devices for use in connection therewith."[11] The first product was a cream to grow hair on bald men, more of the same from the truck of medicinals. The partners pooled five thousand dollars to manufacture a useless but very greasy pomade.[12]

At the time, Pittsburgh was hard-hit with an onslaught of public-health epidemics. In tiny Avalon alone, there were one hundred four reported cases of measles, sixty-four reported outbreaks of typhoid fever, and sixteen deaths from communicable diseases. Typhoid is often carried by contaminated water, and the borough of Avalon placed blame for the disease's alarming spread on nine tainted local springs used for drinking water.[13]

The spike in measles and typhoid, not to mention Inez's failed experiment with G. W. Merritt and his surprise co-mistress, along with the mind-numbing job at Heinz and the wicked Pittsburgh seasons, was enough for Inez to gather what was left of her wits and get herself back to San Francisco. It'd be an investment in the only person she could depend on: herself. To do so, though, required Inez to leave four-year-old Georgie with G.W. and Sarah Ann.[14] G.W. wouldn't allow Inez to leave with his namesake, Georgie, but he'd permit her to take Bobby. If she tried to pack up Georgie, Merritt would sic the police on Inez and haul her to court.

Under the circumstances, if that's what it took to leave infernal Pittsburgh, away from Merritt's clutches, then it'd be worth it. Inez was certain that it would be a temporary arrangement. Sarah Ann would grow tired of raising a child who wasn't hers, and Merritt liked procreating children, not raising them. Inez, Bobby, and Georgie would be reunited sooner or later.

If it made any sense, Bobby was the more mentally agile of the two boys. Inez and everyone else could tell he'd be somebody someday. You knew that with certain children, even at that age. He was smart and likable.

Inez had squirreled enough from her pickle-packing job to pay for passage back to California. She bundled up two-year-old Bobby, kissed little Georgie on the forehead, saying farewell for now, and took the train once again, this time west. She mounted no sales demonstrations of Italian Lotion No. 12 or Mediterranean toilet sponges along the way. Inez had her hands full with Bobby. All she thought about was getting back home.

Just as on her trip to Pittsburgh, there were pulchritudinous women selling their erotic goods, along with hustlers hawking deeds to fictitious bounties of land.

San Francisco comes into view as a ferry approaches from the bay, ca. 1906.

But Inez didn't pay much attention to any of them. She was tired and pining to get back home. Inez met a spirited twenty-nine-year-old Stockton, California, native by the name of Nelly Gaffney, who had taken to train from New York, and the two gabbed like sisters separated at birth. Enterprising Nelly had four steamer trunks full of women's fashions she had bought, and hoped to set up a fancy woman's couture shop in San Francisco. She and Inez vowed to see each other as soon they got settled.

Stepping onto the seven a.m. ferry at Oakland, and traversing the glistening bay, Inez watched as San Francisco came into view, the fog rising with the sun to her back. She held on to Bobby, his arms around her neck, his legs girdling her hips. Telegraph Hill, Russian Hill, Nob Hill, Twin Peaks in the distance, then the un-failing Ferry Building coming closer, the city was welcoming Inez back. She started crying, tears mixing with the saline mist coating her cheeks. This time, Nettie was waiting for them on the long pier jutting into the bay. The two women collapsed into each other's arms without saying a word.

VOL. LIX. No. 1523.   PUCK BUILDING, New York, May 9, 1906.   PRICE TEN CENTS.

Puck

THE NEW FRISCO

A NEW AND FINER CROWN FOR CALIFORNIA.

EIGHT

DREAMLAND, THE PLEASURE PALACE, AND A PAIR OF DEAD BODIES

Inez and Bobby moved in with Nettie, Alice, and brother Walter at 79 Cumberland Street, a half block from the hilly green carpet of Dolores Park in the Mission District. Harry, Inez's other brother, lived somewhere in San Francisco, but Nettie and Alice had lost touch with him. The Ingenthron house had terra-cotta Spanish tiles on the roof and large bay windows facing the street. The five Ingenthrons lived on the top floor. Nettie was ecstatic that Inez was home. Even dour Alice seemed pleased to have her daughter back.

Nettie was still making a meager living as a dressmaker,[1] but she also began dabbling in San Francisco real estate. In 1909, Alice transferred to Nettie the Elsie Street property in Bernal Heights,[2] and in 1912, Walter transferred to her property on Berkshire Street in the Mission District.[3] Nettie was a tightwad, the opposite

The cover of *Puck* in May 1906, showing a hopeful future for San Francisco following the citywide destruction by the earthquake and fire in April 1906.

of Inez, who loved to kick up her heels and spend as lavishly as she could. Frugal Nettie would read by the light of a streetlamp shining into her room. To save water, she'd flush the toilet once a week. Accumulating San Francisco properties, though, seemed to Nettie a smart investment during a buyer's market in the aftermath of the earthquake when skittish owners were dumping real estate like coal down a chute.

It was a propitious time for Inez to return. San Francisco was on the move again, block by block, recovering from the havoc of 1906. What hadn't been demolished by nature had been torn down by man, creating a sheer, vertiginous landscape for the future. San Francisco had the same jaw-dropping geography as ever. No earthquake could change that. Bleak Pittsburgh was a dreary episode Inez would just as soon forget. On clear days, when the fog rose to reveal the city's citadel setting, San Franciscans could make out the distant Farallon Islands, thirty miles west of the Golden Gate, floating like a rising mirage on the horizon. Construction crews worked year-round in the temperate climate. Like resplendent Rome, San Francisco was a city built on seven distinct hills, primed to be transformed into an even greater commercial and cultural metropolis than it had been before earthquake. The city's newly built Victorian and Edwardian homes, the so-called iconic Painted Ladies, would serve as templates for a reawakened sense of civic glory.

As soon as she settled, Inez returned to her lucrative occupation, performing abortions, first working for several established providers downtown, all of them men. Inez didn't return to Dr. West, who since the earthquake had moved his clinic to 1115 McAllister Street. Lurking in the back of her mind was the matter of the medical instruments she had stolen from the glass cabinet in Dr. West's office. Had he noticed? Would he welcome her back? Inez didn't want to find out.

She also realized she didn't need Dr. West any longer. In her absence, Dr. West had run afoul of the law once again. He was implicated in the death of a Santa Rosa woman, Leora Hendrison, who died at St. Thomas Hospital.[4] His name surfaced in a botched abortion of a twenty-two-year-old woman, Laura Taylor, who died at the Central Emergency Hospital.[5] That same year, a third case involved Dr. West and Ruby Soo Hon,[6] who died after Dr. West performed an abortion on her. As with Addie Gilmour, none of these deaths resulted in convictions. Dr. West was taking on too many patients or they may have been too high-risk. He might have been careless and shoddy in his procedures, or he may have been preoccupied by increasing flirtations and indiscretions with his patients. His affection for the pleasures of cocaine also may have escalated. For a time, Inez discovered, Dr. West fled the United States and traveled to Latin America, where he continued performing abortions.[7] In late 1914, at the age of sixty-two, when the dust at home seemed to settle, he returned.[8]

Back in bustling San Francisco, Inez felt a renewed sense of energy. She knew her line of work could bring in prodigious amounts of money. Demand always outstripped supply, and within three years, Inez was able to start her own clinic, working out of a rented home in the Excelsior District. Even though some abortionists advertised their services through transparently worded classified notices in the newspaper, Inez never resorted to spreading word of her expertise that way. She didn't have to. One day she had one patient, the next day three. She attracted them through a network of women. That was the best approach: women talking to women about a kind, sympathetic woman who could take care of their pressing problem. Inez was making as much money every week as she made in three months at the pickle factory. Performing abortions was like printing money. Both activities were illegal, but if you knew what you were doing, you could end up with more cash than you knew what to do with.

As in the aftermath of the gold rush, lucrative business deals abounded during San Francisco's postearthquake building frenzy. Collusion between developers and city officials was rampant in a city already rife with machine politics. San Francisco had become a magnet for carpenters, plumbers, roofers, anyone in the building trades industry, and once again, a plethora of men headed to San Francisco, outstripping the population of women. Anyone who wanted to do business was required to ante up "fees" to a meandering queue of cops, factotums, and elected city officials, each pocketing a vigorish along the way.

In 1911, a forty-two-year-old political neophyte by the name of James Rolph Jr. was elected mayor. It would be the first of five consecutive four-year terms for Rolph, who'd become the longest-serving mayor in San Francisco history. The only reason Rolph didn't seek a sixth term was because he'd been elected governor of California.

If, as the adage goes, every nation gets the government it deserves,[9] then in turn every city gets the politicians it deserves too. If they're any good at their jobs, politicians understand what voters expect and they deliver on those expectations. Extraordinary politicians do more. They transform into the embodiment of the public. How they think, talk, dress, and look reflects the city and people they serve. Their agendas, actions, hopes, and dreams personify their voters'. Their weaknesses are tolerated, even embraced. San Francisco mayor Jimmy Rolph was just such a politician.

The oldest of seven children born to a British immigrant bank clerk, Rolph never went beyond high school. Through street smarts and a likable personality, he

A *Puck* illustration from October 1906 comments on the corruption following the earthquake and fire, showing San Francisco as a woman being tortured on the rack by Greed and various dealers and unions.

became president of two San Francisco banks, president of the Merchants Exchange, director of the San Francisco Chamber of Commerce, and founder of his own shipping and insurance firm, Hind, Rolph & Company. Rolph owned ten windjammers that plied the seas between the Golden Gate and the South Pacific.

Sunny Jim, as he was called by nearly everyone, cut a figure not easy to forget: a ruddy face with a thick mustache, a black silk stovepipe or derby hat over a bald pate, a carnation or gardenia in the lapel of a three-piece white-linen suit, and mirror-shiny black boots. The "sunny" came from the Lee Roberts and J. Will

Mayor James "Sunny Jim" Rolph Jr.

Callahan song, "There Are Smiles That Make Us Happy," a tune that followed Rolph wherever he went, played by a tagalong municipal band. Behind his estate at Twenty-fifth Street and San Jose Avenue, Rolph kept a stable of fighting gamecocks. Rolph was the king of publicity, and the San Francisco newspapers couldn't have been happier. In a corner of his office at City Hall, he installed a life-size cigar-store statue of Tsenacommacah Indian chief Wahunsenacawh, the father of Pocahontas. Rolph boasted that he was a direct descendant of Pocahontas based on his dubious claim that the Indian princess had married Briton John Rolphe three hundred years earlier. American Indians weren't much of a voting bloc in San Francisco, but the Irish surely were, and to appeal to the large Irish constituency, Sunny Jim took to carrying a shillelagh on political outings to show his love for Blarney.

Everything to Sunny Jim was an exuberant celebration. Under Rolph's administration, San Francisco hosted the Panama-Pacific International Exposition of 1915, opened by Sunny Jim, Pied Piper style, leading one hundred fifty thousand San Franciscans from City Hall, singing the words to "I Love You, California," down Van Ness Avenue to the fair gates at Scott and Chestnut Streets.[10]

Rolph presided over the building of the massive gold-leaf Italianate City Hall, with its towering three-hundred-eight-foot dome, completed in 1915. It was (and still is) one of the most extravagant city halls in the world, designed with a hidden stairway that led directly to the mayor's suite for Sunny Jim to squire guests to his office, including his mistress, flapper Anita Page, who retired from the movies when she was twenty-three.[11]

Although Rolph was elected on a platform of eliminating vice and sleaze, such a mandate went only so far in a city with twisted roots that went as deep as San Francisco's. Sunny Jim's promises turned out to be no more than requisite campaign bravado. Rolph himself was the proprietor of his own house of prostitution, called the Pleasure Palace at Twenty-first and Sanchez on Liberty Hill, and the mayor was on a first-name basis with dozens of madams in town. He also became acquainted with Inez. They were neighbors in the Mission District, and one year during a Bastille Day celebration, Sunny Jim escorted Inez inside the New Dreamland ballroom, a cavernous auditorium at Post and Steiner Streets (which years later rock impresario Bill Graham bought and renamed Winterland).[12] Without a politician like Rolph at the city's helm, Inez could never have built her business so grandly.

As Sunny Jim gallivanted around town, Inez was busy circulating her own name, building a base of clients referred to her by other patients, as well as by physicians, attorneys, pharmacists, and nurses. Inez's services were a safety valve for these sympathetic professionals. Most physicians wouldn't risk performing abortions, and few were as experienced as Inez. She rewarded the referring professionals with kickbacks of cash, cigars, or liquor, and everyone made out nicely, including neighborhood beat cops whom Inez paid to look the other way. Word circulated that Inez's services were safe and reliable, and business at her fledgling, woman-run clinic shot up, it seemed, overnight.

The grim years in Pittsburgh had changed her. Now a mother and businesswoman, Inez had become wiser and shrewder. Nettie would say the Pittsburgh patch had hardened Inez. She had turned into a flinty-eyed entrepreneur hell-bent on succeeding at all costs. Inez was never an altruist. She reveled in helping women, but that wasn't at the heart of why she did what she did. Yes, Inez advocated for women through the services she offered, but make no mistake, Inez was in the business she chose to make as much money as she could.

Part of climbing San Francisco's economic ladder was Inez's seemingly innate ability to flirt shamelessly with any man who could do something for her. She thrived on male attention and got it. Now in her mid-twenties, she never went long without the affection of a suitor, often two or three at the same time. Inez was enchanting. She'd toss her Titian mane over her shoulder and demurely smile at any male prospect who might do her some good. Her training at the Palace had primed her; her experience with G. W. Merritt had conditioned her.

Inez still took great pride in her petite figure, although after giving birth twice, she complained to Nettie that men weren't able to fit their hands around her waist any longer. She resorted to weighing herself as soon as she arose every morning; if the hospital scale in her bathroom showed more than one hundred ten pounds, she'd down six raw eggs and a tablespoon of wheat germ, and eat nothing else all day.

Ever on the lookout to accentuate her female charms, Inez talked to Nettie about undergoing elective surgery. Inez had heard about two bizarre cosmetic operations that were all the rage: removing the small toes on both her feet and excising the small ribs on either side of her rib cage. The toe surgery would allow Inez to fit into the stylish high heels of the day; the rib removal would once again allow Inez to showcase her hourglass figure without wearing a constricting tight-laced corset.[13] The only thing stopping her, she told Nettie, was the time off that would be necessary to recuperate from the surgeries. Money was hardly an issue.

"You can't be serious!" Nettie cried.

An exhibit award certificate from the 1915 Panama-Pacific International Exposition.

"Oh, you're such a pill," Inez told her sister, laughing, as the two walked arm in arm across Union Square on their way to Ransohoff's so Inez could try on some hats.

Sometime in the spring of 1912, Inez happened to meet a handsome sea captain by the name of William F. Brown, on shore leave in San Francisco. Nettie knew that it was just a matter of time before Inez would fall for a man, because even though she'd been burned by G. W. Merritt, she needed some stability in her love life, with her business reaching new heights. Men seemed to be constantly buzzing around her wherever she went. Why couldn't disarming Inez pick out a beau who'd treat her right?

To Inez, Billy Brown cut a swashbuckling figure. He was forty-one, fourteen years Inez's senior. The two had known each other before Inez's calamitous years in Pittsburgh. When ashore, Billy had lived several blocks away from the Ingenthrons

Inez Ingenthron, ca. 1917.

in Bernal Heights, at 522 Ellsworth, and on occasion he and Inez had passed each other on the street and conversed.

By all indications, Billy was a bachelor struck by Inez's beauty and sexuality, as well as by her spirited charm and smarts. He found her utterly captivating. Theirs was a whirlwind courtship, and soon Inez found herself pregnant. The couple wasn't married, and as with G.W., the deficit of a marriage certificate didn't bother

The grounds of the Panama-
Pacific International Exposition,
three months before opening
day, 1914.

Inez. She prided herself on being a renegade, and motherhood outside of marriage, particularly if the mother had a hefty cache of savings of her own, was among the best ways a women could thumb her nose at silly convention. Billy was a straightforward, traditional man who didn't quite know what to make of his fetching, iconoclastic, now-pregnant girlfriend. To Inez, looking to reestablish her roots in San Francisco, there was no doubt she would have this child, and in mid-April of 1913, Inez's third son, William E. Brown, was born.

Two years later, two weeks after the Panama-Pacific International Exposition extravaganza closed, Inez and Billy took a streetcar to City Hall and got married on a whim.[14] Within a year, they moved to a larger home, at 163 Lisbon Street, off Excelsior Avenue, so Inez could accommodate more patients.[15] She still had the canvas apron of medical instruments she'd lifted from Dr. West's office, and used them for all of her procedures. To erase their provenance, Inez decided to have her name embroidered on the inside flap of the instruments' carrying case. For this purpose, she used "Inez Brown," her married name, sewn in script with a flourish in black India ink.

Gallant sea captain Billy Brown turned out to be rather ordinary on land. His seafaring days were over, and he didn't care to do much other than sit in an easy chair in the couple's parlor, as a day nurse cared for infant Billy Jr. and youngster Bobby and a parade of rather anxious women was ushered upstairs to Inez's clinic. When she was finished for the day, restive Inez loved to go dancing and be seen at the city's best restaurants, theaters, and operas. Bland Billy wasn't interested in any of these activities. Such inertia wasn't what Inez had had in mind when she married him. At Inez's insistence (some called it "bullying"), Billy secured part-time employment at S. H. Frank & Co., a tannery on Battery Street. The last thing Inez wanted was a deadbeat husband living off her soaring ambition and money.

Billy's occasional work at the tannery was a plus for several reasons, most of all because it left Inez to do whatever she pleased. If she had made the mistake of marrying a loser, she didn't have to become one herself. Inez was a libertine and made no apologies for it, even to Billy. Inez enjoyed being wined and dined, and if her doting admirer wasn't her husband, what the hell was wrong with that?

This prompted great contention from Nettie, who one afternoon told Inez point-blank: "You can't be doing such things. People talk. You're a married woman, for God's sake!"

"Let 'em talk!" Inez shot back with equal fury. "Whadda I care?"

There was no telling Inez anything.

As her marriage unraveled, Inez had her first run-in with the law—not from the abortions she was performing, but from a curious case of seller's remorse. The city had plans to build a school on the Lisbon Street property where she and Billy lived. In 1918, Billy and Inez sold their home to the city for three thousand five hundred dollars to make room for the public school. But as bulldozers arrived to demolish the house for the construction of Monroe Grammar School, Inez changed her mind in a big way. She planted herself at her front door with a loaded shotgun and threatened to blow the head off anyone who made a move to tear down her house. The concrete foundation for Monroe School had already been laid, but Inez was threatening to do away with anyone foolish enough to push her out of her home, even though the city had already paid her. The standoff lasted three months until Police Chief David A. White paid a visit to Inez and told her that she was about to be evicted and that a twenty-four-hour blockade would prevent her from returning to her house. Cops would bodily remove her if she tried to trespass on what was now city property.[16] Inez eventually backed down. She and Billy moved around the corner to 241 Excelsior, where Inez continued to offer abortions whenever a forlorn woman knocked on her door.

There, Inez would have another encounter with police, but this time it wouldn't end as amicably.

Every woman who passed through Inez's makeshift clinic had a story, but Inez never asked the details. She was in the business of fixing mistakes, not commemorating them. For whatever their reasons, Inez's patients didn't want to become mothers at a particular time and under a particular circumstance. All Inez asked was whether patients were certain they wanted to proceed, and when they answered affirmatively, as long as they had the fees Inez required, she went about her task. One patient Inez saw during this time was Edith Suter, an important official of the International

Ladies' Garment Workers' Union. Edith was among a handful of women in the top ranks of a powerful union that had organized fifty-five thousand rank-and-file members throughout the United States.[17]

On May 11, 1920, thirty-nine-year-old Edith was reported missing to the San Francisco Police, and two weeks later, she was found dead inside Inez's home. Inez didn't call the police but contacted the San Francisco Labor Council to notify officials that Edith had died. Inez then sent Edith's body to McAvoy, O'Hara & Co., a funeral parlor on Market and Church Streets, to be embalmed.[18] When police appeared at Inez's door to question her, she told them Edith had come to her complaining of ill health and asking for help. Over the next week, Edith grew steadily worse. Inez then called a doctor, Hans Augustus Mager, who diagnosed Edith with pneumonia. A day later, Edith was dead.

Police took Inez into custody briefly before releasing her, pending the results of an autopsy on Edith's body. City Coroner John Clark found that the labor organizer did not die of pneumonia, as Inez had said, and discovered there had been "every indication that an operation of some kind was performed." But because Edith's body had been drained of blood, Dr. Clark was unable to make a certain determination. He sent tissue samples to a pathology laboratory for further examination.[19]

The next day, police arrested Dr. Mager for filing a false death certificate.[20] Within weeks, after tissue slivers had been examined, a coroner's jury concluded that Edith had died from complications following an abortion, but the city panel was unable to fix responsibility for the procedure. Neither Mager nor Inez was charged, and the case was officially closed.[21]

Even if Inez had been found culpable of performing an abortion on Edith, it's doubtful she would have been charged with a crime. Edith's indiscretion had been her decision not to be pregnant any longer, and her choice to seek out Inez had been based on recommendations distilled from scores of women. As in the case of Dr. West and Addie Gilmour more than three decades earlier, there still was little prosecutorial commitment to pursue criminal charges in such deaths. Most San Franciscans preferred looking the other way. A horrible accident had occurred, but there was no use in placing blame for it. Perhaps a deeper reading was that any woman who got pregnant and sought an abortion implicitly accepted such risks. Even if prosecutors wanted to get tough, getting an abortionist to criminal court was a vexing process, and once there, persuading a jury to render a guilty verdict was next to impossible, particularly if the abortionist was a woman. For prosecutors, trying an abortionist, even when a high-profile victim such as Edith Suter died, depended on testimony from witnesses, and to find a witness to pin Edith's death on Inez or somebody else required time and expense. Except for the poorly paid San Francisco district attorney himself, the prosecutor's office was filled with part-time attorneys who had little incentive to file charges against low-level criminals such as abortionists. Edith's death was an unfortunate turn of events, and that's how it would stay.

A year after Edith Suter's death, the oversize comedian Roscoe "Fatty" Arbuckle, second in popularity only to Charlie Chaplin at the time, was charged with murdering actress Virginia Rappe in a suite of rooms on the twelfth floor of the St. Francis Hotel over the Labor Day weekend. After two sensational trials, Arbuckle was acquitted. To many, Virginia had died from a condition caused by one or more badly botched abortions. An autopsy showed that the actress's bladder had been ruptured and that she had died from peritonitis. No one knows which abortionists may have performed the procedures, but it seems unlikely that Inez had anything to do with Virginia's death. Trying Arbuckle for homicide was more politically expedient for new San Francisco DA Matthew Brady than to suggest that the actress's death had been the result of the mangled procedures.[22]

Other factors conspired to protect Inez too. By now, she had become a growing political force in San Francisco. Cops, public officials, doctors, pharmacists, and lawyers knew Inez, or knew of her and what her business was. She freely gave out favors to anyone who had influence in her insular world. She knew everyone who was anyone in town. Her clinic also had a reputation of being scrupulously clean; Inez was known far and wide as skilled and reliable. Women, and not just a few men, realized how essential her services were, and even at this early stage in her career, Inez had become a kind of public utility, not unlike the city water or fire department, or the municipal railroad.

Along with her swelling success, for the first time in her life, Inez had started to accumulate substantial savings. She began buying expensive clothes at chic downtown emporiums such as Ransohoff's and I. Magnin. Inez still loved hats and took to buying half a dozen, all at the same time. She bought sheer stockings made out of a newly invented material called rayon. She often showed up, without Billy, at pricey downtown restaurants. She enjoyed the food, yes, but her presence—often alone, often with a friend or potential business ally—was always accompanied by requisite fanfare and fuss. It was part of an astute marketing strategy Inez devised to be seen at all the city's high-end establishments. Inez's glamorous looks—and her pocketbook—didn't

Roscoe "Fatty" Arbuckle with an unknown actress on set.

Actress Virgina Rappe,
ca. 1920.

Suite 1221 of the
St. Francis Hotel after
Arbuckle's party, 1921.

hurt such a campaign. Even without the plastic surgery she coveted, thirty-four-year-old Inez was a stunner. She still turned heads wherever she went.

All the while, her nascent business acumen increased. Inez realized that women who came to her in such a precarious, delicate condition deserved surroundings that would put them at ease. An abortionist's office ought to reflect a woman's touch, not the sterile surroundings of a male physician or, worse, a flophouse room rented by the hour. Knowing her competition, Inez began furnishing her Excelsior home's waiting room with tasteful furniture and valuable antiques. She invested in sterling silver tea service sets, Oriental rugs, and family heirlooms purchased from auctioneers. She seemed to be constantly on the lookout for high-end accessories. Inez figured the least she could do was create an environment that honored women rather than shamed them.

At the same time, Inez ramped up her friendships with neighborhood politicians, beat cops, and an occasional newspaper reporter, inviting them into her home for drinks and, on Wednesday evenings, open-stakes poker. She entertained graciously; she was a hostess who anticipated whatever her guests desired. Inez always had two or three Baccarat pitchers filled with silver fizzes on hand—gin, egg whites, sugar, and pinch of lemon juice. Not one to sit on the sidelines, she'd pull up a chair to the card table and get dealt in. She offered cops and pols Cuban cigars. Occasionally, she'd light up a stogie herself, blowing smoke rings that floated above the poker table, rising to the ceiling. The men loved it; the women couldn't believe it.

It made for a show that even Mayor Sunny Jim wanted to be a part of. He'd stop by Inez's house to play a game or two, smoke a Montecristo, and belt back more than several silver fizzes. Prohibition had just been passed, and while the law may have affected others, it had no impact whatsoever on Inez and her boozy friends. Inez's two sons, Bobby and Billy Jr., were transfixed by the eclectic mix of guests. They'd serve appetizers and cocktails in their pajamas until Inez shooed them off to bed.

Inez found herself the star of a nonstop show, which went from the early morning operating on patients till past midnight celebrating with friends, partners in crime, and anyone else with the good sense to join in. She reveled in the limelight she had created.

This, however, was not the case for husband Billy Brown, who wasn't even a supporting player in the fun and games. More often than not he'd be stretched out on the couch in the evenings, snoring. Perhaps from his days at sea, Billy's motto, "Early to bed and early to rise," was the opposite of Inez's let-'er-rip philosophy of "Work hard, party harder."

Opposites might attract in physics and popular romance novel, but not in the case of Inez and Billy Brown. Billy had no imagination. He was stuffy and old-fashioned. He was a weight on Inez's vertical business ascension, and in her mind, it was holding her back. On the rare occasion when Inez would set aside an evening for the two of them, Billy preferred having his dinner at home. He wanted a "wife," hardly Inez's calling. The couple got into arguments that, on occasion, grew into contretemps that turned physical. Inez wasn't afraid of taking a shot at Billy. "Never fight a man with an open hand" was what Alice had taught her. "Use your fists! Make 'em realize you're not a pushover." Inez was volatile. She had a temper. Occasionally, Billy's face showed the results from a poke Inez landed out of frustration.

To Inez, Billy Brown had become a liability, personally and professionally. Guests at 241 Excelsior confused the older man, snoozing on the couch, as being Inez's father. That shamed her to no end. No matter what Inez did, however much she fought and belittled him, Billy was neither going to change nor go away. He had become an immovable force of nature.

So Inez came up with a plan.

She'd kill him.

Extreme, absolutely. Beyond Inez's multifarious abilities, probably not. Inez was through being the victim of any man. G. W. Merritt had burned that into her psyche.

Inez was flying high. She had moments when she thought she could get away with anything, including murder.

So she cooked up a scheme Mabel had once told her about. She'd feed Billy his meals spiked with increasingly larger doses of arsenic. The poison was readily available at hard-goods stores, used in a variety of everyday products, notably pesticides. Unless a forensic scientist knew what he was looking for, its presence in a corpse was virtually undetectable. So common was its use in murder that the French called arsenic *poudre de succession*, or inheritance powder.[23] Arsenic was tasteless, white, and readily dissolved in soups and drinks. Billy would never know why he was getting weaker, until one day his heart would stop. If Billy Brown wanted home-cooked meals, that's what Inez would serve him.

Would the police ever suspect Inez when it came to the death of her husband? Hardly. Inez was everyone's fun-loving, poker-playing confidante who gave cops weekly gifts of cash, booze, cigars, and girls. Who'd suspect Inez of murder?

Inez's granddaughter Caroline distinctly recalled Inez telling her about hatching the murder scheme. "I remember Grandma saying, 'You don't like someone, you poison them. That's the way to get rid of someone.'" Caroline remembered Billy Brown's sister-in-law Hazel Brown years later telling her how Inez had crowed about seasoning Billy's meals with arsenic to do him in.[24]

Week by week, Billy began complaining about his feet and hands tingling or feeling numb. He grew unsteady. His stomach ached after meals. He'd find clumps of hair on his pillow. Billy's breath smelled foul. One afternoon, Inez found Billy in the backyard in a mental fog, talking incoherently. The sea captain wasn't accustomed to being on land for so long. Billy must be going off his rocker. Or so people thought.

William F. Brown died at age fifty on August 5, 1921, two days before his fifty-first birthday,[25] leaving Inez a widow with three sons, two of whom were living with her at the time (the third still in Pennsylvania), and a coterie of loyal friends and associates. The official cause of Billy's death, as listed on his death certificate, was "pernicious anemia," signed by Mission District physician Dr. Morris Evans.[26]

Pernicious anemia is a chronic deficiency of vitamin B12, stemming from failure to absorb the essential vitamin in the gastrointestinal tract. The deficiency prompts a dangerously low level of healthy red blood cells, which can eventually lead to death. When asked to list the method he used to confirm his diagnosis, Dr. Evans wrote on Billy's death certificate "clinical,"[27] shorthand for declaring that the death was determined by what others reported the victim's condition had been, and in this case, the most reliable source was Inez. If that sounds shady, that's because it was. Years later, physicians would recognize pernicious anemia as a convenient cover-up for poisoning.[28]

Inez played the role of a grieving widow to perfection. When asked about Billy's seemingly overnight decline in health, she'd shrug, patting her eyes with a perfumed hanky and sobbing. Inez preferred not to use the word *death*, choosing instead to call Billy's demise "the long sleep."

While there was no conclusive proof that Inez killed Billy Brown, her admission to granddaughter Caroline years later indicated that it surely was a possibility. It was Caroline who talked to Hazel, who contended that Inez had killed Billy. Perhaps Caroline misconstrued what Inez or Hazel had told her. Perhaps Inez fabricated what had happened. Perhaps her murder confession was bravado with no basis in fact. But maybe not.

Meanwhile, Inez inherited Billy's assets, which included a jointly owned house, a bank account, and an annuity from his thirty years as a seafaring mariner. The police never investigated Billy's death. The neighborhood beat cops had more pressing things to do, including showing up for Inez's Wednesday evening parties.

NINE

LUXURY HEELS

Billy Brown had been a mistake. A rebound from Pittsburgh and Inez's ill-fated common-law marriage, or whatever it was, to G. W. Merritt. Sleeping with Billy had been impulsive, bearing his child imprudent, and marrying him foolhardy. Falling for any one of these miscalculations would have been bad, but all three made for a trifecta that Inez came to believe would undermine all she sought to achieve. Why she didn't seek a divorce or separation is something Inez couldn't fully explain, even to herself. Besides being bored with Billy and angry for going as far as she did with him, perhaps Inez knocked Billy off just because she *could*, a challenge renegade Inez had created for herself. The ultimate disrespect for all things conventional. The only person with any suspicions about Billy's arsenic-laced diet was Billy's sister Hazel, but Inez and Hazel were friends, and Hazel's opinion of her brother had been lower than even Inez's. Hazel would be the last to rat on Inez.

In the obituary in the *San Francisco Chronicle*, Billy Brown was lauded with all the plaudits of the recently departed: "dearly beloved husband," "loving father," and "beloved son."[1] Inez didn't know what kind of son Billy had been, but the platitudes about his being a loved husband and father made her laugh—quietly to herself, that is. Better to sing a dead man's praises than tell the truth, Inez supposed.

If the San Francisco Police Department had investigated Billy's death, it likely would have ordered an autopsy. Coroners are the dead's final defense against criminal wrongdoing. Inez had already attracted Dr. Clark's scrutiny over Edith Suter's death. Fifteen months later, Inez would become a prime suspect in another curious death. But no autopsy was performed on Billy Brown's body.[2] At a graveside funeral that thirty-five people attended, almost all friends of Inez, Billy was buried in Cypress Lawn Cemetery, south of San Francisco, in the city of Colma. With the interment went any clue of the cause of his death.

In Inez's business, regret was an emotion that didn't go far. She pulled out her scented hanky once again, shed some crocodile tears, and asked to be dealt in at the weekly poker games. After a two-week hiatus, six beat cops showed up at Inez's home to pick up sealed envelopes with cash payoffs inside. She continued to ply them and anyone else who came by with silver fizzes and cigars, fronting them cash if they ever went bust on a straight to another cop's flush. If their girlfriends ever got in what Inez referred to as "a family way," she'd do them a favor for free. What was there not to like about Inez?

No way were the cops going to investigate her. If you asked them, they'd probably say they weren't disappointed in the least that sleepy Billy was out of the picture. At thirty-five, Inez was still a knockout. What the hell had she been doing with Billy in the first place?

Unencumbered now, Inez marched toward her dream of amassing a fortune as the leading abortionist not just in San Francisco, but in all of California. She knew exactly where she wanted to go and laid out a course of action to get there. Nothing seemed beyond her grasp, and that included men, money, and influence.

For her upcoming birthday on September fifth, Inez decided she had postponed the twin cosmetic surgery procedures she'd coveted long enough. She'd start with her petite size-five feet. She'd get her pinky toes removed so she could fit into pointy heels. Inez found a surgeon at 450 Sutter Street to perform the operation.

This time, Nettie just shrugged her shoulders. She was through trying to tame her sister.

As Inez was to find out, her little toes weren't amputated, but instead were cut open, the bones inside removed, and the flaccid skin then sewn up. The surgery shriveled her pinky toes, creating flaps of excess skin that stayed with her for the rest of her life.

While her feet might have looked a bit peculiar, Inez didn't care. She was able to slip into a growing collection of luxury heels that she adored. A side benefit was that the high heels pushed up her derriere, lifting her breasts and accentuating her curves. The downside was the surgery's recovery, which took Inez out of commission from the clinic for six weeks, during which all she was able to do was hobble around like a sailor with two peg legs. The recuperation was painful but worth it. At least, that's what she told Nettie.

Eight months later, Inez went back to the same surgeon to have the bottom ribs removed from each side of her rib cage. Why wear a painful corset when a surgical procedure could do the same thing? The surgery required a deft, practiced hand since excising the ribs meant the surgeon risked puncturing vital organs, including her kidneys. The bones removed were the twelfth ribs, known as floating ribs because they cover the organs in the back, not the front, of the body. Many surgeons at the time believed these ribs to be extraneous, like an appendix or gallbladder, and their removal was simply a matter of personal preference.[3]

While recovering, the pain in her torso excruciating, Inez survived with a daily regime of morphine. To care for the boys, Inez hired a full-time governess, Henrietta Reynolds. She could well afford the expense, and Mrs. Reynolds did a better job of mothering than Inez could. Even after she was back on her wobbly feet. Inez had more important things to do than play tiddlywinks with Billy or help Bobby with his arithmetic.

Inez's dramatic nature demanded that she be at the center of attention at all times. That made caring for the children difficult. She had little patience. She didn't coddle. As granddaughter Caroline would later say, "You had to make a big fuss over Inez. She demanded the spotlight shine on her. And if you didn't give it to her, you'd suffer the consequences."[4]

Inez was just too busy to trouble herself with the children. Had she ordered enough chemicals, ether, anesthetic? Had she paid off everyone, everyone who mattered? Who might come knocking at her door today? It was a juggling act with Inez constantly tossing more and more balls in the air.

Less two ribs and two toes, Inez was now performing abortions on two or three women a day, taking in as much as seven hundred to a thousand dollars a week. By 1922, she had saved so much that she was able to purchase two tracts of land closer to downtown: one for a custom-built luxury home, the other for a state-of-the-art clinic. She was on her way to seeing her dream come true.

The house would be as large as Inez's personality—five bedrooms, three baths for her, the boys, and servants. She'd have a giant Hollywood bed with tufted fabric stretched on an oversize headboard, facing a wall covered with mirrors so she could admire herself—and anyone else—from a variety of angles. Off the master bedroom would be an immense bathroom with a deep porcelain claw-foot tub and a glass shower with multiple spigots. Inez already had a menagerie of seventy-five hats, and she planned an elaborate walk-in closet to display them and more. There'd be eight horizontal rows, eight vertical rows, making for a total of sixty-four slots. With four or five hats per slot, Inez could manage more than two hundred fifty chapeaus. She'd keep her mink stoles, jackets, and coats in another walk-in closet and the rest in cold storage at H. Liebes on Grant and Post. In the backyards of both the house and clinic, Inez would install concrete incinerators to destroy fetal remains. That was absolutely essential in her line of work.

There'd also be a maze of sliding panels, secret compartments, and removable floorboards to hide everything, from money and ledgers to medical instruments and chemicals. Inez's business was cash-only. Absolutely no checks or credit. As an evening ritual, Inez would count her daily receipts and bind them in thousand-dollar stacks with red rubber bands. She found the activity relaxing and therapeutic. Since banks were mostly off-limits (she couldn't risk a paper trail), Inez would create dozens of places to hide the wads of cash, including in the hems of pleated brocade drapes, a big safe in the hat closet, and in hollowed-out banisters with removable caps. In the basement, Inez would have two adjoining rooms, each with a locked door opened by a different key. Once inside the second room, in the middle of the floor, a hole would accommodate a lockbox that could be filled with cash.[5] She'd also commission a concealed back staircase for getaways.

Inez had already bought a house at 664 Guerrero Street in the Mission District, four blocks from the lot where her grand three-story home would go up. It'd be more than three thousand square feet on a lot double that size. On the second floor, facing the street, would be a series of five graceful arched bay windows that would showcase an elegant sitting room with a fireplace. The entire compound would be encircled by a black wrought iron fence and gate.

Her new home would be perfect, down to its very address: 274 Guerrero Street. Whether by serendipity or design, 274 was the California penal code that outlawed abortion. That pleased Inez to no end. An abortionist living behind a door with the number 274 emblazoned on it.

Ha!

The medical clinic would be located a mile closer into town, at 327 Fillmore Street, up the hill from Haight Street, on the west side of the street in a residential neighborhood, not far from a busy strip of Jewish merchants, bakers, cobblers, synagogues, and kosher butchers.[6] There'd be a ground-floor apartment for either recovering patients or Inez's friends who'd partied too late. Inez would greet patients in an elegantly appointed reception area and office atop a terrazzo staircase, and the operating rooms would be on the second floor.

Following Nettie's lead, Inez soon became a shrewd buyer and seller of real estate. Property was a tangible asset that Inez could use while it continued to accrue value. It also was a way to launder her cash profits. Inez bought real estate at 339 Waller Street and would operate it as an overflow satellite clinic to the Fillmore Street facility. She would ultimately invest in property throughout San Francisco, Oakland, the South Bay, and soon Los Angeles.

With her business booming, Billy Brown out of the picture, and her newly reconstituted feet and ribs, all that was missing from Inez's life was a new steady beau, and in the fall of 1922, that deficit was filled. Inez began dating an Italian national by the name of Charles Antonio Granelli, whom she'd met at a weekend gathering sponsored by the Sons of Italy, which had just opened a lodge, the Vita Nuova No. 1198 on Mission Street.

Charlie Granelli had been born in Parma, Italy, in 1885, which made him a year older than Inez. Like her formal education, Charlie's went only to the sixth grade.[7] And like Inez's parents (and Edith Suter's), Charlie had arrived in the United States via steamship from Le Havre, France. Then known as Carlo, twenty-three-year-old Charlie made the transatlantic passage in 1908 on the USS *Chicago*. Three years after his arrival in New York, Charlie married an eighteen-year-old Hungarian immigrant by the name of Elise Stein. The marriage fell apart, and like tens of thousands of freshly minted Americans, intrepid Charlie made his way across the breadth of America to postearthquake San Francisco to stake his fortune, going into business with his brother-in-law, Alfredo Cesari, who was running a fruit-and-vegetable market called Valley Produce at 258 Washington Street, not far from the Embarcadero and the city's arch of crescent piers.[8] It was to be the beginning of a grand future Charlie envisioned—a chain of modern-day grocery stores.

But it was Charlie's brawn and charm that seemed to woo Inez. By all accounts, he was suave, sartorial, and sophisticated. During a moment of either braggadocio or calculation, Charlie shared his mercantile dream with Inez, who thought he just might have something there. When Charlie's prescient business took off, he and Inez would be complementary to each other. Two distinct and ambitious entrepreneurs joining forces. And, if by chance, Charlie's promising enterprise didn't hit pay dirt right away, that was all right too. His dreamboat eyes, broad shoulders, and continental accent were enough to seal the deal for Inez.

As had happened with G. W. Merritt and Billy Brown, Inez once again found herself pregnant. For someone who knew more than almost anyone about birth control, Inez certainly didn't practice what she preached. Inez might have been hard-nosed and calculating in business, but in her personal life she was carefree and casual. For unknown reasons, this time, on May 23, 1924, the couple married in Napa.[9] No one knows whether Inez contemplated terminating the pregnancy, whether Charlie knew his radiant bride was pregnant, or whether the pregnancy prompted the marriage (certainly for Inez, it wouldn't have). With three sons, perhaps Inez longed to have a daughter. In September, Inez had turned thirty-seven. Charlie moved out of his apartment at 359 Broadway into Inez's palace at 274 Guerrero Street, and five months later, Inez gave birth to a girl, Alice Lorine Granelli, named after Inez's mother.[10]

Soon, Georgie Merritt, Inez's first born, now eighteen, came West to live with Inez, stepfather Charlie, brother Bobby, half brother Billy, and new half sister Alice. In addition to Mrs. Reynolds, the governess, Inez hired a Japanese cook and servant, Mrs. Nake.[11] Charlie Granelli found himself instantly subsumed into a large, ready-made family.

In the evenings, the beat cops continued to stop by, as did Mayor Rolph, along with the usual complement of poker-playing firefighters, referring physicians, pharmacists, and attorneys. Into that testosterone mix often came an occasional prostitute. Boys will be boys, and Inez didn't mind the company.

On a chilly March evening, she noticed one particular working girl, dark-haired with chiseled cheeks, escorted by a cop, who was naggingly familiar. Her name was Mabel Malotte.

"I swear I know you, honey," Inez said, peering across the room at this Mabel.

Inez asked about her family, and suddenly Inez realized who the woman was: her long-lost friend Anna Thompson's niece.

Mabel was the little girl who had accompanied Anna Thompson when Inez performed the abortion in Golden Gate Park in the aftermath of the earthquake. And back further, Anna had brought along little Mabel when the Anna and Inez had met at Westerfeld's Bakery and Anna had told Inez about the manicurist's job at the Palace.

"I can't believe it's you! You're all grown up!" Inez proclaimed, hugging heavily rouged Mabel.

In this close-knit city, it still was a grand coincidence. The last Mabel had heard about Anna was that she had gotten married, moved to the budding metropolis of Los Angeles, and had four children. "We don't stay much in touch," Mabel said. "But as far as I know, Aunt Anna is doin' just fine."

Mabel's life had been a hodgepodge of casualties. She'd been shuttled back and forth between cousins, and dropped out of school, and for the time being, she emphasized, she was "testin' out my options." Whatever that meant.

When Inez raised an eyebrow, Mabel countered defensively, "I got plans for myself," insisting she was trying to get on her feet, not as a call girl, but someday as a madam. "I ain't no call girl. I wanna have me a stock of girls who'll work for *me*."

"Good luck with that, honey," was all Inez could muster, feeling very much like her sister, Nettie, talking to her rebel little sister.

One regular at the Wednesday night soirees was Ed King, a cop who had a penchant for beating up suspects, often immigrants, one of whom had died at his hands.[12] Inez's revolving door of assistants in the clinic also joined the mix, including a nurse by the name of Margie Silver, as well as Myrtle Ramsey, the woman who had hired Inez at the Palace barbershop years earlier. Inez had switched tables on Myrtle. Now Myrtle was working for Inez, helping to calm jittery patients before Inez took them upstairs. She could put anyone at ease—just what Inez's patients needed.

Meanwhile, Charlie Granelli was eager to kick-start his own business venture, and in December, with a bankroll of eighteen thousand dollars, Charlie sailed back to Italy in search of financial backers for his chain of grocery stores. Charlie would later

say the seed money was community property, which he and Inez shared equally; Inez would contend the funds belonged solely to her, and that Charlie had helped himself to them. Whoever was right, the conflict escalated into a madcap domestic brawl.

Actually, the couple's marital problems began spiraling out of control a little earlier, when Inez decided that, in addition to Charlie Granelli, she fancied Joseph F. Burns, a four-term assemblyman who represented the Mission's Twenty-third District. Handsome, blue-eyed Joe, who sported a wavy pompadour, had heard about Inez's parties and stopped by one evening to introduce himself and stick out his palm. Joe and Jimmy Rolph were old cronies. Mayor Rolph stumped for Joe's reelection in 1928, going as far as to compare Joe to Abraham Lincoln.[13] The comparison didn't do much for Joe, who lost the election and retired from electoral politics for good.[14] Instead of commuting back and forth from San Francisco to Sacramento, the state capital, Joe soon found himself spending more and more time at affable Inez's clubby home.

Charlie's version of the facts was that while working tirelessly to attract Italian investors to his grocery-chain idea, Joe Burns had moved into the Guerrero Street house and "usurped his place in his wife's affections." That's how Charlie's attorney put it in an affidavit filed against Inez when he got back. Most galling and insulting were the outrageous gifts Inez had showered on Burns: a four-thousand-dollar diamond ring, an eight-cylinder car, and numerous suits and shirts.[15] And that didn't include the "thousands of dollars" Charlie said Inez had spent on Burns. Apparently, Inez was

Joe Burns.

through with Charlie and was now head over heels in love with the new man in her life. The steamy triangle of abortionist Inez, politician Joe Burns, and wannabe grocery entrepreneur Charlie Granelli made for a deluge of stories the San Francisco newspapers couldn't get enough of. "The love suit," as it was called, placed the bickering trio above the fold on the front page of the *San Francisco Chronicle* on November 4, 1927. None of the stories made mention of Inez's thriving abortion business, but Charlie was described as a "rich S.F. man," and Joe somehow got transformed into a hero whose only crime had been to lend a sympathetic ear to a lonely newlywed whose husband had abandoned her while gallivanting on a European business trip.

In a countersuit, Inez charged that before he had left for Europe, Charlie had agreed that Inez would be able to associate with any man she wanted, as long as she provided Charlie with "sufficient money for his support, pleasure and dissipation and for the support of his relatives." Inez's counterclaim transformed Charlie into a kind of willing cuckold and suggested that he "condoned all improper acts she may have committed." Inez further alleged that Charlie had stolen from her the funds he was using to lure investors. Inez added that Charlie had tried to blackmail her for ten thousand dollars, threatening to go public with Inez's "improper conduct with Burns and other men" if she didn't pay him hush money.[16]

On May 27, 1928, a judge granted Charlie Granelli's petition for divorce. By then Joe Burns, whom the *San Francisco Examiner* had christened the "Love Pirate,"[17] had moved into the Guerrero Street house, replacing Charlie Granelli as Inez's object of affection. There is no record that Inez and Joe, who was six years younger than she, ever married. In the 1930 census, Joe's marital status was listed as single, Inez's as divorced.[18]

The Love Pirate story had legs, especially coming from San Francisco, which was viewed by the rest of America as Sin City. The *Ogden Standard-Examiner*, in the middle of Mormon country, ran a front-page headline, "Wife Reveals Strange Pact With Hubby."[19] The *San Antonio Light* ran the story with the headline: "Hubby Is Given Cash to Let Wife Flirt."[20]

Joe Burns came from a family of six brothers and sisters, and like Inez, had grown up South of the Slot and, also like her, had lived in Bernal Heights. Joe was a founding member of an influential political organization called the South of Market Boys, which helped its members get jobs and elected to public office. For a while, Joe was a teamster, working for the Emporium department store at Fifth and Market Streets[21] before becoming the Mission District's machine candidate for state assembly.

Inez's Fillmore Street clinic was drawing as many as twenty-five patients a week. As was Inez's plan, the waiting-room parlor resembled a high-society tearoom. Once patients rang the doorbell, they walked through an arched entryway to a steep stairway of thirteen steps. Inside, an art nouveau arch of delicate wrought iron flowers and leaves separated two large sitting rooms. Sheer window curtains, with roll-up blinds inside, covered a bank of windows that faced east. The three-story clinic had eight bedrooms, five bathrooms, and was more than six thousand square feet. Like Inez's Guerrero Street home, it had a series of five bay windows on the second and third floors, separated by frieze panels, along with a steeply pitched terra-cotta tile roof. The walls were tannish-white stucco; maroon velvet drapes separated different areas of the first floor. Crystal chandeliers hung in both waiting rooms, with several velvet-upholstered sofas and matching Chippendale-style chairs on either side for waiting patients. Oil paintings hung from the walls, including an impressionistic vista of gondolas tied up at a Venetian dock with a backdrop of twin church spires

The interior of Inez's clinic at 327 Fillmore Street.

and St. Mark's in the hazy distance. A photograph of a beautiful woman in her early twenties, presumably Inez, wearing a bare-shouldered flapper's dress, sat framed on a table. The clinic was filled with antiques, including Tiffany lamps and Persian rugs on a waxed parquet floor. If women were going to get abortions, they ought to be surrounded by taste and beauty. At least at Inez's clinic, they would.

In a copper bowl atop a mahogany table, a stack of business cards read:

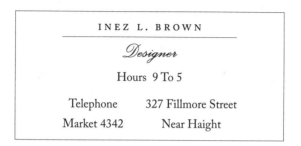

INEZ L. BROWN

Designer

Hours 9 To 5

Telephone   327 Fillmore Street
Market 4342   Near Haight

Two hand-printed signs hung in the waiting room: No smoking please and no talking appreciated. Upstairs in the operating rooms, another sign read: Silence in surgery—this means you.

Occasionally, men accompanied women to the clinic, and sometimes women brought girlfriends or children. Once their wives or girlfriends checked in with Myrtle, the men often went around the corner to the counter at Grant's Pharmacy on Scott and Haight Streets for an ice cream soda.[22] Just as Inez had envisioned, the clinic had a concrete incinerator in the backyard and a secret stairway to the basement apartment that led to an alley.[23]

At her equally elegant Guerrero Street residence, on top of an upright piano, was a three-foot-tall replica of Alexandros's statue, Venus de Milo. Not that the artwork was rare, but an abortionist with a sculpture depicting Aphrodite, the goddess of love and beauty, spoke to Inez's aesthetic and taste. Inez's perceived world was like that. In your face, out to prove she had more class and moxie than anyone else.

Several times a month, Inez summoned designers from Nelly Gaffney's, the couture boutique owned by the woman Inez had met on the train from Pittsburgh to San Francisco. Nelly had finally opened her store: a luxury fashion salon at 354 Post Street, and Inez often went there to shop for dresses, gowns, and lingerie. Inez had recently bought two beloved Pomeranians—Foxy and Theda Bara—and had jeweled collars custom-made for them. (Theda Bara was the name of a silent-film actress who generally played movie seductresses; she starred in *Cleopatra*, *The She-Devil*, and *The Unchastened Woman*.)

With more cash than she knew what to do with, Inez even bought a vintage Pierce-Arrow limousine and hired a chauffeur to take her on appointed errands around town. She had weekly appointments with two astrologers, Katherine Maule and Jean Pearson, both with offices on Sutter Street; they prepared elaborate charts based on the time of Inez's birth and geographical coordinates of her birthplace.

Meanwhile, Inez continued to pour much of her profits into real estate. She often used aliases, occasionally choosing the name Lillian Wilson. The property rolls of her holdings were scattered among five surnames—Ingenthron, Merritt, Brown, Granelli, and Burns (even though Brown and Granelli had been her only legal husbands). Around town, Inez used another alias, Amy Dutch. If federal tax investigators ever were to try to track down titles of properties belonging to Inez, it would be a daunting, near-impossible task.[24] In her daily dealings with assistants at the clinic, Inez employed a kind of linguistic code. *Ni-dash* meant "Don't you dare open your mouth!" and *glantham* meant "cash." The idea was to hide all references to finances. When women were quoted a price for services, it was done in a hushed, whispered tone.

Even if authorities could have pieced together some semblance of Inez's holdings, it wouldn't have included all the cash hidden at the house and the clinic. She once put sixty thousand dollars in a lockbox and buried it in the basement of the Guerrero Street house, only to remember it years later, and when she dug up the box, she found termites had gotten into it and had gnawed through the bills. Another time, she told a maid to take down the living room drapes and have them cleaned, but had forgotten that she had twenty thousand dollars sewn into the hems. The dry cleaners called Inez, told her about their discovery, and Inez rushed to retrieve the cash. She tipped the cleaners five hundred dollars for their honesty.[25]

Although constantly busy, Inez still had time to consult both her astrologers, and took their advice to wear prescribed stones and crystals around her neck and under layers of her clothing. She had her bathroom painted a hue of lily green, dictated by aura diagrams created by the astrologers. One evening at midnight, under a full luminous moon, Inez had her chauffeur drive her to San Francisco's Ocean Beach, in the outer Sunset District, where she threw three stones into the Pacific, walked in a circle, and drew lines in the sand, all exactly dictated by Mrs. Pearson, who had determined that in previous lives, Inez had been either a gypsy or a slave master. Mrs. Pearson wasn't certain which.

TEN

ALL AND EVERYTHING THAT FASHION GIVES

By 1932, Inez had become the leading lady of her own megawatt opus. Throughout California, the name Inez Brown had become synonymous with abortion, even though the procedure was illegal and those convicted could be sentenced to prison for five years per each procedure performed. Through payoffs and favors to cops and politicians, little went on in Inez's world that she didn't control. Almost anyone seeking an abortion, or anyone who knew a woman seeking an abortion, sooner or later got directed Inez's way. Her clinic at 327 Fillmore Street was packed from dawn to dusk. While the listing in the San Francisco city directory under Mrs. Inez Brown didn't specify "abortion services," that was hardly necessary. Just about everyone knew what Inez did. The availability of her services was essential not just to the thousands of women who sought her out but also to preserve much of the social fabric undergirding San Francisco and the rest of the state. Inez was the confidential fixer of inevitable consequences of sexual accidents, miscalculations, indiscretions, as well as of unspeakable crimes such as rape and incest. In the process, Inez had turned into one of the richest and most sought-out women in California.

So successful was Inez's bustling enterprise that by now she employed four full-time assistants, a team that complemented their boss's exacting, hard-charging personality. Myrtle Ramsey met patients at the top of the stairs and took vitals—name, address, medical history, next of kin, how long they believed they had been pregnant.

She also firmly arranged for payment. In the operating room, Inez's assistants were Musette Briggs and Mabel Spaulding, along with part-timers Margie Silver and Madeline Rand. Off and on, Inez hired a woman trained in administering anesthesia whose name was Levina Blanchette. All wore starched nurses' uniforms with matching white caps perched atop bobbed, coiffed heads. Musette usually prepared patients for the anesthetic gas, asking them to count backward from one hundred. By ninety-six, they'd be drifting into a deep slumber. Inez would then start, finishing within fifteen or twenty minutes.

When her assistants weren't attending to patients, Inez had them scrubbing the two upstairs operating rooms, dusting furniture, or waxing the already shiny parquet floors. Inez was a fanatic for cleanliness. She couldn't tolerate anything that wasn't spick-and-span immaculate.

Inez's only male employee was tall, likable Joseph Hoff, her general utility man. Like Myrtle, Inez and Joe went back a long time. As a boy of barely fifteen, Joe had worked as a bellboy at the Palace Hotel, and on the day of the earthquake, Inez had run into him on the fire line. Through the years, they'd kept in touch, and when Inez needed an all-purpose man around the clinic, she hired him. Joe and Myrtle were touchstones of Inez's past; she trusted them implicitly, not an easy virtue for Inez or anyone in her line of work.

While there seemed to be no end to Inez's runaway commercial success, the bloom was starting to droop from the rose of her personal life. The litigious, public aftermath of her marital disaster with Charlie Granelli had begun to collide with her impetuous, headfirst plunge with Joe Burns. Yes, Inez finally had a husband, albeit common-law, who wielded respect through myriad political connections, but the two strong-willed partners argued constantly. Inez had a difficult time getting along with any paramour for any length of time, and Joe was no exception. He took to storming out of the Guerrero Street house and not returning until Inez backed down on whatever argument they were having on any given day. Three or four days later, Inez would purr into the phone, "Oh, Joe, I miss you," signaling that Joe was welcomed back. In a week, they'd be at it again, yelling at each other at the top of their lungs.

During one particularly nasty spat, Joe stomped out of the house, angrily backed the black Packard in the driveway over one of Inez's prized Pomeranians—her favorite, Theda Bara. Joe knew that Inez would be furious. She was accustomed to taking yappy Theda Bara and Foxy everywhere. An apologetic Joe explained to Inez that the little dog had jumped behind the car and, in the process, committed suicide.

Inez paused for a second and then exploded, chasing Joe around the house with a cast-iron frying pan.[1]

Even when they seemed to get along, Inez and Joe maintained an open sexual relationship. Although Inez and Joe lived as husband and wife, Inez openly flirted with men, and on occasion slept with them. Joe did the same with his own ensemble of women who frequented his circuit of horse-racing and card parlors. It was a tacit agreement that seemed to suit them both. Hewing to the straight and narrow, Nettie never understood why Joe didn't walk out for good, but Nettie could never figure out any of Inez's relationships. With Inez's streak of independence and her ever-increasing income, a better question might have been why Inez didn't throw Joe overboard.

As for Inez's four children, Bob Merritt, as Inez had always known, was the charmed son, flashing a big smile wherever he went. Athletic, smart, and handsome, Bob had graduated from the exclusive Drew School, at California and Broderick Streets, then from the University of Nevada in Reno, and was now at student at Cornell University medical school in New York. Older brother Georgie hadn't fared as well. After a stormy, peripatetic childhood with G.W. and Sarah Ann, Georgie

Inez's son, Robert "Bobby" Merritt.

moved to San Francisco in his late teens to live with Inez. He picked up work driving delivery trucks, an ill-fated career choice since he had even by then developed a fierce affection for alcohol. Georgie had a series of accidents, one involving a fifty-seven-year-old woman who suffered a broken arm and head injuries when Georgie lost control of the truck he was driving.[2] That mishap was followed by another while Georgie was driving a milk truck. He ran over a young boy, and to avoid criminal charges and a lawsuit, Inez agreed to monthly payments to the boy's family that lasted for years. Georgie lived for some time in the basement apartment of Inez's Fillmore Street clinic. He married and became a butcher for some time. Inez and Billy Brown's son, William Brown, lived with Inez and Joe at the Guerrero Street house, attended private school, and also became a teamster. Inez's fourth child, Alice Lorine, enrolled in the elite Convent of the Sacred Heart in tony Pacific Heights and later at the Castilleja School in Palo Alto.[3] Inez loved seeing Alice dressed up by Mrs. Reynolds, the governess, in expensive party dresses, looking like a princess. Inez commissioned a large doll's house be built in the backyard for her. Inez's brother, Harry, who on and off lived with her or Nettie, began in his fifties to exhibit signs of what today would be called schizophrenia. Without warning, he'd start playing a concerto, hands flying through the air as though he were Sergei Rachmaninoff, the only problem being there was no piano. Inez's other brother, Walter, drifted away from the family and eventually disappeared. Inez's mother, Alice, lived with Nettie; she grew increasingly erratic and bitter and died in 1936.

With the Fillmore Street clinic operating full bore six days a week, Inez seldom slept more than three or four hours a night. She'd always been an insomniac, even back when the Ingenthrons lived South of the Slot and Inez was terrified of her father and his alcoholic binges, then in Bernal Heights, when pensioners had the habit of climbing into bed with her and Nettie. As an adult, Inez never had the patience for sleep. Too much on her mind, too many things she needed to do. She was in constant motion, interviewing a nurse, receptionist, housekeeper, or servant to fill an opening at the clinic or house; buying more tanks of nitrous oxide, her anesthetic of choice; closing on yet another real estate deal; making sure the beat cops and pols downtown were satisfied; attending to yet another woman knocking at her door, after hours, terrified to go back home pregnant.

With so much cash on hand, Inez invested in another home, this one in the lavish San Francisco enclave of St. Francis Wood. She went on to buy other residences at 1501 Laguna Street, near where the San Francisco Cathedral of St. Mary of the

Assumption stands today, an apartment at 435 Staten Avenue in Oakland near Lake Merritt, and a stunning glass-sided vertical villa with sweeping views of the Golden Gate at 691 Marina Boulevard. Bob Merritt lived in the Marina house after he graduated from medical school, and when he moved out, Nettie moved in.[4]

In the fall of 1936, Inez bought the controlling interest in a sprawling eight-hundred-acre estate known as Burns Ranch in La Honda, in adjacent San Mateo County, forty miles south of San Francisco. The ranch was down the road from Apple Jacks, a hole-in-the-wall bar that would gain dubious fame when writer Ken Kesey thirty years later assembled a band of friends he called the Merry Pranksters who hung out there. Burns Ranch was a bucolic retreat for Joe and Inez, with cooks, horse groomers, and trainers. The couple went there as often as Inez could break away from the clinic. Kentucky horsewoman Suzanne Mason boarded horses at Burns Ranch, including Sun Portland, a thoroughbred that won races at Santa Anita, Bay Meadows, Del Mar, and Tanforan. Mason was the wealthy widow of Silas B. Mason, whose engineering company built colossal public works projects across America, including the Grand Coulee Dam in Washington State, New York's Lincoln Tunnel, and the Chicago drainage canal (which changed the course of the Chicago River).[5] Other horses boarded at Burns Ranch that turned out to be moneymakers included Gold Armor and Pomp Gold.[6]

In addition to the bulging portfolio of real estate and racehorses, Inez bought government bonds for her children. Concerned that too many assets would attract the attention of the Bureau of Internal Revenue, the precursor to the IRS, Inez continued using aliases on property titles and certificates, turning her finances into a gnarled web nearly impossible to untangle. She still had scores of rubber-banded cash bundles secreted in the multitude of properties she now owned that she was afraid she'd lose track of.

Inez found the most satisfying way to dispose of income, of course, was to spend it on herself. When she had finished with the last patient at the clinic, Inez would cut a swath through high-end Union Square shops on torrid buying sprees, often with Foxy, wearing his diamond-studded collar, pulling on her leash. Inez would stop in for chamomile tea and soda crackers with her old friend Nelly Gaffney, trading gossip, while going though trunks full of clothes Nelly had brought from Paris, usually leaving with two or three new outfits and hats. From Liebes furs, Inez bought mink, fox, ermine, seal, and beaver coats for herself and as gifts, even though the weather in San Francisco was seldom cold enough to wear them. At any given time, Inez kept more than two dozen furs in cold storage at Liebes. She had an open account at the city's top jeweler, Shreve & Co. on Post Street.[7] She added so many custom-designed hats, dresses, gowns, lingerie, and bespoke shoes to her wardrobe that her large walk-in closet could accommodate no more. She'd eat lunch at restaurants where society women nibbled on watercress sandwiches and Welsh rarebit. Always on the lookout for antiques and home furnishings, the interiors of each of her homes resembled the pricy showrooms at W. & J. Sloane. Inez bought butter-soft Egyptian cotton sheets for all the beds.

Despite the nonstop spending, Inez had money left over, so she bought Joe a musty Mission Street tavern with sticky counters and floors, called Kavanaugh's, as much of an investment as a way to give Joe something to do. Inez figured it would keep Joe out of her hair, busy in the back room playing California lowball and Klondike while smoking Marca Petri stogies with his friends. If there were loose women among them, that was all right too. Better there than in the Guerrero Street house.

Money was one thing, and between the real estate, couture clothing, furs, glittery baubles, racehorses, and the chauffeured Pierce-Arrow limousine they kept in a garage down the street from the clinic, Inez had more than she knew what to do with. Even with the Great Depression in full swing, Inez had every materialistic thing she could possibly want. The ravages of the nation's economic woes had no bearing on her, just as it had no bearing on hundreds of San Francisco's wealthiest patrician families.

But women from those lineages had more. Which gave Inez pause to consider something that had been weighing on her mind ever since her days as a lowly manicurist at the Palace. Social standing, the vaunted ability to stand out based on pedigree, was a trait more durable than money, which could come and go. The privileged sense of prestige and prominence was a concept foreign to Inez. Could Inez procure money *and* social class?

Inez knew that one of the requisite tickets of entrée to San Francisco high society was the opera. From Mrs. Mason, Inez learned that Louisville's upper crust congregated around the comings and goings of the Kentucky Derby. San Francisco's equivalent was the opera, as highbrow and elite as it got in the City by the Bay. Opera was cultured, frightfully expensive, and strictly blue blood. Opening night was the mandatory, absolute must-attend event for every denizen of San Francisco beau monde.

Inez knew she'd never be a part of the city's old-moneyed establishment, but she certainly could dress like them, and she certainly could comport herself as one of them. So what if she had made her money performing abortions? She had worked hard to get where she was; no one could deny that. At least Inez hadn't cheated, swindled, and lied her way to fame and fortune, as some of the flushest moneyed San Franciscans had. The way Inez saw it, she was a bona fide San Francisco native, and she had accumulated more than enough to partake in the essential festivities of the city's legions of well-heeled.

But if she knocked, would those controlling the door permit her to come in? Inez was more than willing to find out.

She first sought to rent one of the luxe and commodious opera boxes along the coveted Diamond Horseshoe in the new Beaux-Arts War Memorial Opera House. She was summarily informed that those opera boxes had long ago been spoken for. Some of these boxes were more suited for parties than opera and could hold as many as ten people. They also were frightfully expensive, not that Inez couldn't afford the tariff.

Shut out of her first choice, Inez opted for the next best: pricey, prime front-and-center orchestra seats for the season. Their showcase location signaled status and would entitle Inez and Joe to attend the swanky formal opening-night opera soiree. Inez couldn't possibly imagine a better place to announce her transformation, from barbershop manicurist to San Francisco doyenne.

Nineteen thirty-five was a propitious year for Inez and Joe to become opera buffs. This was the year of the San Francisco debut of Richard Wagner's monster fifteen-hour *Der Ring of the Nibelungen* four-part cycle. If not the best known opera in the world, *Der Ring* was certainly the most elaborate and talked about.

For the opening of *Das Rheingold* on Friday, November 1, Inez got her hair done early in the day. She arranged to have one of Nelly Gaffney's seamstresses come to the house to help her dress for the evening. Inez stuffed protesting Joe into a top hat and tails, a costume of sorts that renders men of all shapes and sizes dapper. By late afternoon, Joe, looking a little like Fred Astaire, summoned the chauffeur to bring the Pierce-Arrow from the garage. The limousine presently took its place in the queue crawling along Van Ness Avenue as sheets of rain drenched the Opera Oval opposite City Hall. When it came to their turn, out from the long limo's rear doors stepped resplendent Inez accompanied by her dashing consort, Joe.

Inez strode triumphantly arm in arm with Joe down the red carpet to the opera house portico. She was glowing in a slanted ostrich-feather hat, formfitting off-white Madeleine Vionnet gown, Barguzin sable stole dangling from her shoulders, a brooch of sparkling diamonds, and twin strands of opera-length (of course!) pearls dipping into a décolletage. What good was making a splash if you couldn't soak as many people as possible in the process?

Amid popping flashbulbs that augmented the evening's lightning and thunder,

Inez and Joe made their way into the grand foyer through throngs of couples dressed to the nines, sipping champagne, their eyes agog at the passing parade.[8] As Ninon, the pseudonymous fashion editor of the *San Francisco Chronicle*, enthused, "There is no other occasion which brings forth all that a sophisticated community holds in beauty and feminine luxury—and all in one artistic setting and at one time. It is a profuse, dazzling blossoming of all and everything that fashion gives."[9]

Inez positively floated among the rarified company, which included Mrs. Willian Lindley Abbott, in a Molyneux black gown held up by green and gold embroidered straps; Mrs. Morton Fleishhacker Jr. in a skirt of Grecian royal blue crepe, a beaded sari scarf, and a Dubonnet cape; Mrs. Alfred Ghirardelli in a vanilla satin gown and matching sable wrap; Mrs. Walter Haas in an apricot moiré accented by strappy high-heeled sandals; Mrs. Howard Ransohoff in a blue velvet robe set off with fuchsia flounces; Mrs. Sigmund Stern in a black tulle gown under a floor-length sable; and Miss Yvonne Theriot in a flame-colored skirt and black satin coat with a ribbon of alabaster fox. Nelly Gaffney showed up in a black Chanel dress under a snow-white cape of Canadian ermine.[10]

As Inez and Joe made their way into the perfumed press of the crowd, several women seemed to look askance. A tall, rail-thin woman arched her severely plucked eyebrows into upside down Vs. A full-figured dowager actually sniffed, turning up a rather large proboscis. What were these interlopers doing mixing with us? Just who did these poseurs think they were? At least, that was Inez's take on what they were thinking. If these San Francisco royals actually knew who Inez was, they certainly weren't going to admit it.

The men, on the other hand, didn't seemed to mind the gate-crashers. They smiled genially at Joe and Inez, but that might have been because they had no idea who this ravishing middle-age woman was. Or maybe it was because they did.

In all the hubbub of the evening, several of Inez's former patients, one dressed in a lime taffeta gown and an diamond-pavé tiara, the other in a Marcel Rochas rose-colored dress, strolled by Inez and didn't even bother to acknowledge her with the slightest of nods. Inez knew these women in the most intimate way imaginable, but she said nothing to them. A consummate professional, Inez just smiled. She also realized that her mere presence among the local blue bloods at the opera was a surefire strategy to advertise her services.

Ensconced in their velvet-upholstered seats in row M, Inez and Joe might not have followed all the nuances of the Norse extravaganza unfolding on the proscenium in front of them, but if there ever was an opera that spoke to Inez's own sense of sexuality, power, excess, and audacity, Wagner's magnum opus had to be it.

The impossibly long Ring cycle was a doozy for opera neophytes, so Inez and Joe took a breather from the next installments, but they did make it to the last performance, the epic five-hour, three-act *Götterdämmerung* on November 9. The production starred Kirsten Flagstad, who just as Caruso had done in San Francisco twenty-nine years earlier, wowed the assembled opera cognoscenti. By its blazing conclusion, when murderous Brünnhilde gallops into a ring of flames and the interior of Valhalla is finally revealed, surely Inez could have identified with the Norwegian überdiva onstage, even though Joe by now was snoring ever so lightly at her side. Choruses of *brava* rained down on Flagstad as exulted opera lovers openly wept while tossing scores of bouquets at the soprano's feet.[11] The *San Francisco Chronicle's* opera critic, Alfred Frankenstein, sounding like all true Wagnerians, gushed that he had "a hangover of melody and emotional exaltation that will persist for a long time."[12] In the limousine home that night, while Joe snoozed, Inez was electrified.

The opera and all of its trappings had been an experiment. By breaching an inviolate divide, Inez had defied an unwritten code. She had overstepped ordinary bounds of societal decorum. An abortionist, no matter how much money she had, showing up at the opera? It was as unseemly as it was embarrassing. Inez's appearance might very well encourage an incensed opera patron or two to call someone at City Hall or the Federal Building. Isn't there something that can be done about *that* woman?

Certainly, Inez's over-the-top spending had become a thorn in the feds' side for a very long time, and now she was flaunting it for everyone to see. The Bureau of Internal Revenue couldn't do anything about Inez's abortion services. But it sure could do something about getting its due cut of the hefty profits her clinic took in.

Whether by coincidence or design, within months of Inez and Joe's debut at the opera, the Bureau of Internal Revenue formally charged Inez with underreporting her income. Well, of course, she had. What abortionist declares all the revenue she takes in? Agents from the Treasury Department computed that Inez's income had amounted to the precise sum of $202,956.80 from 1928 to 1935. They estimated that Inez had underestimated her income by more than two-thirds. How the tax bureau came up with such an exact figure is anyone's guess, but to avoid litigation and political fallout, Inez and the Treasury Department quietly agreed to an undisclosed settlement.[13] Inez never acknowledged how she had acquired so much money, but she dashed off a check to cover the delinquent back taxes and fines. And that was that.

The encounter with the feds had been a warning of sorts, a brushback. Inez had been breaking the law for more than a decade, and the police hadn't lifted a finger to arrest her. Inez likely got busted by the feds because someone with some degree of power and influence began exerting political pressure to do something about her. Did that come from her crashing opening night at the opera? It might have.

Cops on the take had warned Inez that she needed to dial it back, to be more discreet. "Don't give the downtown brass an excuse to bust you, Iney," Ed King pleaded with her during a Wednesday evening poker game at the Guerrero Street house. "There's only so much we can do."

Inez folded her arms and let that settle in. The last thing she was about to do was go away, disappearing into San Francisco's vaporous fog. She believed in her mission as an abortionist, and by now, the queue at 327 Fillmore had gotten as long as it ever had been. More and more women had heard about Inez and were utilizing her services. Besides, Inez enjoyed being seen about town, flitting in and out of shops, eating at the city's best restaurants, showing up wherever and whenever she pleased. She had earned that right.

Her reaction to Ed King's admonition was typical Inez: She said she'd double her weekly payoffs to cops and politicians. She'd also seek to bring more of them under her control, widening her circle of graft and influence.

But the tide against Inez slowly started to turn. The feds' 1936 investigation into her finances would presage a series of increasingly troubling confrontations with law enforcement.

In the same year, cops from police headquarters downtown staked out both Inez's Fillmore Street clinic and her Waller Street recovery facility. Through her network of informants, Inez got tipped off to the upcoming raid and was fully prepared for it. To protect her patients, Inez escorted each woman through the private rear stairway and out the back door. When police rushed the clinic, Inez and all her patients were gone; just a receptionist, maid, and janitor remained. Police confiscated two thousand dollars' worth of equipment as evidence, but Inez had taken all her instruments, records, drugs, and cash.

Once inside, the police cleared out Inez's personnel and installed one of their own, a female undercover cop, to take calls from women who wanted to make appointments. The plainclothes officer also greeted patients who had arrived at the clinic to get abortions.

"The women kept coming, and they'd wait all day if necessary," said Police Inspector George Engler, who estimated that on an average day the clinic took in a thousand dollars.[14]

Members of the Bureau of Internal Revenue inspect blank
income tax returns before mailing, January 1939.

The next day, cops in a black-and-white cruiser arrested Inez at her Guerrero Street home. Inez posted bond and was set free immediately, pending a preliminary hearing. Within three weeks, all charges were dropped against her when no patients could be found who'd swear to criminal complaints. Without corroborating eyewitness testimony, putting Inez on trial was impossible.

Unless an abortion produced a dead woman, police generally stayed clear of the clinics in town. Every three or four years, there was a flurry of arrests of some of the other less-connected abortionists in San Francisco, generally to appease an irate neighbor, a zealous churchgoer, or an otherwise offended big shot. Such arrests didn't make headlines, and they seldom resulted in convictions. More than anything, they were a reminder that to avoid harassment, abortionist had to pay out protection money.

When it came to the next rung up in local law enforcement, the district attorney's office, prosecutors seldom filed charges against abortionists. District Attorney Matthew Brady, who had been the city's chief prosecutor since 1918, was a benevolent public servant who looked the other way. Brady's staff of attorneys was part-time, and few did more work than they had to. In the unlikely event charges were ever filed against an abortionist, and a judge found sufficient evidence for the offender to stand trial, more often than not, witnesses had the habit of not showing up in court; if they did, they tended to "forget" details pertinent to the case. A successful prosecution required patients willing to testify, and few women were about to go public with such personal, embarrassing testimony.

Whenever a woman walked into Inez's clinic, she implicitly agreed to a kind of compact: If you successfully perform this illegal operation, I won't reveal your name to authorities. It was a tacit understanding that bound Inez and her patients in a mutual code of silence: I help you out; you protect me. Prosecutors had little leverage in subpoenaing patients to serve as witnesses, and accordingly, any potential case against Inez naturally collapsed. For better or worse, most viewed Inez as offering a kind of public service, and they'd be the last to help shut it down.

Even if Inez *were* brought to trial and there *were* credible witnesses who testified against her, the chances of convincing twelve jurors to convict her were awfully remote. While some San Franciscans might shake their heads at the name Inez Burns, few would deny how essential her services were. On top of this, most juries, at least in San Francisco, didn't convict defendants, especially women, charged with what many considered a victimless crime. Patients came to Inez voluntarily; there was no arm-twisting; it was they who solicited her services. Nor was there the requisite political clout to launch a grand jury investigation into her activities. Inez was too well connected. And if she ever appeared in court, she could afford to hire the best attorneys San Francisco offered.

There also was something else at play. If the largest and most respected abortionist in the state were to be shut down, where would pregnant women seeking abortions go?

Finally, there was one more issue of significance, lurking just below the surface that merits mention. Inez was acquainted with an awful lot of noteworthy people, from cops to the mayor. If she ever went public with what she knew and whom she had paid off, heads could roll, careers put in jeopardy, criminal charges filed. That's one of the reasons she had so many people on her payroll. It was a kind of insurance.

And if Inez ever disclosed the names of the thousands of patients she had performed abortions on, all hell would break loose. Just the thought of such

District Attorney
Matthew Brady.

revelations caused not just a few Californians to get a bad case of the jitters. Inez never anticipated disclosing patient names, but she also wasn't sure what she'd do if law enforcement ever forced her hand.

Without Inez in the mix, women would just seek another abortionist to do the job, and few providers were as experienced as Inez. A certain percentage of pregnant women would try to abort fetuses themselves, often with dire results. Shutting Inez down would ultimately mean that an unknown number of pregnant women who didn't want to carry to full-term would develop serious infections or intrauterine perforations, and some would die. There was no other way around this, except legalizing abortion, but no viable political climate existed at the time to do so.

As with brothels, a kind of prurient aura surrounded abortion clinics, even one as upscale as Inez's, and on occasion, newspapers capitalized on that strange mystique to sell papers. In May 1938, the scrappy afternoon newspaper *San Francisco News*, owned by the Scripps-Howard chain, was looking for a scoop to boost its sagging circulation. *News* editors sent a pair of undercover reporters—a woman and a man—to Inez's clinic, and the newspaper came away with an eyewitness account of what went on inside, under this headline:

S.F. ABORTION MILL
OPERATES OPENLY;
PROPRIETOR BOASTS,
'WE'VE THOUSANDS OF CLIENTS'

Pair Posing as Husband and
Wife Are Assured
Operation Easy, 'but the Longer You
Wait the More it Costs'[15]

One of the undercover reporters, called Miss X in the *News* article,[16] told Inez's receptionist, Myrtle Ramsey, that she was two months pregnant. Myrtle quoted her a price of fifty-five dollars (fifty for the operation and five for the anesthetic). Myrtle told the woman that the fee would jump to eighty dollars if she waited past two months. Miss X made an appointment for the following Friday but never returned to the clinic.

In the article, the reporters concluded their experience at the clinic had been "about as exciting as making a date with a dentist. And about as businesslike."

Hoping to gain more news traction for their story, the reporters had tipped off police, and once Miss X had walked out the front door, police swooped in for a bust, conveniently allowing the *News* to report exclusively on the raid. The scribes had acted as stool pigeons to get their exclusive, and then paved the way for police to bust Inez.

"Who are you? What do you want?" Inez demanded of the officers. "Why don't you just go away?"

Asked to identify her business, Inez replied, "I was trying to rent some rooms."

Inspector George Engler, the same cop who had busted Inez in the previous unsuccessful raid, persisted, and Inez promptly kicked him in the shins.

When a husband of a patient rang the front door buzzer to pick up his wife, Inez shooed him away, yelling, "Get away! This place is hot!"

Inez finally relented to the cops' demands and opened the doors to the operating rooms; two women walked out. Officers examined the room, found it "scrupulously clean and completely outfitted as a hospital," while noting the presence of bottles, bowls, basins, surgical equipment, and a table.

There were thirteen women inside the clinic, and as the *News* dutifully reported, "All of them were attractive and under 30." One woman was able to flee, but ten were determined to be patients. None were arrested. When the patients gave their home addresses, one turned out to be from San Francisco; the others came from Oakland, Monterey, Bakersfield, Hayward, and Napa. The *News* labeled the clinic "a flourishing abortion mill, reputedly the city's most prosperous," and hyped the bust as "the most dramatic raid of its kind in police records."[17]

Inez and part-time nurse Margie Silver were released that evening on five hundred dollars bail. Police got a confession from one patient, a Mrs. Alfred Green, who was twenty-six and admitted that she had received an abortion at the clinic.[18]

Inez and Margie appeared before Municipal Judge Theresa Meikle, the sole woman jurist in San Francisco at the time,[19] but three weeks later, Judge Meikle dismissed all charges against the Inez and Margie because Mrs. Green had changed her mind about testifying. When police tried to track down the other patients, they discovered the women had either given fake addresses or none would swear to a complaint.[20]

A scoop within a scoop developed when the *News* reported that Joe Burns, identified as Inez's husband, was a former state assemblyman. By then, Inez had taken Joe's last name, going from Brown to Burns. When a reporter asked Joe about his wife's profession, he replied with a degree of panache. "Inez is an artist. That's her trade and she won't quit it. She's doing a service to the public, saving people from shame and disgrace. She runs a clean place and takes care of situations doctors can't touch. . . . She doesn't feel she is violating the law."[21] Lest anyone think Joe was involved in the business, he added: "I tend to my business and she tends to hers. I don't pay any attention to what she does."[22]

Within a period of two years, Inez had been twice arrested, but both charges were soon dropped. For the time being, Inez was untouchable.

Emboldened, Inez had earned enough to loosen her rules when it came to favors she bestowed on some of her patients. She saw plenty of repeat customers, and she got angrier and angrier each time they returned. Inez knew that for many of them abortion was their only means of birth control.

"What're you doin' back?" Inez often asked. "Don't let that husband at you again without you using something to prevent babies."

Inez had reprised her role as the Brazilian Beleza. "Use something, for Christ's sake. I don't wanna see you again, you understand?"

When women couldn't afford her asking rate, Inez was stubborn. She'd hardly ever come down in price. Only on the rarest occasions would she give away her services for free. Not that she ever wanted word of her benevolence to get around, or all of her patients would be soon asking for freebies.

Once a woman came in with six unruly kids, and Inez was asked to prevent a seventh. As the woman, wearing a small cross around her neck, left that day with her brood, Inez handed her an envelope with cash inside. "To hell with your husband and the goddamned church. From now on, you look out for yourself." Within a year, the woman was back.[23]

Inez wasn't in the business of birth control, nor was she a counselor or social worker. Her patients knew what they wanted, and dozens continued to stream into her clinic every week. Every once in a while, a few potholes opened up, but Inez was connected enough to either fill them or navigate around them. Her life from manicurist to California's premier abortionist had turned into a wildly prosperous ride.

Until a mean little bastard by the name of Pat Brown got in her way.

PART II

DESIRE

Two young women ride the ferry with the San Francisco skyline in the background in the 1920s.

ELEVEN

MEAN LITTLE BASTARD
AND PROUD OF IT

By 1938, millions of Americans looked toward California as the promised land. Blessed with verdant fields where anything grew, bone-warming winters, and boundless resources and opportunities, California was America's dream state. Although the population of just-beginning-to-sprawl Los Angeles had nosed past compact San Francisco by 1920, San Francisco was still the West Coast's city of record, dwarfing pubescent Los Angeles as the state's capital of commerce, arts, medicine, science, culture, influence, and pleasure. While James Hilton's 1933 best seller *Lost Horizon* had millions of readers abuzz about the whereabouts of its fictional paradise, to many, San Francisco was the real-life version of Shangri-la.

Paradoxically, San Francisco was cosmopolitan yet insular, international but provincial. The forty-seven-square-mile city was at the northern tip of a peninsular citadel wary of outsiders. San Francisco played by its own relaxed rules embraced by ethnic districts adjoining one another in a series of compact contiguous neighborhoods. As Herb Caen, San Francisco's venerated newspaper scribe, put it: "You could walk down the street and nod hello to almost everybody, because you knew almost everybody. It was that kind of town."[1]

Into this outsider-averse metropolis arose Edmund Gerald (Pat) Brown, a second-generation San Franciscan whose ancestors arrived in 1850, the same year California became a state. Pat was the oldest of four children, three boys and a girl.

He was named after his father (Edmund) and the physician (Gerald) who delivered him. On April 19, 1906, the day after the Great Earthquake, Ida Shuckman Brown bundled up her only child three days short of his first birthday, and the two fled to her girlhood home, the hills of Colusa County, to escape the tremors' ensuing turmoil.

Back in San Francisco, when things settled down, the family reunited. Pat's father was simultaneously a flush gambler and a broke spendthrift, either lavishing gifts on his wife and children or drinking and scheming to get back in the game, alternatively high on the hog or brooding in the doghouse. Edmund Joseph Brown was a jack-of-all-trades and master of none. He'd been a bookie, the owner of a photography studio, a Tenderloin cigar store, and a North Beach theater. The Brown family lived just north of the Panhandle to Golden Gate Park at 1572 Grove Street. Young Pat belonged to a generation that valued orators, and, in fact, he got his name because of his public-speaking skills; buddies dubbed him "Pat," a reference to Patrick Henry, whom Brown invoked in a seventh-grade speech to convince parents to invest in Liberty Bonds. The name stuck.

Pat Brown graduated from Lowell High School, then attended night classes at the University of California Extension and a newly established, locally accredited college called San Francisco Law School. He read every issue of *American Mercury* magazine, founded by its two star writers, H. L. Mencken and George Jean Nathan. As a jazz fan, Pat's favorite musicians were Red Nichols and Bix Beiderbecke. In law school, he worked part-time for Milton L. Schmitt, a blind attorney and former state assemblyman. Even though Pat graduated from law school and was admitted to the California bar in 1927, he never envisioned his professional life as an attorney. First and foremost, Pat always considered himself a politician, even though he hadn't been elected to anything—yet.

At Lowell High School, Pat had met San Francisco native Bernice Layne, three years his junior, a bookworm with braids and a toothy smile. They started dating, even though Bernice's parents, Alice and Arthur, took a dislike to Pat's swagger. Bernice's father was an imposing San Francisco police captain born in East Texas who didn't take lightly to any boy squiring any of his four daughters around town. Pat was not to be deterred.

At twenty-three, Pat ran as a Republican for the State Assembly against fellow Republican Ray Williamson. Without much of a platform, Pat came up with a reductive slogan that highlighted just about all he could: "23 Years in the District."

Pat lost miserably, finishing third in the primary in a field of three with six hundred fifty-three votes, barely fifteen percent of the votes cast.[2] It was during the same primary season that Inez's common-law husband, Democratic Assemblyman Joe Burns, even with backing from the then-mayor Jimmy Rolph, would also lose.[3]

The defeat was the first of many of Pat's attempts at getting elected. Nominally working with his two brothers, Harold and Frank, who were also lawyers, Pat handled civil work, often representing labor unions and gambling parlors masking as "social clubs."[4] But that wasn't what drove Pat. What energized him was every opportunity he could manage that called for him to wade into the crush of a crowd no matter how large or small, reaching to shake any hand within arm's reach. He was a wannabe politician yearning to backslap as many would-be voters as he could find.

After ten years of sporadically dating, Pat and Bernice, who had just graduated from Berkeley, set a date to marry at the chapel inside cavernous Grace Cathedral, atop San Francisco's Nob Hill. But at the last minute, they eloped to Reno, where they were married at Trinity Cathedral. Back in San Francisco, the Browns lived in a downtown hotel, then moved to an apartment at 3755 Fillmore, then to 2444 Chestnut Street, both in the Marina District, then to 1461 Shrader Street, a wooden-shingle house in Ashbury Heights, not far from Inez's Fillmore Street clinic.

Like everyone else in San Francisco, Pat was well aware of Inez and her business; he later said, "I knew about the abortion places, because everyone knew about them, I think. So many wives and mothers of that period would have abortions from this gal. . . . So she did a pretty good job."[5] Pat, a Catholic, tried to convince Bernice, a Protestant, to convert. She would have none of it but conceded to raise their offspring in the Church. Their first two children, Barbara Layne and Cynthia Arden Brown, were born in 1931 and 1933, respectively.

Meanwhile, garrulous Pat, politician without portfolio, continued to introduce himself to grocers, gas-station attendants, cops, firefighters, and fellow passengers on the ferry and Muni streetcars for no apparent reason. No apparent immediate reason, that is. Pat was one-hundred-percent, twenty-four-seven press-the-flesh politics, always working a gathering, potential fat-cat donors, or a reporter angling for a mutually beneficial story. The thing was to win. That's why he wanted in on politics, where there are winners and losers, a yes-or-no metric of success or failure with no wiggle room for dispute. As his lifelong friend and fellow prosecutor Thomas C. Lynch would put it, "Pat has always been enchanted by politics, and I don't think he believed he should lose."[6]

By 1936, Pat changed his party affiliation to Democrat, the party that represented San Franciscans by almost two to one, and by 1939, he had set his sights again at getting elected to *something*. He aimed awfully high this time: San Francisco district attorney. Such an aspiration seemed preposterous, a fantasy of ego-driven, bald-faced political ambition. Pat had never tried a criminal case in his life, and now he was seeking to become the county's chief prosecutor, the district attorney of the second largest city in California.

If Pat had any hope winning, it would be based on the shortcomings of his opponent, the incumbent DA Matthew Brady, known by friends and foes alike as Good Ole Matt, who'd been San Francisco DA for the previous twenty-one years. Brady, sixty-three, was ripe for picking off. "He is reported to have practically no legal ability but surrounds himself with capable assistants who carry on work of the office," said a 1935 FBI memorandum. That appraisal was charitable. The FBI assessment noted that Brady was "reputed to be easygoing and kindly and wholly lacking in force and aggressiveness in law enforcement." One FBI informant, Police Captain Charles Dullea, who in several years would be named police chief, characterized Brady as a "'softy,' too easily influenced." The classified FBI report raised questions about Brady's morals and suggested he might be a "chaser." It said that Brady was reputed to be a "heavy drinker, and when drinking to excess, is said to associate with people of low and questionable character." The file suggested that Brady had the support of the "so-called underworld" without going into detail.[7]

The district attorney's office had been a way for Brady and his cadre of cronies to cash in on some of the cushiest jobs corrupt city government offered. When a criminal allegation traveled from the police department to the DA, Brady would assign the case to one of his attorney friends in private practice, who got paid based on the number of hours he said he put in. The expression "partner in crime" in prewar San Francisco was an apt description for how the district attorney's office dealt out these cases to select lawyers. So egregious was the practice that the San Francisco Bar Association charged Brady with being dishonest and lazy, concluding that he had faked payroll vouchers to pad his friends' bank accounts.[8]

Brady was corrupt even by San Francisco standards, and that said a lot. "Brady wasn't worth anything" was how Tom Lynch, a federal prosecutor at the time, characterized the him."[9] The district attorney allowed hundreds of bookie operations and card parlors to flourish through a system of bribes to cops and higher-ups. When it came to houses of prostitution openly doing business (including the Pleasure Palace owned by Mayor Rolph), Brady also looked the other way. As long as such bordellos were relatively free of crime and disease, Brady and hardly anyone in San Francisco seemed to care. The most famous belonged to Sally Stanford at 1926 Franklin Street in Pacific Heights; Stanford's business was as flagrant as Inez's. Another well-known brothel was House of Joy on Columbus Avenue. Taverns such as Dew-Drop Inn, Roddy's Fish Bowl, Play House, Silver Dollar, Havana Club, Swing In Club, and Club Kamokila employed B-girls who, while drinking watered-down cocktails, would tease and cajole men into buying liquor, and then fleece the barflies with the thickest wallets. It wasn't all that different from what used to happen at the old Barbary Coast, although this time around few of the dupes ended up in the ships bound for China. Good Ole Matt was no Marshal Dillon. But few San Franciscans expected him to be or he wouldn't have been elected to six straight terms.

Brady and Inez hadn't been close friends, but they knew each other and they surely respected the influence each wielded. In the power equation, Inez likely exercised more than Brady. She had too many friends in high places, and she knew too much. She had too many names in her little black books for a get-along DA like Brady to threaten her. Her ledgers included the names of cops, businessmen, Hollywood starlets, politicians, and lawyers, some of whom were now judges, not to mention the names of hundreds of former patients, some from prominent local families. Inez had too much firepower for Good Ole Matt to force her hand. And since there was little pressure to shut her down, Inez's clinic had turned into an institution.

Brady represented the old guard in San Francisco, and Inez prided herself on knowing what it took to stay on the right side of those pulling the strings. Inez paid more in protection money each week than she did for her tanks of nitrous oxide, drugs, operating tables, instruments, sterilizers, sheets, and blankets. Any change to the city's old guard meant trouble for both Brady and Inez, who was just as entrenched in San Francisco as Brady was.

Pat Brown was cut from a wholly different cloth than Good Ole Matt. Pat was a young man in a hurry. He was hungry. The Catholic Church had drilled into Pat how immoral abortion was, but that wasn't why Inez knew she had to be wary of this politician on the come. Pat was a reformer, looking toward creating an entirely new constituency of progressive San Franciscans who might be persuaded to stick it to venerable Inez, turning her into a Hydra of sloth, sin, permissiveness, corruption, and everything else that Pat hoped he could tie to Brady.

Pat got an assist from Good Ole Matt himself, under investigation by the grand

Edmund "Pat" Brown, ca. 1939.

jury for graft. This was way too golden an opportunity to pass up, so Pat summoned an impromptu press conference to trumpet what he cried was a brewing "red-hot" scandal, that Brady would be charged with misappropriation of fifty thousand dollars in public funds. But the next day, the pro-Brady *San Francisco Examiner* revealed that one of the grand jurors, Edgar A. Hills, was Pat's campaign manager, and that it was Hills who had leaked news of the alleged impropriety to Pat.[10]

Like most elections in San Francisco, charges flew fast and furious. DA Brady had the endorsements of all four daily newspapers, and that left Pat and three other challengers fighting among themselves, diluting viable opposition to Brady. One candidate, John G. Reisner, made a deal with Pat, pledging that if Reisner could convince the other two candidates to withdraw, Pat would drop out too, thereby consolidating the vote against Brady behind Reisner. The goal was to oust Brady at all costs. Reisner got the two challengers to quit, but Pat reneged on the deal, saying he never had any intention of quitting the race. Pat repaid Reisner with a lawsuit, charging that he wasn't a resident of San Francisco but actually lived in Marin County.[11] The California Supreme Court ruled against Pat's claim two weeks before the election.[12]

Ultimately, all the political machinations didn't make for much of a difference. Pat lost to Brady, racking up 92,442 votes compared to Brady's 135,282.[13]

The election had been far from a cliff-hanger, but Pat had garnered nearly one hundred thousand votes, an impressive turnout for a newcomer in his first real campaign. It was like giving heroin to an addict. The loss energized never-say-never Pat, and on election night, he vowed that he would challenge Brady in four years.

The grand jury delayed releasing its findings until after the election, and in mid-December, threw the book at Brady. The panel found that Brady's office had inadequately investigated criminal cases, that indictments were carelessly prepared, and that deputies were more interested in their own private practices than in serving the public. Brady's response was, "The grand jury would perform a more valuable service by minding their own affairs instead of telling public officials how to conduct their duties."[14]

Pat couldn't have written a better comeback. An attractive and progressive new voice in San Francisco was off and running.

TWELVE

NO PIECE OF CAKE

While San Francisco and the rest of the nation staggered through the final years of the Great Depression, hundreds of pregnant women each month kept coming to the dignified sitting rooms at 327 Fillmore Street. Married and single women, women with children, women with none. Housewives, teachers, nurses, secretaries, waitresses, stewardesses, students. It didn't make any difference. Inez was open six, sometimes seven, days a week, and business was booming.

Poor economic conditions translate to spikes in crime, suicide, spousal abuse, malnutrition, alcoholism, and abortion.[1] Inez was performing as many as fifteen abortions a day and could take in as much as thirty thousand dollars a month at a time when the economy was at a virtual standstill. If Inez's friends walking the beat, in City Hall, and at the newspapers had had anything to do with helping Good Ole Matt coast to a fifth term, Inez wasn't complaining. With Matt Brady as DA for another four years, Inez's insurance policy would continue as long as she continued paying premiums in payoffs and influence peddling. Four years was a long time in Inez's line of work. All the hubbub from the bluenoses at the opera had long died down.

Who knew what would happen if and when Good Ole Matt stepped down or got cut off at his wobbly knees? If Pat Brown ran for DA in 1943, then Inez would figure out what to do when it happened, if it happened, and if he won. Inez knew enough influential people to make the election of Pat Brown no piece of cake, an expression Ogden Nash, the erudite funnyman of the era, had just coined. Cops,

Dr. Adolphus Berger.

prosecutors, judges, politicians, newspapermen all had a way of turning up some of the most embarrassing information about people they didn't like.

Inez had other insiders she could lean on, two in particular. Both ran in the shadowy world of real-life noir San Francisco. Like cockroaches, they avoided the sunlight and scurried whenever it appeared. They knew things and could get to people of influence. One was A. A. Berger. Actually, Dr. Adolphus Arthur Berger, better known to friends as Dolph. Berger had beady eyes and an Adolf Hitler mustache. He'd been the city autopsy physician from 1927 to 1933—not a bad connection if you were in Inez's line of work. Berger had appeared in court more than four thousand times.[2] After Berger left the city's employ, he worked as an autopsy surgeon for the US Marshal's office and later for the Navy.[3] Berger knew everyone's dirt. That was the business he was in. Another insect Inez was acquainted with was a spiny private detective by the name of Eugene "Pop" Aureguy. In 1934, Aureguy had gotten

Constance May Gavin $1.2 million from the estate of Comstock silver heir James L. "Big Jim" Flood when Aureguy helped prove she was Flood's illegitimate daughter.[4] Aureguy used to be a William J. Burns Agency detective but quit when the murders he was assigned got too easy to figure out.[5] Inez would employ both Berger and Aureguy in a variety of ways.

Along with the dismal prospects of crusader Pat Brown running once again for district attorney, Inez couldn't help realizing that the social contours of San Francisco were changing, and that these, too, would have consequences for her business. A host of factors were commingling to alter San Francisco at its very core.

Coit Tower, a striking two-hundred-and-ten-foot shaft that resembled an art deco fire-hose nozzle (even though the architect said the resemblance wasn't planned), opened as a public monument in 1933. Paid with funds left by eccentric socialite Lillie Hitchcock Coit, a cigar-smoking volunteer firefighter herself, and situated atop Telegraph Hill, the fluted cylinder was a piece of architecture that immediately set San Francisco apart from all other American cities. Iconic Coit Tower instantly became an integral part of the city's landscape. Wide-eyed tourists made a beeline for the three-hundred-and-sixty-degree view from the top.[6]

The city's two biggest architectural statements, though, were right around the corner. They would have more practical purposes than a concrete tower in the shape of a spout. Two bridges six miles apart, built within a year of each other, were about to change everything about San Francisco and, with it, the nation.

For almost a hundred years, ferry service cutting through the salty bay breeze was a leisurely luxury for almost everyone who wanted to get to and from San Francisco. Outside of arriving from the southern peninsula, ferries were the only way to get in and out of San Francisco from the north or the east. By 1935, the entire Bay Area was growing too fast for San Francisco to stay so geographically inaccessible. Despite the Depression, automobiles were picking up in popularity; on a typical Sunday evening, the wait to cross the Golden Gate divide on the car ferry could be as long as three hours.[7] Each workday, fifty thousand commuters arrived in San Francisco at the foot of Market Street, making the Ferry Building the busiest terminal outside of London's Charing Cross Station.[8]

The ambitious solution: build two long bridges, one connecting San Francisco with Oakland and points east, the other connecting San Francisco with Marin County and points north.

The eight-mile-long San Francisco–Oakland Bay Bridge took three years to finish at a cost of seventy-seven million dollars and was opened in 1936. The 1.6-mile Golden Gate Bridge cost thirty-five million dollars and was opened a year later. With the two bridges now completed, transit to and from San Francisco was easy and efficient. Crossing the choppy bay by ferry was no longer necessary. The bridges instantly put San Francisco at the epicenter of the region; the city was no more than an hour's drive from anyplace within a fifty-mile radius. Commuter communities in the East Bay and North Bay sprang up. An interurban train, called the Key System, now traversed the lower span of the Bay Bridge, delivering tens of thousands of workers to downtown. The Caldecott Tunnel, which opened in 1937, bore a highway through the hills east of Berkeley; the Waldo Tunnel, which also opened in 1937, bore a highway through a steep grade in southern Marin County. Both served to whisk more and more commuters to San Francisco. Whereas in the past the only ready suburbs to San Francisco were south of the city in San Mateo County, now

The San Francisco–Oakland Bay Bridge during construction, ca. 1937.

there were three more accessible counties—Alameda, Contra Costa, and Marin—from which workers could commute to San Francisco with ease.

Of course, it would be the Golden Gate Bridge that would steal everyone's heart, as well as brighten the wattage of the spotlight on San Francisco. In any intrastate rivalry, Los Angeles could never pull from its hat anything as sublime as this wondrous bridge. The engineering feat of bridging the Pacific portal to San Francisco Bay with the longest and tallest suspension bridge in the world was a staggering achievement. From its trademark International Orange hue to its soaring art deco towers, the bridge was an instant icon. The American Society of Civil Engineers would rank the Golden Gate Bridge as one of its Seven Wonders of the Modern World, and in the process the bridge became a national symbol of freedom.[9]

A procession of cars driving through Waldo Tunnel on opening day,
February 27, 1937.

Along with the Bay Bridge, the Golden Gate Bridge escalated the flow of cars and trucks, and therefore residents, visitors, and workers, stampeding into San Francisco every day. Officials were initially worried that neither bridge would pay off the bonds that made each possible, but the number of vehicles from opening day was so great, the revenue so large, that tolls on both spans were soon *lowered*: on the Bay Bridge, from sixty-five cents to twenty-five cents; on the Golden Gate, from fifty cents to twenty-five cents.

While the city's population stayed relatively the same, the populations of the three counties immediately north and east expanded by more than ten percent between 1930 and 1940, and during and after World War II, that growth expanded exponentially.[10] Could Inez continue to flourish with impunity in this new iteration of

The Golden Gate Bridge
under construction, ca. 1934.

INDIAN COURT

FEDERAL BUILDING

GOLDEN GATE INTERNATIONAL EXPOSITION

SAN FRANCISCO 1939

Starting JUNE 15th

FEDERAL THEATRE

TREASURE ISLAND

A CAST OF 100

SWING MIKADO

Sensational Success
HOT FROM NEW YORK

DAILY PERFORMANCE 8 P.M. (EXCEPT MONDAY)
PRICES 25¢ - 50¢ - 75¢ PLUS TAX

THE BIG HIT OF THE
GOLDEN GATE INTERNATIONAL EXPOSITION

A DIVISION OF THE WORKS PROGRESS ADMINISTRATION

BLANKET DESIGN OF THE HAIDA INDIANS · ALASKA

INDIAN COURT

FEDERAL BUILDING

GOLDEN GATE INTERNATIONAL EXPOSITION

SAN FRANCISCO 1939

PUEBLO TURTLE DANCERS FROM AN INDIAN PAINTING · NEW MEXICO

INDIAN COURT

FEDERAL BUILDING

GOLDEN GATE INTERNATIONAL EXPOSITION

SAN FRANCISCO 1939

the modern American city? Small-town San Francisco soon would be transformed into a metropolis filled with legions of anonymous workers, who were streaming into the city every day. On one hand, the metamorphosis would favor Inez and her business by giving more patients ready access to her; on the other, it would lift the sealed cocoon that had protected Inez and allowed her to flourish for so long.

In part to celebrate this brand-new connectivity to San Francisco, a grand world's fair was appropriately planned at the halfway point between Oakland and San Francisco. The Golden Gate International Exposition was to be located on Yerba Buena Shoals, dredged and magically reborn as Treasure Island, a four-hundred-acre pancake of land said to be the largest engineered island in the world. The '39 Fair would be a reprise of San Francisco's great Panama-Pacific International Exposition of 1915, deemed a success by everyone involved. "The exposition must be unique, it must be educational, it must be beautiful, it must be entertaining. If these qualities are present, then it will be successful," wrote Angelo J. Rossi, who succeeded "Sunny" Jim Rolfe as San Francisco's mayor, in *The New York Times*, announcing the fair to one and all.[11]

Opening on February 19, 1939, the exposition was a quixotic attempt to say goodbye to the ravages of the Depression and embrace the San Francisco of tomorrow. The fair's theme was the Bay Area's ties to Asia and the Pacific Islands, in part to draw attention to a new airplane service from San Francisco to the Orient. The fair had competition three thousand miles in the other direction, with the New York World's Fair that same year. No matter. San Francisco's Gateway of the Pacific featured stage-set buildings that shared a cringeworthy resemblance to the fascist architecture of Mussolini's Italy and Hitler's Germany. To less geopolitical minds, the temporary buildings bore a striking resemblance to Emerald City, displayed in Technicolor that year in *The Wizard of Oz*, which wowed everyone who saw it.[12]

It was hard not to be swept up by the hoopla of the fair. Less a vision of the future and more a nonstop cavalcade of commercial goods to make visitors believe the present was the greatest time ever, the fair was a statewide advertisement to make people forget they didn't have enough money to buy any of it.

President and Mrs. Roosevelt visited, as did any other celebrities who would attract paying visitors, including musicians Benny Goodman, Eddie Duchin, Duke Ellington, and Count Basie, swimming sensation Esther Williams, *Tarzan*'s Johnny Weissmuller, funnyman Eddie Cantor, singer Bing Crosby, and ventriloquist Edgar Bergen and sidekick Charlie McCarthy, along with revues like the *Follies Bergère*.

Sally Rand

GOLDEN GATE INTERNATIONAL EXPOSITION

6

An attraction called Sally Rand's Nude Ranch (the *D* in Dude was crossed out) featured forty-seven women wearing not much but cowboy boots and G-strings, playing badminton and horseshoes as fairgoers ogled through plate glass.

Joe Burns bought into the hype, as did Alice Lorine, Inez's fifteen-year-old daughter by Charlie Granelli. Inez went along for the ride, eager to take a day off from the busy clinic. Emma Nevada, the singer whose hair Virgil had cut and whose nails Inez had buffed back at the Palace barbershop was Empress of the Fair.[13] Inez was always up for perambulating in a new outfit, so Joe drove the Packard to Treasure Island with enthralled Alice Lorine sitting in between the two of them up front. An abortionist, her teenage daughter, and a former politician turned card-parlor owner, off to take a peek into the future of the world.

Joe was particularly keen on seeing a wild stunt that was scheduled for that summer day. Walter Mails, the San Francisco Seals public relations man, had come up with a promotional stunt to commemorate what Mails had dubiously proclaimed as the "hundredth anniversary of baseball." Seals catcher Joe Sprinz would catch a baseball dropped from the Goodyear blimp Volunteer, hovering eight hundred feet above Treasure Island. Sprinz was the Seals' starting catcher and had once caught for fastballer Dizzy Dean. If anyone knew how to catch a baseball, it had to be Sprinz.

On the day of the event, August 3, 1939, the sky was light blue, not a cloud anywhere, but it was the kind of backdrop baseball players hate, what they call a "high sky." Without clouds, there's no way of gauging distance, and the glare against the blue sky makes tracking a ball nearly impossible. Especially one dropped from eight hundred feet.

The first ball rocketed into the stands, causing two thousand spectators to cover their heads and scream. The second ball was off target and plunged fifteen inches into the newly installed sod.

The crowd was silenced in anticipation for the next drop. At first, the ball looked like a tiny dot, but as it got closer, the orb started to resemble a cannon ball headed straight for Sprinz's head. At the last second, Sprinz put up his catcher's glove, more to protect himself than to catch anything. The ball promptly pummeled Sprinz's skull, fracturing his jaw in twelve places, splitting his lip, smashing his nose, and knocking out five teeth.

"Wow!" Joe marveled. Alice Lorine covered her eyes. Inez just shook her head.

"I thought the blimp fell on me," Sprinz said from his bed at St. Joseph's Hospital that evening.[14]

Joe and Alice Lorine said they were pleased they had witnessed what turned out to be one of the highlights of the entire fair; Inez could have cared less. Filing through the Food and Beverages Building on their way out, the three passed the H. J. Heinz exhibit, and it was there, where Inez perked up and took notice. A smiling young girl was handing out little green pickle pins with the name Heinz embossed on it. Inez took one. For a second or two, the trinket transported Inez back to her days in Allegheny City, working in the pickle building, squeezing garlicky pickles into clear-glass jars with the red pimento garnish laid on top, all the while as G. W. Merritt and his wife were living down the block, and Inez was scampering to feed little George and Bob. That thought segued to all those potions, elixirs, and ointments from the back of G.W.'s horse-drawn wagon, with Inez dressed up in scarves and flowing dresses like a gypsy, the Brazilian Beleza, hawking Italian Lotion No. 12. What a transformation she had created and witnessed. About the only salutary benefit from those ancient days was that she still used olive oil. Whenever the opportunity arose.

The combination of Joe Sprinz missing the baseball dropped from the heavens and the Heinz pickle swag was a harbinger of sorts for Inez. Inez was waiting for that wannabe, opportunistic gangbuster Pat Brown to get elected. Or not to get elected. There wasn't much else she could do, except try to pull some strings downtown with her politician friends while continuing doing what she was doing, providing as many abortions to as many women as she could, while she could. And wait for the ball to drop.

Inez suddenly grabbed for Alice Lorine's hand as the trio made their way back to the Packard.

"Who wants ice cream?" Inez asked.

THIRTEEN

OFF HER BACK

If the police and the district attorney were afraid to go after Inez, the feds certainly weren't. The Bureau of Internal Revenue wanted a bigger slice of Inez's income than it had been served three years earlier. The bureau still believed that Inez was living way too large for the paltry income she'd been reporting. Part of why the feds went after Inez again was because of her seemingly constant, on-parade presence in San Francisco. She had an uncanny habit of showing up everywhere, at the city's priciest restaurants, emporiums, and nightclubs. On October 1, 1939, Inez dragged Joe to a recital starring twenty-three-year-old violin virtuoso Yehudi Menuhin at the War Memorial Opera House. They saw Alfred Lunt and Lynn Fontanne in a play called *There Shall by No Night*, by Robert E. Sherwood at the Curran Theatre. Inez enjoying being seen and recognized. She didn't mind in the least when people whispered behind her back or pointed her out. In many ways, she thrived in this demi-spotlight. The other reason the Bureau of Internal Revenue went after Inez a second time was because of a pugnacious pit bull of an assistant US attorney by the name of Thomas C. Lynch. Inez stuck in Lynch's craw—because she was an abortionist *and* she was enjoying gallivanting around town proclaiming to everyone what she did for a living. Or maybe it was because he just didn't like anything about Inez. The tenacious prosecutor would return to Inez's life for years to come. They would become thorns needling each other for two decades.

The government charged that Inez owed forty-four thousand dollars in unpaid taxes, yet had paid just $157.25, and in October 1939, a federal grand jury indicted Inez for tax evasion. She pleaded guilty, was fined ten thousand dollars, and paid another undisclosed sum to settle the case. Harold Louderback,[1] the federal judge who accepted Inez's plea, said, "Never in my history on the federal bench has so little information been given the court. For some reason, there seems to be a great reluctance to tell what Mrs. Burns's business was." When Judge Louderback drilled Inez about her occupation, she only replied, "I'm a housewife." As part of the plea bargain, Louderback summarily sentenced Inez to two years in federal prison, but the negotiated deal called for a suspended prison term.[2]

At the same time as Inez's guilty plea in federal court, the San Francisco Police Department was jolted by its "biggest shakeup . . . in decades, reaching from the roof to the very foundations," as the *San Francisco Call-Bulletin* put it.[3] The *San Francisco Chronicle* called the housecleaning of the thirteen-hundred-officer police force the most extensive department reorganization in thirty years.[4] Chief William J. Quinn, a thirty-four-year veteran, was fired and replaced by Captain of Inspectors Charles Dullea, who had trashed District Attorney Brady to the FBI several years before. Sandy-haired Quinn had been a holdover from the days of Mayor Rolph, and had been chief during the 1935–'37 investigation of police graft and corruption. Quinn never attended Inez's Wednesday evening poker games, but he certainly knew cops who did. New police chief Dullea and Pat Brown were friends and would become even closer political allies. Another mover and shaker in town, stentorian Walter McGovern, president of the three-member police commission, had engineered the ouster of Chief Quinn, and praised new top cop Dullea as "the greatest peace officer in America."[5] McGovern, a shrewd criminal defense attorney and former state senator, would also return to make an imprint on Inez.

As the dust was settling inside police headquarters, America soon became embroiled in a world war that commenced when Japanese aircraft bombed the US naval base at Honolulu's Pearl Harbor early on a Sunday morning on December 7, 1941. San Francisco was the largest and closest mainland city to the attack, and overnight, it became the epicenter of the US war effort. Nets were affixed below the four-year-old Golden Gate Bridge to guard against Japanese submarines breaching the San Francisco Bay. GIs manned antiaircraft guns on the cellblock roofs of Alcatraz Federal Prison in the middle of the Bay, waiting for Japanese fighter planes that never came. The entire state of California was on alert, but San Francisco was thought to be the most likely target. Citywide blackouts were common. More than 1.6 million military men and women were assembled to ship out to the Pacific from the Bay Area. Troops used Golden Gate Park, the newly built Cow Palace, and Crissy

The corner of Montgomery and Market Streets on December 8, 1941 after the attack on Pearl Harbor.

Field around the clock to practice maneuvers.[6] Newly commissioned naval shipyards ringed the bay and operated twenty-four hours a day.

San Francisco was bursting at the seams with war-related economic development. In addition to GIs, the city was packed with tens of thousands of recently arrived workers, and the number of factories had increased by a third. Women, collectively dubbed "Rosie the Riveter," were for the first time employed in factories producing munitions and war supplies, replacing men fighting overseas. Predominately white Catholic San Francisco, with a preponderance of Irish and Italians, became a vaunted destination due to the abundance of blue-collar jobs now available. All of

Two women take a break from their wartime jobs at the Southern Pacific Railroad Company, February 1943.

the activity made for a glut of young, transitory men in San Francisco, which—once again—resulted in a multitude of unplanned pregnancies, serving as yet another boon to Inez's already stretched-to-capacity business.

So frenzied was the San Francisco–based war effort that a national advertising campaign urged tourists to stay away. "This city and its region are too busy and crowded now to entertain you," one advertisement read. "War workers and Army and Navy personnel are taxing to capacity our hotels, housing, restaurants, transportation, and other facilities. Unless your need is imperative, please do not come to the San Francisco Bay Area until the war is over."[7]

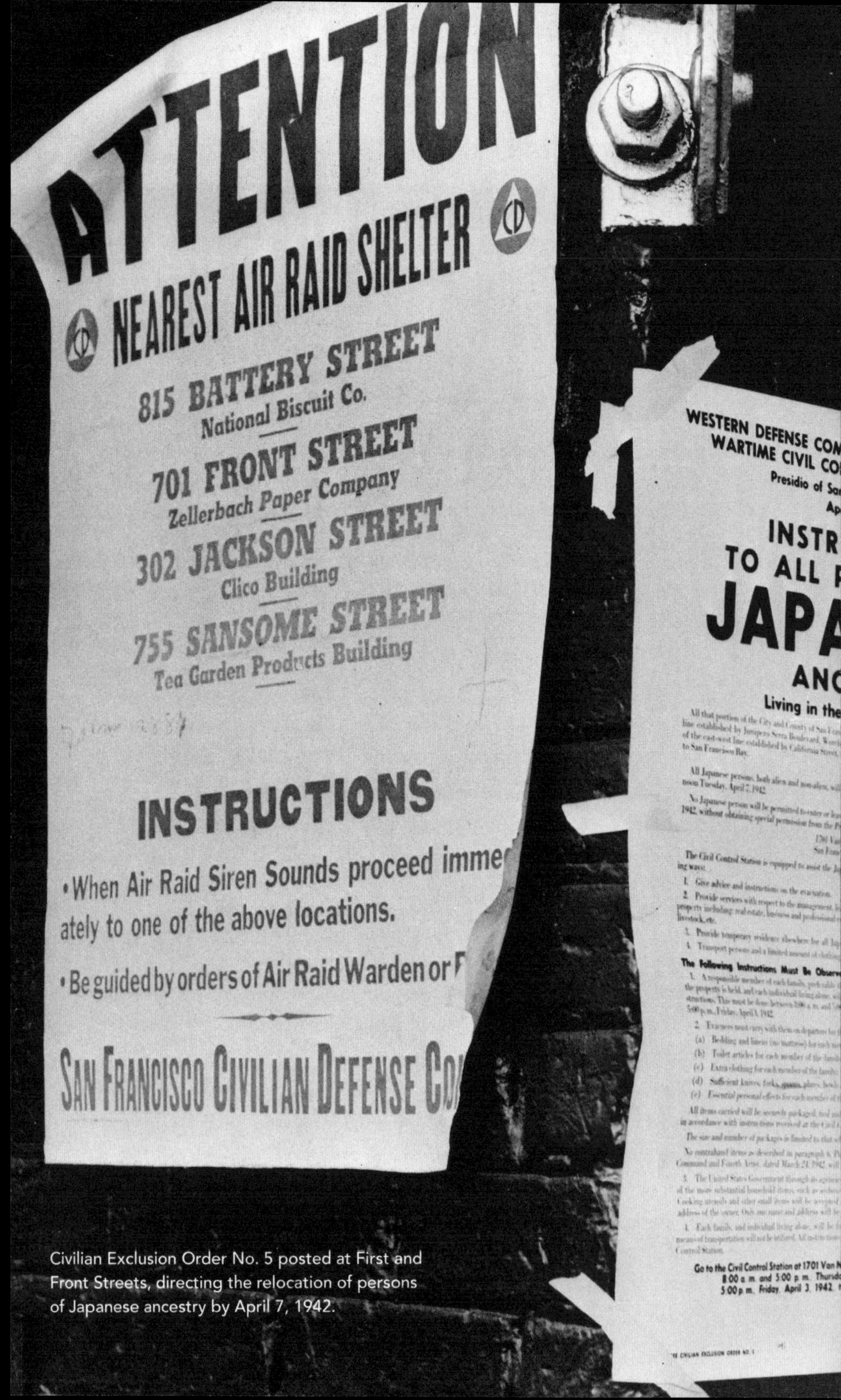

ATTENTION

NEAREST AIR RAID SHELTER

815 BATTERY STREET
National Biscuit Co.

701 FRONT STREET
Zellerbach Paper Company

302 JACKSON STREET
Clico Building

755 SANSOME STREET
Tea Garden Products Building

INSTRUCTIONS

- When Air Raid Siren Sounds proceed immediately to one of the above locations.

- Be guided by orders of Air Raid Warden or F

SAN FRANCISCO CIVILIAN DEFENSE CO

WESTERN DEFENSE COM
WARTIME CIVIL CO
Presidio of Sa
Ap

INSTR
TO ALL
JAPA

AND

Living in the

Civilian Exclusion Order No. 5 posted at First and
Front Streets, directing the relocation of persons
of Japanese ancestry by April 7, 1942.

NOTICE

Headquarters
Western Defense Command
and Fourth Army

Presidio of San Francisco, California
April 1, 1942

Civilian Exclusion Order No. 5

San Francisco citizens take to the streets, August 1936.

A Japanese-American family makes their way to a relocation bus at an Army control center, 1942.

A Japanese shop owner hangs a sign in the window after the store was closed following orders for civilians of Japanese descent to evacuate to War Relocation Authority centers for the duration of the war, March 1942.

At the same time, local women were urged to go out of their way to welcome the influx of soldiers; after all, these brave young men would be putting themselves in harm's way for democracy. Some would die overseas; when servicemen sailed westward under the Golden Gate, it might very well be their last glimpse of America. The least San Francisco women could do was comfort GIs while they were in town. That was the unmistakable, flag-waving message wartime propaganda telegraphed.

Entertaining servicemen, showing them a good time, was considered an enviable patriotic duty. One women's club in San Francisco, the National League for Women's Service, exhorted women to do whatever it took to make soldiers feel at home. "[F]ar away on boats of every description and in lands of jungle, baking sand, and far-flung prairies are 'boys' who know that the National League for Women's Service cares, knows what boys want, and treats them as men, not adolescents," the organization encouraged its members in no uncertain terms.[8] It came as no surprise that thousands of wartime flirtations resulted in unintended pregnancies, and Inez became the city's go-to fixer.

While her business was going through the roof, Inez still continued to keep her eyes on reformer Pat Brown, who by now had told friends he intended to run once again against Matthew Brady for district attorney, in 1943. Inez knew that if Pat ever pushed Brady off his perch as district attorney, there'd be hell she'd have to pay.

Bernice and Pat's third child, Edmund G. (Jerry) Jr., was born in 1938, and their fourth, Kathleen Lynn, soon followed. The Browns had just moved to 460 Magellan Avenue, a home built in 1920 in San Francisco's burgeoning middle-class Forest Hill District. Pat made it no secret that practicing law bored him. It required him to work as an attorney, and ambitious Pat had far greater aspirations than being a lawyer.

He applied to be an FBI special agent and was interviewed on May 18, 1942, but Pat abruptly withdrew his application in the middle of the interview, telling the interviewer that he wanted to spend more time with his family and that he needed to make more money than the bureau was offering.[9] Pat threw his name in the hat for the position of head investigator at the War Department in Washington, DC. A week later, he wrote a letter inquiring about working at the Federal Reserve Bank of San Francisco. In December, he lobbied Governor Culbert L. Olson to be appointed a municipal judge.[10] None of these jobs came through. At the time, Pat had neither the experience nor connections, but he sure had the drive.

He was a wannabe politician through and through, and if he was serious about running again for DA, he'd have plenty of spadework ahead of him. He'd have to

California Governor Culbert Olson, May 1940.

curry favor with donors and make as many political allies as possible. As a kind of politician-in-waiting, Pat attended the 1940 Democratic National Convention in Chicago as a delegate. On the train east, he chatted up Governor Olson and the traveling entourage of Democratic candidates, as well as the state's other delegates. The schmoozing paid off. Back home, Pat was able to wangle three political sinecures: director on the Golden Gate Bridge and Highway Commission, which oversaw the new span connecting San Francisco with Marin County; member of the California Code Commission, charged with updating the arcane numbering system of state laws and statutes; and an appeals member for the Selective Service System's local board 87, where favors went far and were remembered forever. Even if he didn't run against incumbent Brady in November, the appointments would bulk up a thin résumé. Pat now could boast that he was engaged in genuine government service, entry cred for any would-be politician.

Meanwhile, District Attorney Brady had a pesky problem on his hands. Howard Hughes's film *The Outlaw* made its premiere at the Geary Theater on February 5, 1943, and, in the process, introduced curvaceous come-hither Jane Russell to the world. The

Actress Jane Russell in a risque photo for *The Outlaw*, 1943.

Chronicle's critic Dwight Whitney thoroughly panned the film, writing that "it is really no story at all. Nothing happens worth mentioning."[11] But it wasn't the plot that drew curious moviegoers. It was the mega-image of a pouting Jane Russell, plastered on billboards in San Francisco, that seemed to send local bluenoses up the wall. Reacting to complaints from church groups, Brady's office prepared criminal warrants to remove the eighteen-square-foot advertisements, saying they depicted "a seminude young woman lying in a haystack in a wanton pose with a pistol in her hand."[12] Hapless Brady had fallen for the oldest game in any publicist's playbook. Unwittingly, he had transformed the billboards into advertisements that no one could take his or her eyes off of. On one hand, Brady was soft on abortion, gambling, and prostitution, but on the other, he was a staunch guardian of "community morals"—a fitting description for how San Francisco looked at such things. All the while, Pat was taking notes.

By mid-1943, Pat had weighed all of his options. Centrist Republican Earl Warren, a former law-and-order district attorney in Oakland and state attorney general, had won the governor's mansion the previous November. Warren had announced to friends that he would allow his name to be placed in the Republican primary for president. Although Warren was a Republican, Pat admired him. The broad-shouldered prosecutor's ascendancy to the governorship, and perhaps to the White House, showed Pat that a career trajectory starting with district attorney wouldn't be a bad route to take for himself. Three thousand miles away, former New York prosecutor and now governor Thomas Dewey was trying the same thing.

In early September, thirty-eight-year-old Pat made good on his promise to challenge Brady once again. Pat declared that San Francisco had "the greatest future of any city in the Western Hemisphere" and, at the same time, faced "the greatest crime problem in its history." He labeled Brady "incompetent," implying that Good Ole Matt was the cause of the city's descent into sloth and sin.[13] In contrast to a tired Brady, seeking an unprecedented seventh term as DA, Pat's persona was that of a fresh, energetic, reform-minded prosecutor ready and able to do whatever it took to upend the status quo. Go get 'em, Pat!

Voters would be as much deciding to hire Pat as to fire his sixty-eight-year-old opponent. Pat promptly took out a third-of-a-page advertisement in the *San Francisco Chronicle* and proclaimed himself a "man of high character, [who] is physically and mentally fit to fill the important office for which he is the candidate." Under a youthful and bespectacled visage, wonky-looking Pat listed an army of bipartisan support, including past and current leaders at the Chamber of Commerce, labor groups, the Elks, the United Irish Societies, the Junior League, and the Young Democrats. Pat was the San Francisco of the future—young, energetic, a crusader. In an only-in–San Francisco juxtaposition, Pat's ad ran below one for Mr. Del LeRoy at the "world-famous" transvestite nightclub, Finocchio's in North Beach.[14]

Not one to reject anyone who could help his cause, Pat tried to solicit support from crooked lobbyist Artie Samish, who controlled much of the city's and state's gambling and liquor interests, but Samish refused to write him a check.[15] Pat could have turned this into a badge of political integrity, but Samish's help would be important for other elections down the road. Pat's biggest donors were building contractor William A. Newsom II and William M. Malone, the Democratic chair of the state and county committees. He also got donations from San Francisco real estate mogul Louis R. Lurie, one of Hollywood studio boss Louis B. Mayer's closest friends and investors.[16]

With the election around the corner, Inez had real cause to be worried. Her police consiglieri duly informed her that Pat's driving personal agenda was to create a statewide persona. The basis of his political ideology was one-note: to propel his career as fast as he could, to do whatever it took. District attorney would be Pat's first stop. Hell, one cop told Inez over a game of deuces wild that he wouldn't be surprised if Pat Brown became governor, senator, even president someday. He was a young man in a hurry.

All the cops said the same: If busting Inez could help Pat politically, then that's what he'd do. Pat didn't care about the morals of what Inez was doing. If he cared about morals, he would have become a priest. Pat was a zealot for himself; he was on a ferocious mission to succeed. Best to double down on getting Good Ole Matt reelected, the cops told Inez, and the best way to do that would be to stir up as much as she could against upstart Pat. Inez knew several newspapermen in town. Sooner or later, everyone needs a favor, and Inez's home was always open to any kindred soul.

A week before the election, the *San Francisco Examiner* revealed that Pat had drawn up incorporation papers for two gambling clubs, the Menlo Park Club and his father's old cigar store, the Padre Club on Eddy Street. The pro-Brady newspaper reported that Pat had advised club operators not to testify before the county grand jury investigating them.[17] So much for holier-than-thou Pat Brown parading around as Mr. Clean.

The fact is that many in San Francisco's old-money establishment were unnerved with what havoc Pat might wreak on a city that operated perfectly well. Upstart politicians can be liabilities because they are untested, too eager to please.

Who is for
EDMUND G.
BROWN

For District Attorney

●

We unhesitatingly recommend to the voters of San Francisco the election of EDMUND G. BROWN as District Attorney. He is a man of high character, and is physically and mentally fitted to fill the important office for which he is the candidate.

B. F. (Andy) ANDERSON
Accountant;
Past Commander, George Washington Post, American Legion

HAMILTON BARNETT
President, Young Republicans

T. D. BOARDMAN
Past President, Commonwealth Club of California; Member, Board of Freeholders that drafted San Francisco's charter

VIC E. BREEDEN
R. H. Moulton & Co.;
Treasurer, San Francisco Chamber of Commerce

DANIEL W. BURBANK
Burbank &·Laumeister, Attorneys

DANIEL F. del CARLO
Vice President, Golden Gate Bridge and Highway District; Business Representative, S. F. Building and Construction Trades Council.

ALLAN E. CHARLES
Lillick, Geary, Olson & Charles, Attorneys; Past President, Barrister's Club, San Francisco

JOHN W. CLINE, M. D.
Immediate Past President, San Francisco County Medical Society

DAN COLLINS
Holt & Collins, Investment Brokers;
Past President, South San Francisco Parlor, N. S. G. W.

BARTLEY C. CRUM
Attorney; General Chairman, Citizens' Committee for Edmund G. Brown for District Attorney

CHARLES de YOUNG ELKUS
Bacigalupi, Elkus & Salinger, Attorneys;
General Chairman, Conference on Children in Wartime; Member, Juvenile Probation Committee

WENDELL T. FITZGERALD
Morrison, Hohfeld, Foerster, Shuman & Clark, Attorneys

HERBERT HANLEY
Chairman, Republican County Central Committee

BERT W. LEVIT
Former Special Assistant to U. S. Attorney General at Washington, D. C.; Past President, California State Junior Chamber of Commerce

PERCY V. LONG
Former City Attorney of San Francisco;
Chairman, Juvenile Probation Committee

RICHARD LYNDEN
President, Warehouse Union, Local 6, C. I. O.

J. WARD MAILLIARD, Jr.
Member, Board of Harbor Commissioners;
Past President, San Francisco Chamber of Commerce; Former Police Commissioner of San Francisco

JOSEPH MURPHY
Advertising Manager, "Organized Labor"

CHARLES R. PAGE
Fireman's Fund Insurance Company;
Former Chairman, San Francisco Civil Defense Council

HOMER POTTER
Williams-Wallace Company;
Past Exalted Ruler, S. F. Lodge No. 3, B. P. O. Elks

MICHAEL RIORDAN
President, United Irish Societies

MRS. WILLIAM LISTER ROGERS
Past President, Junior League of San Francisco

ALBERT A. ROSENSHINE
Attorney; Past President, Commonwealth Club of California

RICHARD L. SLOSS
Sloss & Turner, Attorneys;
Vice Chairman, San Francisco Conference of Christians and Jews

ALFRED STERN
President, Young Democrats

MRS. HAROLD TURNER
Past President, San Francisco Center of the California League of Women Voters

This advertisement bought and paid for by a group of citizens determined to establish efficiency in the District Attorney's office

Five weeks before the election, the *San Francisco Examiner* spoke for many when it praised Brady as "tolerant and humane at all times, but sternly inflexible in his prosecution of criminals and his warfare against organized crime" under the headline "Brady's Splendid Record."[18] In an editorial the day before the election, the newspaper doubled down, labeling Pat Brown unfit to be district attorney.[19]

The locally owned *San Francisco Chronicle* and the Scripps-Howard *San Francisco News* endorsed Pat, as much to tweak the *Examiner* as to take a chance on a novice. It was time to toss Brady out of office, the *Chronicle* editorial said, adding that the twenty-three-year veteran "has been utterly devoid of initiative." The newspaper said Brady's office was "limp with lethargy. Its vision is backward. . . . San Francisco no longer can afford this. The world is moving too fast."[20]

Pat Brown tried to fashion himself as the first of San Francisco's modern politicians. Glib and photogenic, he made his pitches through expensive, slickly produced ads, to which Matt Brady didn't know how to respond. Flat-footed, lumbering Brady charged that Pat had spent more than thirty-two thousand dollars for billboards, direct-mail advertising, radio time, and newspaper-display spots, which was more than the salary of the district attorney over the course of an entire four-year term.[21] Pat spent an unheard-of sum of money in the race for district attorney, an ostensibly nonpolitical office. His campaign slogan was "Crack down on crime, elect Brown this time."[22]

It was a phrase that struck fear in many. "The campaign against Brady is a campaign of desperate men," the establishment *Examiner* vented to its readers in a large-type, unsigned editorial a week before the election[23]—as sure a sign as any that crusading Pat was a force to be reckoned with.

Matt Brady followed the paper's vitriol by calling Pat Brown a puppet of underworld bosses. Brady said Brown had "submerged whatever righteous scruples he possessed," adding that Brown was capitalizing on "the enmity and resentment that it has been my inevitable fate to have built up for having performed my sworn duty against the influences of the underworld."[24] It was a last-resort effort from a drowning politician.

On election day, with photographers in tow, Pat voted first thing in the day, so a photo of the smiling and confident candidate casting his vote would appear in that day's afternoon newspapers. Still, Pat was such a nervous wreck that Bernice suggested he try to settle his nerves by playing a round of golf at Lincoln Park Golf Course. But at the first tee, Pat muffed the shot and dribbled the ball three inches.[25]

He made phone calls after his round of golf and visited with friends and supporters. During the evening, Pat got to his Market Street campaign headquarters even before votes started coming in.

With Pat's relentless glad-handing, along with voter enthusiasm at throwing out sleepy Good Ole Matt, Pat eked out a victory by a little more than seven thousand votes out of almost two hundred thousand.[26] Pat joined newcomer Roger Lapham, who was elected mayor. Pat Brown had just been elected to one of the most powerful political offices in California.

To his supporters on election night, Pat trumpeted, "At times the campaign just closed grew extremely bitter. Charges were made by Mr. Brady and his supporters, which, I am sure, they now regret. I take this opportunity of assuring them that I approach my new responsibilities entirely without malice and without vindictiveness."[27] It was pure Pat: No one had ever said Pat *would* proceed with malice and vindictiveness. Pat and his entourage of young Turks repaired to Vanessi's, the popular North Beach restaurant known for martinis and osso bucco.

Sworn into office by Municipal Court Judge Daniel Shoemaker in the grand rotunda of the beaux arts City Hall on January 8, 1944, Brown gave a law-and-order preview of what was down the road: "The Office of District Attorney deals with human nature at its worst . . . with crime, vice, and humanity gone wrong. Its primary obligation is to protect society from its rebellious and predatory members. It must move vigorously and impartially in the prosecution of crime. It must seek the full penalty of the law against deliberate, malicious, and unrepentant offenders. . . . The prosecutor must not become the persecutor, seeking vindictive punishment and exulting in its infliction."[28]

Back at her Guerrero Street home, taking a chamomile-and-rose-hips bath in her claw-foot tub, Inez rolled her eyes. Pat Brown was a politician, but a man too. Her job would be to find out his weak spot. Every man had one.

It didn't take Pat long to come out swinging. Just one month in his new office in the Scatena Building at 550 Montgomery Street, Pat had hired a team of nine young and aggressive attorneys, including Bert W. Levit; Norman Elkington; and the most troubling, his chief deputy, Thomas C. Lynch, the former assistant US attorney who had prosecuted Inez for income-tax evasion. Lynch was an SOB, at least to Inez he was.[29]

The Brady years had been hands-off, and now this Pat Brown would be sticking his mitts into everything. Vice would be first because the results are always the most visible—and the least permanent. Pat immediately went after bookies to show that despite who his father had been, the district attorney's office wouldn't be compromised. Governor Warren had signed into law a bill that made bookmaking no longer punishable as a misdemeanor, but as a felony, which meant prison time. Bookies would no longer be able to pay a fine and be back taking bets the same day. As a test to see how rigorous Pat would be in enforcing Warren's get-tough antigambling law, bookies on the first Friday in March organized a citywide start-up of their operations again. It was an in-your-face challenge to Brown to see who would blink first.[30] Brown's office responded by charging four notorious bookmakers with the new felony law.[31]

Most troubling to Inez was that Pat had transformed himself into a prosecutor preaching from the pulpit of morality. At least that's what he was doing publicly. It was a new concept in live-and-let-live San Francisco. Pat sought to connect the dots of crime to factors few at the time ever bothered to consider. Perhaps because of his Catholic upbringing, one factor Brown cited as an indicator of crime was San Francisco's divorce rate. Coming from a district attorney, the cause-and-effect connection was curious. In his first crime prevention report, Pat's number-one recommendation was a call to reaffirm the sanctity of marriage. Extolling family values, Pat preached, "People must be made to realize that the marriage contract is sacred. In every case where a divorce action is filed in the superior court and there are children of the marriage, a full and complete report should be made to the court before the decree is granted showing the actual and real cause for the divorce."[32] Pat was now sounding less like a district attorney and more like an archbishop. This could not augur well for Inez.

Next, his office began assembling intel on more than twenty-five notorious bars where venereal disease was being spread, and moved to revoke the bars' licenses.[33] Pat went after bars that refilled liquor bottles.[34] He followed by prosecuting the madams of brothels, including the notorious El Rosa Hotel in the Tenderloin.[35] That kind of prosecutorial fervor was more bad news for Inez.

Meanwhile, Mabel Malotte, Anna Thompson's niece, had turned into quite a businesswoman herself. By now, she was running a budding call-girl service from a house on Bay Street, near Fisherman's Wharf. Mabel was always good for sending a couple young girls to Inez's place for the Wednesday evening get-togethers. Inez didn't know if Anna would be proud of her niece, but she, too, had become an entrepreneur like Inez and could call herself a success. For the time being, it seemed that

Mabel's house of prostitution would be spared from Pat's dragnet. Mabel's clients were upscale businessmen, and Mabel, like Inez, maintained a scrupulously clean operation.

No matter. Pat's first acts were prima facie evidence that the new district attorney and Inez would sooner or later be at war. It was just a matter of time. If Pat was cracking down on bookies, divorce, VD, tainted alcohol, and prostitution—and divorce and communicable diseases were legal—then it was just a matter of time before he'd get to Inez and abortion.

San Franciscans quickly grew accustomed to their new about-town DA, who held weekly press conferences, his photo appearing with regularity in the newspapers. Pat showed up everywhere. Like former mayor Rolph, a manically extroverted Pat chatted up everyone wherever he went, whether eating Swedish pancakes at Sears Fine Foods or riding the Powell Street cable car over Russian Hill and down to Fisherman's Wharf. He took questions as often as he could for an hour-long interview show he called "Your District Attorney in Action" on radio station KJBS. The program was a real-life complement to the popular radio crime drama at the time, *Mr. District Attorney*, which aired on KPO. If listeners confused Pat with gruff-talking prosecutor David Weist in *Mr. District Attorney*, that was fine;[36] the show's motto was "Champion of the people, defender of the truth, guardian of our fundamental rights to life, liberty, and the pursuit of happiness."[37] Who could be against that in a district attorney?

Megawatt Pat thrived on the limelight. He'd intentionally walk into the wrong hotel ballroom fifteen minutes before he was scheduled to deliver a speech, only to be "persuaded" to toast a pair of unsuspecting newlyweds or to welcome a herd of Colorado cattlemen to the city he loved. It was all part of Pat's manic drive to make himself a celebrity at all costs.

Pat aligned himself with pretty much anyone to snatch a vote—or, better, a bloc of votes. Pat did whatever it took, and there weren't many things that took more than he was willing to give. Pat epitomized two quotes his political archrival Jesse M. "Big Daddy" Unruh, the speaker of California's Assembly, would make famous a generation later: "Money is the mother's milk of politics," and referring to lobbyists, "If you can't eat their food, drink their booze, screw their women, and then vote against them, you have no business being up here."[38] With the exception of the women part, that pretty much summed up Pat.

Just one year into his first elected office, Pat had already set his sights on running for state attorney general, following in the path of his mentor, Earl Warren. Like Warren, Pat needed to radiate his name beyond the insular confines of the Northern California city that had elected him. For statewide office, Pat would need to launch a campaign stretching the length and breadth of coastal California, the creeping megalopolis of Los Angeles, and the state's fertile interior. It would be a formidable task.

With purpose and foresight, Pat took to transforming himself into a Prosecutor for the People, or "a mean little bastard," as he would call himself.[39] He amped up his campaign against cops who winked at bookmakers, gambling parlors, and whorehouses. Corruption reigned supreme throughout the state, Pat championed, and he'd tell anyone in earshot that he was the man to make dazzling California deserving of the nine million worthy inhabitants who now called it home.

That made Pat an unpredictable commodity to those who didn't like surprises in their politicians, and it was precisely because of how fast his trajectory had gone vertical that the FBI began collecting surveillance intelligence on Pat. Beginning in 1939, the FBI started what would eventually turn into a five-inch-thick dossier on him. FBI Director J. Edgar Hoover didn't know exactly where Pat was headed— always troubling to kingmakers—so he directed his field agents to find out.

A notation in one FBI memorandum categorized the upstart as, "Some person close to Brown stated he is impulsive and ambiguous in both speech and actions and as a result gets in 'hot water' on occasions." Another memo cited a source who said, "Brown is lacking in character, ability, judgment, integrity, and cannot keep a secret." A third memorandum suggested "Brown appears to be 'playing both sides' at the present time. He is reported to be honest but is looking toward the future in a political way, being anxious not to make enemies of any side."[40] The advisory concluded by urging all bureau dealings with Brown to be handled "with caution because it appears he is more interested in obtaining personal publicity than serving the ends of justice." In summary, the memo suggested, "Brown is reputedly not too capable an attorney but sincere and unquestionably has high political ambitions."[41]

The classified FBI memo wasn't wrong. What Pat needed to realize those ambitions was a cause that would catapult him—a rousing issue that would create a statewide name to match his colossal hunger. He would need to generate headlines, statewide name recognition, and, most of all, money. Jesse Unruh's first law of politics.

Surely Pat was a natural at attracting press coverage, but he'd also need to make sure he was in sync with public sentiment, or he'd be a one-term DA. Don't go too fast, his advisers urged him. Slow down. Assess what the public wants and will tolerate. "Somebody said to me, 'Don't try to clean up San Francisco all at once. If you do, the people of San Francisco will regurgitate, and they'll throw you out with it.' So I'd wait for an incident."[42]

That incident would be police corruption, something Inez had lots of experience with through the thick envelopes beat cops picked up each week at her Guerrero Street house and Fillmore clinic. Graft, payoffs, bribes—that's what Pat would make as his cornerstone to building statewide recognition. And if a flagrant abortionist got taken down in the process, that'd be fine too. A small but necessary skirmish on the way to greater fame.

"The abortionists we had to go after because we felt they were corrupting the homicide bureau," Pat said. "The abortionists, whether they killed anybody or not, were under the jurisdiction of the homicide squad. We had evidence, although we could never prove it, that the police were getting four hundred dollars a day. We found documents with 'Police: $400' or 'Protection: $400.' So we had to go after them on that."[43]

A close friend of Pat's, Norman Elkington, whom Brown had appointed as one of his first deputies, put his own perspective on why Pat soon went after Inez with such a single-minded vengeance.

What was scandalous in San Francisco wasn't getting an abortion, Elkington allowed, but "the political corruption that it entailed. Policemen were corrupted, politicians were corrupted from the highest level down to the lowest. The queen bee of abortions in San Francisco was Inez Burns. Brown made statements that this was going to be ended, but they paid no attention to him."[44]

Closing down Inez and ending the chronic system of bribing cops and politicians would be just the beginning of Pat's mandate to fan his political career. He sicced Inez's nemesis, First Deputy Tom Lynch, on her. "One of the first orders of business when Brown became DA was to go after Inez Burns," Lynch would say. Lynch allowed that ninety percent of Inez's clients were middle-class women, but he threw out the window any notion that Inez provided a public service. "She didn't have those lofty ideas. She was after the money. She was as greedy as she could possibly be."[45]

By the way of Tom Lynch, Inez would be Pat's ride to statewide office. Pat and Inez would become *agonistes*, a word from ancient Greek that means persons engaged in public struggle. Two opposing forces seeking to prevail when there was room for only one.

It would be a ruthless fight to the finish.

FOURTEEN

THE NATURE OF THE BEAST

Either Pat Brown was a pack rat or he believed every scrap of every letter, every doodle he ever sketched, every lunch engagement noted in his calendar, any and all of it, would be of vital importance to someone someday, chronicling the long arc of Pat's variegated political life. Pat's papers, speeches, notebooks, posters, and calendars are kept under lock and key in the vast, hermetically sealed repositories of the Bancroft Library of the University of California, Berkeley. All of it is contained in seven hundred sixty-one brown cardboard cartons, which take up almost one thousand linear feet. The papers include thousands of letters asking for voters' support or thanking donors for their contributions. Every judge, every University of California regent, every high-ranking police officers' appointment seemed to merit a letter of congratulations from Pat. He seemed to leave out no one. From early in his career, Pat spoke to fraternal organizations of every stripe and color, from the Knights of Pythias and the Order of DeMolay to the St. Francis Guild and the B'nai B'rith. All to propel him higher and higher.

Like all politicians, Pat was constantly receiving gifts from constituents to remind him of their importance and munificence, which in 1946 included a crate of Mendocino pears; a pencil from Ranier Brewing Co.; a box of Yuba City Persian melons; season passes to the Blumenfeld, Empire, Golden Gate, Newsreel, and Paramount theaters; neckties; candy; passes to Playland at the Sea and the Cliff House at Lands End); a subscription to *Fortune* magazine; an antique vase; a bag of Oroville oranges; wine and brandy from the Bank of America's legal department; holly and mistletoe; a money clip (from the manager of the Pantages Theatre in L.A.) on behalf of comedian Bud Abbott; a tin of ham; multiple cases of liquor; a quart of cream from Dairy Belle Farms; and dozens and dozens of golf balls.

Pat's papers are numbingly exhaustive. There is a parking ticket for one dollar his wife received, along with a letter he wrote to suspend his Book of the Month Club delivery for the month of May. Included in the repository is a standing order to buy monthly fifty-dollar war bonds. A copy of his 1938 state income tax is included, which showed a net income of $5,016.67. On May 8, 1943, Pat paid one dollar for a set of the *Encyclopedia of the Popes*. He was a member in good standing at St. Cecilia's Church, at 2555 Seventeenth Avenue. He applied for his daughter Cynthia to matriculate at the Convent of the Sacred Heart (where Inez's daughter, Alice Lorine, had also been a student), and wrote his son Jerry at summer camp not to forget to "brush your teeth, wash your hands and face, and say your prayers at least three times a day." Pat added that he hoped Jerry had "not gotten into any fights, but, if you have, I hope you haven't lost them."[1]

Pat was flattered by his circle of admirers, getting larger and larger seemingly by the day. Some supporters reflected Pat's deep political spadework, such as George A. Engelhardt, the elevator operator at the Huntington Hotel on Nob Hill, who wrote, "I voted for you, and know you will live up to your campaign promises."[2] Another came from A. H. Jacobs, a Washington Street produce wholesaler, who wrote, "You certainly defeated a strong opponent, a man who was well entrenched (or should I say interred) in his twenty-four-year-old office."[3]

But most were correspondence to and from men about town who wanted in early on a career that was going places. Everyone knew the office of district attorney was Pat's starting line, but no one knew where the finish line would be. Budding San Francisco trial attorney colorful Mel Belli, two years younger than Pat, was one who wanted to hitch a ride, and went out of his way to engage Pat in every way, including on a number of manly outings, which Pat seemed to relish.[4]

The Bancroft Library collection includes thousands of pieces of ephemera that in its entirety reveals insights into the man who would seek to make Inez his own personal bounty. Pat accepted all the support he could attract, and that included accommodating San Francisco's archconservative religious elements, who—finally—could see in Brown a moral wedge that had been nonexistent in Matt Brady's tenure as the city's chief prosecutor. Nine days after Pat's election, he received a letter from the Reverend John Compton Leffler, backslapping him on his victory. "I congratulate you with a great deal of enthusiasm because I believe you mean it when you say this city will be given the kind of law enforcement which it has not had in many years," wrote Leffler. Sister Euphrasia of the Nativity wrote Pat from the Carmelite Monastery in Santa Clara that the convent's sisters had been praying for his victory; Pat replied that his intention was "to serve the people in my official capacity in as Christian a manner as possible. . . . With the help of God, I shall be able to overcome the great problems that lie ahead of me as District Attorney of a City that is fast becoming one of the most important Ports in the world." The archbishop also wrote to Pat to schedule a meeting.[5]

Pat's nemesis, Inez, didn't exactly have an army of vocal public supporters cheering her on. Few abortionists did. But Pat did get a letter or two, condemning his actions whenever he crowed about putting abortionists behind bars.

"I am told Inez Burns never lost a patient. The poor or unmarried people who now require abortions will have to turn to surreptitious doctors who will probably lose some of their lives. I am not blaming you, but I do ask that you consider the nature of the system," wrote San Francisco resident Tertius Chandler, a detractor of Pat's campaign of family values. "Cleanups like this have gone on for years. As you know, a district attorney can make his reputation cleaning up a situation like this, then two years later another attorney, or even the same attorney, can do the same thing all over again and make another reputation. Nothing gets really done that way except to lower the standard of living of the unlucky folk who have to use the humble outlets." Pat dutifully responded to Chandler, saying he'd welcome a visit to discuss the matter, although no such meeting apparently ever took place.[6]

FIFTEEN

PILLARS OF MONEY, FOUNTAINS OF PAYOFFS

After less than a year as San Francisco district attorney, Pat was seriously angling for a larger office. He'd always seen great things for himself and now had the means to accomplish them. Governor Earl Warren would be up for reelection in 1946, and Attorney General Robert Kenny, a Democrat, had announced his intention to challenge him. That in turn would leave Kenny's job open, and while Pat hadn't yet amassed much of a record as a prosecutor, he'd positioned himself as the leading candidate to replace Kenny as California's top crime fighter. State Democrats met in San Francisco and gave Pat the nod to run as the Democratic candidate for Kenny's spot. It wasn't Pat's sparse record as DA that captivated the audience of seasoned politicians wary of comers; it was the power of his oversize magnanimous personality. Pat relished the opportunity to diffuse any and all naysayers in the crowd. Even this early in his grand political trajectory, Pat had become a politician's politician, striking deals and compromises right and left, at the same time exuding to one and all a heaping dose of charm and tact.

Los Angeles District Attorney Fred Napoleon Howser, a Republican, would be Pat's opponent in the fall election. Like Brown, Howser was thirty-eight and had served less than a year as DA.[1] Like Pat, Howser, too, was a politician who'd pretty much do whatever it took to get where he wanted to go. In a wacky campaign strategy, California Republicans that year were hoping that voters might mistakenly cast their ballots for attorney general wannabe Howser, thinking they were actually voting for someone else—a popular incumbent lieutenant governor with the nearly identical name of Fred Houser. California gambling and liquor czar Artie Samish, who had turned down Pat's earlier entreaty for support, banked that voters would be confused enough to cast their ballots for the wrong man.

Samish, who would eventually spend time in Alcatraz Federal Prison for tax evasion, had launched Fred Howser's career when Howser was elected to the State Assembly and Samish was able to maneuver Howser onto the Assembly's Public Morals Committee as chairman. "I knew the voting public wouldn't be able to differentiate between Fred Houser and Fred N. Howser, so I told Howser that he should run for attorney general," Samish unabashedly wrote in his memoirs. At three hundred pounds, lobbyist Samish was smooth and slippery, controlling a slush fund of more than a million dollars. Samish picked politicians and promptly molded them into errand boys; he called the system his policy of "select and elect."[2] Samish was so powerful that he once told state investigators, "*I* am the governor of the legislature. To hell with the governor of the state."[3] Bankrolled by crooked Samish and his bottomless coffers of money and influence, the well-funded Fred Howser would be a tough opponent for Pat to beat for attorney general.[4]

With the confusing pair of soundalike candidates on a Republican ticket headed by well-liked Governor Warren, Pat would need a surefire way to snare statewide headlines to promote his name beyond the clubby confines of San Francisco. So Pat came up with a repeat message he tried to sell everywhere he went: Pat Brown was a tireless, crime-fighting DA cleaning up a permissive city that had swung way too tolerant. Pat was the man the entire state of California now needed. The only problem with the campaign rhetoric was that Pat hadn't accomplished much. His only accomplishment had been promises.

Although Pat was a Catholic and personally opposed abortion, religion hardly motivated him. It was votes, or the potential of them, that spoke to Pat. He knew there'd be votes if he went after Inez, but only if he did it in a roundabout way. San Franciscans might be loath to admit it, but if pressed, most would begrudgingly acknowledge Inez's utility. It was a fact of life that her services were necessary in a society where human error often trumped wisdom. Inez was a necessary safety valve, and few in San Francisco were ready to close her down. So Pat came up with a two-fold strategy: first go after San Francisco's runaway police corruption, then, and only then, set his sights on going after Inez. He'd proclaim that Inez was a flashing neon sign advertising San Francisco's deep-seated graft and corruption. It had only been because of bribes and payoffs that millionaire Inez had been able to flourish for so long. Two decades of cops and officials paid to look the other way had turned Inez into a powerful political figure in San Francisco. Without complicity from those in power, Inez never could have reached the heights to which she had soared. Pat's play, then, would be first to hit on graft, and then to let the fallout infect and destroy Inez. Inez was the natural outgrowth of unabated sleaze on the part of cops and City Hall. It would be a one-two punch.

Pat knew he had to raise a ruckus that could be heard the length and breadth of the state, from Redding to Barstow, to drown out Fred Howser's doppelgänger name and Samish's free fall of cash circulating his candidate's scrubbed reputation. Not only would Pat have to contend with the confusing Howser/Houser gambit, but he'd also have to buck Earl Warren's runaway popularity and his wide coattails. Pat couldn't do much about the latter, but he could try to clear the air about the duplicity Republicans had engineered when it came to his opponent's name. Pat took out newspaper advertisements warning voters not to confuse Howser with Houser and, while he was at it, urging Californians to cast their ballots for Brown, "the honest candidate."

Pat traveled from San Francisco as often as he could in an attempt to drown out Howser's well-funded campaign. Back home, Inez continued to reel in more friends and supporters to her side. Her political instincts were long honed by an army of loyal informants. She knew as much about the comings and goings at City Hall and the Hall of Justice as Pat did. Probably more. Every Wednesday evening, Inez heard from her parlor cabinet of cops and political confidants. One of Joe Burns's sisters was married to Police Sergeant Glen Hughes, and another cop, Stephen J. Flahaven, lived at 333 Fillmore, a couple of doors north of her clinic.[5] Fire Captain Ed Dullea, the brother of Police Chief Charles Dullea, often showed up at the gatherings, as did Mabel Malotte, when she could, and when she couldn't, she'd send over a girl or two, and no one seemed to mind in the least. Like Inez's clinic, Mabel's bagnio remained open for business through a multitude of well-placed bribes, and the two women happily shared their intel.

Inez got around, not just in political and police rank-and-file circles, but by necessity within the local medical community. A large percentage of her clientele came from referring physicians, as well as dentists and pharmacists. One regular at Inez and Joe's gatherings was Dr. Claude Cleveland Long, who had also had a

Mabel Malotte.

long history of performing abortions, dating back to 1923. In 1937, Dr. Long had been arrested after a twenty-six-year-old San Francisco mother died as the result of an abortion he performed.[6] The ensuing trial of Long, his wife, Isabel, and a nurse, Ann Fisher, was graphic and explosive, with charges of jury tampering and bribery. Inez's associate, Dr. Adolphus A. Berger, the former city autopsy physician, testified on behalf of Dr. Long.[7] But the jury found Dr. Long guilty of manslaughter;[8] he remained free for four years but lost his appeal and eventually served time at San Quentin.[9] Out of prison and out of the abortion business, he sent patients to Inez, who had more experience than Dr. Long ever had. In the weekly mix at Inez's place, Dr. Long was an inveterate bettor on racehorses, although he didn't have much of a track record, thus his nickname, Dr. Long Shot. Always with a *Racing Form* rolled up in his back pocket, Dr. Long used to play the piano in Inez's parlor while singing a variety of show tunes, including "Bewitched, Bothered and Bewildered" from the 1940 Rogers and Hart musical *Pal Joey*. Others who joined the weekly retinue included San Francisco physicians Ernest Rogers and Maurice Eliaser, along with a dentist by the name of Lloyd Commins.[10]

Another regular on Wednesday evenings was Inez's accountant, Joseph Anton Felix, who went by the first name of Bud. Well-to-do Bud Felix lived at 2925 Lake Street in the ritzy Sea Cliff neighborhood, and later at 2101 Pacific, in a stately Pacific Heights building, in between Lafayette Park and Broadway. Bud was Inez's financial adviser, and maintained an office in the Mills Building on Montgomery Street in San Francisco's financial district. The two often met for hours, mapping out Inez's investment strategies. Tall and slender, with steel-gray hair and rimless glasses, Bud Felix often stayed to talk money after Inez shooed everyone home. If the fog wasn't out, they'd stroll in the backyard garden or talk over coffee in the breakfast room. Born in Switzerland, he and his wife, Martha, were significant philanthropic players in the Jewish community in San Francisco. Martha was a leader in Hadassah, the National Council of Jewish Women, ORT, and annual campaigns to raise funds for Israel bonds. The Felixes hobnobbed with Mae and Ben Swig, the owner of the Fairmont; Eleanor and Ben Deitch; and Barbara and Jay Semelman, all pillars of moneyed San Francisco society.[11]

Other members of Inez's inner circle included Warren Shannon and his new third wife, Gloria. For twenty-five years, Warren had been a member of San Francisco's Board of Supervisors and had served as acting mayor on numerous occasions. He'd been appointed to the board in 1919 by Mayor Rolph and served consecutive terms until 1944. On Inez's recommendation, Inez's son Bob, who by now had set up his own medical practice, had operated on Shannon for ulcers in 1939.[12] Warren was a large, fleshy, red-faced Irishman who favored wool suits and three-point crown-fold handkerchiefs. He had one eye, and during poker games, he liked to pop his glass eye out and polish it with a handkerchief.[13] Because of an automobile accident while in her twenties, Gloria was partially paralyzed and had a brace on one of her legs. She had a preference for chinchilla wraps and tilted halo hats festooned with feathers. Gloria liked to boast to anyone who'd listen that her profession was "the movies," but everyone thought she was ditzy.[14]

The consensus among Inez's circle of friends was that after a loud and fussy skirmish, Pat Brown might actually win statewide office. And if that ever came to pass, Pat would be happily gone from San Francisco, installed in Sacramento as attorney general, and, before much time, setting his sights toward the governor's mansion to replace Earl Warren, who was looking to be a viable candidate to make a run at the White House. By then, all of Pat's tough-talking prosecutor bravado would turn to a statewide agenda, and Inez would become a fading image in Pat's rearview window as he roared ahead with his career. With Pat out of town, Good Ole Matt might even run for DA again, wiping clean all the muck Pat had smeared everywhere. And if not Matt Brady, then someone else whom Inez could work with. Pat Brown's tenure as district attorney would have been a blip, a momentary aberration. The oppressive San Francisco fog would lift to reveal a clear, sunny day once again for Inez and for her queue of jittery patients, not just worried about their upcoming medical procedures, but about looking over their shoulders for crusading cops out to arrest the only woman who could help them.

While Inez was undoubtedly the most popular abortionist in the state, there was creeping competition from not just lesser-known operators in San Francisco and Los Angeles but also from clinics across the border in Mexico. Abortion was illegal in Mexico, too, but that had never stopped anyone from opening a clinic, whether in Mexico, the United States, or elsewhere. Dozens of clinics in Tijuana at the time targeted American women with their services and lower fees. Considering the expense, trouble, and time involved with traveling south of the border, not to mention most clinics' sanitary conditions, such trips weren't worth the risk for many women, especially those in Northern California. Still, the Mexican facilities were yet another sign of how lucrative the abortion trade was, as well as the never-ending necessity for such services.[15]

Inez continued performing as many as fifteen to twenty abortions a day, even though she knew that Brown's lieutenants, deputies Tom Lynch, Bert Levitt, Andrew J. Eyman, and Norman Elkington, along with Police Chief Dullea and his minions, were now watching her every move. Inez had become a de facto yet essential part of Pat Brown's campaign. Something was bound to happen sooner or later. Pat and Inez were playing a cat-and-mouse waiting game.

"Let 'em just try to shut me down," Inez told Joe one evening. When Inez got fixated on something, she never let go. Joe knew that, so did Inez. "Just let 'em try. Do they really know who they're dealing with?"

It sure sounded like Inez was bruising for a showdown. She wasn't about to let any man, let alone a politician posturing as squeaky-clean, dictate what she could or couldn't do. It wasn't just about money; it was also pride in what she had accomplished. Not to mention all the women who continued to make a beeline to her clinic every day.

On the rare afternoon when Inez wasn't working, she and Mabel often met, and the two would go on what became legendary shopping sprees. Both had plenty of cash to get rid of, and Union Square merchants didn't mind in the least assisting them in that noble cause. Inez and Mabel would spend hours at Ransohoff's and Nelly Gaffney's, making a spectacle of themselves as a flurry of salesgirls fluttered around them with dozens of dresses, hats, and fur coats as each woman tried on item after item after item in private fitting areas.[16]

It was during one early evening after Mabel and Inez had finished a frenzied afternoon of shopping, when the two women found themselves inside the Papagayo Room at the Fairmont, nursing drinks. Inez was dressed to the nines, wearing a beaver coat, a flowing chiffon dress, and a dramatic forest-green turban. On the ring finger of her right hand, she had on a large ruby and diamond ring.[17] Mabel had to take leave to oversee another drama, her girls primping for the evening crowd, and she kissed Inez goodbye. That's when Inez spotted Gloria and Warren Shannon, sitting at a table across the room.

After kisses all around, Inez noticed that carefree Warren appeared uncharacteristically troubled. He fidgeted with the silverware. The weight of the world seemed to be weighing on his ample shoulders. He was perspiring and repeatedly patted his forehead with his handkerchief. Inez just hoped he wouldn't pop out his eyeball and start polishing it.

After some prodding, Warren allowed that he was experiencing a financial reversal of sorts. Inez wasn't sure of the details, but here was a once-prosperous man, a trusted friend, who had fallen on hard times. He had stepped down from the Board of Supervisors the same year that Pat Brown had been elected DA; that's when Warren's fountain of payoffs must have dried up, Inez figured. After listening to his sad story of woe, Inez invited the couple to move into the first-floor apartment of the clinic, at 325 Fillmore. Gloria could work at the clinic, Inez promised.[18] Inez welcomed the company. Warren's connections couldn't hurt, and however loopy Gloria was, Inez always could use an extra woman upstairs.

If any trouble ever erupted at the clinic, Inez usually turned to Joe Hoff. Inez kept a thirty-eight-caliber revolver, hidden in one of the sliding-wall partitions, if she or Joe ever needed it. That hardly ever happened, but it was reassuring just the same. After a busy day, Inez's receipts could be as high as three thousand dollars in cash, and that didn't include everything hidden in the nooks and crannies.[19] It'd make for a nice haul should some goon try to strong-arm her. Inez couldn't exactly call her friends at the Northern police station should she need help—at least that kind of help.

Because the clinic was so well known and Inez took in so much, every once in a while Inez became accustomed to contending with an unsavory character dumb enough to think he could muscle in on her success. Or worse, that he could twist her arm into working for *him*, turning Inez into some kind of financial goombah. Such a venture, of course, was preposterous, and anyone who was the least bit acquainted with Inez knew it. Considering whom Inez knew and how long she'd been in business, only a fool would even suggest it.

One such fool was a thirty-six-year-old gangster by the name of Nick DeJohn, who'd been banished from Chicago for being nuts enough to butt heads with Chicago mobster Al Capone. DeJohn, who was born Nicholas DiGiovanni, had relocated to sleepy Santa Rosa, fifty miles north of San Francisco, where he reinvented himself as Vincent Rossi, a "retired furniture salesman." DeJohn brought his wife and four children, and every Sunday they made a big deal of celebrating mass at St. Rose Catholic Church on Tenth Street just north of downtown. Besides DeJohn's nearly impenetrable accent, neighbors scratched their heads over a colossal diamond ring he wore on his pinky and the yacht-size Chrysler Town & Country car he drove around town.[20]

DeJohn and two other Chicago hoodlums had made the miscalculation of skimming profits from one of Capone's businesses, selling olive oil as a front for narcotics.[21] Capone's minions retaliated by stuffing one of DeJohn's associates into a sewer pipe and locking the other in a trunk until he froze to death.[22] DeJohn wisely skipped town and headed West. But tending to his rose garden on Santa Rosa's Bryden Lane didn't provide enough excitement for the erstwhile gangster. That's when DeJohn made inquiries about the abortion trade in San Francisco and found his way to Inez's place on Fillmore Street, where he had the moxie to try to extort a cut from her profits.

It was a crude, ill-advised attempt to shake down Inez. To sweeten the deal, DeJohn told Inez he'd throw some business her way (as though she needed any). Everyone would make out fine, DeJohn promised, rubbing his right fist into his left palm, smiling like a jackass wearing a pinkie ring with a seven-carat diamond in it.

Inez didn't like anything about DeJohn. He smelled of cigarettes and his musky cologne stunk up the clinic's parlor. Inez hated men who wore perfume; they always were hiding something. Besides, when DeJohn opened his mouth, he reeked of anchovies. Inez didn't know which was worse, the cologne or the anchovies, but the medley was making her sick to her stomach. In a contest between the nauseating DeJohn and the holier-than-thou Pat Brown, Inez probably would have chosen Pat, and that was saying something.

Inez motioned for Joe Hoff to come closer. She whispered a few words into his ear. Joe nodded and backpedaled out of the parlor, only to reappear moments later with the snub-nosed thirty-eight pointed at DeJohn's chest.

Inez told DeJohn never to show his ugly, smelly mug ever again, and if he did, she'd make sure it'd be filled with lead. He'd end up floating in China Basin or rolled down Devil's Slide into the Pacific never to be seen again. A shouting match ensued, but it ended abruptly when Inez pointed her index finger at DeJohn's chest, and Joe held the revolver against his right temple.

"You wanna leave alive through the front door or dead through the back?" Inez asked, as though inquiring whether he preferred sweet or dry vermouth.

When DeJohn paused, as though considering his options, Inez added, "You know, I got an incinerator in the back, and I can make you"—at which point she looked at DeJohn head to toe—"all of you, disappear just like that," she said, snapping her fingers.

"You *ca-piche?*"

That took care of Nick DeJohn. For the time being, that is.

In the coming months, DeJohn and a sidekick named Gus Oliva went to a few also-ran abortion clinics in and around town in an attempt to make Inez pay for her impudence. The pair scored with Alta Anderson, her daughter Mae Rodley, Gertrude Jenkins, and Anita Venza, who worked out of a dilapidated Victorian house at 1097 South Van Ness Avenue. The four women were already trying to move on Inez's overflow clientele, and they shortsightedly bought into DeJohn's plan to help them do it.[23] As long as DeJohn stayed clear of Inez, Inez didn't care what the hell he did.

With Pat Brown on the hustings trying to get elected attorney general, Inez continued to focus on consolidating her financial success. When the clinic was running on all cylinders, she was raking in as much as fifteen thousand dollars a week. Even if Inez took off two weeks a year, her take could amount to seven hundred fifty thousand dollars a year. And that was a conservative figure, since some days she performed as many as twenty abortions, and Inez had a sliding scale, charging well-heeled patients more. That was only right, Inez reasoned. It subsidized poorer girls, who needed abortions the most and could barely afford to pay anything. How much Inez had accrued since she started her business was anyone's guess, but surely it topped fifteen million dollars. Little had gone to the Bureau of Internal Revenue, even after the penalties and the back taxes were paid off. Her expenses were hush money, personnel, equipment, supplies, and property taxes. The rest was profit.

For rest and relaxation, on weekends, Inez and Joe began entertaining more and more at the ranch in La Honda, run by Joe's brother, Jim, and his wife, Kitty. By now, Inez had several grandchildren, and when Inez and Joe drove to Burns Ranch, they often took them along.

William Brown, Billy's son, lived with his wife and their two children in the tony San Mateo County community of Atherton, at 401 Selby Lane, in a fourteen-room, seven-bath English Tudor mansion, not far from where newspaper magnate William Randolph Hearst lived when he wasn't holed up in his Xanadu castle in San Simeon. Inez had bought the property outright with cash in 1939. The estate had a carpet of manicured grass, an elaborate garden and a grove of fruit trees, the layout designed by Thomas Dolliver Church, one of the nation's premier landscape architects, and was maintained by a full-time gardener, Alfred, who pruned a multitude of rosebushes and sweet corn.[24] For granddaughter Caroline Brown, Inez bought a Shetland pony to ride at the ranch and in the Atherton house's backyard.

Inez bought son Bob Merritt and his wife, June, another magnificent estate in Atherton, this one at 116 Tuscaloosa Avenue, around the corner from the Brown family compound. Bob was Inez's favorite, and she had also bought him and June a San José house in the Rose Garden neighborhood on Morse Street, as well as another house in San Francisco at 550 Darien Way in Balboa Terrace.[25] In addition, Inez bought Bob's medical equipment when he first opened his practice in San Francisco at the Flood Building at 870 Market Street in 1937. Inez showered her daughter-in-law June with a diamond-encrusted watch and three fur coats—a mink, a beaver, and a seal coat. She gave the couple a sterling silver service for eight from Shreve & Co.[26]

To get to Burns Ranch, Inez and Joe, along with grandchildren William and Caroline, would drive on narrow mountain roads, the four of them singing "You Are My Sunshine," "Stella by Starlight," and "Little Alice Blue Gown." Joe loved to mimic the bellhop in the Philip Morris cigarette radio commercials, singing "Call for Phillip Morris!" so often that William and Caroline in the backseat would groan, "Not again!" Joe gave everyone a fright when he'd announce that he knew the hairpin-turn route so well that he could drive it with his eyes closed, and he'd open them only after the grandchildren screamed. Joe had a reputation for being a lousy driver on the straightaway, so closing his eyes on these winding back roads was asking for trouble, and everyone knew it.

Inez was able to import some glamour to the ranch through crooner Joaquin Garay. He was part owner of the Copacabana at 2215 Powell Street near Fisherman's Wharf, which doubled as a nightclub to showcase his own talent and to invite friends up from Hollywood.[27] Inez fronted shirtsleeve relative Tommy Harris to start House of Harris, a nightclub at 555 Sutter Street, billed as "San Francisco's Finest Supper Club." Through Garay and Harris, Inez had met burlesque comic Pinky Lee, who made several trips to Burns Ranch. Pinky was a funnyman who could compose the silliest and most ribald lyrics on the spot, bringing the house down. Other entertainers Inez invited included comedians Jerry Lester, Mae Williams, Frances Faye, and Tommy Farrell; singers Dwight Fiske and Burl Ives; hypnotist John Calvert; and a fez-wearing magician by the name Gali-Gali, who plucked squawking chickens out of thin air.

Back in San Francisco, granddaughter Caroline was spending more and more time with Inez and Joe. The three of them went out to dinner often, going to some of the most expensive restaurants in San Francisco, including Ernie's, Normandie, El Patio, and the Papagayo Room (where Caroline marveled over a pair of talking parrots) at the Fairmont.

For days on end, Caroline didn't go back home to Atherton, choosing to stay at

A poster advertising performances by entertainer Joaquin Garay at the popular Copacabana restaurant.

Inez and Joe's house, and often helping out at the clinic. Her attendance in school was spotty, and instead, little Caroline's job was to serve tea and cookies to the women in the waiting room. Sometimes, Inez baked the cookies, but just as often she'd send Musette or Myrtle over to her favorite bakery, Blum's, on the corner of Polk and California, and Caroline would serve sweets on a silver tray. For a treat, Inez would buy Blum's coffee crunch cake for just the two of them to savor.

Seeking to launder more and more of her income, Inez increasingly looked toward Los Angeles. On a trip there in 1938, Inez went house hunting and fell in love with a bungalow in the Hollywood Hills, adjacent to where bandleader Xavier Cugat and his wife, Abbe Lane, lived at 2277 El Contento Drive. Inez's home was southeast of Mulholland Drive, along the twisty, narrow, wooded streets of the neighborhood. Inez and Joe got to know Cugat and Lane, and went to parties at their home. There they met Fred Astaire and Rita Hayworth, who had starred with Cugat in *You Were Never Lovelier*, filmed in 1942. A year earlier, Inez had bought for first son, George, and his wife, Cecilia, a four-bedroom Los Angeles home at 1008 Hilts Avenue in the Westwood neighborhood near UCLA.[28] Inez kept her name off the title and put the property in Cecilia's name, ostensibly because of the fatal San Francisco delivery-truck accident George had been involved in years earlier.

Inez's nod toward Los Angeles was part of a cagey business expansion she hoped to pull off. Inez, Joe, and occasionally little Caroline would take the Lark, a deluxe all-Pullman-car Southern Pacific express train that left San Francisco in the evening and pulled into Los Angeles's Union Station the following morning at seven. They'd spend the weekend there, partying with Hollywood A-listers, and then return to San Francisco Monday or Tuesday.

Back home, Inez often summoned her favorite dressmaker, Molly Bergens, from Nelly Gaffney's shop, to measure both Inez and Caroline for clothes, down to their underwear. Inez had no modesty and would strip naked to be measured, as red-faced Caroline stood by, blushing from her grandmother's immodesty. For the Wednesday evening gatherings, Inez allowed Caroline to stay up late, serving drinks, cigars, and cigarettes. Caroline loved these nights with her grandmother holding court, talking about everything, from politics and booze to opera and politics. At age fifty-seven, Inez was still electric.

SIXTEEN

UNAPOLOGETIC

Arresting Inez and trying to close down her clinic became too tempting an opportunity for Pat to pass up as he traveled the state stumping in what had turned into an uphill battle to get elected attorney general. If Pat was going to mount any credible challenge against the Samish-anointed Fred Howser, Inez would have to go and she'd have to go big. The bigger the bust, the grander any subsequent trial; the bigger the splash, the better for Pat's political destiny.

Pat still didn't know his way around a criminal courtroom, so if Inez was to be brought down, it wouldn't be he who'd try her. Instead, Pat would rely on his pit bull of a first deputy, Tom Lynch, who had prosecuted Inez for tax evasion when he was an assistant US attorney. Lynch was champing at the bit to go after Inez again. "She was an ex-whore," Lynch would later say, reflecting on the twists and turns of his career. "The sooner she could be destroyed, the better."[1] Pragmatic Pat wasn't so doctrinaire. If shutting Inez down could help him and his career, then off with her head.

A decade earlier, when Inez had rubbed shoulders with San Francisco society at the War Memorial building, she'd been a curiosity, an aberration that opera socialites surely must have thought would have been vanquished by now. But in the intervening ten years, Inez had only flourished, growing richer and more powerful and influential. She had proved she had staying power. Her Fillmore Street clinic had become a statewide institution. All the while, Inez had continued to flit around town as though she was San Francisco's singular grande dame. No doubt, San Francisco heiresses in glittering jewels and flowing gowns were beneficiaries of ill-gotten gains, but those doyennes were from old-line pedigree families, not someone who had grown up dirt-poor and did what Inez did for a living. Inez's ubiquitous presence around town was embarrassing to more than a few heavyweights and their wives, and no one seemed to mind when Pat announced he intended to close down Inez. If they needed her services, they'd find her.

While abortion providers may have been essential to making society function smoothly, they also assumed a certain stigma, not unlike Inez's longtime friend Mabel Malotte and her house of prostitution on Bay Street. There was something unsettling and unsavory about both those professions despite their evergreen utility. Each business scratched the surface of human desires. In any society, there's an abundance of lawbreakers large and small, and deciding who to bring to justice always carries social and political implications. Former district attorney Matt Brady knew this. That's one of the reasons why he had stayed away from Inez and Mabel. As long as no one got killed on their premises, Good Ole Matt found no reason to go after either. But Mabel's profile hadn't been nearly as large as Inez's. Along with a solid standing as *the* city's fixer of "women's problems," Inez had also established an indelible citywide reputation: Rumors circulated of her profligate spending, poker playing, party giving, bribe paying, and profanity spewing. Then there were the stories of what went on at the secluded Burns Ranch: entertainers, exotic dancers, rafts of call girls. And the gossip: that Inez was an unapologetic libertine, a free spirit, a woman who played by a wholly different set of rules. Tales spread about how Inez had borne children out of wedlock, how she slept with men half her age even though she was the wife of a former state assemblyman. There were whispers of how Inez talked about sex, and worse, how she enjoyed it, even bragged about it. That she performed acts that drove men wild. That no woman's husband was safe around her. Some compared Inez to Wallis Simpson, the Baltimore seductress reputed to have stolen King Edward VIII through sexual prowess. All of these tongue-wagging accounts might even have been true. For Inez, they were badges of a kind of devil-may-care source of pride.

"To hell with 'em all," she said to Nettie over a cup of tea and biscuits one evening at the Guerrero Street house. "They're just jealous." From experience, all Nettie could do was shrug her shoulders and advise Inez to be careful, which didn't mean much when it came to her sister.

That Inez for decades had provided sterile and safe abortions wasn't Pat Brown's concern. That she had saved hundreds of women's lives from the unskilled hands of disreputable abortionists didn't seem to register with him. The show had gone on long enough, and Pat was more than happy to step in and bring down the curtain. What Inez had been doing was illegal, and Pat's first charge as district attorney was to enforce the rules of the land. If that sounded lofty and right, well, that's exactly how Pat wanted it to sound and play.

Pat's first bit of business was to convene a grand jury. In 1945, the procedures surrounding California grand juries were largely the same as they are today. Persons under investigation have no right to an attorney. Grand juries are usually convened in January and last through the end of the year; come the new year, a new grand jury is summoned with a new foreman and set of jurors. All testimony is cloaked in secrecy, and as such, the courtroom is locked and closed to the public; no public transcript is made of the proceedings. Subpoenaed witnesses can be compelled to answer all questions. The only attorney present is usually a prosecutor presenting evidence of alleged criminal wrongdoing. Verdicts need not be unanimous.

The rationale behind the draconian measures is to move quickly to trial, bypassing a preliminary hearing at which a judge may or may not decide whether the people have met the burden to bind a defendant over for trial. In San Francisco at the time, superior court judges nominated one hundred forty-four potential grand jurors, and the final number was winnowed to nineteen, usually well-heeled community leaders. Their nominal charge was to ferret out corruption within city government.

Could anyone possibly believe Inez *wasn't* guilty of bribing the police and pols so she could carry out her business? Almost everyone in town knew a woman who had gone to Inez, or knew a woman who knew a woman who had gone to Inez; and pretty much everyone was aware of the system of payola by which she had managed to stay open so long. Bringing Inez to her knees would be a piece of cake. Or so Pat figured.

His plan was to present straight-up evidence to the grand jury, get an indictment, then try Inez in superior court, obtain a guilty verdict, and remand Inez to state prison. At a press conference announcing his campaign to nail her, Pat estimated that Inez, along with other abortionists in San Francisco, had performed eighteen thousand abortions a year. That compared to fourteen thousand births annually, Pat said, feigning righteous shock and moral outrage to the assembled.[2] The city's abortion trade amounted to five million dollars annually, he railed. No wonder Inez had become one of the wealthiest women in California.

While grandstanding had always been among Pat's greatest strengths, he'd need credible evidence that would stand up in court, even if it was for a grand jury tilted to the prosecution. A dramatic raid would be Pat's preferred route, and that's what he, Tom Lynch, and Police Chief Dullea planned in the summer of 1945.

Two days before the raid, Inez received an urgent telephone call, then quickly hung up and shouted to everyone, "We gotta get outta here!"[3] When police cruisers careened down Fillmore and screeched to a halt in front of 327, the clinic was empty. Inez, her four assistants, and all her patients had already exited through two trap-doors,[4] and with them went Inez's instruments, anesthesia, tanks, cash, and ledgers. When police barged in, the clinic resembled a quiet, smartly appointed home.

Flummoxed, Pat and Dullea raided the clinic a second time, but this bust also fizzled, when like the first, Inez got tipped off, and when cops arrived, no one was there.[5]

Three weeks later, during the evening hours of September 26, 1945, police stormed the clinic a third time, and this time they netted gold. Cops found surgical records and a card index of patients, although police would later say that most of the records had either been destroyed or removed. Inez had already gone home, but Joe Hoff was still there and taken into custody. When police asked Joe what his job was, he offered straight-faced, "To dust off the furniture."[6] Two homicide inspectors had stormed the clinic, Frank Ahern and Al Corassa, along with Assistant District Attorney Andrew J. Eyman.

Not finding Inez, Ahern and Eyman raced to Guerrero Street while Corassa stayed behind. Police Inspector Ahern found Inez upstairs on the second floor, frantically tearing up pages pulled from a brown ledger book. He ordered her to stop and put the ledger down, which she did. Ahern then told Inez to open the big safe in the walk-in closet where she stored her hats.

"My god," Inez said to Ahern. "What are you trying to do to me? I'd rather die first before opening the safe."

A momentary standoff ensured, during which neither Inez nor Ahern budged. They just stared at each other with dagger eyes. When neither blinked, Ahern drew his revolver.

That prompted Inez to say calmly, "You can put that away."

Inez played the hand she knew. It was just the two of them. Why would this cop be different from any of the others?

Inez checked Ahern, a straitlaced, barrel-chested forty-five-year-old cop with a square face and chiseled chin who could have come from central casting. Ahern slowly put his gun back in the holster. That was more like it. Now maybe we can get somewhere, Inez figured.

"You wanna see what's inside?" she said, nodding toward the safe. "You wanna see why everyone comes to me? You wanna see what I'm worth?"

Inez was playing with Ahern.

"What's it worth for me to open it?"

"Just open the damn safe and shut up," Ahern told her.

"Let's see what you're made of, Inspector."

Ahern didn't like where this was going. "Open the damn safe," he said.

"You talk that way to all the ladies?" Inez replied.

"You open it here or we take it downtown," Ahern said. "Either way, this safe of yours is gonna git opened."

"I suppose you're giving me no choice, then?"

"Open the goddamn safe now!"

Inez went into the closet, knelt down, and peered at the big dial, spinning it right, then left, back left, then right again. As Inez spun the dial, both she and Ahern could hear the tumblers click, a clean, satisfying sound to both Inez and Ahern. When she was done, Inez cranked the handle down and to the right, and . . . nothing.

Inez pulled on the handle and still nothing.

"Dammit! I got this big safe and I can't even open it!" Inez said as much to herself as to Ahern, leaning over her shoulder.

Ahern figured Inez was bluffing, but truth was that Inez had never memorized the combination. Safes were a big production. That's why she preferred hiding cash anywhere but in the big, black safe. She had learned her lesson, though. At one time, she had had so much money scattered in so many places that she'd forgotten where it all was.

"With your permission," she said, getting up and going to her bedroom, then opening up the top drawer to a mahogany dresser and retrieving a folded piece of paper. Ahern followed Inez, taking out his gun again and holding it to the small of her back.

"You sure you wanna see what's inside?" Inez asked, as the two walked back to the closet.

"I said open the damn safe," stony Ahern repeated.

Inez knelt down again and turned the dial. "I got these two numbers reversed. I *always* do that!" she said more to herself than to Ahern.

This time when she cranked the handle, the heavy door swung open.

Perspiring, beads of sweat popping up on his forehead, Ahern took a flashlight from his belt, bent down, and shined it inside.

"Holy God!" Ahern said, scanning the safe's interior.

He'd never seen so much money. There were more than two dozen three-inch-thick bricks of cash, each tied with a red rubber band. Ahern counted each stack out loud. There were twenty-seven.

When he finished totaling them, Inez looked Ahern squarely in the eyes. Their noses were less than six inches apart.

"Drop the whole thing," she said, lowering her voice to a whisper, "and all this cash is yours."

Ahern didn't reply.

Did he want more?

"I'll make it three hundred thousand. And no one's ever gotta know. Between you and me. That's an *awful* lot of money, inspector."

"You want in?"

By now, Ahern's forehead was soaked. Inez could see his temples pounding.

"I don't do business that way," he shot back.

"Then how *do* you do business?"

When Ahern said nothing, Inez said, "I'll sweeten it by fifty thousand more. You ain't never gonna git another offer like this. In your lifetime. You better think long and hard about this, Inspector."

"I don't gotta think long and hard about nothing. You're getting charged with bribing a cop. And a lot more. Now clear away."

Inez didn't like this at all. This guy didn't want to play.

"You got any idea how many cops I've paid off?"

"Well, this cop ain't takin' part in that game."

"I can count on one hand the number of cops I *haven't* paid off. Just who do you think you are?"

Inez gave Ahern a moment to man up.

When nothing came forth from Ahern, she shook her head in disgust. "You know what? You're a damn fool! That's what you are. You'll never have to work another day in your life! Take the money for Christ's sake! What the hell's wrong with you?"

"Tell it to the judge," Ahern repeated and grabbed Inez by her arm.

The two of them walked down the steps to the parlor. Ahern handed Inez off to a pair of cops, then went back upstairs to the closet to scoop up the bricks of cash, putting them in a lockbox next to the safe. He threw in the two notebooks and paper chits, which, as he glanced at them, revealed names and scribbles of figures. He could make out the numbers: seven hundred thousand. All the while, cops from

Central had arrived and were rampaging through the downstairs, knocking over lamps, turning over tables and chairs, tracking mud on Inez's vintage Persian rugs. One cop brushed against Inez's marble Aphrodite, and as the statue teetered, about to topple over, Inez lunged to save.

"Damn you!" she said.

These cops were storm troopers, flexing their brawn, impervious to all that was civilized and enlightened. "Stop it!" Inez screamed. "Look what you've done! You're destroying my home! Get the hell out!"

The cops ignored her and continued their assault. One seemed to be tapping on the wooden walls, then fingering the curtain hems, and stamping on the floorboards. He was searching for hidden cash. Who had tipped him off about *that?*

"Do you know who I am?" Inez yelled to the cops. She got so agitated that Ahern had to come down and put handcuffs on her.

Joe finally arrived from Kavanaugh's and tried to calm Inez, though without much success. "Look what they'd done, look what they've done," Inez kept on saying. All Joe could do was shake his head.

Inspector Ahern took Inez to the Hall of Justice in one of the police cruisers, sirens blaring. Joe followed them in the Packard.[7]

Score one for Pat Brown.

After Ahern met with Pat that evening, Pat called a press conference the next morning and gloated over all the cash Ahern had found. There was no question where it had all come from—proof of Inez's wildly successful abortion business. Pat made no mention of Inez's bribe even though Ahern had told him all about it. Whether it would be before a grand jury or twelve jurors in a courtroom, Inez's offer to a cop was too good to let fly now. Pat knew there was a time and place for everything.

Pat allowed to the covey of reporters surrounding him that, along with the cash, Ahern had confiscated handwritten ledgers with, he said, "the names of several thousand women and notations of money paid," as well as "case history cards of patients" and "receipts for oxygen, ether, and other anesthetics."

But many of the records were missing, and once again, Pat realized that Inez must have been tipped off about the raid for a third time since neighbors on Fillmore Street said they saw her dash away with bags and boxes from the clinic in a black sedan moments before cops had arrived. There was something else curious: Even before any arrests had been made, Inez's attorney, James F. Brennan, and bail bondsman Edward "Red" Maloney had already made their way to the Hall of Justice and

(Left to right) Police Inspector Frank Ahern, Deputy District Attorney Jack Eyman, District Attoney Pat Brown, Deputy District Attorney Tom Lynch, November 8, 1945.

had been waiting for Inez to be brought in and booked, so they could immediately spring her with a two-thousand-dollar bond. Someone had tipped off Brennan and Maloney, too.[8]

From both the clinic and house, Ahern and the other police officers had confiscated an astounding seven hundred fifty thousand dollars.[9] At the clinic, they discovered a secret sliding panel in the rear of a clothes closet that led to the downstairs apartment, which had served as a getaway for Inez, her employees, and patients. All the cash and materials police confiscated amounted to the kind of evidence that prosecutors dream about. Inez was dead-to-rights guilty and Pat now had the proof.

Or so he thought.

After the raid, police did what they'd done when they'd busted Inez and Margie Silver at the clinic seven years earlier. Undercover female officers set up shop as though nothing had happened, answering the phone and making appointments. Thirty-three women called in four hours. Several women, noted by police as "well-dressed," showed up at the front door, but they hurried away when they realized that something wasn't quite right.[10]

Within two weeks, with the surfeit of evidence secured, a gleeful Pat Brown sought indictments from the grand jury for "suspicion of conspiracy to commit an abortion," subpoenaing a multitude of witnesses, including Inez's employees and suppliers. Meanwhile, Inez and four employees were arraigned before Municipal Judge Edward Molkenbuhr.[11] All pled not guilty.

Pat was working two separate tracks to get Inez and her codefendants behind bars: using the grand jury to proceed directly to trial and—the more usual route—presenting evidence to a municipal judge in a preliminary hearing. The charges against Inez and the four others were felonies, punishable by two to five years in prison *for each offense*. Depending on how many abortions the district attorney's office could prove that Inez and the others had performed and whether the prison terms would be served concurrently or consecutively, Inez and the others could be sentenced to state prison for a very long time. Consecutively served prison terms would be unlikely but absolutely possible.

Then something extraordinary happened.

Despite the overwhelming evidence against Inez, the grand jury on October 3, 1945, refused to indict Inez or any of her employees. At a subsequent press conference, Pat Brown had to endure the indignity of explaining how a "no bill" from the grand jury could possibly have happened. "I do not intend to dismiss the case," Pat said, stammering for the first time in his life. "I have no comment to make—at this time—on the grand jury's refusal to act. All available evidence was put in."

Les Vogel, foreman of the grand jury, as well as the owner of an immense Chevrolet dealership at the corner of Market and Van Ness Streets, said there just wasn't enough evidence to warrant an indictment, and then abruptly walked out of the press conference as though he had just remembered he had a cake baking in the oven at home.[12]

The spotlight now was on Pat. He was a candidate for statewide office, which undergirded why he had gone after Inez in the first place. Inez was central to his getting elected attorney general. All Pat needed was for Fred Howser to make hay out of this fumbling misstep. Artie Samish was probably laughing like a hyena somewhere. Pat had been caught flat-footed.

Pat's natural swagger came back the next day. "This case is going farther than anybody thinks," he teased reporters at another press conference, not getting into specifics. Pat trumpeted that records seized at Inez's properties showed "the names of a number of prominent San Francisco women," along with dates when abortions were performed and fees paid, adding that many of Inez's patients had come from throughout the state, "including Hollywood."

Then came the clincher.

Pat paused for dramatic effect, barely able to conceal his glee. The reporters leaned in.

Pat announced that he'd been approached by "persons in public life" who told him "how it would be politically dangerous to press the case" against Inez. Pat added that these persons, who had to remain unnamed, were people "with whom Mrs. Burns definitely had connections," and they were applying pressure on him. Pat dug in deeper, saying he'd been threatened with "coercive measures," whatever that really meant.[13]

"We cannot tell all we know right now," Pat said solemnly. "But we have plenty."

Then for the denouncement: "This office is not going to be bought!" Pat boomed. "I can tell you that!"[14]

It sounded like a real-life episode of *Mr. District Attorney*.

Politics being politics, Pat could have made up all these so-called threats. Pat never said who was pressuring him and he never went after anyone he said was strong-arming him. What were the means of the threats? On the telephone, in person, through intermediaries? No one ever found out.

Whether real or manufactured, the straw man tactic worked. Pat came across as the crime-and-racketeer-busting reformer. If this year's grand jury didn't indict Inez and a judge wouldn't bind Inez over to be tried in superior court, then Pat would convene yet another grand jury more to his liking. And if that didn't work, he'd convene another and another.

From her corner, Inez had plenty to blab far and wide. Hundreds of patients had given her insider information—who had impregnated them, under what circumstances, who was footing their bill. Inez could sing about which politicians and cops she'd paid off, for how long, and for how much. She could leak names of prominent patients Pat had intimated at his press conference. That'd only be as a last resort, though. Going public with names would cause tremors the likes San Francisco hadn't experienced since the Great Earthquake.

If Pat Brown pushed hard enough, Inez would push back. Even harder.

PART III

TREACHERY

(Left to right) Musette Briggs,
Inez Burns, Joe Hoff, Myrtle
Ramsey, and Mabel Spaulding.

Warren and Gloria Shannon.

SEVENTEEN

TRAITORS!

Brand-new Municipal Court Judge Harry J. Neubarth had the fortune, or misfortune, to be assigned to the much-anticipated preliminary hearing against Inez and her four clinic employees: Musette L. Briggs, Joe Hoff, Myrtle Ramsey, and Mabel Spaulding. Known as "Happy Harry" since he was a baby, Neubarth, forty-four, had been former district attorney Matthew Brady's chief deputy, and had just been appointed to the bench by Governor Warren. Two years earlier, Neubarth had been the lead prosecutor in a notorious case against jazz drummer Gene Krupa, charged with possession of two marijuana cigarettes, which sent Krupa to jail for eighty-four days.[1] Neubarth was a law-and-order judge, an ace-in-the-hole for Pat Brown and the prosecution.

That's one of the reasons it was so surprising that Tom Lynch and Pat would put together such a thorough, point-by-point case against Inez and the four other defendants so early in the process. Prosecutors don't need to tip their hand to the defense this early, at the preliminary-hearing stage; instead, they would usually present just enough to guarantee moving forward to trial. The plethora of evidence and testimony ordinarily would be aired at the superior court level. Surely, Neubarth would find just cause to try Inez. So why did Lynch lay out practically the state's entire case this early?

Maybe it was that Pat and Tom didn't want to take any chances after their debacle with the grand jury. Maybe they were just getting their ducks lined up in preparation for the big trial in superior court. One of the reasons for the full-court press had to be Pat's practiced routine of fanning a blizzard of pretrial publicity.

The prosecution's star witness was a twenty-one-year-old Oakland housewife by the name of Jerri Marsigli, who testified that she'd been referred to Inez by two Sutter Street bartenders known only as Delano and Bruno.[2] Mrs. Marsigli said that several minutes into the procedure she decided she "was not going through it." Inez advised the sedated Mrs. Marsigli that she was at the point of no return and wouldn't be allowed to leave until the abortion was completed. Nonetheless, Mrs. Marsigli bolted upright from the operating table, got up, and walked straight out the front door of the clinic, only to have a miscarriage several days later.[3]

A second patient, whose name was not disclosed, testified that after paying one hundred dollars, she underwent an abortion at Inez's clinic with no ill effects. Her testimony duly noted by the judge, the woman stepped down from the witness stand and left the courthouse. Twenty minutes later, while hurrying along Kearny Street near Clay, she took notice of a middle-aged man tailing her. He wore a fedora and a dark gray suit with a navy-blue tie. The man approached the woman and sharply grabbed her arm. "You'd better be careful," he said. "You're gonna be sorry. You're gonna be in for a lot of trouble."[4] Shaken, the woman returned to the courtroom and reported to Judge Neubarth what had happened.

When Lynch heard about the shakedown, he told Judge Neubarth that his wife, Virginia, had also received a threat, but at their home and on the telephone. "Tell your husband he'd better mind his own business," a male caller told Virginia Lynch, then abruptly hung up.[5] Judge Neubarth cautioned anyone to report further incidents of harassment directly to him.

Lynch and the prosecution presented a long line of state witnesses. Edward (Scotty) Scott, the owner of Grant's Pharmacy on Haight Street, testified that he had supplied ether and other anesthetics to Inez three to four times a month. Joe Zich, a truck driver for Ohio Chemical & Manufacturing Company, testified that he had dropped off tanks of oxygen and nitrous oxide to Inez's clinic on a regular basis. Herman Weniger told the court he had manufactured the two sets of stainless steel medical instruments seized in the September twenty-sixth raid.[6]

Lynch's case was proceeding like clockwork. To everyone in the courtroom, there was no way Judge Neubarth wouldn't bind the five defendants over for trial in superior court.

Then Inez's attorney, James Brennan, dropped a bombshell.

On the afternoon of the second day of the hearing, Brennan rose to his feet and announced to the judge, prosecution, press, and a gaggle of court watchers something that stunned everyone—except Inez.

Homer Davenport, father of
Gloria Shannon.

Brennan declared that Warren Shannon, Inez's friend and the former president of the San Francisco Board of Supervisors, and his wife, Gloria, had tried to extort money from Inez in exchange for their silence.[7]

The revelation was so shocking that for a moment there was silence in the courtroom. No one could quite believe his ears. Then everyone started talking at the same time, and Judge Neubarth had to bang his gavel, not once, but three times to quiet the chambers.

The charge of blackmail was outrageous, not just for what it was, but for whom Brennan said had made it.

Warren Shannon, sixty-five, had been one of San Francisco's best-known political figures for decades. He cut a distinctive figure around town: six-foot-two, two hundred fifty pounds, thinning gray hair, and blind in one eye. His wife, Gloria, forty-one, was the daughter of the late Homer Davenport, who had been one of the nation's preeminent political cartoonists, whose sketches used to run in Hearst newspapers coast to coast, including the *San Francisco Examiner*. Homer Davenport and President Theodore Roosevelt had been friends.[8]

On top of that, Inez had known Warren Shannon for years. She used to welcome him at her home, drank silver fizzes with him, played poker with him, and had offered him some of the best Cuban cigars money could buy. Along with cops, firefighters, doctors, dentists, and other politicians, Warren had been a member of Inez's parlor cabinet. When he met his third wife, Gloria, Inez had welcomed her too. The Shannons were the couple Inez had eaten dinner with at the Fairmont earlier in the year, and because of that encounter, Inez offered them her downstairs apartment at the clinic rent-free. Inez had given Gloria a job as a receptionist upstairs. And this is how they repay her?

Attorney Brennan declared to the court that Gloria Shannon had told him that she had seen everything that went on in the clinic and would sing about it—unless Inez paid her thirty-five thousand dollars.

Two days later, Gloria Shannon called a press conference and announced that she was writing an exposé about working in Inez's clinic, and titling it *San Francisco Slaughterhouse for Babies*. Gloria said that she and her husband had moved into Inez's apartment and that she had accepted Inez's job offer for the sole purpose of writing about what transpired upstairs.[9] The Shannons had set up Inez with their sob story that evening at the Fairmont, and seen-it-all Inez had fallen for it.

Gloria Shannon seemed to be fashioning herself as a journalist in the muckraking spirit of Nellie Bly, the reporter who had exposed a New York women's insane asylum,

(Left to right) Warren Shannon, Tom Lynch, Gloria Shannon, and Pat Brown.

or Upton Sinclair, the crusader who shocked the world with his account of meatpacking plants in Chicago.[10] Gloria Shannon said her manuscript contained purloined snapshots and records from Inez's clinic. She said she had already shopped her explosive account around and was eager to get it published. "It has been shown to lots of people, not only here, but down in Los Angeles and Hollywood, as well," Gloria crowed to the press.

Did the exposé contain names of high-profile patients or politicians on the take? she was asked. How did her eyewitness account incriminate Inez beyond the facts everyone knew?

Those were hole cards Gloria wouldn't flip over.

Unless Inez could come up with thirty-five thousand dollars, Gloria would seek to publish her potboiler, which she touted as "incendiary." At least, that's what attorney James Brennan told the court.[11]

When presented with their blackmail offer, Inez told the Shannons to go to hell, but likely used much stronger language. The nerve of her!

Gloria Shannon was someone to remember. Heavyset with coiffed dark-blonde hair, she walked with a pronounced limp, the result of an automobile accident during which her onetime fiancé had been killed.[12] She liked to talk, and when she got going, she didn't stop. The *San Francisco Examiner* characterized her as "volatile,"[13] but a better description might be "unhinged."

Even before Gloria and Warren had come up with the idea of the tell-all, Warren had tried to shake down Inez. Earlier in the year, he'd tried to force Inez into buying five hundred cases of whiskey, the origins of which were murky. When Inez refused, Warren grew testy and asked her again, more insistently this time, to come up with eight thousand dollars for the booze. At that point, Inez later recalled, "I began to see the handwriting on the wall."

When Inez refused, Warren tried another tactic. He told Inez he wanted to start a Hollywood nightclub with Gloria acting as the emcee in a role similar to that of Texas Guinan, the actress and entrepreneur who ran the 300 Club, a speakeasy in New York during the 1920s. For this, Warren demanded thirty-five thousand dollars from Inez. When she refused, Warren lowered his demand to twenty-five thousand dollars. For this, he said Gloria would destroy the diary she had kept while working in Inez's clinic.[14]

"My manuscript raises the question of who permitted her to operate all these years and how much did they get out of it,"[15] Mrs. Shannon teased a reporter about her exposé in search of a publisher. Hyping her story to attract more commercial interest, Gloria allowed that the abortions she said she witnessed were "brutal affairs," during which women who were unruly were slapped, pulled by their hair, and "treated abominably."[16]

When Inez refused to submit to the Shannons' blackmail, the couple responded by reporting Inez to the Bureau of Internal Revenue, on the condition that the Treasury Department reward them with ten percent of any funds recovered.[17] It was a proposition the federal bureau politely turned down.

Did Gloria and Warren Shannon have any idea whom they were dealing with? Did they have any clue whom Inez knew, what the stakes were, or what Inez was capable of?

The spiraling drama had everyone speculating—and that was before what was to happen next.

The Shannons vanished.

Immediately, there was speculation that the couple had been murdered or muscled out of town by the mob on orders from Inez. All of San Francisco held its breath for the missing couple to surface, dead or alive.

What a hand Pat Brown had just been dealt!

Pat directed Police Chief George Dullea to issue an all-points bulletin to find the missing Shannons. Both were all-in.

It turned out the couple's disappearance was a well-concocted publicity stunt so Gloria could further fan her account of what she said she saw inside Inez's clinic. The couple's disappearing act was a pay-to-play scheme to draw even more attention to Gloria's unsold alleged true detective story.

The Shannons hatched their extortion scheme once Gloria saw how much cash Inez was taking in. After working three months, Gloria told Inez that she and Walter were getting back on their feet financially. They appreciated Inez's goodwill and thanked her. They moved out of the apartment and into the Lake Merritt Hotel in Oakland, driving there in the 1938 Buick sedan Inez had given them as a present.[18] It was at this point when the Shannons opted to play the blackmail card, and after Inez rebuffed them, the pair slipped out of the Bay Area on a mysterious two-week southwestern odyssey, first to the Padre Hotel in Bakersfield, where they registered as Mr. and Mrs. Cooper, then to Hollywood, Las Vegas, the Texas border, and Ensenada and Chihuahua, Mexico, all the while telling anyone who'd listen that they were on the run and fearful for their lives.[19] Gloria and Warren surfaced in El Paso, Texas, where Gloria told a newspaper reporter that the title of her forthcoming exposé had grown exponentially to *My Memories in the Midstream of Life After an Intimate View of San Francisco's Slaughterhouse for Babies*.

"It's loaded to the hilt with dynamite," Gloria said. "I don't know where it's going to blow me, but it's going to blow. San Francisco has danced to Inez Burns's tune for twenty years at least. It's time to call another tune. Like Margaret Mitchell and 'Gone with the Wind,' this is my first masterpiece," Gloria told the *San Francisco Examiner*. "I have in it 12,000 words now. Before I get through it will probably be two volumes."[20]

Gloria wrote a friend that she had offered her account to several magazines, including *Literary Digest* and *True Stories*, and that by doing so, "this proves that it is not blackmail."[21]

Oh.

P. T. Barnum had nothing on Gloria Shannon. She soon had an entire state eating out of her hand. The newspapers loved reporting on the on-the-run couple; the Shannons were a terrific circulation booster. Pat Brown didn't mind, either—so much so, that he doubled down on the Shannons.

Pat wasn't exactly sure what Gloria had on Inez, but whatever it was, it wasn't going to hurt him. When the Shannons surfaced in Phoenix, a week before

Patrons of Hotel Westward Ho relaxing
on the grounds in the 1940s.

Christmas, Pat Brown and Tom Lynch got on a plane and flew to meet them. With a nod from Pat, so did the San Francisco reporters chasing the story. The Shannons, Brown, and Lynch met for three hours at the Hotel Westward Ho's coffee shop, as reporters milled around outside, smoking cigarettes and checking their watches. When the meeting finally concluded, Pat held an impromptu press conference to announce that he had "learned plenty," but as was his routine, he couldn't elaborate other than to say, "Mrs. Shannon asked me to meet them here in Phoenix because she was afraid some harm might befall her once she arrived in San Francisco."[22]

Pat announced that he personally was committed to providing the Shannons with around-the-clock police protection when they returned to San Francisco (whether they needed it or not). For her part, Gloria Shannon promised the reporters that her soon-to-be-published revelations would "finish abortions in the United States and the butchery that goes with them." She closed with a line spun from a very bad pulp-fiction magazine: "I'm Rasputin Jr. I'd get chummy with Jack the Ripper. I'm not afraid of any living person."[23]

While all this was going on, back at the preliminary hearing in San Francisco, Police Inspector Frank Ahern had testified about the bribe Inez had offered him upstairs at her home. "Mrs. Burns asked me to take some of the money in the safe and let everything go," the officer testified.[24] Ahern told the court the piles of cash amounted to $289,217.[25] This was the first public disclosure of Inez's attempt to bribe to Ahern and it, too, made headlines.

The preliminary evidence against Inez was overwhelming, and on December 5, 1945, Judge Neubarth surprised no one when he ruled that Inez and the four other defendants would be tried for felony conspiracy to commit abortion, as well as practicing medicine without a license. Two potential defendants in the case were excused, part-time clinic employees Madeline Rand and Virginia Westrup, for "lack of evidence."[26] Both women had traded their alleged culpability to turn state's evidence.

Trials with so many defendants—there would be five—are not daily legal fare. Prosecutors try to turn defendants against each other by offering plea deals, including immunity, in exchange for incriminating testimony. But no way was Pat Brown going to offer any deal to Inez. She was to be his prize. That's why Pat had busted Inez in the first place—to get the headlines that would bury his opponent Fred Howser in the upcoming election for attorney general.

It was her codefendants that had Inez worried; any of them might flip against her to save themselves from a prison term. Each was playing a game of chicken: It was a test of nerves and loyalty, perhaps with the perception of fear tossed in for good measure. A friend of Inez's utility man, Joe Hoff, said, "I asked him to have a beer when I saw him in a bar, and he nearly jumped off the stool."[27] In the end, all four defendants stayed true to Inez.

Even for the well-connected Inez, shimmying out of the charges would be near impossible, and Inez responded the way any defendant with money does: She shopped around for the best attorney, one with pull and prestige, far more than stand-in James Brennan had.[28]

Although her safe had been emptied, Inez still had plenty. She asked for names from her brain trust of Wednesday-evening confidants. At the time, San Francisco's biggest defense attorneys were Vincent Hallinan and Jake "The Master" Ehrlich. Both were occupied. Hallinan was lead counsel in a blockbuster case, defending socialite Irene Mansfeldt, charged with murdering her husband's nurse, with whom she suspected he was having an affair.[29] Ehrlich had his own headline-grabbing trial, defending Alfred Leonard Cline, charged with murdering nine wealthy widows he legally married in eight states by insisting they drink a glass of buttermilk laced with rat poison.[30]

Inez ultimately chose Walter McGovern, a native San Franciscan born in Rincon Hill, who had been a state senator, as well as the head of the city's police commission. McGovern was a smart and strategic choice. Besides being a gifted attorney, he was allied with the city's old political guard. McGovern was as well connected as anyone in San Francisco. A Civil War and California history buff, he apprenticed as a law clerk before being appointed assistant district attorney; when elected state senator, he received the largest majority recorded from his downtown district.[31] As the president of the three-member police commission, McGovern oversaw a reorganization of the department, although from all indications, that meant officers and brass were shuffled through a revolving door and stayed in the same place. A Republican, McGovern had been a California delegate to the national convention that nominated dark horse Wendell Wilkie for president against Franklin Roosevelt in 1940.

But most of all, Walter McGovern hated Pat Brown.

Large and portly with a flat moon face, McGovern had the nervous tic of twisting a gold signet ring he wore. He had bellows for pipes. Everyone inside a courtroom not only heard what McGovern said, but listened. The *San Francisco Chronicle* called McGovern, sixty-two, "one of the city's great trial lawyers."[32] Columnist Herb Caen went further, labeling McGovern "one of the greatest trial lawyers in the country."[33]

(Left to right) Inez Burns, Mabel Spaulding, Myrtle Ramsey, Musette Briggs, and Joe Hoff.

Facing off against Walter McGovern in superior court trial would be Tom Lynch, Inez's longtime antagonist. If anyone had a vendetta against Inez, Pat Brown included, it was Lynch. He'd been one of Pat's first hires in the DA's office. Lynch was forty-two and, like everyone else in town, had forever known of Inez and what she did for a living. With slicked-back, jet-black hair, Lynch had a coiled alertness about him. Lynch and Pat had been best friends for more than two decades. They had met their wives together on a hiking trip in Yosemite.

Tom Lynch and Pat Brown were each other's yin and yang: Tom was detail-compulsive, and Pat was broad brushstroke; Tom had to work to turn on any charm he could manufacture, while charm oozed from every pore of Pat's body; Tom was an intellectual, while Pat's effusive personality trumped any necessity for depth.

But if the *People v. Inez Burns et al.* was going to be the momentous trial de-signed to showcase Pat Brown to the rest of California, why didn't Pat try the case himself? If Lynch won, the victory surely would belong to Pat. If Lynch lost, it'd be Lynch who had squandered away the win.

But there was the undeniable issue of experience: Pat had none in a criminal courtroom, whereas Lynch was a career litigator. Perhaps as important, Pat had bet-ter things to do with his time than try a complicated case with five defendants, with a statewide election around the corner.

Broad-stroke Pat's métier wasn't in the courtroom, anyway. The last thing he needed was the daily burden of preparing an elaborate case, managing scores of witnesses. That was lawyers' work, and Pat hired attorneys to do the grueling work of going to trial. Pat was more interested in playing to the court of public opinion. He had an election to win.

The trial was set for mid-February 1946, which gave a host of other hustlers, in addition to the Shannons, time to milk the matchup for whatever they could. Charles Rand, the husband of Inez's former clinic employee Madeline Rand, who'd been dropped as a defendant in exchange for her testimony, tried to sell Pat Brown information about who had tipped off Inez to the police raids of the clinic, an offer Brown refused.[34] The brother of one of Inez's patients also came forward, telling Inez's old attorney, James Brennan, that his sister had "been ruined" by getting an abortion at Inez's hands; he demanded twenty thousand dollars in hush money or he'd go public with his story.[35] It was another offer Pat turned down.

As Lynch and his investigators were beating the bushes to find as many of Inez's patients and former employees as they could, they thought they'd scored big when they located anesthesia nurse Levina Blanchette Queen, who had worked on and off for Inez for years. But when they showed up at her door at 2070 Tenth Avenue in the Forest Hill neighborhood, Mrs. Queen was so terrified of the prospect of testifying against Inez that she scaled a rear fence while wearing just a nightie and fur coat, and went missing. Police issued a warrant for Mrs. Queen, calling her a fugitive from justice. She had seemingly disappeared.[36]

On December 28, 1945, Warren and Gloria Shannon finally arrived back in San Francisco, Gloria's explosive manuscript in tow. That same day, they said wormy private detective Eugene Aureguy, now on retainer for Inez, had cozied up to them and threatened them, offering them "all the money you need" if they agreed not to testify against Inez. When they balked, the Shannons said Aureguy issued them a warning: "It's better to be a horse's neck than to be a dead horse."[37] Whatever it meant, it wasn't good.

As the year drew to a close, Warren Shannon was asked whether as a member of the board of supervisors for two decades and as San Francisco's acting mayor, he had known about Inez's clinic, and his answer was absolutely yes. "So did the chief of police," Shannon proclaimed, as did "the people of San Francisco. When twenty or thirty women are going into a place every day, it's bound to attract attention. That sort of information spreads around."[38]

All of San Francisco seemed poised for the upcoming trial. It would be a referendum not just for or against Inez Burns, but for or against abortion. Like San Francisco's unrelenting fog and persistent hills, everyone had accepted Inez as part of the city's landscape. Tens of thousands of women had trusted Inez for decades. Now, rather suddenly, Pat Brown and Tom Lynch were about to declare that everything Inez had done for all these years ought to be considered wrong and illegal. And as punishment, Inez ought to be sent to prison.

Pat was glowing with such a prospect, waxing rhapsodic about the trial and where it might take him. "My objectives in the Burns case are two: first to convict Mrs. Burns; and second, to probe into the ramifications of this case and find out just how these things happen. I want to know all about it. I'm going to find out too. I'm not kidding."[39]

Meanwhile, as Gloria and Warren Shannon were celebrating New Year's Eve at a North Beach café, a man known only as Frenchy silently accosted Warren, placing a shiny silver bullet on the bar in front of Warren and then disappearing into the cool night.[40]

EIGHTEEN

THE OTHER SHOE

If the revelations of the Shannons' extortion attempts, the couple's subsequent disappearance, and their peripatetic Southwest odyssey to spark a bidding war to sell Gloria's exposé was one shoe, then the actual publication of her tell-all account was the other shoe. And it didn't just drop. It exploded.

The *San Francisco Examiner* ran the first installment of Gloria's eyewitness account on January 20, 1946. Perhaps the other outlets she had offered the manuscript to hadn't been as taken by the scoop as she and the *Examiner* editors were. There's no record of what the *Examiner* paid Gloria, but it was likely much less than the thirty-five thousand dollars the Shannons had tried to squeeze from Inez to kill the story. To whip the revelations into shape, *Examiner* editors hired Elenore Meherin, a popular Hearst writer and author of *Chickie*, a jazz age romance about a stenographer who dreams of marrying a millionaire.[1] But whatever Meherin did wasn't enough, or maybe it was too much.

Gloria Shannon's first-person tale appeared in the Sunday newspaper above the fold and above the mast, in screaming block letters:

MRS. WARREN SHANNON EXPOSES
INEZ BURNS' HOUSE OF HORRORS

Tells Inside Story of Girls' Suffering and Woman's Greed
Those Lacking Money Told 'Earn It on Streets'

MRS. WARREN SHANNON EXPOSES INEZ BURNS' HOUSE OF HORRORS

Tells Inside Story Of Girls' Suffering And Woman's Greed

Those Lacking Money Told 'Earn It on Streets'

Here is the inside story of an abortion "mill" with all its sordidness—its tragedies—its callousness—and its undermining of public officials and underlings through the "payoff."

In the hope of arousing public consciousness, Mrs. Gloria Davenport Shannon, member of a distinguished American family, daughter of the famed political cartoonist, has made available to The Examiner a manuscript of her personal observations of the abortion "mill" of Inez Burns.

This is the first chapter of what is probably the most unusual story ever written of one of America's important social problems—a problem not unique to San Francisco but present in every large city in the United States.

By GLORIA DAVENPORT SHANNON
Copyright by Hearst Publications, Inc., 1946

Every fifteen minutes a baby went to its death. A river of blood ran out of that house.

It is such a quiet looking place. The curtains are newly laundered. They are crisp and home like. And the tan stucco has a modest aspect. You'd think honest people lived there, kind and happy people.

Things more appalling than murder went on. For this is the House of Death. This is the Inez Burns' Abortion Mill at 327 Fillmore street. Inez Burns whose business cards read, Inez L. Brown, Designer, but who proudly and openly boasted, "I am the greatest abortionist in the United States," and whose intimates include men who hold and who have held key positions in San Francisco life.

Cleanliness Ends at Door

You've read stories of girls butchered. You recall the scene in "An American Tragedy," when Clyde leads the girl a later kille to that sordid back alley in the hope of getting rid of their unwanted baby. You've read of men in bloody smocks operating without anaesthetics, and the ferocious old women endure to kill the child of their unsanctioned passion.

The Burns' establishment is not of this type. It has a clean, pleasant exterior. It is in a respectable neighborhood of fine homes, except the rare few who refuse it, are given a anaesthetic.

With these, the difference between 327 Fillmore Street and other slaughter houses for the unborn, ends.

There's no decency, no cleanliness, no human consideration in women endure to kill the child of their unsanctioned passion.

'Surgery' on Top Floor

The sheets on those beds are used for ten days without being changed. One girl gets out. Before the bed can be soothed, another topples in. The towel on the operating table be changed only when it is red with blood. Disinfectants are not permitted in the laundry, since there may not be clothes. Soap is curtailed. The water in which the unseasoned linen has been boiled is used to scrub the kitchen floor.

In this establishment, the main operating room is on the top floor. This is set back and escapes a hasty glance from the street.

A strange, clever, lonely woman, wickedly tempered with deft hands and torrential energy sits on a stool before the narrow table and for six hours every day, butchers women.

This woman sells death. Some pay $100—her minimum for murder. Some pay $300. For the nervous shock, for menace to health and the crime against society, no reckoning is made.

Inez enjoys her work. She sits on that stool and eats lunch with the reek of a young girl's blood in her nose. A friend walks casually in and tell a joke. A bank clerk nods at the table while Inez finishes an operation. He idly discusses a wife he has drawn for the children of the abortionist. A policeman in full uniform enters and is told to go right on up. Nobody cares for the girl or woman so shockingly posed.

'Smile, Damn You, Smile'

Girls of 16—frightened, bewildered kids—clutching their mothers—in cheap patent leather bags, come up those steps in mute forced—a symbolic thirteen steps for them, they rely are. Short while ago, those girls, full of "oomph" coquetter, were baptized at Playland as they whirled on roller coaster with the boys they thought they loved. were wise kids who knew the score and never dreamed r Life with its ruthless consequences would catch up on them.

They're not hard boiled or sophisticated as they climb to the table and face the contemptuous eyes of Inez Burns. mile, damn you, smile!" Inez orders as the mask is slipped g the blanched, cowering face. Sobbing or laughing, re are terrified and obey.

Wives too, come up those steps. Sometimes they bring ding of their 2 with them. Tragedies take play in the kitchen the frail jests of the attendants; hearing the moans of tim as an unborn brother or sister is dispatched. Often a boy and girl approach the place together. Boy is never admitted. He goes to the drug store across

(Continued on Page 14, Col. 1)

Von Wiegand says:

U. S. Must Lead World or Bow to Russia

By KARL H. VON WIEGAND
Head of American Foreign Correspondence
Written Exposes for the Hearst Newspapers

WASHINGTON, Jan. 19.—AMERICA, LOOK TO YOUR LEADERSHIP IN WORLD AFFAIRS! LEAD or give up pretensions!

Stop giving away the world and your own country.

Spiritual, moral, economic and material world leadership was WON for America and THRUST INTO THE HANDS OF AMERICAN STATESMEN by the victories and sacrifices of OUR BOYS on land, sea and in the air in the great war.

THAT LEADERSHIP IS IN GRAVEST DANGER FROM EXTERNAL RIVALRY AND PRESSURE AND INTERNAL WEAKNESS, VACILLATION AND UNDERMINING.

I have called attention to that before, and cited proofs.

My few days in Washington after fourteen months in a Europe which has turned to COMMUNISM and SOCIALISM, not to TRUE DEMOCRACY for which we fought, have impressed me still more with the

(Continued on Page 7, Col. 1)

San Francisco Examiner

AN AMERICAN PAPER — AMERICA FIRST — FOR AMERICAN PEOPLE

Monarch of the Dailies

VOL. CLXXXIV, NO. 20 — COCC — SAN FRANCISCO, SUNDAY, JANUARY 20, 1946

Sensational Expose Aids Vice Inquiry

Book Gives Names

By RICHARD T. HYER
As District Attorney Edmund G. Brown cleared the decks yesterday to widen his abortion investigation into a full scale expose of vice and corruption, a wealth of new information was made available to him through Gloria Davenport Shannon's sensational book.

Publication of the unique document, which is an eye-witness account of what went on in the Burns' alleged surgery mill at 327 Fillmore Street, begins in today's Examiner and will continue in daily installments.

PROBE LIST.

Although certain names are being withheld pending completion of official investigations, all of the information will be placed in the hands of Assistant District Attorney Norman Elkington, whom Brown has placed in charge of the expanded inquiry.

It includes, in addition to its shattering descriptions of the actual operations at 327 Fillmore Street, episodes and deals which involve five doctors not yet brought into the probe.

Two of these physicians are Navy doctors. Two more are East Bay physicians. The fifth is a San Franciscan.

The astonishing narrative also involves a major San Francisco hospital and one of its amenities with the Burns establishment.

KEY FIGURES.

Its key figures include a number of persons who hold, or have

(Continued on Page 4, Col. 1)

Mass Russ Suicide

Ordered Home by U. S. Army

FRANKFURT (Germany), Jan. 19.—(AP)—Ten Russians committed suicide and twenty-one others injured themselves at Dachau today in protests against attempts to repatriate them to Russia, United States headquarters announced.

Headquarters said that "some, at least," of the 271 Russian nationals being repatriated from Dachau had served in the German armed forces.

PUT ON TRAIN.

Most of the Russian nationals who loaded aboard a train for Russia yesterday afternoon, headquarters said, but one group objected strenuously.

Gen. Joseph T. McNarney, commander of United States forces in the European theater, said the United States was determined to fulfil its Yalta promise to return Soviet nationals "by force if necessary," and had sent the gas to subdue the recalcitrants.

THE CIE.

When the melee ended thirty-one were taken to hospitals with injuries which the announcement said were self inflicted, either by hanging or throat cutting. Ten of these died.

Details of the incident were not fully reported here by General McNarney said:

"As part of an agreement with the Soviet Union at Yalta, the policy of the United States has been to facilitate early repatriation of Soviet citizens. More than 2,000,000 already have been repatriated from western Germany, leaving perhaps less than 20,000 in the United States zones.

"Although—this program of repatriation may in some cases involve use of force, which in certain isolated instances may result through fear and hysteria in self-destruction, it is necessary to point out the United States Governmental policy is firm, clear and resolutely stated, and that as the easier commander we orders have been to carry out my government's decisions."

The Tragedy Of Truman

(Number 1 in Series of Four)

By SAMUEL CROWTHER

On the night of Thursday, January 3, President Truman, speaking over the radio from the White House, asked the American people to join with Sidney Hillman's Political Action Committee in bringing pressure upon the Congress to enact a program of legislation which would socialize America and foreclose what remains of American freedom.

Principally Mr. Truman urged that the despotic powers granted on the pretense they were needed for war, be strengthened and extended into peace.

He asked that the Office of Price Administration's (OPA) powers to dictate the price at which a citizen may buy or sell his goods and services be confirmed into the far future.

Asks Laws to Extend Power

In addition, he asked for the passage of laws extending the already vast Federal bureaucracy through new or bigger agencies to look after employment, medical care "antidiscrimination" and "full employment."

And finally he asked for a bill to settle labor disputes by referring them to fact-finding boards which he would appoint.

The program advanced by President Truman is, with the exception of the "fact-finding" boards, the program of the PAC-CIO.

It is even more drastic than that of the popular front which reduced a once powerful France to a mere shell that collapsed at a touch by the Germans. It is even more drastic than the British labor program which has reduced that once great nation to a mendicant bitterly standing on the international street corner snarling for alms.

The American people have wanted to believe in Harry S. Truman. They have wanted to believe in him as a plain American who would never yield to the superman delusion and who would battle to rid the White House of the despotism which a series of rubber stamp Congresses and the war had lodged there.

The people have hoped and prayed that President Truman would use the transition from war to peace to mark a transition from control OF the people to control BY the people.

Our Nation Is in Crisis

In the beginning the Truman words were fair and heartening. Now it stands revealed that Harry S. Truman, no matter how good were his original intentions and no matter how good are his present intentions, is President of the United States in name only.

Today our Nation is in crisis. There is no point in being optimistic or pessimistic. Those words are worn out. The facts are plain.

We have passed, with the speed that night follows day and with scarcely a twilight, from being the world's deep

(Continued on Page 2, Col. 1)

U. S. Threatens Koreans in Fighting

Warns Nation May Be Put Under Trusteeship

By HOWARD HANDLEMAN
SEOUL (Korea), Jan. 19.—(AP)—The American occupation officials today ordered the Korean people to cease violent political demonstrations after two persons were killed, seven wounded and 120 arrested in disturbances last night and early today.

Lt. Gen. John R. Hodge and Maj. Gen. Archer L. Lerch warned the Koreans that unless the rioting is stopped, Korea will be put under the trusteeship she is seeking. The main burden of the disturbances occurred at dawn today when 200 Korean policemen

(Continued on Page 5, Col. 2)

Iran Asks UNO To Sift Row With Russ

Charges Meddling in Internal Affairs

LONDON, Jan. 19.—(AP)—Iran appealed to the United Nations Security Council today to investigate its dispute with Russia over the presence of Russian troops in the Iranian province of Azerbaijan.

Iranian delegate Nasrullah Entezam said his delegation had submitted a letter asking an investigation of what the Russian delegation contends is "Soviet interference with the internal affairs of Iran."

J. N. O. Masik of Australia, who probably will call a meeting to consider the issue. The appeal to the UNO was

(Continued on Page 5, Col. 2)

Russ Persecuting Catholics in Ukraine, Pope Pius Charges

By MICHAEL CHINIGO
International Staff News Service
VATICAN CITY, Jan. 19.—Patriarch Alexis, head of the Russian Orthodox Church, and Ruthenian faithfuls to defection from the Catholic Church.

In launching "wounds" inflicted by peoples of the persecution, the Pope expressed deep anxiety and early today.

Lt. Gen. John R. Hodge and Maj. Gen. Archer L. Lerch warned the Koreans that unless the rioting is stopped, Korea will be put under the trusteeship she is seeking.

(Continued on Page 5, Col. 2)

Steel Strike Starts; U. S. Seizure Remote

East Bay Mill Picketed

All production was halted yesterday at the Columbia Steel Company plant at Pittsburg in Contra Costa County when CIO Local 1440 of the CIO Steel Workers Union struck before the scheduled hour.

Bethlehem Steel Company reported operations proceeding normally at its South San Francisco plant, where the union prepares to strike at 12:01 a.m. tomorrow.

The union said three steel fabricating companies in Alameda County met union wage demands and will continue to operate.

Steel workers' pickets appeared unexpectedly at gates of the Columbia plant Friday night.

EXPLANATION.

Joe Milnor, union general agent, said the action was taken after the company moved an ice box and large quantities of food into the plant. He said the company refused to meet with the union to arrange an orderly shutdown.

"We have no intention of operating the plant," said Charles Hone, company spokesman. "If an ice box was moved in it was an old one and will be used to store food for the general superintendent, department superintendents and their assistants, who will remain on duty as a fire watch."

The union permitted its members to remain at their jobs until the last blast furnace was tapped at 4 a.m. yesterday.

CLOSE FIGURE.

Closed in addition to the furnaces by the strike of an estimated 2,200 men were a rolling mill, rod mill, wire mill, wire rope mill, sheet mill and casting foundry.

A. F. Campo, representative of CIO Local 1367 at Oakland, said contracts granting the union a 25 cent hourly increase were signed by the Judson Steel Corporation, Pacific State Steel Corporation and Jacuzzi Pump Company, fabricators whose steel employment is 600 men.

Negotiations will continue centered in the eighty-two-day old East Bay area machinists' strike awaited the vote this afternoon

(Continued on Page 2, Col. 1)

Kaiser, CIO Sign Pact

WASHINGTON, Jan. 19.—(AP)—Henry J. Kaiser signed up today under President Truman's compromise wage plan to keep his California steel plant in operation while the bulk of the industry got set for an economy-shaking shutdown Monday.

The CIO steelworkers, meanwhile, reported that they were dickering for additional breaks in the industry front against their demand for a boost for at least 18½ cents an hour.

Kaiser's contract assured continued operation for his plant at Fontana, Calif.

JUMP GUN.

Elsewhere 750,000 CIO steelworkers were ready to walk out of 1,300 steel plants as of 12:01 a. m. Monday in a crucial recon-version struggle. Some jumped the gun.

An official close to the presidentially-sponsored negotiations which collapsed yesterday said there was no indication that the White House would initiate any new steel move such as Government seizure before the walkout.

President Truman had suggested the 18½ cent increase as a compromise between the Union's 19½ cent demand and the United States Steel Corporation's counter of 15 cents. The corporation accepted here as representing the entire industry concentrated in the East and Midwest, turned it down as too high.

(Continued on Page 2, Col. 2)

Twenty-nine Hurt In Trolley Crash

LOS ANGELES, Jan. 19.—(INS)—Twenty-nine persons were recovering in their homes today from slight injuries received when two street cars collided last night at the north end of the Broadway tunnel.

All were treated at the Georgia Street Receiving Hospital for their bruises and sent home.

28,000 Pacific Vets Due by February

YOKOHAMA, Jan. 19.—Eighth Army headquarters announced today that approximately 28,000 low-point Pacific veterans will be on their way home by the middle of February.

Away 3 Palaces

TOKIO, Jan. 19.—(AP)—Emperor Hirohito was granted permission by General MacArthur today to give away three palaces, worth nearly $1,000,000.

Hakone Palace, valued at more than $250,000, was bestowed on the Kanagawa prefecture. Hamo-Detached palace, valued at $350,000, was given to the city of Tokio. Akasaka Palace, valued about $130,000, went to the city of Kobe. Lands accompanying each gift are worth an estimated $13,000.

Hirohito to Give

THE WEATHER
San Francisco Bay Region—Partly cloudy. Light variable winds.

The lurid details contained in what was billed as the first in a series were as yellow as any newspaper has ever printed, even for the founder of yellow journalism himself, William Randolph Hearst. In an explanatory note that preceded the story, the pretext for publishing the account was explained this way:

"This is the first chapter of what is arguably the most unusual story ever written of one of America's important social problems—a problem not unique to San Francisco but present in every large city in the United States."

Then came the outrageous opening:

"Every fifteen minutes a baby went to its death. A river of blood ran out of that house.

"It is such a quiet looking place. The curtains are newly laundered. They are crisp and home like. And the tan stucco has a modest aspect. You'd think honest people lived here, kind and happy people.

"Things more appalling than murder went on. For this is the House of Death. This is the Inez Burns Abortion Mill at 327 Fillmore Street. Inez Burns, whose business cards read, Inez L. Brown, Designer, but who proudly and openly boasted, 'I am the greatest abortionist in the United States!' And whose intimates include men who hold and who have held key positions in San Francisco life."

And Gloria Shannon was just warming up. She went on to describe Inez as "a strange, clever, lonely woman, wickedly tempered but with deft hands and torrential energy [who] sits on a stool before the narrow table and for six hours every day butchers the unborn.

"Inez enjoys her work. She sits on that stool and eats her lunch with the reek of a young girl's blood in her nose.

"This gayest, friendliest, most beautiful of cities has become the Mecca for mothers both married and unmarried who wish to get rid of their children. Here abortion is protected, here it is safe to kill the unborn, here a woman openly boasts she is the greatest American peddler in illegal death.

"Abortion—getting rid of a little human thing that might come to love the flowering hillside, that might rejoice in a gallop through the woodlands as I had rejoiced; a child whose laughter is that loveliest of music—I could as readily have taken a knife and slit the throat of the mother I adored as I could contemplate killing a little unborn soul."[2]

The story instantly commanded everyone's attention, including Inez, who responded by writing a three-page letter to the editor of the competing *San Francisco*

Chronicle, delivered "by special unidentified messenger." On lavender-tinted stationery, Inez wrote in neat cursive penmanship that Gloria Shannon's allegations were "nothing but vicious lies, ravings of a woman gone insane over money." Rebutting an allegation in the story that Inez advocated a permissive lifestyle, Inez remonstrated, "I have never advised any girl to do anything immoral."

But the absolute worst calumny alleged in Gloria's barbed account had nothing to do with morals or what Inez did for a living. What rankled Inez the most was Gloria Shannon's vilification of Inez's clinic as "squalid." Inez couldn't let stand such vilification. Inez shot back: "I cannot tolerate dirt and filth. Anyone acquainted with me knows that is true."

Inez was livid at the Shannons' betrayal, now in black and white for everyone to see. She'd been double-crossed and stabbed in the back at the same time. Inez wrote that she had known Warren Shannon for decades. "He has had many meals and drinks at my home. The Shannons aroused my sympathy. I was kind to them. Gloria pleaded for help and assistance. She had no place to live and was heavily in debt. I took them in and bought them a car because Warren was an old man with one eye; his wife is also a cripple, and they were broke. She begged me for shelter. I took them off the streets. As a reward they tried to blackmail me."[3]

Inez braced for more to come. Sunday's installment was only part one.

Day Two of the series, Gloria Shannon pulled the pin on another grenade:

MORE HORROR HOUSE REVELATIONS
MRS. SHANNON TELLS HORROR HOUSE VISIT
INEZ BURNS QUOTED ON HUGE PROFITS OF MILL

The second story in the series mixed God, America, and procreation in a kind of apocalyptic vision of right gone horribly wrong.

Gloria portrayed herself as a naïf ushered into Inez's cold, dark demiworld by recounting a discussion she had with Warren upon first meeting Inez:

"Did the woman really earn $5,000 a day for murder: People knew about it, but no one did anything?

"'Of course they know it,' Warren answered. 'Everybody in San Francisco knows about it. She'd been operating twenty years.'"

Gloria detailed one particular incident:

"I remember one woman who defied her. She was about twenty-eight. She wore the blue dungarees and carried the goggles of a woman shipyard worker. She climbed to the table with grim set face and unseeing eyes.

"'Where's that smile?' Inez demanded.

"'The girl turned on her like a tigress.

"'Listen,' she said, 'you're getting your price. And I'm not laughing for anyone.'

"She was strapped to the board. The anesthetist went to adjust the mark. 'And I'm not taking any anesthetic, either!'

"'I don't want you to suffer,' Inez snapped.

"'It's none of your business what I suffer. . . . Just get to work!'"

Gloria's prose quickly turned from yellow to purple. *Newsweek* reported that "horrified" readers "gagged" at the story, flooding the newspaper with hundreds of letters of protest. The deluge got so heavy and so one-sided that from his castle in San Simeon, Hearst himself called the *San Francisco Examiner* executive city editor who had overseen the project, forty-two-year-old Joshua Eppinger Jr., and told him to kill the series immediately. And that probably wasn't fast enough. In a wire to Eppinger, Hearst wrote that the newspaper's editors ought to hire a woman to guard for "decency and good taste."[4]

It's doubtful that Hearst would have applauded Inez or her profession. Hearst wasn't a religious man and no documents exist to reveal his views on abortion. But this surely was one crusade Hearst wasn't willing to trumpet. When Day Three's installment was set to run on Tuesday, the series was nowhere to be found, with nary an explanation to readers about what happened. It was as though the first two installments of Gloria Shannon's jagged exposé had never appeared.

That hardly mattered. The visceral impact of the stories had already ripped through San Francisco and the rest of the state, alerting readers to an upcoming trial that would pit good versus evil, Godliness versus heathenism, a civilized future desperately fighting to triumph over a sordid monstrous past. The pair of newspaper accounts telegraphed to everyone that San Francisco was about to confront the scourge of abortion head-on, and what was about to happen would be something no one ought to—or could—miss.

Pat Brown couldn't have asked for more.

Meanwhile, presiding Superior Court Judge Edward P. Murphy started putting together a new grand jury for 1946, which Pat hoped would be more sympathetic to his cause against Inez than last year's "no bill" tribunal had been. Silver-haired Henry C. Maginn, fifty-seven, well connected in Democratic Party circles, and a member

Inez, September 22, 1945.

of the city's requisite social associations, the Stock Exchange Club and Olympic Club, was named grand jury foreman.[5] Maginn was the kind of civic leader Pat could count on. Gloria Shannon was scheduled to be the panel's first witness, but figuring that the erratic Mrs. Shannon might turn the grand jury into a circus, Pat put her off for the time being. Not to be deterred, Gloria told *San Francisco Chronicle* columnist Herb Caen, "When I appear before the grand jury, they'll gimme the Academy Award."[6]

Given the firepower that her first two stories had ignited, Gloria ratcheted up her case and profile by soliciting support from San Francisco's clergy, sending out a battery of letters to priests and ministers in town, writing that the "abortion mill at 327 Fillmore Street has been destroying the lives of six to seven thousand babies yearly," and the revenue earned from Inez's "monstrous work [is] in excess of a million dollars yearly." Gloria ended her elegiac missive appeal by writing, "I am pleading with you and your church for unborn babies, for decency, for morality, and for humanity."[7]

When the grand jury convened, Inez and Joe were ordered to testify, but they refused; Pat could have compelled the couple to appear but didn't press the matter. Inez would be front and center at the upcoming criminal trial next month, and Tom Lynch was itching to begin pressing his case. "We could go to trial tomorrow," Lynch boasted. "We believe we have a strong case. It is our intention first to try Mrs. Burns and those people who were in the Fillmore Street place every day. Then, if our investigation warrants, we will ask for indictments against the smaller fry and the occasional workers."[8]

Meanwhile, Pat's second deputy, Norman Elkington, reported that to scare him from pursuing his case before the grand jury, on the evening of January 24, 1946, he received a threatening call from a gruff-sounding, unidentified man.

"OK, wise guy," the call started. "Would you like to know what the odds are on you around the town?"

"Yes, I would," Elkington replied.

"It's ten to one neither you nor Brown outlive Brown's first term of office."[9]

The case against Inez never got far in the grand jury. Although the secret body continued to meet and discuss issues of police corruption, nothing seemed to come out of it. As opposed to the grand jury, the criminal trial would be public with plenty of witnesses testifying on the record. It'd be a surefire way to sell papers, giving street-corner newsies reason to yell, "Read all about it!" It'd also be a surefire way to sell Pat to the rest of the state.

On February 18, Tom Lynch would get his first crack at Inez. He'd be joined by other big-city prosecutors across postwar America, seizing on a vaguely perceived mandate to close down abortion clinics in other cities, which like Inez's had operated for years. In postwar America, abortionists had suddenly become public enemies, just as menacing as bank robber Willie Sutton and gangster Al Capone. Although abortionists had been around forever, they seemingly had to be banished *now*. It was as though scores of district attorneys throughout the nation had all gotten the same memo, delivered over every prosecutor's transom, that the time was ripe to stamp out abortion once and for all.

Across the bay in Oakland, the *Tribune*'s walk-up to Inez's headline-grabbing trial teased readers, proclaiming that Inez's case "may prove one of the most sensational in San Francisco court history."[10] Not to be outdone, the *San Francisco Chronicle* pulled out all the stops, calling the upcoming trial "an event in the life of San Francisco, which potentially may compare with the beginning of an atomic chain reaction."[11]

Neither Gloria nor Warren Shannon, it turned out, would ever testify. By mid-March 1946, they had packed up and moved to New York, skipping out on paying their attorney and a swath of creditors. They were never seen again in San Francisco. Perhaps they had been muscled out of town. Or maybe they had just milked Inez for all that they could.

NINETEEN

BUSTER BROWN
TO THE RESCUE

Inez's attorney, Walter McGovern, wasn't a Shakespearean actor, but he could have played one. His speech was lofty, ornate, and eloquent. Listening to McGovern was like riding a roller coaster: slow, arduous rides going up, thrills and chills coming down. He was a master of elocution, aware of every breath, pause, and intonation whether asking a waitress for a cup of coffee or petitioning a judge for summary judgment. When choosing a word, he'd dangle it before his audience, suspended in midair, to be pondered, appraised, and weighed for all its meaning and intent.

Like Inez, an awful lot of people in San Francisco knew Walter McGovern. Oversize and bulky, sixty-one-year-old McGovern wasn't graceful. He had a flabby girth that posed problems when inside a courtroom. He lumbered around like an awkward bear. McGovern had traveled the world and prided himself on an encyclopedic knowledge of arcane facts that he liked to sprinkle any and all conversations with. He once killed a rattlesnake in rural Trinity County by stomping on it and then flattening it into a pancake. A San Francisco native, McGovern studied law at Jesuit College in Seattle, where he met his wife, Kathryn. They had no children, perhaps significant, perhaps not, in a case involving abortion.[1]

Forever parsimonious in extolling anything positive about his opposition, all Tom Lynch would concede publicly about McGovern was that "he knew his way around town." Laconic Lynch was all business all the time. He rarely smiled. He was no-nonsense, "straight as a walking stick," as a colleague put it. Precise and clipped, he was trained to drill meticulously and methodically to arrive at his version of the truth. The vexing questions of the nuance of innocence or guilt never diffused Lynch's single-beam vision. There were law-abiding citizens and then there were criminals, and society was served only when the latter were put behind bars. That was his job

Walter McGovern.

as a prosecutor. Let academics debate the cause and effect of crime, the etiology of criminality. For Lynch, by the time a defendant had arrived in court, it was a matter of laying out cold, hard facts to convince a jury of the offender's guilt. Lynch had been orphaned after his San Francisco–native mother died when he was two and his Irish immigrant father was killed in an accident when young Lynch turned nine. He was the product of an all-Catholic education, from grammar school through law school at Santa Clara University.[2] These, too, were facts that may or may not have had significance in a trial involving an abortionist.

If it had just been McGovern and Lynch facing off in Department 11 in San Francisco's musty Hall of Justice, the matchup would have made for terrific drama, but with Lynch serving as Pat Brown's proxy in a statewide scrimmage against Fred Howser, the courtroom would become full-blown theater with a panoramic cast of witnesses coming and going for two weeks. Genial Pat would pop in and out of the courtroom, glad-handing, smiling, nodding at the judge, attorneys, witnesses, reporters, cops, and everyone else who might make it to the voting booth next June for the primary and November for the general election.

Presiding over the cavalcade was Judge William F. Traverso, a fifty-year-old jurist who had been Earl Warren's first judicial appointment when the governor named him to the municipal court bench; two years later, Warren elevated Traverso to superior court. Traverso would stand for election just months after Inez's trial, so he, too, would be front and center in the public proscenium. A first-generation American, Traverso had graduated from the University of San Francisco Law School; he too was a Catholic, a World War I veteran, and a member of the Golden Gate Speranza Lodge of the Masons.[3]

Just prior to trial's opening on February 18, 1946, Inez came down with what was variously described as the flu, a cold, a virus, or, most ominously, food poisoning. No one quite knew what exactly Inez had picked up, or even if she had contracted anything at all. Perhaps it was just a case of nerves. For her entire adult life, Inez had been both a health nut and a hypochondriac. The malady she complained about might very well have been a ruse to delay the trial in hopes that Brown and Lynch would get cold feet and negotiate a plea deal. Fat chance that was going to happen. Both were chafing at the bit to get their hooks into her and the four other defendants. Their careers depended on it.

Inez and Joe had spent the previous week at their Hollywood Hills home. Inez maintained that she had been under the constant care of a physician, who had pre-

Joe and Inez.

scribed for her a new drug called penicillin. Figuring that Inez's alleged ailment was a tactic to postpone the trial, Pat sent Tom Lynch and Deputy DA Andrew J. Eyman to Los Angeles, where they hired their own physician, Dr. J. Park Dougall, to examine Inez, who was pronounced thoroughly fit to appear in court. Out of options, Joe and Inez drove their brand-new Buick up Highway 101 on the way to San Francisco. By the time they reached Santa Barbara, Inez said she felt a panic attack coming on, so they stopped and found a physician, who prescribed a sedative. The drug seemed to steady her nerves, and after several hours, Inez and Joe got back on the highway headed north.

For the opening day of the trial, Walter McGovern hired a private nurse to attend to his client's medical needs. Whether Inez's malady was real or imagined made no difference. Dressed in a crisp white nurse's uniform, Margaret Brown sat next to Inez in the courtroom, every few minutes adjusting a tiny pillow against the small of Inez's back to ease any discomfort. Inez, who was fifty-nine, looked pale and haggard. Any physical symptoms she may have been experiencing certainly did not match the sparkling couture Inez was wearing that day: a blue back-pleated peplum dress, accented by a white hat designed by New York fashion designer Lilly Daché. The dress was only partially visible since Inez kept a thick sable coat draped over her shoulders during most of the day. Whether the fur was for fashion or to guard against the courtroom's chill was unclear. Joe Burns, sitting next to private investigator Pop Aureguy in the first row behind Inez, wore a handsome dark three-piece wool suit. Through much of the day, Joe held on to the brim of a fedora that rested on his lap. Aureguy appeared nervous, patting perspiration from his puffy checks with a wrinkled handkerchief. He got up often, excusing himself, leaving the courtroom; two or three hours later, he'd return. It was like that all through jury selection.

Without wasting any time, shortly after nine a.m., Walter McGovern promptly rose to his feet and asked Judge Traverso for a week's continuance. "I don't need to be cruel or inhuman to anyone," the judge replied apologetically. "But we must proceed unless in the opinion of a competent physician she is physically unable to attend the proceedings."[4] McGovern hemmed and hawed, but proffered no such medical diagnosis, and jury selection commenced.

Judge Traverso nodded to the bailiff, who retrieved fourteen prospective jurors, solemnly filing into the courtroom. McGovern and Lynch chose from a pool of one hundred would-be jurors; each attorney would have thirty-five preemptory challenges. The judge excused one prospective juror right away when she announced her name, May Shannon, the sister of Warren Shannon. Another potential juror, Bessie

San Francisco Chronicle

THE CITY'S ONLY HOME-OWNED NEWSPAPER

FOUNDED 1865—VOL. CLXII, NO. 35 CCCCAA SAN FRANCISCO, TUESDAY, FEBRUARY 19, 1946 DAILY 5 CENTS, SUNDAY 15 CENTS

COMPARATIVE TEMP[...]

	High	Low	
San Francisco	59	48	New Yo[...]
Oakland	57	43	Chicag[...]
Los Angeles	72	44	New Or[...]
Sacramento	58	37	Washin[...]
Seattle	50	30	Salt La[...]
Reno	57	21	Pensac[...]

JURY SELECTION BEGINS IN BURNS ABORTION TRIA[L]

Public Library 3L5 (CM) 30Mar66 Fifth Ave & 42nd St NEW YORK N 1

[T]HIS [W]ORLD [T]ODAY

[...] BRIER

[w]alk down from the [...]lls, going east, you [...] to a rocky hillock [...] Pnyx. In the fifth [...]re a stone platform, [...]re are a few crum[...]s. Here the Athe[...]ns used to harangue [...]ers, who apparently [...] the rocks round[...]elled the equivalent [...]" and "Booooo!" Af[...]y all went down to [...]r public square, and [...]btless in the Agora [...] the equivalents of [...]e in, and even long-[...]bartenders saying, [...]t, Jack!" to every-

[...] that's roughly the [...]went in Athens, and [...] it had a modern [...]there were plenty of [...] in those days, al[...] to lead The People [...]la. The social strati[...] not unlike ours, for [...] the conservatives, [...]oligarchs, and the [...]hom Pericles was a [...]ample, and the radi[...]ere included in the

[...] issues, of course, [...] somewhat different [...]ours, but like ours, [...]olden Age began to [...] brassy, the issues [...]rossed with the war- [...]nvolved in the con[...] Peloponnesian War

[...]s was the instru[...]ich the demagogues [...] it was theoretically [...] So the brilliant and [...]blades, and his occa[...]s, Nicias and Cleon, [...]n faction to faction [...]eath of Pericles, and [...]n the Pnyx, and the [...] that The People got [...] shellacking, and lost [...], their greatness and [...] into the bargain.

[G]reek story, dazzling [...]dy colors of human [...] great intellect and [...]y, with heroism and [...]th violence and de[...]th, is the very best [...]our own time, first [...] detailed record has [...]ously preserved, sec[...]se it is exceedingly [...]pe, and so, easy to

[...]n this rocky hillside [...]t the first modern [...], the utter cynic

[Continued] on Page 4, Col. 1

[M]ore than [1]000 [PL]AYS every [PFA]NSTIEHL [Pho]nograph [N]eedle

[...] your money's worth [...] Pfanstiehl! Not only be[...] plays so long withou[t] [...], but it plays so well. [...] protects records. Made [...] metal and polished to [...] precision, Pfanstiehl [...] in a lucite case, wait[...] add life and lustre to [...] records.

[...]d by Sherman, Clay

$1.50

[SHERMA]N, CLAY & CO. [...] Sutter Streets [...]co 6, California

[Sen]d me __ PFANSTIEHL NEEDLES at $1.50 each

[...]ate

[Ch]arge account ☐ Check ☐ [O]rder ☐ C.O.D. ☐

[...] Sales Tax in California

[Sher]man, Clay

[S]AN FRANCISCO Kearny-Sutter-2539 Mission Street

SAN JOSE [...]hart 89 So. First Street

[...]TO FRESNO

First Day In Court

Only Two of 70 Challenges Are Used Up

Inez Brown Burns, leaning on the arm of a nurse, went to trial in Superior Court here yesterday on a charge of conspiracy to commit abortions.

By late afternoon, the jury box was occupied tentatively by nine women and three men, but the pace of questioning indicated that a final jury may not be selected until Wednesday or Thursday.

Together, the defense and prosecution have 70 peremptory challenges. Only two were used yesterday, and Judge William F. Traverso excused four other jurors, one of them Miss May Shannon, a sister of former Supervisor Warren Shannon.

WILL CASE SPREAD?

Both defense and prosecution came out slugging as the trial got under way. Since the arrest of Mrs. Burns and her co-defendants last September, both sides have freely predicted the case would "spread out" once it came to the trial stage.

Chief Prosecutor Thomas C. Lynch brought the names of seven San Francisco and East Bay physicians into the case for the first time in questioning prospective jurors. He asked the veniremen if they were acquainted with the doctors, but did not tell why the question was asked.

Lynch also asked the prospective jurors if they knew Shannon, or his wife, Gloria. During her Municipal Court hearing, Mrs. Burns accused Shannon of attempting to shake her down for $35,000.

POLITICAL TALK

Former Police Commissioner Walter McGovern and Former Assistant District Attorney John R. Golden, the defense attorneys, leveled away on District Attorney Edmund G. Brown in their questioning of the jurors.

Both mentioned the fact that Brown's younger brother, Frank, is a member of the District Attorney's staff, and reference was made to Brown's purported political aspirations to be State Attorney General.

McGovern, who was denied a continuance of the case Saturday on the plea Mrs. Burns has the flu, lost another motion for a postponement when the trial was called yesterday morning.

Judge Traverso offered to talk over the question of Mrs. Burns' health in his chambers at the noon recess, but McGovern did not appear for the appointment. He said he would check after court with the woman's physician, and may possibly ask again this morning for a continuance.

Mrs. Burns' co-defendants are Mrs. Myrtle Ramsey, Mrs. Musette Briggs, Mrs. Mable Spaulding and Joseph M. Hoff, all accused of being assistants in the operation of an alleged abortion mill at 327 Fillmore street.

Shelley Will Run For Houser's Job

SACRAMENTO, Feb. 18—State Senator John B. Shelley, San Francisco today formally announced his candidacy for Lieutenant Governorship, now held by Frederick F. Houser.

The San Franciscan made his announcement at a luncheon meeting of the Democratic members of the Legislature. He is president of the San Francisco Labor Council, AFL, and has served eight years in the Senate.

Senate Passes 5 Billion Bill

WASHINGTON, Feb. 18 (AP)—Minus funds for a west wing addition to the White House, a supply bill carrying more than $5,000,000,000 for various Federal agencies was passed today by the Senate.

Biggest item in the bill is more than $4,000,000,000 for the Veterans Administration to provide hospitalization, disability compensation and other payments for World War veterans. The measure also included funds for Federal aid highways.

Rain Due Today, And a Cold Snap

Umbrella weather will return to the Bay Area today, the Weatherman said last night.

It will be colder with fresh to strong southerly winds this morning. The outlook is similar for most of Northern California.

Tomorrow will bring clouds and occasional showers.

If you're Sierra bound, you'll find [...]

Truman Wage-Price Policy Is Explained

Food, Shelter, Clothing Price Line Can Be Held Under Plan, Says Bowles

New Economic Stabilizer Warns, 'Inflation Boiler Near Exploding Point'; Will Speak on Radio Tonight

By the Associated Press

WASHINGTON, Feb. 18—Chester Bowles assured the Nation today that under President Truman's new wage-price policy the prices of the three essentials of life—food, shelter and clothing—can be held at about their present levels. But he solemnly warned the House Banking Committee that co-operation of the entire Nation is necessary—that the inflation boiler is dangerously near the explosion point, "with our entire economic future at stake."

Bowles also arranged to go on the radio tomorrow night to explain the Administration's new wage-price policy. He will speak over CBS.

The broadcast will be carried here over KQW at 7:45 p. m. (PST) today (Tuesday).

Zenas L. Potter, adviser to Bowles, told the committee OPA believes "that all controls but rents can be eliminated next year."

"If the OPA act is extended," he said, "we can decontrol ourselves out of existence . . . Rent control can then appropriately be transferred to other agencies or to the States."

FIRST APPEARANCE

Bowles, making his first appearance as Economic Stabilizer, climbed Capitol hill to appeal to Congress for a continuation of price controls, which are due to expire June 30.

"The lobbyists and the profiteers are licking their chops," he declared. "It is going to take firm and decisive action—it is going to take teamwork and support on every hand—if we are to hold this country on an even keel."

But Bowles told the House Banking Committee Mr. Truman's new wage-price policy is "a program that will work" and will turn back the inflation pressures.

It does not mean a retreat to a new and higher price line, he said. Moreover, he declared:

"To those people who are betting on inflation in the stock market and in the commodity markets, let me say, 'You are betting on the wrong horse. There isn't going to be any inflation. We're going to hold the price and rent line as we've held it since May, 1943—all the speculators, lobbyists and pressure groups to the contrary notwithstanding!'"

PREVENT HOARDING

Also, he gave "notice to speculators" that he intends to use all the power at his command to prevent hoarding.

"This is one thing we simply must not tolerate," he said.

Bowles called upon Congress to "stop the inflation in the real estate market" as a necessary step if the new homes-for-veterans program is to succeed. He asked for continuation of food subsidies.

Bowles departed from his prepared text to take a poke at the National Association of Manufacturers, which he said "wants to let prices go up and get production, and then let them collapse." He declared, "That doesn't make sense to me. It didn't work after the last war when he had no price controls."

Spectators, filling all seats in the committee room, crowded the walls and sat on the floor to hear Bowles plead the case of the new wage-price policy.

Bowles spent most of the morning reading his formal statement, and when members asked that he come back in the afternoon to answer questions he advised he "had a date" with Mr. Truman at 3:15. He offered "to call up the President and cancel it." Instead, the committeemen asked him to return tomorrow.

(Bowles' summary of Truman's new economic policy appears on Page 22.)

Truman Has a Spy List, Too

Report Names Over 100 Who Worked With Foreign Ring

By THOMAS F. REYNOLDS

(Chicago Sun Washington Bureau)

WASHINGTON, Feb. 18—President Truman has a secret report listing names of more than 100 men and women in this country who directly or indirectly have co-operated with a foreign spy ring attempting to "crack" the secrets of atomic energy here and in Canada.

The FBI, who submitted the list, has had this organization under surveillance for almost a year and can begin making arrests any time the White House authorizes action, it was learned tonight.

The espionage organization was activated by agents of Soviet Russia, according to informed officials.

The espionage activities inside the United States, it was indicated, dwarf those carried on in Canada. Spy activities in Canada resulted last week in a special statement by Prime Minister W. L. Mackenzie King, a sweeping series of arrests, and appointment of a royal commission to take evidence from suspects. (Further arrests are reported on page 4.)

NOT SUCCESSFUL

Informed officials said tonight, however, that while the ring was "moving toward" basic data on the manufacture of atomic weapons, it was unsuccessful in procuring that information.

The Canadian investigation is expected to divulge that while agents transmitted overseas data which they believed bore on the atomic secret, they were actually duped into sending scientific mumbo-jumbo calculated to intrigue nuclear scientists but in the long run to confuse them.

Activities of the ring are understood to have precipitated a highly embarrassing situation at the White House and State Department. President Truman and Secretary of State Byrnes are said to be none too anxious to order arrests, in considerable part because this country is presumed to have its own agents working in Russian areas who would be subject to instant reprisals.

THE TIPOFF

The situation is more confused by the apparently well-authenticated report that the operations of the ring in this country was first "tipped off" by a British intelligence agent working here.

As a consequence the Big Three are confronted by a situation where their counter-intelligence is working so effectively that their intelligence is becoming embarrassing.

Until either Mr. Truman or the Secretary of State give the signal, the FBI will not be able to tighten the noose around the 100-odd people who have been under surveillance for upward of a year.

One well-informed official said there was no reason to believe any basic atomic data had been picked up. The only major data acquired by the ring was understood to be the secrets of the radio proximity fuse for anti-aircraft shells—a major weapon developed during the war by U. S. Army scientists.

These secrets were said to have been picked up in Canada. Whereas Canada is not manufacturing the fuse, shells for many of its anti-aircraft outfits were equipped with the weapon, and basic data was available in government offices there. The Royal Commission is expected to base its most serious charges on the unauthorized transmittal of information on the prox[...]

Lie Will Leave For U. S. Soon

OSLO, Norway, Feb. 18 (Reuters)—Trygve Lie, Secretary General of the United Nations Organization, returned to Oslo today and said he would go to New York within two weeks. He was met by the British, United States, Soviet and French Ambassadors.

Raskob Resigns From DuPont

WILMINGTON, Del., Feb. 18 (UP)—John J. Raskob, New York, today resigned as vice president and director of the E. I. duPont de Ne[...]

THE POPE ARRIVES—Pope Pius XII (with hand upraised) is shown here approaching Consistory Hall at the Vatican yesterday where he attended the secret consistory of the Sacred College of Cardinals, during which 32 prelates were elevated to the college. Left to right: Msgr. Enrico Dante, carrying the Pontiff's allocution decla[ring the inst]igation of the new princes of the church; M[sgr.] Callori di Vignalle, attendant; Pope Pius, and [...] Venini, attendant. For additional pictures of [the] four American Cardinals, see page 3.

Less Butter, Is Producers' Prediction

There will be less butter available this year than ever before.

The public appetite for "luxury" dairy items, aided by pockets lined with war-time high earnings, has resulted in a diversion of whole milk to more profitable production fields.

California's butter production, about 70,000,000 pounds in a pre-war year, fell to 30,000,000 in 1945 and will fall to less than 10,000,000 pounds this year.

THE ECONOMIC CAUSE

This is a view of the current butter demand-and-supply picture as seen by Paul McClure, chairman of the butter committee of the Pacific States Butter, Egg, Cheese and Poultry Association, now in session at the Fairmont Hotel.

"The whole answer is that milk producers can make more money by selling their milk for use in ice cream, whipping cream, cheese, and other luxury items," he said.

McClure said the current ceiling price for a pound of butterfat destined for butter production is 53 to 55 cents, as compared to 85 cents to $1 for other uses.

He said the only means by which butter production can be stimulated is to raise the price of churning cream by 10 or 15 cents a pound.

Increases of 6 to 18 cents per pound in butter prices, proposed last month by the Department of Agriculture, met with immediate disapproval of OPA Chief Chester Bowles.

'MORE COWS'

McClure's view was seconded by G. A. Brown, a butter committee member from Portland, who said:

"In my area (around Portland) the consumption of milk has increased 65 per cent over prewar figures, and the consumption of cream is even higher. There simply isn't [...]

Richard J. Warner, chairman of the California Dairy Advisory Board, to the overall shortage of dairy products.

"Our cities and population have grown," Warner said, "and it's time our cow population started to increase, too.

"We have room for three times as many cows as we now have on the Pacific Slope, and not to use it is a waste of land."

PRICE RISE PREDICTED

Hobart Creighton, chief of the poultry branch, Production and Marketing Administration, Department of Agriculture, said he does not know how current price-adjustment policy differences between his department and the OPA are going to work out.

"The Department of Agriculture tries to keep the prices up for the farmer and the OPA tries to keep them down for the consumer," he declared.

Joseph B. Danzansky, the Association's Washington representative, predicted a break-through on some price controls.

"Nobody knows what is going to happen to price controls," he declared, "but there will be a definite break in price levels, Mr. Bowles to the contrary."

At today's closing sessions of the convention, the various committee reports will be made, officers will [...]

Traffic Death No. 30

The black flag flies again—there was a traffic fatality yesterday in San Francisco. The white flag will fly tomorrow if there are no traffic deaths today.

(See Story on Page 11)

32 Prelates Eleva[ted] To Rank of Card[inal]

Spellman Vows to Serve Ma[nkind] Against Menace of Atomic [...]

By United Press

ROME, Feb. 18—Thirty-two prelates of 19 nations were elevated to the sacred purple of Cardinals in ancient Rome today, with Francis Cardinal Spellman of New York vowing to serve mankind against the war-born atomic doom menacing the etnire temporal world.

Spellman received notification of his cardinalitial honors while sitting in the packed hall of the historic apostolic chancery side by side with the three other Americans similarly honored—John Cardinal Glennon of St. Louis, Samuel Cardinal Stritch of Chicago and Edward Cardinal Mooney of Detroit.

Pope Pius XII, in raising the churchmen to the Sacred College, said the new Cardinals were selected for their prudence and wisdom from five parts of the world and through these qualities "convey the peoples to the pastures of eternal truths."

SPELLMAN'S APPEAL

In his first statement upon becoming Cardinal, Spellman called upon the world to make a right-about turn to God to avoid the destruction that in another form [...]

and another ag[...] Carthage into th[e] [...]

Amid all the [...] and tradition of t[he] Church carrying [...] rites, Spellman [...] world's dangers b[...] fate of atom-blast [...]

Before and as[...] tional messengers [...] carried to the oth[er] [...] the notification [...] to the sacred pur[ple] [...]

IMPENDING TR[...]

One messenger [...] tragedy at the La[...] lege, where Jos[e] [...] Rodriguez of Ch[...] notification from [...] then was rushed [...]

Continued on [...]

Pope on [...]

Pope Pius XII [...] cial radio ad[dress] [...] (Wednesday) fro[m] [...] be heard over KP[...]

The Chronicle Index

THE W[EATHER] Showers [...]

Peabody, acknowledged that she might be a "third or fourth cousin" of Gloria Shannon but didn't know which. Miss Peabody was also dismissed.[5]

As jury selection continued, defense counsel McGovern embarked on what would become a crusade that would last for the duration of the trial: Pat Brown's political aspirations. McGovern's strategy may have appeared puzzling in a case of five defendants charged with performing abortions. But McGovern dug in his heels right from the beginning, and as he proceeded point by point, his motives became increasingly clear.

The first question McGovern asked would-be juror Charles D. Signorelli was whether Signorelli supported Brown for attorney general.

"I didn't know he was running," stumbled a surprised Signorelli.

"Lots of other people don't either," McGovern said not missing a beat, then striking the accountant from the jury.[6]

McGovern asked another potential juror, real estate agent Jacob Barman, who said he had supported Pat Brown for district attorney, whether Barman was planning to volunteer to work on Brown's bid for attorney general.

"Not yet," Barman volunteered, smiling, which also prompted McGovern to excuse him from the jury.[7]

In addition to jurors' political leanings, there also was the moral issue of abortion, at least how much jury candidates would admit under questioning. The judge excused sixteen prospective jurors based on their expressed personal beliefs on the subject. Leah R. Hamilton, the wife of a physician at the University of California, was struck from the jury pool when she voiced opposition to any and all laws prohibiting abortion. A salesman who said he didn't believe any baby ought to be brought into the world if the child was unwanted was removed. A housewife who said abortion under any circumstances was "outright murder" was also excused.[8]

The prosecution and defense went through seventy-one prospective jurors before coming up with a final draw of seven men, five women, and two alternates. Ten of the jurors were married, one woman was single, another woman was divorced with five grown children. Four were parents.[9]

Once the jury was impaneled, McGovern caused another stir when he announced to the court that against his advice, Inez would take the witness stand in her own defense.

"I'd love that," piped up Lynch, an uncharacteristic ejaculation from the by-the-rules prosecutor, which brought down Judge Traverso's gavel.

Jurors in first trial; Mrs. Linder, seated fourth from the left.

"Please, Mr. Lynch," the judge cautioned him.

The court adjourned for the day, but sometime during the evening or night, Inez's clinic was ransacked, although nothing appeared to have been taken. The intruders clearly knew what they were doing and how to get around inside. They were thoroughly familiar with the clinic and surrounding property. They entered by cutting a precise hole through a panel in the back door to the second floor and went directly to Inez's office where she kept records. They emptied desk drawers and picked through file cabinets, scattering hundreds of sheets of paper on the floor. Whether the thieves found what they were looking for was unknown. Perhaps they weren't looking for anything but instead tossed the clinic to intimidate Inez. But who were the intrud-

ers? Someone scared that the name of a particular patient might surface during the trial? Religious zealots harassing Inez in the wake of Gloria Shannon's exposé and her antiabortion screed? Mobster Nick DeJohn and some of his goombahs sending Inez a message to cooperate with him or else? Maybe even private investigator Pop Aureguy wanted to feign a burglary in order to fan the flames of what Inez knew and what would happen if Pat's push came to shove. Such a tactic hardly was beyond the play-for-keeps Aureguy.

Tom Lynch opened the prosecution's case with two surprise witnesses. The first was Kathryn Bartron, a part-time anesthetist who had once worked at Inez's clinic. But as soon as Miss Bartron's name was called, she fainted and, in the words of sheriff's matron Rita Copeland, became "hysterical."[10] After a recess, Miss Bartron seemed to recover and was once again summoned to the witness stand. Resolutely avoiding Inez's steely gaze, Miss Bartron testified that she had been employed at the clinic from 1934 to 1936, and returned in 1943, working four afternoons a week. She identified photographs of clinic equipment and detailed procedures Inez and the codefendants followed before, during, and after each abortion was performed.

McGovern was furious and rose to object. "If her testimony is correct, then this woman is a felon!" McGovern boomed so that everyone in the courtroom and in the hallway outside could hear. "She is a coconspirator!" McGovern demanded that Judge Traverso strike all of Miss Bartron's testimony.

Judge Traverso motioned counsel to approach. If testimony from Inez's former employees were ruled inadmissible, then much of the people's case against Inez and the other defendants would collapse. Those in the courtroom discerned a heated, muffled exchange among the three men. McGovern twisted his signet ring, his chins wobbling; Lynch nodded, allowing a tight-lipped smile that in anyone else wouldn't be considered a smile at all. Judge Traverso suddenly waved the attorneys back. He overruled McGovern and instructed Miss Bartron to continue.[11]

When it was McGovern's turn to cross-examine Miss Bartron, the jury learned that she had often stayed overnight at Inez's home, had been taken out to expensive dinners numerous times by Inez and Joe, and had received opulent gifts of furs, dresses, and jewelry from Inez.

"Did you thank her for them or are you thanking her now?" McGovern asked, sounding like a principal scolding a particularly vexing student.[12]

Miss Bartron looked down, embarrassed. She muttered something to herself that was inaudible.

Then she fainted again.

Pat Brown, who had quietly slipped into the courtroom after the recess, leaped up from his seat and rushed over to Miss Bartron in the witness box. Pat couldn't help himself from springing into action. He unfurled a crisp handkerchief and patted Miss Bartron's forehead. Miss Bartron soon regained consciousness. Holding her hand, Pat looked toward Tom Lynch, instructing him to pour a glass of water, and after helping Miss Bartron to a chair, Pat offered the witness a sip.

McGovern stared at the district attorney's impromptu gallantry in front of the packed courtroom and couldn't help himself from grinning. "Buster Brown to the rescue," he cracked in a stage whisper to his cocounsel, John Golden, a reference to the popular cartoon-boy mascot. Everyone heard the remark, including Judge Traverso, who banged his gavel and warned McGovern against such outbursts.[13]

The prosecution's second surprise witness turned out not to be much of a surprise. Madeline Rand, one of the original codefendants who had turned state's evidence, described her recollections of activities inside the clinic, testifying that she often attended to twelve or more patients a day. Once again, McGovern jumped to his feet. Mrs. Rand's testimony was tainted and prejudicial, McGovern charged. Besides breaking the law herself, making Mrs. Rand culpable of the same crimes Inez and the other defendants were charged with committing, McGovern told the court that Mrs. Rand's husband, Charles, had tried to sell information to Pat Brown's office.

"Didn't you tell Mrs. Burns after the arrest that if you didn't get three thousand dollars you'd go to the district attorney's office?" McGovern asked the witness. "Isn't it true you have an intense dislike and hatred for Mrs. Burns? Didn't Mrs. Burns accuse you of stealing money out of women's purses?" It was a quick, rat-tat-tat, one-two-three punch to Mrs. Rand and the prosecution.

Mrs. Rand denied all the accusations but admitted that she did go to Inez's former attorney James Brennan after the raid to get what she said Inez owed her in back pay.[14]

McGovern theatrically threw up his hands, effectively destroying any credibility that Mrs. Rand had left. He again charged that Mrs. Rand and Miss Bartron both were "coconspirators turned informers," and as such their testimony must be ruled inadmissible. McGovern called for an immediate mistrial, a motion the judge summarily and neatly denied.

Buoyed by Judge Traverso's string of favorable rulings, Lynch proceeded to call to the witness stand a procession of Inez's former patients. This is what many in the courtroom seemed to have been waiting for—a kind of public shaming. A hush permeated through the court. Here were scarlet women under oath confessing their indiscretions and the illegal remedies they sought to rectify their lapses in judgment. Each woman made her way through the courtroom door to the witness box, the clicking of high heels against the floor seeming to punctuate the courtroom's anticipation.

The first was a twenty-two-year-old Oakland woman, who testified that when she showed up at the Fillmore Street clinic, she was informed that the fee for an abortion would be one hundred twenty-five dollars. The woman had only one hundred dollars but was told that if she could come up with twenty-five more dollars, Inez would perform the procedure the next day. The woman returned with the extra cash, handed it to Musette Briggs, and was shown to a room where Inez, Mabel Spaulding, and Myrtle Ramsey were present. After the procedure, the woman developed complications and came back to the clinic. Joe Hoff drove her to nearby Saint Francis Hospital, took her through a rear door, where a doctor there diagnosed her with appendicitis. The woman never registered at the hospital, gave nurses a fake address, and recovered after a ten-day period, she testified.[15]

Next, a woman from Daly City, described by a reporter as a "blond and dimpled" mother of four, testified that she made two visits to the clinic, in 1941 and 1944. The woman pointed out Mabel Spaulding as the employee who told her the fee for the first procedure would be seventy-five dollars. "I only had sixty-five dollars, so she took that. It was all I had," the former patient testified. For the second procedure three years later, the required payment had jumped to one hundred dollars, but the woman testified, "I had only eighty dollars, so she took that."[16]

On cross, McGovern asked if the woman's husband was in the courtroom, and when she said yes, McGovern directed her to point him out. A tall, uneasy man dressed in a suit, sitting in one of the back rows of the gallery, stood up, awkwardly shifting his weight from foot to foot. It wasn't clear what McGovern had in mind except to show how average and ordinary Inez's patients and their spouses looked.[17]

A third prosecution witness called to the stand was a waitress described as "a pretty dark-eyed girl with wavy brown hair." Separated from her husband for six months, "Mrs. D. K." testified that she had been living near Redding, California, when she became involved with a miner in the area. She got pregnant, relocated to Oakland, where two East Bay physicians referred her to Inez's clinic. There, she paid one hundred dollars for an abortion, she testified.[18]

After some prodding by Lynch, the woman said that several days earlier an unidentified man and two women had approached her outside the Oakland restaurant where she worked and tried to intimidate her into not testifying, telling her that by doing so, she'd be criminally liable for submitting to an abortion. McGovern tried to strike that portion of the woman's testimony, but here, too, he was unsuccessful.[19] It wasn't clear who had tried to intimae the witness, whom the trio might have worked for, or even if the incident ever actually took place.

When Judge Traverso adjourned for the day, Pat Brown called several of his favorite newspaper reporters into his office at the Scatena Building and, while huddled around his big desk, told them that every one of the prosecution's witnesses had reported to have been intimidated through phone calls and "pressure put on their family and friends."[20] Whether braggadocio, speculation, or fact, the charge prompted holy hell from Walter McGovern the next day. "Your Honor, I have no hope—no hope—that anything can shut Mr. Brown up. But in as much as the jury is not being locked up and has ready access to the newspapers, such statements are manifestly unfair to the defense." McGovern had a point. Brown was strategically floating prejudicial hearsay by suggesting that Inez and her defense teams were attempting to muzzle witnesses. Whether or not true, it was a baseless accusation since Pat offered no evidence. The judge said as much, reminding jurors that they had taken an oath to be impartial and that the "case must be tried solely on the evidence."[21]

Lynch now entered a second phase of his case, presenting witnesses who had provided services or supplies to Inez. One was J. Franklin Dare, the owner of a laboratory at 2288 Market Street, who processed patients' blood tests. From a one-month period in 1943, Dare presented records of three hundred fifty-six women, which broke down to fifteen to twenty patients a day. The names of the patients were not read aloud but entered into the court record.[22] This, too, produced no small amount of anxious anticipation.

McGovern slowly perused the list of names, flipping through page after page after page. He took his time. Thirty seconds, a minute, two minutes, during which no one said a word. It was as though the entire courtroom was collectively holding its breath. McGovern nodded his head slowly as he read to himself. He seemed to be memorizing the women's names for some future purpose, which was unclear at the moment. When McGovern came across a name that caught his eye, he paused. He took to squinting through his bifocals, raising his eyebrows, and then puffing out his checks with an exhalation of spent oxygen. When McGovern finished going through the voluminous list of names, he looked up at the jury, the judge, and finally Lynch. He hesitated another ten seconds for more effect, and then lamented that the names made him "preoccupied—some of them are so *very* familiar." That McGovern had just familiarized himself with the names of hundreds of women who had undergone abortions left everyone in the courtroom breathless.[23]

At this midway point, Inez seemed to have fully recovered from whatever was, or was not, ailing her when the trial had begun. Each day, she wore a hat more flamboyant than the day before. Some days she removed her fur coat, other days she didn't, clutching it as though it was a shawl fashionably draped over yet another dress or suit that Nelly Gaffney had helped her select.

On Wednesday at noon, as much to take a break from the still courtroom air as to be seen in public, Inez and her codefendants strolled around the corner to Big Ben, a popular fish grotto at Montgomery and Merchant Streets for lunch. Inez made a fuss about where the tuxedo-clad maître d' sat them all until he found a round table in a far corner. Just as they were about to order, Inez peered across the dining room, and who should she see sitting in a booth, hunkered down with Pat Brown, but her old attorney James Brennan, who had represented her in the preliminary hearing. Brennan was the lawyer who had told the court of Warren and Gloria Shannons' attempt at blackmailing her.[24]

What the hell was Brennan doing with that son of a bitch? What could they possibly be talking about? And why the hell were they in such a public place?

In Pat Brown's political world, Inez knew there were no coincidences.

Inez pushed aside her plate of sand dabs, no longer hungry.

Back from the stomach-churning lunch recess, Lynch had saved the best for last, Inspector Frank Ahern, the cop's cop Inez had tried to bribe in her upstairs hat closet. When the San Francisco native who had risen from patrolman to inspector tried to recount the episode, McGovern once more rose to his feet and objected, but Judge Traverso immediately overruled him. When Lynch asked Ahern how he reacted to Inez's offer of cash, the inspector bristled, put off that Lynch would even suggest that Ahern might have considered the bribe.[25]

Lynch introduced into evidence the two brown dime-store notebooks that Ahern had found in Inez's bedroom. A reporter in the courtroom referred to the notebooks as "two sticks of dynamite" as they were gingerly passed from juror to juror for inspection. The first notebook listed more patient names, the clinic's daily receipts, payoffs to cops and others, along with penciled-in figures of Inez's monthly overhead—three thousand seven hundred fifty dollars. The second notebook was a kind of employee handbook labeled "Inez's Advice," which contained tips that included, "Never take a patient you think you cannot face again," "Follow your hunches," and "Don't forget the black list."[26] Scrawled on the back of the notebook were the names of nine California physicians who had referred patients to Inez.[27]

McGovern vigorously objected once again. He didn't want any of this in the court record. He tried to knock down Ahern's testimony. He voiced his objections to the kid gloves he said Lynch was wearing while questioning the inspector, terming it "Mr. Ahern's self-canonization."[28] To McGovern, witness Ahern wasn't being treated like a cop, but like a hero.

McGovern itemized a list of objections to the show, to which Judge Traverso responded:

"Each and every objection is denied."
"Each and every motion to strike is denied."
"Each and every motion of Mr. Lynch is granted."[29]

McGovern sat down, a fourth chin drooping from his face.

"The state rests, Your Honor," Lynch announced in a smug, satisfied way.

Lynch had called thirty witnesses and had entered fifty-nine exhibits, including a hospital bed, jars of pills, tanks of oxygen and nitrous oxide, trays of medical instruments, and a series of hypodermic needles, all seized by police from Inez's clinic. It was a tsunami of devastating and damning evidence.

Judge Traverso now turned to the defense. Finally, it was Walter McGovern's turn to present his case.

McGovern stuck a finger in the collar of his starched shirt to scratch his prickly neck. He adjusted his rimless glasses and clumsily positioned himself in front of the jury box. Jurors could see the creases deepen in McGovern's forehead. He paused for a moment, during which he said nothing. Forget a pin. You could hear a feather drop.

Then he slowly pivoted to the judge. "In view of the total insufficiency of evidence, Your Honor, we rest too."[30]

Say what?

The jury, the prosecution, the packed courtroom, even Judge Traverso, wondered what McGovern was up to as he lumbered back to his chair and lowered himself in it, as gently as he could, and even so, the chair creaked.

Without mounting a defense, nary a single witness or exhibit—including Inez, whom McGovern had promised would testify—McGovern seemed to be saying that his clients had no defense.

Judge Traverso appeared as shocked as everyone else. He tried to keep his reaction in check, nodding to Lynch to begin his closing. Lynch hadn't a clue that he'd be called on this soon.

"We have forced every single link in the chain," said Lynch, his restive momentum returning. "Not one single person has come upon this stand to deny one single word of the testimony. There is not one single shred of contradiction."

Speaking assuredly, Lynch continued. "It was a cold-blooded business proposi-

Frank Ahern inspecting Inez's ledger, March 5, 1946.

tion. Mrs. Spaulding took the money and put it in her tin box. Then she turned the patient over to Joe. He said he dusted around the place. Joe the duster did his dusting with a microscope. Then the patient was sent upstairs to surgery. Sometimes Mrs. Burns did the work and sometimes Mrs. Briggs performed the operation. Mrs. Ramsey was there to help them both. All five worked together as one unit."[31]

Summing up, Lynch said, "No woman was asked how badly she needed an operation, or if it was necessary to save her life. The price was set, and if they didn't have it, they were turned down. It was take it or leave it."[32]

Lynch spoke assuredly for another twenty minutes, and when finished, Judge Traverso smacked his gavel and adjourned for the day. Leaving the courthouse, Walter McGovern somehow appeared undeterred. He told head-scratching reporters and onlookers that the prosecution hadn't proven its case either "legally or in substance." When asked to elaborate by the bewildered crowd, all McGovern said was, "Wait for tomorrow."

TWENTY

AMBITION FEEDS
ON STRANGE FOODS

At nine the next morning, Walter McGovern arose from his creaky chair, faced the jury, and pronounced that Pat Brown and Tom Lynch's case against Inez and the others was, pure and simple, "a political conspiracy." Brushing aside reams of incriminating testimony and a truckload of exhibits the prosecution had filled the courtroom with, McGovern appealed to something more basic: civic responsibility. He instructed jurors, "If you would do for the public of San Francisco a distinct and just service, you will return an immediate verdict of not guilty."

Considering the case Lynch had painstakingly built over the last week, it was an audacious entreaty. And the jury hadn't even heard what McGovern had in mind.

Two words—Pat Brown—would be McGovern's salvo to save Inez and the others from prison. If the jury voted to convict, it'd be a wholesale indictment of justice led by a power-hungry, career-driven politician. Although Pat hadn't shown up in the courtroom since he'd dabbed Miss Bartron's forehead with his handkerchief, everyone in Department 12 knew who'd been calling the shots for the prosecution. Pat had engineered the state's case from beginning to end with one person in mind: Himself. It would be these twelve jurors who'd propel Pat to where he wanted to go, to where he was destined to go. That's how McGovern painted the entire case, at least.

"Don't make these defendants the goats on the sacrificial altar of the political ambitions of Mr. Brown!" McGovern bellowed, the beginning of a nonstop oration that would run the next three hours. "He is using these women as a springboard to attain higher office through publicity! Don't be pawns in a dirty, political fight!" McGovern called Inez a victim of a vicious attack by the "district attorney's wolf pack." Inez was nothing more than a tool to burnish Pat Brown's insatiable lust for power. The trial, McGovern said, was "Brown and Lynch versus Burns et al., and not the People of the State of California versus Burns et al."

That was for openers.

McGovern proceeded to quote the Bible and Dante's *Divine Comedy*, sprinkling his speech with American, Scottish, and Irish history. Nodding sympathetically towards Inez, who on cue produced a spray of tears, McGovern said, "Hasn't she been punished enough? Hasn't she suffered enough? Look at her poor, wracked body. She is past the noontime of life, past the summer. The shadows of her life are falling toward the east. Obviously she hasn't a great deal of time to stay here."

And McGovern was just warming up.

He blamed the people of San Francisco for arresting Inez and the other four defendants, and said if they are sent to prison, then the people of San Francisco ought to join them. McGovern described Inez as others had for years: "She was operating a public utility. If she is punished, I say the overwhelming majority of the people of San Francisco are equally guilty. How can the ladies and gentlemen of San Francisco excuse themselves? How can the people look at her as she sits there and say that for fifteen years she had gone and done these things and not say, 'We permitted you to do it'?"

McGovern declared what everyone, including the prosecution, knew to be true. "Public opinion had permitted this establishment to run for fifteen years as a necessary evil." Inez's clinic "was running wider open than the City Hospital," McGovern said, charging what prosecutors are loath to admit: "Laws are enforced by public demand." And since there had been no demand to close Inez for so long, why was there such a sudden demand now?

Coincidence? Hardly.

The answer, said McGovern, was Pat Brown's stop-at-nothing ambition, first as district attorney, then, if he won in November, as attorney general, and, after that, as high as Pat could jump. Or as high as voters allowed him to jump.

"We ask you to refuse to take orders in this political conspiracy. I ask Mr. Edmund G. 'Buster' Brown why did he fail, neglect, omit, or refuse to take any action against these defendants for twenty months, if what he says about them is true? How did it happen, Buster, that if in twenty months these things went on and you are the fighting district attorney—God save the name!—you didn't do anything about it except walk around with the keys in your pocket?" McGovern dismissed Brown's hand-picked staff of yes-men prosecutors as a bunch of "peanut politicians" and "tricksters."

"If, during the twenty months since Brown took office, things were as he says they were, why didn't he send one of his satellites out to Mrs. Burns and tell her, 'You have to stop'? If he had been less of a peanut politician and more of a statesman, that's what he would have done." McGovern paused to let that sink in, all the while twisting his gold signet ring. "As Dante says, 'Ambition feeds on strange foods.'"

You didn't need to be a fourteenth-century Italian scholar to ponder the nuance of that loosely stitched quote. McGovern was building his case, whether specious or not, point by point, and it seemed to be working. Two jurors, both women, nodded their heads as McGovern finished his first stanza.

All this was child's play compared to what was to come. McGovern switched from Pat Brown's career lust to a topic few San Franciscans dared even to talk about. But since the inception of World War I, the matter had been on almost everyone's mind.

Calling San Francisco the "Port of Last Fling," McGovern said, "Women are the particular victims of war." Many young women "were patriotic and wanted to do something for the men" headed "across the Pacific sea, where danger lurked. Other women went into bars and were seduced. They made a mistake. They became victims of seducers."

San Francisco women had been encouraged to "welcome" the tens of thousands of GIs who descended on San Francisco during the war years. Should these women have to pay the price for doing what should be of no surprise to anyone? Should they be mothers against their will, raising children without fathers? Should they be asked to bear such a responsibility when they have no desire to do so? If authorities had thought Inez's clinic was so insidious, then why had it been allowed to flourish for so long?

To ask these questions was to answer them, McGovern told the jury.

Consider "some girl close to you, who was the victim of an assault by a man whose race, color, or physical background she did not know. If you were responsible for that girl, would you allow her to bring this child into the world or to stop it?"

McGovern paused a full ten seconds, letting that unnerving image sink into the white jurors' minds, playing it for all it was worth.

Next, McGovern tore into the prosecution's witnesses, labeling them "stool pigeons, double-crossers and informers." He went full bore, comparing them to real-life turncoats: Benedict Arnold, the American general who defected to the British during the Revolutionary War;[1] Leonard McNally, who betrayed Robert Emmet, the Irish nationalist, hanged, beheaded, drawn, and quartered by the British in 1803;[2] and John de Menteith, who informed on William Wallace of Scotland, the leader of the Wars of Scottish Independence, executed in 1305.[3]

The trio was a prelude to, once again, tearing into Pat Brown, comparing him to history's ultimate traitor.

"Judas had the decency to hang himself after he betrayed his master," McGovern intoned to the jury, bowing his head as though he was praying.

McGovern said that the persons who had sold Inez medical equipment and devices were just as guilty as Inez and the other defendants, since they all knew what the supplies were being used for. Inez was a scapegoat, a convenient way for all of San Francisco to wash away its collective guilt.

But it was for Brown whom McGovern reserved the deepest enmity. He praised Pat's predecessor, former district attorney Matthew Brady, recently appointed as a municipal court judge, and called the current district attorney's office a "headquarters for the subornation of perjury in this community." McGovern dismissed Pat as a "wasp, flitting from flower to flower, and stinging as he goes." He charged the prosecution with "coaching" witnesses. He called Tom Lynch and second chair Andrew Eyman publicity-seeking "gumshoes," warning, "The prosecution is trying to use you and fool you." McGovern exhorted the jury to teach Brown and the toadies around him a lesson. "You will do San Francisco a good service if you bring a verdict of not guilty and thus throw back into their laps a case conceived in political ambition and carried out for political ends."

Regarding laws prohibiting abortion, McGovern railed that returning a not-guilty decision would be a "protest verdict," the "only method of registering disapproval of the state statute making abortion a felony." Then, opening his hands, palms outstretched in a gesture of supplication, McGovern glanced back at Inez and the four other defendants, and softened his tone, appealing to jurors to "be as considerate as you can to these fellow human beings."[4]

Looking spent and mournful, dripping in perspiration, McGovern mopped his forehead and closed with, "Judge as you would be judged," from the New Testament's Matthew 7:1–2.[5]

Everyone in the courtroom seemed to exhale together.

Knowing Walter McGovern as he did, Tom Lynch had suspected all along what the defense counsel would try, so he set out as best he could to clip McGovern's righteous wings. Lynch's first mandate was straightforward: to convince jurors to focus on the law. After all, this was a court of *laws*, and Inez and her four employees—not Pat Brown—were on trial for breaking them. It was that simple. "This case cannot be tried on passion, sympathy, or prejudice," Lynch started. "Mrs. Burns was *not* engaged in a public utility for the public welfare. Name-calling is the oldest dodge in the world to camouflage a case which has no other means of support." The defense, Lynch charged, "castigated the police, the district attorney's office, and myself. But *we* are not on trial. All the evidence and the testimony here have been against Mrs. Burns."

As for McGovern's broadside against Pat Brown, Lynch couldn't let those aspersions against his friend and boss go unanswered. McGovern's goading had succeeded. "Mr. McGovern refers to Mr. Brown's illustrious predecessor in the district attorney's office. He was in office for twenty-four years. You can write your own conclusions," Lynch snarled, letting jurors ruminate about Brady's quarter-century-long reputation for graft and corruption.[6] It was an adversarial way to close, but McGovern had gotten the best of Lynch in that regard. Lynch scanned each juror's face, thanked them for their service, and sat down. He seemed pleased with his performance.

Judge Traverso gave jurors a series of complicated and, at times, convoluted instructions that lasted a long eighty minutes. The instructions amounted to reiterating Lynch's admonition that the jury was to reach a verdict based solely on whether the defendants broke the law and on that alone and nothing else. Public opinion, gossip, rumors, newspaper accounts, or personal philosophy had absolutely nothing to do with rendering a fair and impartial verdict, the judge preached. Even if members of the jury disagreed with current laws prohibiting abortion, jurors should not register such beliefs when weighing the evidence in the case. Unanimity was the key here, the judge said. There were ten separate verdict forms—guilty or innocent for each defendant—and for each defendant all jurors must reach a consensus. If a decision were split on any defendant, then a hung jury would be declared on just that defendant, and it would be up to the district attorney's office to try that case and that defendant again. If the district attorney chose not to retry that case, the defendant would go free.

At eleven forty-two Friday morning, the fate of Inez and the four other defendants rested with the jury.

Their first bit of business was to elect a foreman, and jurors chose Jacob Abrams, a retired machinery salesman who lived near Stern Grove in the southwest corner of the city. Then the jury went out to lunch. When they returned, at two fifteen, jurors sent a note to Judge Traverso, asking to take a look at Inez's curious notebooks filled with names, her check stubs, and the hospital records of two of the witnesses who testified they had been hospitalized. Both Lynch and McGovern interpreted these requests as positive signs. Lynch figured jurors wanted to examine the exhibits before pronouncing the defendants guilty; McGovern assumed jurors were questioning the veracity of what the witnesses had testified. Another interpretation was that jurors just wanted to see for themselves if they recognized any of the names of women who had received abortions at Inez's clinic.

At four ten, the jury solemnly filed into the courtroom. It didn't seem to either side that jurors had reached a verdict yet, and they hadn't. Foreman Abrams asked Judge Traverso a basic but essential question: "Just who is legally permitted to perform abortions?"

The judge responded by reading aloud section 274 of the penal code: "Any person, licensed or unlicensed, cannot perform an operation except to save a human life."

Abrams didn't look satisfied. "That doesn't cover what we have in mind," the foreman said.

Judge Traverso appeared perplexed. "There's still doubt after hearing this section?"

Abrams nodded.

"I'll interpolate then," the judge responded, saying no one can perform an abortion in the state of California, even a physician, unless the life of the woman is in jeopardy. At least legally no one can.

Each of the jurors seemed to understand and they filed out of the courtroom once again to resume their deliberations.

At five fifteen, foreman Abrams again sent word to Judge Traverso, this time to inform him that jurors were so divided that they were deadlocked. Judge Traverso told Abrams and the other jurors "to keep trying." The jurors went out for dinner at six and resumed their deliberations at eight.

At nine twenty, foreman Abrams reported again that the jury wasn't able to agree on a verdict. Judge Traverso again ordered jurors to try and reach a consensus. At ten, with no further word from foreman Abrams, Judge Traverso ordered bailiffs to escort the jurors to the five-hundred-room Hotel Whitcomb on Market Street, a marvel of Edwardian architecture that had survived the 1906 earthquake and fire. The judge urged jurors to "get a good night's sleep."

The next morning, jurors reconvened in the Hall of Justice, but by midafternoon, they still hadn't arrived at a consensus. Inez and the four defendants remained in the courtroom, encouraged by Walter McGovern's building enthusiasm. "This is one time when no news is certainly good news," he told them. The experienced litigator had a point. If the state's evidence had been so clear-cut, as Tom Lynch had assured the jurors it was, then they wouldn't have needed more than an hour or two to convict. By now, the jury was going on thirty hours of deliberations.

At five that afternoon, a Saturday, jurors once again returned to the courtroom. This time, foreman Abrams got specific: The jury had deadlocked eleven to one for conviction. A total of eighty-five ballots had been taken, and no one was willing to budge.

Judge Traverso had no choice but to dismiss the jury, calling them "hopelessly deadlocked," parlance for a hung jury, and all five defendants were free.

Walter McGovern smiled and clasped Inez's hand. Musette Briggs hugged Mabel Spaulding. Joe Hoff jubilantly raised both hands above his head as though he had just been declared the winner of a prizefight. Joe Burns, joined by Mabel Malotte, clapped, and when friends and relatives of the other defendants followed, they were silenced by the judge's gavel.

What had happened in the jury room?

After the first round of balloting, the vote had been eight to four to convict all defendants. Subsequent ballots settled at ten to two to convict, with Jean Hibbitts, a housewife who lived not far from where Inez had grown up, one of the holdouts. The other holdout was Anna M. Linder, a widow of an attorney and the mother of five grown children, four of them in the Armed Services. After a fitful night at the hotel, Mrs. Hibbitts came around to the majority Saturday morning, but foreman Abrams said Mrs. Linder could not be swayed. The four other women on the jury had taken Mrs. Linder into a corner and had gone over the evidence with her point by point but to no avail. The eleven jurors got so exasperated with Mrs. Linder's recalcitrance that they resorted to eating their meals at one table, leaving Mrs. Linder to eat at another table alone.

One of the jurors, Leland J. Badaracco, an insurance broker who lived in the Sunset District, said the deadlock was a "great miscarriage of justice." Another juror,

William Gillespie, a Bank of America teller from West Portal, said, "We could have jumped from the window one by one or collectively, and it would not have moved that woman," referring to Mrs. Linder. Another described the standoff as so tense that he thought one of the jurors "was going to strangle" Mrs. Linder.[7]

The stunning verdict and its implications radiated beyond the Hall of Justice. Someone set a fire to Inez's clinic just hours after the jury announced it was dead-locked. The arsonist had drilled holes in the upper and lower flats of the clinic, and two mattresses were set on fire, one on the first floor, the other on the second floor. Like the break-in before the trial, there was little damage to the clinic. The motive for the fire seemed to be to intimidate. Exactly *who* wasn't clear.[8]

The next day, Pat Brown threw several body punches at the jury, grumbling to the press, as had become his habit, of nonspecific "sinister influences." He character-ized the lack of a verdict as a "gross miscarriage of justice," and said the prosecution had presented "the best and most carefully prepared case" since Brown had assumed office.[9]

The larger picture was Pat's ongoing race for attorney general, and how allowing Inez and the four others a pass would play statewide. A district attorney whose office couldn't convict an avowed abortionist with evidence galore . . . well, how was Pat going to put real crooks and thieves behind bars?

He needed to turn this misadventure around, but in the meantime, innuendo would be Pat's friend. "From the day I first walked into the grand jury with this case, until this trial jury was dismissed, I knew there were influences interfering with the administration of justice," Pat grumbled to a bevy of reporters he called to his office. Pat paused to let them keep up. "There are influences that go hand in hand with the tremendous power wielded by the Burns woman."[10]

Pat Brown didn't name names, but Pop Aureguy, McGovern's private investigator, was among the targets of Brown's specious invective. Once during the trial, Mrs. Linder, the sole holdout, was looking for a taxi ride home after Judge Traverso had adjoined for the day when Aureguy rolled up in his Buick and asked if he could give her a lift since they both lived in the Marina District (Mrs. Linder at 3314 Broderick Street, Aureguy at 3601 Baker Street).[11]

"Mr. Brown's dire thoughts, which he implied today, are not clear," Aureguy replied in his typically cryptic manner. "When he makes them clear, we will be able and willing to answer whatever statement or charge he makes regarding our conduct in the Inez Burns trial."[12]

Inez and Musette Briggs.

There was no question that Pat would retry Inez and the other defendants. He had no choice, considering what his Southland opponent for attorney general might do with the defeat. Tom Lynch trumpeted that he would call "ten to twenty" additional prosecution witnesses the next time. To make the case stronger, Pat said he'd ask Mayor Lapham for an additional twenty-five thousand dollars to fund an "extensive investigation" of Inez and a lesser-known San Francisco abortionist, Dr. Charles B. Caldwell.[13]

Meanwhile, Pat tore into Walter McGovern, targeting McGovern for asking jurors to overlook the law and "base their decisions on emotion."

"He can't get away with that kind of stuff," Brown fumed. "I don't mind when he attacks me or my motives, but when, as an officer of the court, he asks the jury to pervert its oath, that's going too far."

McGovern responded, calling Pat "a little whippersnapper."

TWENTY-ONE

DISTRUST

As Pat Brown and Tom Lynch were planning their courtroom strategy to retry Inez and the others, Jerri Marsigli, the twenty-one-year-old Oakland housewife who had testified against Inez in the preliminary hearing, landed in San Francisco's Central Emergency Hospital, the victim of poisoning. Mrs. Marsigli had apparently tried to kill herself by swallowing ammonia. At least, that's how the police reported the incident. She'd been found unconscious in a flophouse hotel in San Francisco's seedy Tenderloin District, at 380 Eddy Street.[1]

But it turned out that Mrs. Marsigli hadn't tried to commit suicide at all. She had discovered she was pregnant once again, and because Inez's clinic was temporarily shut down during the trial, Mrs. Marsigli decided to do the job herself. Women tried lots of ways to self-abort, from intentionally falling down stairs to ingesting household cleaners, ammonia being the most popular. Other abortifacients included castor oil, turpentine, and lye. Coat hangers were the most commonly used objects, and generally imparted the most catastrophic results.[2] Mrs. Marsigli recovered, but her desperate attempt pointed to the extremes women would go to in order to terminate an unwanted pregnancy. Mrs. Marsigli had gone through the wringer with the district attorney's office: her subpoena to appear in court; time off from work; the indignity of testifying about her personal life, not to mention how Mr. Marsigli felt about his wife being questioned in open court. Even if she had waited, Mrs. Marsigli could hardly have gone back to Inez, and the last thing on her mind was shopping around for yet still another abortionist.

With Inez's trial over and still no conviction, Inez quietly went back to work. The way Inez figured it, why not? Pat Brown and Tom Lynch hadn't been able to convict her, so why should she pack up her medical instruments and deny her services to thousands more women? The cat was out of the bag. If someone by chance hadn't heard about Inez and what she did at 327 Fillmore Street, then they certainly knew by now. If the trial had hurt Pat's statewide reputation, it had made Inez's soar. Pat could have asked a judge to issue an injunction against Inez, but what good was that going to do?

Just as they had before the 1945 raid, pregnant women started showing up once again at the clinic each morning, first singly, then in groups. There, they found the front door locked with nary a note posted to it, but the same woman-to-woman network that had gotten them to Inez's clinic in the first place now directed them to her home on Guerrero Street, a twenty-minute ride on the 22-Fillmore. Would police try to raid the house? She'd had already been charged with violating California Penal Code Section 274, and another trial was scheduled in superior court in early spring. So, why *shouldn't* Inez continue while she could? Working out of her home was just another way for Inez to stick it to Pat Brown, Tom Lynch, Judges Traverso and Neubarth, Frank Ahern, and all the rest who had tried to put her behind bars. As if incarcerating Inez would somehow stop women from seeking abortions.

She also could use the money. The three hundred thousand dollars that Inez had tempted Inspector Ahern with had been impounded, and the Bureau of Internal Revenue was breathing down Inez's neck to assess what properties she owned, when they were purchased, and how much in assets she had, all in preparation to present her with yet another tax bill. There was also the not-so-trifling issue of her attorney, Walter McGovern, who definitely hadn't taken on the five defendants' cases pro bono. McGovern expected to get paid, and with another trial around the corner, Inez needed more cash for his retainer.

It was during these in-between months when my friend, twenty-one-year-old Corinne Patchen, had met a soldier at a USO dance, and the two took an immediate liking to each other. The soldier was handsome in his crisp military uniform and pressed garrison cap. He would ship out in a week, and over the next five days, Caroline and the soldier spent as much time together as the enlisted man's training schedule allowed. On his last night in San Francisco, the two ate at Flor D'Italia in North Beach across from Washington Square. Corinne and the soldier returned to her studio apartment on Russian Hill, where the soldier spent the night. Six weeks later, Corinne discovered she was pregnant.

Corinne was referred to Inez by a North Beach attorney, and it was in Inez's parlor at the Guerrero Street house one afternoon in May 1946 that the two met. Corinne ended up not having an abortion at Inez's or anyone else's hands, and her son was born seven months later.[3]

That same spring, Pat's Brown's request to Mayor Lapham for the twenty-five thousand dollars to reopen his investigation into Inez's clinic got halved when it came before the Board of Supervisors. With some of those funds, Tom Lynch and Andrew Eyman, the deputy district attorney who had been Lynch's second chair at the trial, flew to an undisclosed location in the Midwest on a wild-goose chase to uncover what they said would be additional evidence against Inez but refused to elaborate. Meanwhile, columnist Herb Caen wrote that Pat Brown planned to fly to New York to meet with reprobates Warren and Gloria Shannon to figure out how their testimony might add to the prosecution's case.[4]

Pat's plate by no means was filled with just Inez's trial; there was the usual assortment of felonies, including murders, that all big-city prosecutors handle. But Inez's case was special. It showcased not only Pat's touted moral code of family values, but also allowed him to focus on rampant police and government corruption, marketable items in the upcoming race for the state's top legal gun. It allowed Pat to shine as the crusading real *Mr. District Attorney*. Certainly, that ought to translate to votes. Besides, Pat had his lieutenant Tom Lynch to handle the tedious spadework of a trial.

Pat thus charged headfirst toward the June primary, a necessity since Republican Fred Howser had entered both the Democratic and Republican primaries, which was permitted at the time. Howser's supporters, led by Artie Samish, had bottomless pockets and didn't mind spending whatever it would take to defeat Brown. To counteract any fallout from the disastrous trial against Inez, Pat preemptively lobbed a fusillade at Howser, charging that his campaign treasurer, T. Kirk Hill, used to be the director of a company that owned a string of offshore gambling ships in Southern California, and that as Los Angeles district attorney, Howser had been soft on shutting them down. Of course, Brown himself had a long history of connections with gambling interests, from his father's gambling club to his years as a private attorney representing card parlors and bingo halls. These gambling venues just hadn't been as large and as lucrative as the Los Angeles gambling ships.

The statewide election was shaping up to be tough to win for Pat. Republican Earl Warren was an immensely likable governor up for a second term, and Attorney General Robert Kenny, a wonky and ineffective campaigner, headed the Democratic Party ticket for governor. Pat had doubts whether any Democrat would be able to cut in on Warren's long swath of coattails.[5] Still, with the retrial of Inez scheduled for mid-May, just weeks before the primary, the timing couldn't have been better. Pat needed statewide recognition, and a well-publicized victory could afford him press and headway against Howser.

This time, Pat's office would be trying not just one abortion case, but two, both opening on the same day. In addition to Inez et al., Andrew Eyman would be trying Charles B. Caldwell, a Market Street physician, for the Christmas Day abortion death of Signa Bredeson, a thirty-nine-year-old Ingleside mother of two. Competing abortionists make strange bedfellows, and while Caldwell and Inez knew each other, they weren't friends. Inez saw scores of patients every month, and even though Caldwell was a physician, she had more experience than he or nearly anyone anywhere.

Lynch didn't let on what he was planning the second time around, with the exception of adding to the number of Inez's former patients he planned to have testify. "We laid our cards on the table in the first trial—we think we had a strong hand then, and still think so," Lynch said, in a typical admit-nothing preview of his case. "We'll play these cards again."[6]

The judge this time would be forty-two-year-old Herbert C. Kaufman, viewed by fellow jurists as a kind of whiz kid. Kaufman graduated from Berkeley and San Francisco's Hastings College of Law, and had been admitted to the bar when he was just twenty-one. Appointed to the municipal bench in 1938 by Republican Governor Frank Mirriam when he was thirty-four, Kaufman ran for superior court judge five years later. His campaign slogan had been "Justice delayed is justice denied"; Kaufman charged that his opponent, a seventy-two-year-old judge by the name of John J. Von Nostrand, took as long as two years to render his decisions.[7] Breezy Kaufman had the reputation as hardworking and efficient. He had an impressive and ready intellect. He was a Mason, a member of the Improved Order of Red Men, the Elks, the Eagles, and the Moose, and was an avid fly fisherman who spent weekends at the Russian River in Sonoma County angling for bass and bluegills.[8]

As the second trial opened, jurors this time were chosen out of a pool of eighty candidates, with each side given thirty-five preemptory challenges. For her close-up in court, Inez showed up wearing a forest-green chapeau and matching suit with a straight skirt she found at Nelly Gaffney's. Inez ditched the fur for a three-quarter-length chocolate-brown knit wool coat.

Right from the beginning, everyone who paid attention to such matters could see that Judge Kaufman was more of an intellectual than Judge Traverso. He was

Superior Court Judge Herbert C. Kaufman.

more thoughtful when it came to issuing rulings from the bench. Judge Traverso had banged his gavel the moment McGovern rose to object; Kaufman waited, listened, and pondered. As he had done prior to the first trial, defense counsel McGovern objected to a raft of Lynch's questions to prospective jurors, including, "Do you think abortion should be legalized?" and "Would you be prejudiced if it is shown that women went to these defendants for abortions voluntarily?" This time around, though, Judge Kaufman sustained almost all of McGovern's challenges. What a difference. Herb Kaufman was the kind of judge Walter McGovern could get behind.

During voir dire, the compact, insular world of San Francisco, where everyone was related, knew each other, or knew someone who knew someone else who knew a prospective juror, revealed itself once again. The husband of a woman in the jury pool had once been sued by McGovern; another would-be juror knew Pop Aureguy; another had played golf with a deputy district attorney in Pat Brown's office; another worked in the same insurance office as a juror from the first trial. All were excused.

Then there was the matter of political philosophy. A bacteriologist from the University of California declared he was against any law prohibiting abortion, no matter what the evidence would prove. He was discharged, as were two other men who readily agreed. All this airing of personal opinion prompted a mild rebuke from Judge Kaufman. "A citizen has no right to form such opinions on hearsay or on anything except legal evidence in a court of law," the judge lectured the dwindling pool of jurors. "This sort of thinking is contrary in our duties as citizens and has no place under our democratic system." Perhaps intellectually, yes, but practically, no. Every juror has a storehouse of opinions that forms a foundation of beliefs independent of what gets introduced in court. It's impossible to partition such core beliefs so they don't bear on the evidence presented in a court of law. Every trial attorney knows this. The trick, if you're a litigator, of course, is to get a glimpse of those beliefs before choosing each juror.

One potential juror, Viola Swartz, volunteered that she was opposed to abortions for personal economic reasons. Judge Kaufman looked puzzled, and asked her why.

"Because my husband is in the baby food business," Mrs. Swartz announced rather indignantly. She was promptly excused.

The back-and-forth pleased the defense for another reason besides giving hope to McGovern that Judge Kaufman seemed impartial. McGovern needed to give private investigator Pop Aureguy enough time to dig up anything he could in each prospective juror's background to indicate whether he or she might be friend or foe. Aureguy was being paid by McGovern to profile those who would sit on the jury. What potential jurors admitted in open court was an element in any trial; what they believed in private was another. McGovern wanted to stall for as long as he could for Aureguy to find out anything he could about potential jurors that might signal a predisposed opinion on the matters at hand. All day long, Aureguy popped in and out of court, whispering into McGovern's ear about whatever he had uncovered about each man and woman in the jury pool.[9]

After four days, both sides agreed to a jury of eight women and four men. McGovern had used fifteen preemptory challenges, Lynch fourteen.[10]

As testimony began, Lynch called many of the same witnesses, including former employees of the clinic, patients, deliverymen, salesmen, and police officers, but this time he produced several new witnesses. A San Leandro woman, who went to Inez for an abortion, testified that Inez had boasted, "You needn't worry. I've been doing this work for twenty-five years, and there's never been a slipup," an admission neither side disputed.[11] The admission could play to either the defense or the prosecution.

In responding to an objection from McGovern, Inez's defense got a huge boost when Judge Kaufman announced that testimony from Inez's former patients must be viewed as coming from "coconspirators," or "accomplices," and as such ought to be considered with "distrust." In the first trial, Judge Traverso had allowed such testimony despite McGovern's strenuous objections. McGovern viewed this turn as pivotal for the defense.

There was more good news for McGovern. Judge Kaufman ruled that he wouldn't allow into evidence Inez's two ledgers, with the names of patients and physicians, the twin "sticks of dynamite" passed among jurors during the first trial. The judge's reason for exclusion: The notebooks were private and there was no proof they were written by Inez or that they even were her property.

McGovern liked this judge. He wasn't a part of the Pat Brown machine. Herb Kaufman had a mind of his own and wasn't afraid to exercise it. He was what a judge was supposed to be. McGovern was feeling so good about his prospects this time around that he asked Judge Kaufman for a directed verdict of acquittal. The judge denied the motion, of course, but this time without a scowl.

As in the first trial, McGovern mounted no defense. His position was the same as before—that if Inez and her employees were convicted, then all of San Francisco ought to be convicted for allowing her business to flourish for so long. The impact of the war had caused an increase in the number of unwanted pregnancies and women who got pregnant shouldn't be blamed. Many of them had gotten carried away. Many were victims. Why should they be saddled with the financial responsibility of offspring they neither wanted nor planned for? Why weren't men being held responsible for the pregnancies that they had created? In fact, McGovern intoned, the people of San Francisco owed Inez no small degree of gratitude for providing such an essential service to women of the city, state, and nation.

Just as McGovern was driving home his case with dramatic crescendo, a heckler in the courtroom stood up and shouted, "What church is this in?"

"I beg your pardon," McGovern responded, turning toward the interloper.

The man repeated the question, but by then a bailiff had grabbed the man's arm and was escorting him out of the courtroom. McGovern turned to the jury and quipped, "He must have fallen out of his high chair when he was a baby."[12] Perhaps an ill-advised comment, but a rejoinder that nonetheless prompted several jurors to laugh.

In his closing this time, McGovern offered that the five defendants weren't ogres, but compassionate caregivers whose essential services were in demand. Once again, while twisting his signet ring, McGovern preached the words of sages, philosophers, and poets. McGovern told the jury, "When your time comes to die, you will do so more easily if you have tempered justice with mercy," a line borrowed from either Portia's discourse in *The Merchant of Venice* or Clarence Darrow's defense of Nathan Leopold and Richard Loeb in 1924.[13]

When Tom Lynch rose, the prosecutor reaffirmed that the case was nothing of the kind that McGovern had portrayed. The matter was open and shut, a simple issue of law, not necessarily of justice. He alliteratively termed McGovern's defense a combination of "sarcasm, sympathy, solicitude, sophistry." Did Inez and the four defendants break the law or not? Lynch asked. There was nothing nuanced or complicated about that. The answer could be decided in a matter of minutes, Lynch declared to the jurors.

The jury filed out of the courtroom at three twenty-seven in the afternoon. The first bit of business was electing a foreman, and that responsibility fell to John O. Wagner, a traffic manager of the Emil Clemens Horst Co., San Francisco exporters of hops and hop-picking machinery. The jurors then took a dinner break. At eight forty-five, back in the jury room, foreman Wagner buzzed the judge. He had a request.

Could Judge Kaufman provide the jury with a dictionary? Not a law dictionary, but an ordinary dictionary of the English language. Wagner gave no indication what word or words the jurors wanted to look up.

Judge Kaufman said he had never before been asked by a jury to procure a dictionary, and since nothing in the state code mandated that such a request be granted, he denied it. Wagner looked disappointed but said he understood, and then told the judge that jurors wanted to break for the evening; they repaired, as did the first jury, to the Hotel Whitcomb at 1231 Market Street. They had thus far deliberated three hours and forty minutes. As in the first trial, Walter McGovern took this as a positive sign.

The next morning, jurors reconvened, but by noon they still hadn't reached a verdict. Tom Lynch, running scared, declared perhaps prematurely, "If this jury fails to agree, there definitely will be a third trial."[14]

Despite Lynch's bravado, to try Inez and the others a third time would pose an enormous risk to the prosecution. If the second jury was also unable to return a verdict, it would send a clear and convincing message that unanimity may well be impossible in this particular case. It also wouldn't auger well for Pat Brown, who in less than ten days would be facing Fred Howser in the June primary. And further, even if this jury was somehow able to reach a guilty verdict, the defendants would likely serve no more than the midterm of a two- to five-year prison sentence. Yet Lynch and Brown were treating Inez and her codefendants as though they were being tried for a capital crime. No one figured exactly how much public money had been spent on the two trials thus far, but it was substantial in terms of time, capital, and resources. Was getting a guilty verdict against Inez and the other four worth all that Pat Brown and Tom Lynch were willing to pay for it?

At seven after nine Tuesday night, on May 28, 1946, foreman Wagner and the other jurors filed back into the courtroom. By now, they had deliberated for twelve hours. Both Lynch and McGovern studied each juror, paying close attention to any sign that might signal a verdict.

One juror, Hazel Mayo, looked directly at McGovern and ever so slightly tilted her chin. Both attorneys saw the body language, but only McGovern nodded back to Mrs. Mayo. He reached for Inez's hand and squeezed it.

The judge directed his attention to foreman Wagner, who stood and announced that the jury was in "hopeless disagreement." Judge Kaufman shook his head and grimaced, then polled each juror and asked whether there was any hope, any hope at all, for a verdict. All said no.

"I'm going to ask each of you again. Do you see any hope that you might all agree on a verdict?"

This time the nos were more emphatic.

The judge said he had no choice but to thank the jurors for their service and dismiss them.

Inez and the other defendants let out a cheer, which prompted Judge Kaufman to silence them with his gavel. In the hallway, the foreman Wagner said jurors had divided themselves seven to five for conviction through twenty voice votes and four ballots. No one would budge either way. The sticking point was the judge's admonition that prosecution witnesses had to be viewed with distrust. Hearing that, the five jurors who favored acquitting Inez believed that the prosecution had no case. They just couldn't convince the other side. Those convinced of the defendants' guilt couldn't persuade the other side to switch their allegiance. The breakdown had been six women, one man, for conviction; three women, two men, for acquittal.[15]

The word jurors wanted to look up in the dictionary was *distrust*; that was how Judge Kaufman had cautioned the jury to view the parade of prosecution witnesses. The judge had been very clear: Testimony from such witnesses must be viewed with not just skepticism, but with *distrust*.

In the hallway, Tom Lynch again vowed to retry Inez and the others, even without conferring with Pat Brown, who was nowhere to be seen.

Two hung juries and Pat didn't have anything better to do than have Tom Lynch bring Inez and the others to trial for a *third* time? And if that jury couldn't reach a verdict, would there be another trial, and another, and another? When was all this going to stop? When did prosecution turn to persecution?

"That son of a bitch Brown isn't going to let this go, is he?" Inez said to McGovern as the two got ready to leave the courtroom. This time, she didn't bother to keep her voice at a whisper. Inez was angry. McGovern couldn't disagree with her.

If two sets of twelve strangers couldn't agree on the merits of the case, then maybe no jury would—or should—agree. Perhaps the people had already spoken.

If Inez had anything to rejoice that evening, it was the percentage of jurors who favored an outright acquittal. The first jury had divided eleven to one to convict. The second jury had split seven to five to convict. Inez was gaining in numbers. If Pat Brown and Tom Lynch were bullheaded enough to pursue a third trial, let them bring it on. Maybe a third airing of the case would be the charm.

In the meantime, it was time for a big party at sprawling Burns Ranch. Inez, Nelly Gaffney, Mable Malotte, Joe, Walter McGovern, Pop Aureguy, Mabel, Myrtle, Musette, Joe, a half dozen cops, Drs. Long Shot, Eliaser, Rogers, Commins, some friendly attorneys, along with fifty more friends, were going to celebrate—if not a win, then not a loss. Inez's *aide de camp* at the ranch, Fats Selmi, had invited a young comedian by the name of Pinky Lee, who'd make one and all drown their woes and sorrow. For the time being, that is.

TWENTY-TWO

THE BRIDGE OF SIGHS

As Tom Lynch was preparing for an unprecedented third trial against Inez, Pat Brown had to decide how he was going to handle a petty and irksome case of obscenity. This time, the offender wasn't Jane Russell's busty anatomy, but a book, Edmund Wilson's *Memoirs of Hecate County*, a sordid tale of suburban sex, scandal, and salaciousness. Ever the protectors of family values, the Hearst papers had started a fussy campaign to ban the book, which did nothing except rocket the Doubleday novel to the best-seller list.[1] Weighing the implications the case might have on the upcoming election, Pat instructed Police Chief Dullea to order two police officers to buy a copy of the novel with the purpose of arresting the bookseller. The DA's office then filed criminal charges against Stuart F. Cunningham, manager of Lieberman's Book Store at 723 Market Street.[2]

At the subsequent obscenity trial, the jury deliberated three hours and failed to reach a verdict. "We will try it again and again," Deputy District Attorney Vincent Mullins declared. "We are dealing with a principle as well as this vile book." Just as he had done with Inez's trial, Pat Brown planned to retry the obscenity case against the hapless bookseller. That trial was scheduled for December. Win or lose, it would be after the election for attorney general, so for Pat the hung jury bought him time.[3] In June, Republican candidate Fred Howser had scared Pat, nearly knocking him out in the Democratic primary; Pat survived only by the skin of his teeth, barely advancing to the general election.[4] It was now on to November by the narrowest of margins.

Pat knew there wasn't much of a correlation between a district attorney's conviction rate and his electability, particularly to statewide office. For prosecutors, politics and likability superseded performance in the courtroom, where Pat rarely ventured anyway. Pat hired lieutenants for that. The trenches were for career prosecutors like Tom Lynch. Pat sought to be the general. How competent Pat actually was as a prosecutor had far less bearing than the public's perception of his competency. As the candidate, Pat had deals to make, backs to slap, speeches to deliver, and donors to be soothed and courted. Pat didn't want to provide Howser and his chief sponsor, Artie Samish, with any ammunition. Inez had been so flagrant in her lawbreaking that convicting her and the others ought to have been a cakewalk. Or so Pat had thought before the two embarrassing hung juries. Getting a guilty verdict had turned more than just political. It had become personal, turning into a matter of pride, honor, and no small amount of machismo.

A dead-to-rights female abortionist had walked all over Pat and Lynch. Inez had been breaking the law for decades, plain and simple, and two juries of San Francisco residents somehow couldn't summon the requisite gumption to declare her and her employees guilty. Ever the politician, without a statewide election around the corner, Pat might have capitulated for expediency's sake. But the stakes were too high to fold now. Convicting Inez, Pat fulminated to reporters, was essential to rid "scandal and corruption in the community."[5] He had bet his reputation and political future on it.

With the third trial set to open in September 1946, the public titillation of bringing an abortionist and her team of assistants to trial had begun to wear thin. It might have been just as well, if you were Pat. The newspapers and public were getting tired of eavesdropping on a third performance of what essentially was the same drama, actors, and material. From the prosecution's point of view, though, retrying the case raised all kinds of peril. Why risk still another hung jury—or a straight-up not-guilty verdict? Each successive jury had edged closer and closer to declaring Inez and the others innocent. And even if Lynch could secure a conviction in trying Inez again, there always was the possibility of an appeal, based on an inadvertent misstep from the judge or the prosecution. Being a prosecutor is akin to being a surgeon. Every time a prosecutor goes into court, there's inherent, unforeseen risk, no matter how certain and straightforward the case appears from the outset. If the legal system is rigged, it is rigged for the defense, as it should be.

The occasion was thus ripe for Lynch and McGovern to come up with a quiet deal for Inez and the four other defendants. The two trials had already gone on far too long, sapping Pat Brown's resources and Tom Lynch's time for more than a year. The political capital expended on the two trials had been ridiculous, not to mention the actual costs in dollars. As long as Lynch could save face for himself and Pat, and as long as Inez and the others would avoid prison, then both the prosecution and defense could celebrate at the end of the day. So behind the scenes, that's exactly what Lynch and McGovern set out to do: to make this case somehow disappear through a negotiated plea bargain.

Both attorneys agreed that the five defendants would plead guilty to misdemeanor charges of practicing medicine without a license in exchange for neither jail nor prison time. There would be fines for their misdeeds, but no mention of performing abortions.

Negotiating such a deal would allow for everyone to return to the more pressing issues of the day. Pat Brown and Tom Lynch wouldn't be folding. Let another DA tangle with Inez and her abortion clinic after Pat got elected attorney general in November. McGovern could get back to his prosperous practice of law and get out from under the burden of another trial. A settlement would put Inez's legal hydra back in a bottle. That Brown and Lynch would agree to such a plea bargain showed how absolutely desperate the prosecution was to dump the whole matter, despite all of Pat's righteous pronouncements otherwise.[6]

Both sides breathed a sigh of relief—until Lynch and McGovern ran into a roadblock. When informed of the proposed deal, the superior court judge assigned to the trial, Robert McWilliams, blinked. He refused to sign off, rendering the plea bargain dead. This infuriated Walter McGovern, who charged that Judge McWilliams ought to have disqualified himself from hearing the case in the first place. McWilliams had been a prosecutor with the US Attorney's office, which had twice gone after Inez for income-tax evasion. McWilliams had prosecuted Inez as had Tom Lynch for the feds. To McGovern, McWilliams was as biased against Inez as Lynch and Brown were, but McWilliams this time would be presiding as the judge over her trial. If this didn't smack of a perversion of justice, McGovern didn't know what did. Judge McWilliams responded by throwing up his hands and further recusing himself from the case.[7]

With their carefully constructed deal off the table, Lynch and McGovern had no choice but to square off for another trial.

For Lynch, the defeat in the first two trials hadn't been for lack of evidence. Inez was guilty of the charges; both sides had conceded to that. It was the jurors who had refused to put aside their notions of whether abortion was right or wrong. In the first trial, the rub for the prosecution had been the one holdout on the jury, Anna Linder. Perhaps Mrs. Linder had voted her conscience, but perhaps she had been persuaded to vote her conscience. Had private investigator Pop Aureguy gotten to her with money or some other incentive to be the sole holdout? Pat and Lynch had their suspicions. In the second trial, Judge Kaufman had started off on the wrong foot for the prosecution by declaring that witnesses must be considered coconspirators and therefore viewed with "distrust." The brainy Judge Kaufman had bent over backward to be more than fair to the defense. How could Lynch have won that case when the judge had called into question the testimony of eyewitnesses who had been inside Inez's clinic? With that kind of ruling, the prosecution had been lucky that Inez and the others hadn't gotten an outright acquittal.

With no plea bargain, Pat Brown and Tom Lynch would need a reptilian judge who would ride hard on Walter McGovern and all of his eloquent pronouncements that if Inez were declared guilty then all of San Francisco must share in her guilt. That had nothing to do with the law. Lynch had been right when he declared as much. But experience had shown the attorneys that few juries ever base their verdicts strictly on the law. Deciding guilt and innocence had as much to do with the emotional attachments jurors form with both sides as with anything else. There also was the issue of equating prosecution witnesses with "distrust," as Judge Kaufman had put it. For the prosecution to win, that judicial opinion had to be quashed. What prosecutor would ever be able to convict a defendant if state witnesses had to be viewed with misgivings and suspicion? These witnesses Lynch had called to testify weren't criminals who had been in prison for years, summoned to court in exchange for a shot at freedom. They were mild-mannered druggists, medical-supply company owners, manufacturers, former employees, and once-pregnant women who had gotten themselves to Inez's clinic for abortions. Their testimony was essential to the prosecution's case and ought to be viewed as such. Pat Brown and Tom Lynch needed a jury who would understand that, and they needed a judge who'd look at the law the way they did.

They got more than they had hoped for in a jurist by the name of Edward P. Murphy, who appointed himself to sit in judgment over the next trial. Pat Brown, Tom Lynch, and Judge Ed Murphy were three peas in a pod.

Murphy was the tough-talking presiding judge of the superior court, the judge who doled out cases to other judges on the bench. He also happened to be the same judge who was presiding over the concurrent grand jury investigation of Inez and police corruption.

Appointed municipal court judge at age thirty-seven, six months later Judge Murphy was elevated to the superior court. A Nevada native, he was an avid hunter. Judge Murphy was a linguist who spoke German, Spanish, Italian, and French; that might make him a good match for the longwinded, erudite McGovern. Judge Murphy grew up in Sacramento and earned undergraduate and law degrees, like Lynch,

Superior Court Judge
Edward P. Murphy.

from the Catholic Santa Clara University.[8] Stocky and stern, from his perch on the bench, he had the habit of peering over horn-rimmed glasses and staring down anyone who disagreed with him. He ruled his courtroom as though it was his living room.

As the trial commenced on September 17, 1946, in Department 11 of the Hall of Justice, Judge Murphy streamlined jury selection so completely that it was over almost before it began. The vexing legal arguments Judge Kaufman had entertained were summarily ruled out of order by the punctilious Judge Murphy. When McGovern asked a prospective juror about her attitude toward birth control and abortion, Judge Murphy instantly smacked his gavel, sustaining the prosecution's objection. Such a line of questioning was irrelevant in Judge Murphy's courtroom.

"I want a jury today!" Murphy exclaimed to both counsel on the first day, sounding more like a spoiled child demanding a pony for Christmas than a judge.[9]

This time, the pool of jurors was chosen from one hundred twenty-five candidates. The defense excused eighteen in peremptory challenges, the prosecution twenty-four. When assembled under Judge Murphy's fast-track expedited rules, the jury consisted of seven women and five men; it included an Army officer's wife, two accountants, a shipfitter's wife, a bank teller, a doctor's wife, two housewives, a steamship company employee, and a jewelry store employee. Once they were seated in the jury box, Judge Murphy swiveled his large leather chair toward them and delivered an hour-long sermon, warning jurors that "certain forces" may try to influence their verdict. "If any person approaches you, you must get in touch with me immediately—at any hour of the day or night, at my home or office." If that wasn't enough to intimidate the jurors, the judge warned, "You cannot simply say, 'I do not like this law and will not abide by it.' If there is anyone who feels that way, speak up. No offense will be taken. It is your duty to speak."[10] Judge Murphy wasn't about to preside over a replay of the first two trials. He was in charge of overseeing a trial in which the verdict had all but been declared.

One juror, Henry C. Tinney, timidly raised his hand, and volunteered that he knew Police Inspector Frank Ahern. The judge immediately replaced Tinney with an alternate.[11] Then, just as Lynch was readying his opening, Judge Murphy dismissed one more juror, Thomas J. Furner, a cashier, when a deputy district attorney, John Rudden, happened to step into the courtroom and recognized Furner as a defendant in an upcoming hit-and-run case down the hall. Judge Murphy promptly replaced Furner with the second alternate juror.[12]

But by then the jury had already been sworn in and impaneled. In Walter

McGovern's mind, no judge could replace a juror at this point. It was too late. The trial had already begun. Juror Furner had been charged with (but not convicted of) a vehicular felony. That wasn't grounds for a judge to bounce a juror in any event. Judge Murphy had overstepped his judicial bounds, McGovern told the court.

The ramifications of such a potential misstep were huge. McGovern asked that all charges be immediately dismissed against the five defendants, and that they be set free at once. If McGovern could show that Furner had been dismissed from a lawfully constituted jury and that the trial had indeed already commenced, then the sacred legal principle of double jeopardy would attach to the case.

Judge Murphy didn't see it that way.

He promptly denied McGovern's motion, ruling that no witnesses had yet been sworn or called, so the trial hadn't yet started, and therefore, double jeopardy was not in play.[13] McGovern harrumphed but sat down, tucking his objection into his back pocket.

With another juror chosen to replace Furner and the jury once again impaneled, Judge Murphy informed jurors that they would be sequestered for the duration of the trial at the Hotel Whitcomb, however long that would be. Jurors would be prohibited from seeing their families for the length of the trial, as well as for their deliberations. Three deputy sheriffs would be posted as guards at the hotel to protect the jury from all outside contact.[14]

By all counts, the judge's sequestration order was a remarkable measure. Even in murder trials, few juries were ever sequestered, except during their final deliberations. Although Pat Brown had repeatedly fulminated there had been evidence of jury tampering during the first two trials, those staticky charges never went anywhere. Pat had never proffered anything to support them. Furthermore, not only was sequestering a jury expensive, it also often sped up verdicts, since jurors generally wanted to return home and to work. Judge Murphy's extraordinary sequestration mandate was the first time such a measure had been imposed on any San Francisco jury since the Preparedness Day bombing trials in 1916, thirty years earlier, when two defendants had been charged with the deaths of ten people and the wounding of forty bystanders; the penalty at the time had been death by hanging.[15]

Was sequestering the jury in a comparatively minor abortion trial really necessary?

Incredulous with Judge Murphy's strong-handed ruling, McGovern registered his objection, but the judge bulldozed him. "I intend to make the case foolproof," Judge Murphy declared,[16] sounding more like a prosecutor than a judge sworn to be impartial.

As the gala San Francisco Opera season opened with another Wagnerian opera, this time *Lohengrin*, so did Inez's third trial, along with an unusual and oppressive fall heat wave, as tens of thousands of American Legionnaires were about to descend on San Francisco for their annual national convention. To Judge Murphy, the issue in his courtroom was simple and straightforward: Were Inez and her codefendants guilty of performing, or assisting to perform, abortions? Jurors were to decide up or down. There would be no in between, no debating finer points. Put the defendants on the chopping block; armed with a sharpened carving knife, Lynch would go about his job under the supervision of flinty-eyed Judge Murphy. Case closed even before it opened.

The prosecution's first witness was Madeline Rand, Inez's former employee who had turned state's witness. Miss Rand, twenty-six, testified that Inez performed at least fifteen abortions a day; she also identified a raft of medical instruments and supplies the police had seized from Inez's Fillmore Street clinic.

Time ran out before McGovern could cross-examine, and since the first day of the trial was a Friday, the jurors were sent to the Hotel Whitcomb for the weekend. On Saturday, sheriff's deputies took jurors to a movie, and on Sunday, the deputies escorted them to a football game between the San Francisco 49ers, playing in their debut season, and the Brooklyn Dodgers, held at Kezar Stadium in Golden Gate Park. The 49ers won 32–13.

Monday was the hottest day of the year, a scorching ninety degrees. Well, at least scorching for San Francisco. Lynch got to the courthouse early and started filling up the courtroom with examination and operating tables, anesthetic machines, tanks of oxygen and nitrous oxide. The courtroom looked like a crowded hospital-supply showroom. When it came to the lineup of prosecution witnesses that day, three of Inez's former patients suddenly chose not to testify. Nerves had gotten the best of them. Or maybe it had been Pop Aureguy. One said her testimony would "incriminate and degrade" her. Two others "suddenly disappeared," as Lynch put it, and could not be found anywhere.[17]

Lynch wasn't taking any chances this time around. A total of thirteen of Inez's former patients were standing or sitting in the hallway outside the courtroom. Some were nervous and fidgety, others stoic and ready to meet their fate. No one knew their exact motives, except that they had been interviewed and coached by the prosecution, and had been subpoenaed to appear in court, and that there was just no other way around it. Figuring out the order of which women would testify took some time, as well as some last-minute cajoling from Lynch and his assistants, and there was a delay in getting witnesses to the stand. This did not sit well with Judge Murphy.

"Please get those people in here quickly!" the judge barked.

"We are, Your Honor," Lynch replied as compliantly as he could under the circumstances.

"Well, it isn't quick enough!" the judge snapped.[18]

The staccato sound of high heels clicking against the floor once again punctuated the courtroom as woman after woman proceeded to the stand to tell her story. The packed courtroom leaned forward in anticipation of each woman's scarlet testimony.

The women were followed by Edward Scott, the druggist who previously testified that he had sold large quantities of pharmaceuticals and medical and surgical supplies to Inez for years. Scott was followed by William Sinclair, a bank teller at the Bank of America branch on Fillmore Street, who told the court that Mabel Spaulding on occasion had made cash deposits in a running account apparently for incidentals.[19]

Outside of showcasing the prosecution's witnesses, Judge Murphy had little patience for much. He refused all attempts by McGovern to introduce anything that wasn't black-letter law. San Francisco residents' long-standing acceptance of what Inez did for a living was patently relevant, the judge ruled repeatedly, each ruling affirmed by a resounding thwack of his gavel.

If all these rebuffs weren't enough for Walter McGovern's chins to droop even more, the prosecution called a surprise witness.

Tom Lynch had located the "lost" Levina Blanchette Queen, Inez's former anesthetist who had disappeared after police appeared at her Forest Hill home almost year earlier, eluding cops by climbing over the back fence, dressed in a nightie and fur coat. Forty-two-year-old Mrs. Paul Queen, labeled a "chic brunette" by the *San Francisco Chronicle*, had skipped town and had been a fugitive ever since. A warrant had been issued for her arrest. The Canadian native had eluded police while on the lam, hopscotching from Salt Lake City to New York to Miami to Quebec.

As soon as Levina Queen took the stand, Inez whispered furiously to McGovern, who cupped his hand over his mouth and Inez's. Mrs. Queen was a witness who clearly alarmed Inez. She knew things. She'd been granted immunity for her testimony, and to earn that immunity, she would have plenty to testify about. While getting settled in the witness stand, Inez tried to stare Mrs. Queen down, and for a moment, the two women's eyes locked. But even Inez's snarly glower couldn't keep the witness from spilling her guts.

It was a brutal round for the defense. Mrs. Queen testified for more than an hour. She said she earned three hundred dollars a month while employed by Inez, adding that she saw Inez, Musette Briggs, and Joe Hoff perform anywhere from twenty to forty abortions a day. Mrs. Queen told the court that three physicians frequently showed up at the clinic and also performed abortions on the premises too. She went into graphic detail about the procedures, which she testified she saw firsthand after administering anesthesia to the patients.[20]

Inez continued staring daggers at Levina Queen, which seemed to have no impact whatsoever on Mrs. Queen's testimony.

Inez was appalled that yet someone else she had trusted—once again, another person she had befriended and on whom she had bestowed gifts galore (including the fur coat Mrs. Queen had been wearing when she fled from police)—would so savagely turn on her. It was a redo of Gloria and Warren Shannon, Madeline Rand, and all the others. Even the procession of once-pregnant women Inez had ministered to, they, too, had turned against her. These women had come to *her*, many of them with tears in their eyes, begging Inez to help them out of their awful predicament. And this was how they repaid her? Was there no honor left in the world?

It all proved once again what Inez had known for almost her entire life: She could trust no one. That's what she had learned long ago, from her father, from G. W. Merritt, William Brown, Charlie Granelli. But they were men. These toxic witnesses sitting across from her now, testifying against her in this courtroom, were women. What had happened to the underground woman-to-woman network that had sent tens of thousands of women to Inez for decades? Was there no loyalty, no sense of sisterhood that these women shared? All Inez had done was what these women had implored her to do, safely and without complications.

Inez's elegiac reverie was interrupted when McGovern could take Mrs. Queen's bruising allegations no more. He rose to object—to both Mrs. Queen's graphic testimony and to the fact that in testifying, she was also implicating herself in the alleged crimes she had committed. "Sit down, Mr. McGovern!" Judge Murphy told him. McGovern had no choice. He had been muzzled.

On cross-examination, McGovern made it a point to refer to Mrs. Queen as "madam." It was uncertain whether McGovern meant to associate her with a house of ill repute or whether "madam" was an honorific to address a witness who had just admitted that she had assisted in performing hundreds of abortions herself, thus making her testimony suspect and self-serving. She was a tainted witness, a coconspirator, and because of that Mrs. Queen's account must be viewed with distrust, McGovern argued once again.[21]

Again, Judge Murphy scolded McGovern "to sit down!"[22] The judge lowered his nose, peered over his spectacles, and instructed the jury that every word of Mrs. Queen's testimony would be allowed into the court record. Judge Murphy had taken a giant flyswatter and flattened big, blustery Walter McGovern with one swipe.

When it was the defense's turn to present its case, once again, McGovern introduced no witnesses or evidence. Neither Inez nor any of the other defendants would take the stand.

"The defense rests, Your Honor," McGovern said, this time wearily and mournfully.

For the state's close, Lynch let his cocounsel, Deputy District Attorney Bert Hirschberg, present the people's case. Perhaps thirty-nine-year-old Hirschberg would have more luck than Lynch had had in the closings of the first two trials. Perhaps jurors needed a face other than Lynch's scowl to nudge them toward a guilty verdict.

Hirschberg said that not a single allegation against Inez and her codefendants had been disproved or denied by the defense. While the prosecution hadn't provided the jury with a film of what went on inside the Fillmore Street clinic, Hirschberg said it had surely produced the players: Inez, the star; Musette Briggs and Myrtle Ramsey, the understudies; Mabel Spaulding, the "custodian of cash"; and Joe Hoff, the handyman who took care of everything else. Inez's business had nothing to do with helping women in need, Hirschberg told the jury. "It was an abortion mill, a racket, a big racket. In the name of the State of California, stop this travesty of justice by returning verdicts of guilty against each of these defendants."[23]

As he was about to begin his own closing, McGovern took his time ambling his bruised yet oversize frame toward the jury box; it was all a practiced part of McGovern's courtroom theatrics. By now, he had gotten some of his strength back from Judge Murphy's rebukes. The judge didn't decide the case; it would be the jurors. They were the judges McGovern would appeal to.

McGovern stood for several seconds, scanning the jury, then glanced back at Inez and the others. He twisted his signet ring. With a pained expression on his face, McGovern sighed heavily, took a labored breath, and began.

He started with Judge Murphy. McGovern's play was a calculated tactic to split the courtroom into two camps: the avuncular McGovern, the elegant Inez, her four loyal assistants on one side; on the other side, the imperial Judge Murphy, the career-hungry Pat Brown, his lackeys Lynch and Hirschberg, and a lineup of self-serving witnesses who were muscled by the state into testifying against the sole woman who had helped them when they needed help the most.

By sequestering the jurors from their families, Judge Murphy had used the same tactics that "in totalitarian countries ... is called protective custody," McGovern charged. He recalled that the grand jury, presented with the same evidence as in the criminal trial, had failed to indict Inez or any of the other defendants. "Why was that?" asked McGovern rhetorically, raising the timbre of his voice. Several of the jurors widened their eyes at the tone and volume of McGovern's grandiloquence.

Before getting into the meat of the case, just in case any jurors were on the morality fence when it came to the issue of abortion, McGovern had a ready-made answer. He said a not-guilty verdict would not equate to "approval" of what the defendants were charged with doing. McGovern expressed contempt for the district attorney's office for filing charges against Inez in the first place. Pat Brown, McGovern railed, prosecuted Inez for one reason: "to further his political ambitions." As for Tom Lynch, McGovern said, he put "aside the robes and ethics of his profession to don gumshoes and do police work." McGovern reiterated his objection to the prosecution's lineup of "turncoat" witnesses and demanded that they be viewed as coconspirators. He quoted philosophers, sages, and poets, this time not so much to defend Inez and the others, but to vilify the judge and the state's prosecutors for their unrelenting campaign to pervert justice.[24] After seventy minutes, McGovern staggered back to his chair, his face a sponge of perspiration.

It was now Judge Murphy's turn. After shooting an icy glare at McGovern, he cautioned jurors against making their decision with "pity, compassion, or prejudice." If jurors were convinced the law had been violated, then a verdict of guilty was required. Up or down, yes or no, innocent or guilty. There would be no in-between. McGovern rose to object, calling the judge's draconian instructions the "most adverse" he'd ever heard, but Judge Murphy once again admonished him, "Sit down, Mr. McGovern!"[25]

Judge Murphy knew expediency was essential, for reasons extraneous to the facts at hand in the case. If the jury were to deliberate for more than two days, they'd have to be moved from the Hotel Whitcomb, and Judge Murphy had no idea to where. The American Legion convention, with its one hundred fifty thousand conventioneers, was set to open in San Francisco Tuesday, and every single hotel room in the city had been booked for months. The management at the Whitcomb had informed the court that the Legionnaires' reservations would take precedence over the sequestered jurors. The jury would have to reach a verdict within two days or the case against Inez and the others would fall apart, since there'd be no place to put the jury. There also was the issue of the jury alternates. Two had already been seated as part of the twelve-person jury, leaving no one in reserve. If a juror got sick and couldn't perform his or her duty, then the case would turn into a mistrial. Once again.

Just as the Nuremberg trials were going full steam across the Atlantic, and a prolonged butchers' strike was making meat scarce on San Franciscans' dinner tables, the jurors at four twenty Thursday afternoon filed into the jury room to begin their deliberations. They elected Sverre C. Kloster, an oil company executive accustomed to efficiency, to be the foreman. Not wasting any time, by five, Kloster sent a note to Judge Murphy, requesting to view photographs of the clinic, along with Inez's patient notebooks and bookkeeping records seized by police, both of which the Judge had allowed into evidence this time. The jury promptly broke for dinner at six.

At ten fifty, foreman Kloster buzzed the bailiff. Jurors had reached a verdict.

McGovern, Inez, and the four other defendants stood as the verdicts were read. The jury found Inez and each codefendant guilty on all counts.[26]

The courtroom erupted in a tangle of voices. Reporters raced to get the news in the Friday morning papers. Friends and relatives of the defendants shook their heads in disbelief. Lynch pumped Bert Hirschberg's hand. Walter McGovern whispered to Inez about an appeal, adding that their chances were very good. McGovern's objection, he mentioned furiously to Inez, was based on the sacred principle of double jeopardy, and they'd go all the way to the Supreme Court if necessary, he promised. Inez wasn't so certain.

McGovern asked to poll the jurors individually and all affirmed the unanimous guilty verdict, with the exception of Elizabeth Moses, the wife of the physician, who spoke so softly that McGovern asked her to speak up. After some hesitation, Mrs. Moses barely squeaked yes.

Judge Murphy didn't waste any time and ordered the defendants into the custody of the sheriff, rejecting out of hand a motion from McGovern that the five be allowed to remain free on bail.

In the hallway, speaking for the jury at nearly eleven that night, the foreman Kloster said, "I hope I never have to go through it again."[27] He said jurors initially were divided eight to four for conviction, but after dinner, they shifted nine to three for conviction, then twelve to zero on the last ballot. Discussions turned into arguments, which centered on whether the crimes the defendants were charged with ought to be considered crimes, despite Judge Murphy's directive otherwise. At one time, one juror shouted to another, "All right, lady! You keep your opinion and I'll keep mine!"[28] In the end, all twelve jurors hesitantly agreed to agree.

Inez, Mabel Spaulding, Musette Briggs, Myrtle Ramsey, and Joe Hoff were led across what locals called the Bridge of Sighs, a span connecting the Hall of Justice to the county jail. The newspapers got a series of terrific photos of the defendants being booked and fingerprinted with Inez wearing a fur coat. The five spent the weekend in jail.

On Monday at two in the afternoon, sheriff's deputies led Inez and the others back into the courtroom to hear the judge's sentence. Inez's sister, Nettie, and son Bob Merritt were there, sitting with Joe. As Inez was brought into court, the three caught her eye. Inez was sobbing. She couldn't help herself. If Judge Murphy had any emotion toward Inez and the other defendants, it was scorn. Tears weren't going to sway this judge. Inez fully realized that. She was crying because she knew that her entire world was about to collapse.

When the judge asked the defendants if they had anything to say before he pronounced sentence, each looked expectantly toward McGovern, who reiterated that the court had erred in allowing juror Thomas J. Furner to be excused.

"We want the record to show that we are opposed to and protest against this court proceeding to pronounce judgment upon these five defendants on the grounds heretofore stated, and, to summarize, that they were not tried according to the principles of common law that subsequently were written into the Constitution of the United States and the Constitution of the State of California," It was an earful, but McGovern wanted to lay out the heart of what would become his defendants' appeal.[29]

Judge Murphy clenched his jaw, peered over her glasses, and said nothing.

"I am ready to pronounce judgment," he finally intoned, not deigning to respond to McGovern.

Inez and the other defendants stood.

Judge Murphy sentenced each to "not less than the minimum nor more than the maximum." That meant two to five years in state prison. The women would be sent to the California Institution for Women at Tehachapi; Joe Hoff would be remanded to San Quentin State Prison.

McGovern summarily asked Judge Murphy for a stay of execution, pending appeal. At the least, McGovern hoped, the five defendants could remain free on bond. To no one's surprise, Judge Murphy refused.

"Does this mean bail in *any* amount?" McGovern asked as nicely as he could under the circumstances.

"In *any* amount," Judge Murphy responded.

"This court is adjourned," he concluded, then banging his gavel and disappearing into the recesses of his chambers in a flourish of a swirling black robe.

Denying bail for defendants charged with performing or assisting to perform abortions? Walter McGovern thought Judge Murphy's final ruling was particularly severe. Not to release five defendants, four of whom were older than fifty (Inez, Mabel, Myrtle, and Joe), was particularly extreme considering the crime they had been convicted of. Perhaps it was the only way the judge knew to guarantee that Inez and the others wouldn't be back in business the next day. Surely it was to show how utterly repugnant Judge Murphy must have thought each of the defendants was. That along with a rebuke to impudent Walter McGovern for showing such nonstop judicial impertinence.

Before sheriff's deputies took the five defendants away, Nettie, Bob, and Joe, along with the relatives of the four other defendants, crowded the front of the courtroom. Each of the women was crying softly. Even Joe Hoff got teary-eyed, despite his job of being the one employee whose job was to take care of everything, and this certainly was one of those times. Nettie reached out to grab her sister's hand, but a sheriff's deputy pushed her away with a paw as large as a ham.

"Damn this blubbering," Musette Briggs finally snorted as the deputies steered her toward the Bridge of Sighs. "It's ruining my mascara. Gosh, what I wouldn't give for a cup of real coffee. That stuff they serve in this can—I wouldn't give it even to Lynch."

The next day, the *San Francisco Chronicle*'s page-one story started this way: "One of San Francisco's oldest and best-known institutions came to the end of the road yesterday."[30]

TWENTY-THREE

HYPOCRITES!

For Pat Brown, the verdict against Inez was a sweet victory he savored in abstentia. Pat hadn't been in San Francisco for either the verdict or the sentencing. Instead, he had flown to San Diego to attend the state bar convention, where he hoped to pick up support for the November election less than five weeks away. Priorities were priorities. When contacted by a newspaper reporter, a jubilant Pat enthused that with Inez's conviction under his belt, he'd now go after lesser-known abortionists, pledging that the Burns verdict allowed him "an opportunity to resume where we left off. . . . Now we'll see what we have and go into it."[1] Pat also floated the proposition that if Inez wanted to sing about what she knew, he'd be open to recommending a shorter prison term.[2] That optimistic entreaty never got very far. Perhaps Inez wasn't interested, maybe Pat didn't get what he was hoping for, Judge Murphy wouldn't rubber stamp any deal, or possibly no offer was ever proffered.

Two days after Judge Murphy had pronounced the defendants' prison sentences and confined the five to jail without the option of posting bail, Walter McGovern was able to persuade State District Court of Appeal Judge John T. Nourse to let them go free—for the time being. After Judge Nourse intervened, bond for Inez, Mabel Spaulding, and Joe Hoff was set at five thousand dollars each; for Musette Briggs and Myrtle Ramsey, two thousand dollars each. McGovern vowed to take the case to the California Supreme Court, and to the US Supreme Court, if necessary. That would take some time, but at least the five would be permitted to leave jail. It was a small victory, but a victory nonetheless.

McGovern got busy filing his appeal, which contended that by dismissing juror Furner and replacing him with an alternate after a jury had already been sworn in, Judge Murphy had in essence started a new trial, placing Inez and the other defendants in jeopardy for a second time. It was an appeal based on a rather arcane technicality, but that's what appeals were. If an appellate judge agreed, the five convictions would be overturned.

Meanwhile, Pat Brown was busy gallivanting up and down the state acting like a new man. Convictions do that to prosecutors, even though Pat didn't have much to do with this one. Tom Lynch had gone after Inez and her employees thrice, and finally all his work had paid off. It was now Pat's turn to gloat. The elected official always got his due—whether it was credit or blame. The day after Inez and the others posted bail, Pat promptly opened his Southern California campaign for attorney general with a combative radio broadcast, charging that opponent Fred Howser was a dupe of mobster offshore gambling interests. The accusation didn't come out of nowhere; Howser and his benefactor, Artie Samish, were long thought to be crooked, but a confident Pat Brown had now taken off the gloves and had come out swinging. Howser duly responded by saying that Pat had descended "into the political mud bucket."[3]

Even though Inez had been convicted, the San Francisco grand jury still had plenty of business to conduct. There wasn't any purpose in the grand jury's issuing an indictment against her now. But one of Pat's deputies, Norman Elkington, puffed nonetheless, "The case is far from closed, since we intend to take collateral matters before the grand jury shortly."[4] A curious aside came when grand jurors had the opportunity to examine Inez's "little black books," introduced into evidence during the first and third criminal trials. Poring over them, grand jurors noticed the notation "Emily" repeatedly scrawled in the ledgers. No one could figure out who "Emily" was and how she possibly could have received so many abortions, until police realized that "Emily" must have been code for a patient who erroneously thought she was pregnant. The woman would pay for an abortion, undergo anesthesia, submit to a phantom operation, and would then be told that the procedure had gone well with no complications.[5]

While roaming the state trolling for votes, Pat was pushing the grand jury to issue indictments against the legions of cops and city officials who for years had been on the take from Inez. If Pat could finger police officers and politicians who had protected her, he'd have more political ammunition, maybe enough to defeat Howser. When Pat had run against Matthew Brady, his platform had been to rid San Francisco of graft and corruption, a staple of the City of Seven Hills dating back to the gold rush. If Pat was going to get anywhere in post–World War II California politics, he'd knew he'd have to personify himself as the reform law-and-order candidate leading the state into a new era of clean government. That branding had worked for Earl Warren, whom Pat deeply admired, and Pat banked on it working for himself. Inez's conviction had helped; a series of grand jury indictments against crooked cops and pols would help more.

Pat surely had an ally in Judge Edward Murphy, the pugilistic jurist who also presided over the grand jury. Even though they sat on opposing sides of the bench, Pat and Judge Murphy checked in often with each other. Judge Murphy's name appeared in Pat's own handwriting six times in Pat's red-leather-bound personal calendar for 1946, unearthed in the voluminous Berkeley repositories of his papers. The first mention, "Call Judge Murphy," appeared on April sixteenth, between the first and second deadlocked trials. A July ninth lunch between Pat and Judge Murphy was canceled, but the next day, Brown wrote himself a reminder to "Call Judge Murphy." The last mention is a November twentieth notation that reads, "Judge Murphy," seven weeks after he sent Inez and the others to prison.[6]

No one knows what the subject of these meetings was, or even if they ever took place. Pat could have met Judge Murphy on other occasions never recorded in his calendar. The two likely talked on the phone. There may have been other political players at these encounters, including opposing counsel. But a district attorney meeting with a judge numerous times in an ex parte fashion raises questions. Judges are sworn to be impartial; repeat meetings between a judge and a district attorney during an ongoing criminal trial ought to be viewed as suspect, the specter raised of the tilting of judicial scales toward the prosecution. Judge Murphy made no secret on which side he stood when it came to the *People v. Inez*. In his court, Lady Justice carried a scale and a sword, but she surely didn't appear blindfolded.

There were other hints of backroom dealing and influence peddling when it came to Inez's trial. Levina Blanchette Queen, the anesthetist who helped clinch the verdict for the prosecution, it turned out, had a host of unusual connections. While employed by Inez, Lavina Blanchette had gotten married in 1944, and none other than Police Captain Arthur Christiansen signed the marriage certificate as a witness. As the captain in charge of the police department's Northern station at 841 Ellis Street, just a mile and a half away from Inez's clinic, Christiansen was suspected to be one of the top cops on Inez's payroll.[7] Captain Christiansen later succeeded Pat Brown's own father-in-law, Arthur D. Layne, as supervising captain of the police department. That was for openers.

It also turned out that the San Francisco official who had presided at Levina Blanchette's marriage to Paul Queen was Herbert C. Kaufman, the same superior court judge who had presided over the second trial involving Inez and the four other defendants.

But there was more.

Inez herself was Levina's second witness at the wedding; she had signed the marriage certificate on behalf of Levina and Paul Queen.[8] It sure seemed cozy—a police captain, a superior court judge, and the best-known abortionist in California huddled in a windowless chamber in City Hall, all there together to make an abortion-clinic employee's wedding official.

Then, just two weeks before the third and successful raid on Inez's clinic, on September 17, 1945, Levina was sworn in as a naturalized US citizen in the US District Court in San Francisco.[9] Then, three months after Inez's conviction, Levina Queen's husband pled guilty to a felony of altering state gasoline-tax-refund certificates, and the prosecutor was Tom Lynch, and the judge was William Traverso, who had presided over Inez's first trial. Paul Queen got a slap on the wrist, probation, and a thousand-dollar fine.[10] What a surprise.

Did Levina Queen have anything to do with the timing of the successful police raid on Inez's clinic? Might probation and the fine for Paul Queen have been payback for his wife's bruising testimony against Inez and the other defendants? And why did Levina suddenly decide to return to San Francisco after being at large for more than a year? Might Pat Brown and Tom Lynch have offered her a deal she couldn't refuse?

And finally: Levina and Paul Queen lived at 2070 Tenth Avenue; the jury foreman in the third trial, oil company executive Sverre C. Kloster, lived three blocks away at 1783 Tenth Avenue in the Sunset District.[11] Sure, San Francisco is a compact city, but was that proximity merely a coincidence? Did the three know each other?

Now that Inez and her accomplices had been found guilty, it seemed as good a time as ever for heads to roll in the police department for the first two botched raids of Inez's clinic, ostensibly thwarted by a posse of cops on Inez's dole. That happened, sort of, when the chief inspector of the homicide division, eighteen-year veteran Alvin Corrasa, was demoted to the robbery detail. Other than Pat Brown and Tom Lynch from the DA's office, only five cops were supposed to have had advance knowledge of the raids: Police Chief Dullea, Captain of Inspectors Bernard McDonald, Inspectors Ahern and Corrasa, and Captain John Engler.[12] Had Al Corrasa been the crooked cop or was he taking the fall for someone higher up? Had Corrasa leaked word of the raid so Inez could clear out before the cops arrived?[13]

The grand jury once again began investigating allegations of tip-offs and corruption.[14] There was talk of payoffs Inez had made to grand jurors and witnesses, accusations again volubly fueled by Pat's office. But the grand jury chose to duck indicting anyone—not Inez, no one from the police department, Hall of Justice, jail, or City Hall, or anyone else thought to be a recipient of Inez's munificence, despite reams of evidence to the contrary.

Investigating graft in San Francisco was like disappearing down Alice's rabbit hole. No one knew where it might lead, so it was best not to go anywhere even near the abyss. Following money and influence was a risky proposition in a city as wired to favors, privilege, and bribes as San Francisco. Grand jury foreman Henry C. Maginn proclaimed that jurors were "tired of hearing nothing but suspicions and rumors," and without any smoking gun, he said that he had no alternative but merely to note the matter of alleged corruption in the grand jury's annual report. "That is all there is left for us to do," Maginn said lamely.[15] When released in January 1947, the grand jury's report contained not a single word of Inez, police tip-offs, or bribes.[16] What a surprise.

The three-member police commission followed suit with its own whitewash.[17] "If the grand jury with all its powers cannot unearth enough evidence for an indictment, I don't see how the Police Commission with its limited ability can do any better," said President Jerd Sullivan, effectively washing the commission's hands of any and all dirt.[18]

So the raft of cops who for years had been informants for Inez got a pass. Cops don't rat on cops, a basic rule of blue survival. Even governmental bodies explicitly charged with overseeing cops didn't rat. An iron ring protected Inez, from the police department's Northern station to the Hall of Justice downtown.[19] That's what payoffs were supposed to ensure, and in Inez's case, they couldn't have worked better.

As the November election got closer, Pat was giving stump speeches from Eureka to San Diego, trying to throw as many wrenches as he could into the well-oiled gears of the Republican machine that Earl Warren had for more than a decade greased.[20] Pat stepped up his charges against Howser, accusing him of permitting a notorious bootlegger to operate the *Lux*, a gambling ship six miles off Long Beach, to which hundreds of fun-seeking Los Angelinos were ferried nightly.[21] Pat charged that Howser's campaign manager was the former business partner of the ship's owner.[22]

Howser responded with restraint, staying clear of citing his opponent's own peccadillos—that Pat's father had run a notorious gambling den and that Pat had represented a slew of gambling parlors when he'd been in private practice. Howser could have mentioned Pat's two recent extravagant trials that resulted in hung juries, but it was probably best to stay clear of Inez for a variety of reasons. "Let me say to my opponent, who has conducted a smear campaign," Howser did say, "that had I been so inclined as to descend to personalities there is a wealth of material available for my own use, but I haven't seen fit to indulge in a campaign of innuendo." Front-runner Howser didn't want to throw gasoline on a campaign he thought he had already contained. Taking the high road, Howser proclaimed that the voters of California have "the good sense and intelligence" to repudiate such tactics."[23] The next day, two of Pat's key Southern California staff, former Assemblyman Maurice Atkinson and former State Supreme Court Chief Justice Louis W. Meyers, abruptly resigned from the Brown campaign, citing "differences of policy."[24] Atkinson soon came out for Howser, charging that Brown had "inconsistencies bordering on hypocrisy."[25]

The conservative *Los Angeles Times* endorsed Howser in the race. That wasn't a surprise, but when all four of Pat's hometown newspapers also endorsed Howser,[26] it was a slap in Pat's face that stung. How effective could Pat's vaunted hometown family-values campaign have been—with Inez's ultimate conviction its crown jewel—if San Francisco's press barons were backing a district attorney four hundred miles away?

Gaming tables inside the gambling ship *Lux*, 1946.

Pat shouldn't have taken the brushback personally. The endorsements were a matter of party-line politics and the Republican publishers who owned the San Francisco papers. The only sizable newspaper in the state that was Democratic was the *Sacramento Bee*, and while the McClatchy-owned flagship paper endorsed Pat, its impact was negligible.

For what it was worth, Pat did get a vote of confidence from Catholic churches up and down the state in the wake of Inez's conviction, with clergy fanatically urging parishioners not only to cast their ballots for Pat, but to go out and convince other Catholics to do the same. Parishes circulated an over-the-top editorial that appeared in *The Southern Cross*, the organ of the Diocese of San Diego, in which Pat was called "brilliant" for his "courageous battle" against Inez.

"Brown declared that a sentence of not guilty would have established San Francisco as the abortion capital of the nation. There must be great rejoicing in Heaven to know that there are men, leaders in this country, who, unmindful of the criticism of so few people, determinedly ferret out the unethical quacks who commit murder for a price. A voluntary abortion is nothing but intended murder. It is the most ungodly slaughter of innocent and defenseless babies. Basically there is no difference between the voluntary killing of a three-year-old child and the taking of the life of a viable or unviable fetus. We cannot acclaim too loudly such men as Attorney Brown. May his efforts spread to all other American cities."[27] It almost seemed as though Gloria Shannon herself might have penned the clerical missive.

Alas, such righteous fervor wasn't enough to overcome Howser's decidedly secular momentum, even with his shady backing. The preelection betting odds in San Francisco put Howser beating Brown by a four-to-one margin.[28] The bookmakers weren't off by much.

Come November fifth, Brown lost his bid for attorney general, as did almost every other Democrat running against Earl Warren's muscular ticket. Pat received 1,038,528 votes to Howser's 1,367,036 votes, which translated to a forty-three to fifty-seven percent loss for Pat. Governor Warren coasted to an easy reelection, amassing close to two million votes to crush Democrat Bob Kenny. It was the most votes any candidate had ever received in California history.[29]

While he roundly lost the election, Pat still had a job, and as district attorney, he immediately began looking to 1950 to challenge Howser again, glad-handing and campaigning any group willing to listen to him. In December, Pat delivered a speech at the annual meeting of the San Francisco Elks. Two weeks later, he addressed a fundraiser for the Hebrew Nursing Home, joining his ally Superior Court Judge Edwin P. Murphy at the St. Francis for the evening. Inez's longtime friend, singer Joaquin Garay, performed at the benefit.[30] He had entertained her guests along with Pinky Lee several months earlier at her ranch in La Honda.

Pat's crime-busting, family-values political persona stayed intact as he tried to climbed back to mount another statewide campaign. He went after chiropractors with phony diplomas; he closed down a Tenderloin hotel for prostitution, the first time the city's Red Light Abatement Act had been enforced since 1941; he pursued cops who fixed parking tickets; and he busted corner grocers selling cigarettes at cut-rate prices.[31] These were minor *Mr. District Attorney*–type maneuvers, but actions nonetheless that voters talk about. Along with several murder trials his deputies handled, Pat continued to hone his métier, which was to glad-hand anyone he ever ran into, along with lining up as many potential donors as he could.

As for Inez, in part to pay Walter McGovern, she and Joe were forced to sell her pride and joy, the Fillmore Street clinic in February 1947. The bottom apartment, at 325 Fillmore, reopened as the Hillside Guest House, a kind of hotel/short-term rental inn.[32] For a time, the top two floors served as the office of a so-called nutritionist, Rolf Alexander, a New Zealand native who was charged with practicing medicine without a license. As far as anyone knew, Alexander, the author of *The Doctor Alone Can't Cure You,* didn't perform abortions, but illegally prescribed controlled substances to his patients.[33]

Not to be deterred, Inez, on bail, awaiting her appeal, still attended to pregnant women who sought her out, now at her Guerrero Street house. If anyone knew anything about women in the precarious state of being pregnant and not choosing to give birth, it was Inez. It didn't make any difference how much the procedure would cost, or even how dangerous it would be; women still would do anything to interrupt an unwanted birth. Even with a prison sentence hanging over her head, Inez still reigned as the abortionist of choice in San Francisco.

And at this point, there was little police could do to stop her. Although Inez had been found guilty and sentenced to prison, neither Pat Brown nor Tom Lynch relished the prospect of trying her for yet another violation of penal code 274. They had already made their point. So, until she was sent off to prison, police made a separate peace with Inez continuing to perform abortions.

In the meantime, there were other abortionists Pat thought ought to be given a lesson. One was a mother-and-daughter team, Alta Anderson and Mae Rodley, along with Gertrude Jenkins. The trio operated a ring police busted in January 1947. Their operation—with two facilities, one at 1097 South Van Ness Avenue and the other in Colma's Garden Village District, south of San Francisco—had the protection of Nick DeJohn, the unctuous mobster with fishy halitosis who had tried to shake down Inez two years earlier. While Inez was tied up in court, the three women had hung out a shingle to meet the demand that Inez couldn't handle at the moment, with a little something special. Their gimmick was "curb service." Arrangements and payments were made at the San Francisco office, then patients were picked up by limousine at prearranged locations on San Francisco street corners and shuttled to the Colma clinic, where the procedure would take place.[34] The tweak was American capitalism at its best, reflected in a sign that hung upstairs at the San Francisco facility: "If you do your business right, you may have your business in the woods, but the public will make a road into you."[35]

The enterprising Alta Anderson, whose trademark was big, floppy hats, was so successful with her chauffeured abortion services that she opened a third clinic across the Bay in Oakland. Jenkins was a two-bit rival of Inez, and had been arrested, tried, and acquitted four years earlier for an abortion-related death of a thirty-seven-year-old woman. When police busted the San Francisco clinic, they found a Victorian house filled with secret compartments, concealed sliding panels, and a big safe—all standard fare for an abortion facility at the time. Anderson, Rodley, and Jenkins were represented in court by San Francisco's leading criminal defense attorney, Jake "The Master" Ehrlich, whom Inez had tried to hire before she chose Walter McGovern. In lieu of payment, Ehrlich took ownership of the Colma property with Anderson's deed transferred to his name.[36]

Four months later, the abortion trio's godfather, sleazy Nick DeJohn, was executed gangland style, garroted with fishing line, and found in the trunk of his Town & County sedan in San Francisco's Cow Hollow District. DeJohn had eaten a pasta dinner the night before at La Rocca's in North Beach, and diners there remembered a large man flashing a thick wad of bills more than once. Whoever killed DeJohn took his monster diamond ring and diamond-encrusted watch, likely as trophies, along with the cash. When police discovered his body in the trunk, all they found was seventy-seven cents in his pocket.[37]

Chronicle columnist Herb Caen eulogized DeJohn this way: "In Vanessi's the other night a couple of characters were talking about the late Nick DeJohn, still a favorite topic of the gibble-gabble. 'Y'know,' said one, 'Nick wasn't such a bad schmo. He never bothered the little guys. The only people he cut in on already had too much dough, anyway.'"[38]

With a prison term hanging over her head, Inez had finally turned toxic to the

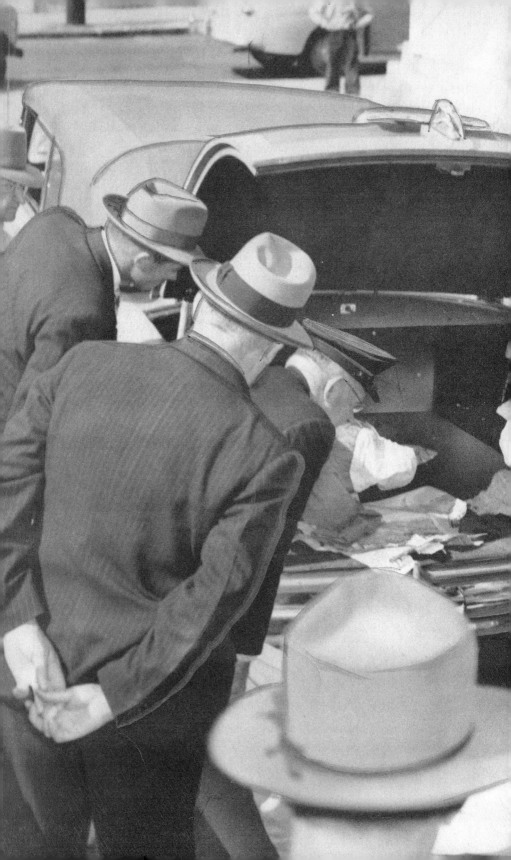

San Francisco Police examine gangland murder of Nick DeJohn.

legions of cops she had supported and entertained for years. If you wore a blue uniform, it was too risky to associate with Inez any longer. She and Joe still held their Wednesday night soirees, and had friends down at the ranch for weekends, but these were decidedly tame affairs. Inez had finally turned down the dial. Nettie often stopped by the Guer-rero Street house, as did Nelly Gaffney, and on occasion the three shared soda crackers and chamomile and rose hip tea served in Inez's Royal Copenhagen china service.

On February 25, 1948, the district court of appeals rejected Walter McGov-ern's writ for Inez and the others. McGovern promptly appealed to the California Supreme Court, and one month later, that court announced that it had declined to hear Inez's case.[39] With their state appeals exhausted, Judge Murphy could now—with glee—order Inez, Mabel, Musette, and Myrtle to the California Institution for Women at Tehachapi, and Joe Hoff to San Quentin. The quintet had enjoyed eigh-teen months of freedom since the guilty verdict, and Judge Murphy thought that was far too much time for convicted felons to be free.

"Every right guaranteed under both the federal and state constitutions has been accorded these people," Judge Murphy said to a packed courtroom. "This is the end of a long, gruesome, bloody and macabre road."[40]

The defendants' only remaining hope was that the US Supreme Court would rule in their favor. For that, McGovern turned to Simeon E. Sheffey, a Harvard-trained San Francisco attorney, who submitted his brief to the court on August 9, 1948.

There was no denying the fact any longer: Inez and her four accomplices were going to prison. Walter McGovern had done all he could.

The day before she was to turn herself in, Inez needed to take care of some final business. She had to safeguard her still-ample funds for when she got out. Banks were hardly a viable option, and the last time Inez had buried cash in her basement, it had been gnawed to pulp by termites. Inez had maxed out on real estate; she needed all the liquidity she could muster.

Her first stop was Nelly's house, at 2518 Gough Street, and in the front parlor, Inez gave Nelly an oversize brown envelope containing fifty thousand dollars and told her to keep it until she got back from Tehachapi.

"Don't worry, Iney. It'll be safe with me. And stiff upper lip, hon. Chin up. They'll wanna break you, but they don't know what you're made of. You'll get through this. I know you will."

Sweet Nelly. Of all of her friends, Nelly was the one Inez trusted the most. She was a regal woman who had all the money in the world and, like Inez, had earned every penny of it.

Inez's next trip was to Atherton to see her son Bob Merritt, now forty. If she couldn't rely on Bob, then whom could she rely on?

She would have preferred that Bud Felix hold the money for her, but Bud demurred. Mabel Malotte was out of the question; her brothel on Bay Street surely wasn't safe, with strangers traipsing in and out every night, not to mention the prospect of a police bust. Her two other sons, George and Billy Jr., weren't in the position to hold that kind of cash, and Alice Lorine, Inez's daughter by Charlie Granelli, was now all grown up, married to an Annapolis man, and Inez didn't want to lean on her. Nettie was too straight an arrow for this task. And forget about Joe. He'd drink it, or lose it playing cards or on the ponies.

Bob's medical practice was flourishing, but Inez knew his wife, June, had an appetite for clothes and jewelry. Inez had provided the couple with a series of rent-free homes, not to mention her paying for Bob's medical-school education back East and setting up his medical office. Inez had showered June with jewelry and fur coats. Inez gathered the rest of her cash, hidden in the hems of curtains, in sliding compartments, lockboxes, and wall partitions. It amounted to a staggering nest egg of a half a million dollars. Still.

"Keep this for me, Bobby. I'm going to need it when I get back. But promise me this: Whatever you do, don't mention the money to June."

Whether most husbands could keep such a secret from their wives is speculative, but Bob nodded, not wanting to start a tiff between his mother and his wife. "Don't worry about a thing," he told Inez. "The money's safe with me." Inez had her doubts, but what choice did she have?

The two hugged, and as Bob walked his mother back to the idling Packard with Joe in the driver's seat, Inez turned to him.

"I don't want you to visit me," she said to Bob, her tone flat without emotion. "I don't want *anyone* seeing me in prison. I don't wanna be remembered like that."

US Route 99 running through
the Tehachapi Mountains in the
San Joaquin Valley.

PART IV

RUIN

(Left to right) Musette Briggs and Inez Burns go to jail, March 31, 1948.

TWENTY-FOUR

STIFF UPPER LIP

At daybreak on March 31, 1948, hours before the hazy morning fog would lift, Joe drove Inez to the Hall of Justice, where she would meet Mabel, Myrtle, Musette, and Walter McGovern. The four women had decided to dress up for the occasion, as though they were going to the opera or perhaps the theater. They were wearing expensive wool suits, high heels, nylons, and gay hats perched on newly coiffed heads of hair. Mink coats covered Inez's and Mabel's outfits; Myrtle and Musette wore mink stoles. Each woman carried a smart white Imperial-brand train case, gifts from Inez. Just because the four were going to prison didn't mean they weren't ladies.

Walter McGovern took care of the formalities, going through a stack of forms and asking each of the women to sign an endless stack of affidavits. He persuaded Inez and the others to remove the furs, and after some back-and-forth, the women relented, reluctantly handing them over to McGovern, who stood with the coats and stoles stacked on his outstretched arms up to his multiple chins. He said he'd keep them for the women for when "they returned," tactfully leaving out any mention of where the quartet was headed or for how long they might be gone.

"You'll have them back in no time, especially if our appeal before the US Supreme Court is heard," McGovern said, trying to be cheerful, although he knew such petitions seldom proved fruitful. "They'll be safe with me."

"They better be!" Inez cracked, cutting through the stale air. "They're expensive, and I've already paid you plenty!" That was the Inez everyone knew. McGovern laughed, as did the others.

COUNTY JAIL
N.º 1

COUNTY JAIL
N.º 1
VISITING HOURS
1 P.M. to 3.30 P.M.
DAILY

DANIEL C. MURPHY
SHERIFF

Though the matching train cases were stylish, Walter McGovern knew they were hardly appropriate. Best to pick your battles with Inez. He'd be the last to say such accessories weren't necessary where the women were going.

Joe seemed more anxious and fidgety than Inez. He looked like he'd been stabbed in the heart, and when the sheriff's deputies said it was time to leave, he was choking back tears. He took out a handkerchief from his wool jacket pocket and patted his face, more it seemed to cover his emotions than for anything else. "Don't you go gettin' any crazy thoughts in that head of yours, Joe Burns. I'll be back before you realize I was ever gone," Inez said, promptly giving him a kiss on his flushed cheek. "Now, on your way. I'll be fine." Inez remember what Nelly had counseled her, "Stiff upper lip."

With that, the sheriff's deputies drove the women to the Ferry Building at the foot of Market Street. Accompanied by two deputies, the women boarded the No. 51 Southern Pacific San Joaquin Daylight, which left the Embarcadero at exactly seven forty-five, crossed the fog-shrouded Bay Bridge to Oakland, then headed toward the Sacramento Delta, Benicia, and Stockton, south through Modesto, Turlock, Merced, Fresno, Bakersfield, and, finally, at six fifteen that evening, arrived at their destination: a dot of a town called Tehachapi (pronounced Ta-HATCH-a-pee) at Railroad Mile Marker 361, where the six disembarked.

In the meantime, Joe Hoff had been driven nineteen miles north across the Golden Gate Bridge, accompanied by two sheriff's deputies to San Quentin, where he was stripped, deloused, given a crew cut, issued a denim prison uniform, and ushered to "fish row," where new inmates were housed.[1]

The Tehachapi train depot was a one-story, redwood-shingle Type 23 Southern Pacific station built in 1904. In front, on Tehachapi Boulevard, a prison-transport bus idled while a male correctional officer, drawing on a cigarette, waited. He looked bored, as though he'd been doing this job of prisoner transport forever. A plume of exhaust spewed puff by puff from the bus's rattling tailpipe, which rose into the high desert air as though it were a series of smoke signals.

Inez, Musette, Mabel, and Myrtle were joined by five other women, who had either arrived on Train No. 55 from Los Angeles, or had gotten on the San Joaquin

(Left to right) Sheriff Homer Kelly, Inez Burns, and Musette Briggs, March 31, 1948.

Daylight from points further south. The San Francisco sheriff's deputies handed over their charges to four Tehachapi matrons who'd been waiting for them inside the depot.

"What *are* you girls wearing?" one of matrons asked, more a raised-eyebrow observation than a question. "And what in the world is in those little suitcases? You ain't gonna need any of that inside." The three other matrons shook their heads in unison, one of them in a not-very-welcoming way.

Speaking for the new inmates, Inez piped up, "We thought we might add some class to the joint."

Well, the matron in charge didn't like that at all. "You best watch yourself," she said crossly, turning to Inez. "Wit' a mouth like that, you gonna git into big trouble. I can tell you that right now." Then as an afterthought, she added, "You oughta know better, a girl yo'r age. Miss Holzschuh don't like her girls actin' up. No siree, she don't. You remember that."

Inez wasn't sure who Miss Holzschuh was or whether she cared. She ignored the matron's comments and boarded the bus. No use getting into a fight, at least no use now.

The prisoner-transport driver stamped out his cigarette with the heel of a scuffed boot. Now he'd seen it all. Women going to prison in fancy clothes, each carrying a miniature suitcase.

"We ain't got all day," he said. "Git a move on it!"

"Step up, girls," another matron said. "One inmate per row. And no talkin'. You girls in prison now."

The bus rumbled down to Curry Street, went south for eight blocks until it got to Valley, and from Valley, it stopped at Three Mile Corner, brakes squeaking, then bounced along a dusty road that went alongside fields of what looked like orchards. The bus windows were open and sucked in a dry, dusty breeze.

"This is *nowhere*," Musette leaned forward, whispering to Inez.

"Maybe that's why they put a prison here," Inez deadpanned. At forty, Musette was the youngest of the four, and sometimes she said the dumbest things.

"You two!" the head matron hissed. "You shush!"

The California Institution for Women was the first prison in the state designed to house female inmates. Before it opened, female felons used to be incarcerated in San Quentin, but by the late 1920s, the Q was getting overcrowded, and female inmates rightfully needed a place they could call their own. Located in the wind-swept Cummings Valley between the Mojave Desert and the San Joaquin Valley, Tehachapi was where the Kawaiisu Indians once roamed. *Tehachapi* comes from the Kawaiisu and means "sweet water and acorns."[2]

When Inez, Mabel, Musette, and Myrtle arrived that dusky evening, it was the beginning of spring, and spring in rural Kern County was something to behold. Not that anyone on the prisoner-transport bus was in the mood to appreciate nature's robust palette of color—the scarlet buglers, purple beardtongues, and red-orange hackberries that had just pierced the hard, dry earth. That included the driver, who brought the bus to an abrupt stop at the eastern edge of the valley, at the prison entrance, where two stone turrets flanked an ornate iron gate. A guard opened both halves of the portal and waved the bus through.

By the time Inez and the others arrived, Tehachapi had become an integral part of popular American culture. Hollywood had transformed the California prison into a holding pen filled with tough, beautiful dames in for killing men who had done them wrong. In John Huston's 1941 film, *The Maltese Falcon*, Humphrey Bogart's Sam Spade says to Brigid O'Shaughnessy, played by Mary Astor, "If you get a good break, you'll be out of Tehachapi in twenty years, and you can come back to me then. I hope they don't hang you, precious, by that sweet neck."[3] In Billy Wilder's *Double Indemnity*, Fred MacMurray tries to sell Barbara Stanwyck on murdering her husband by offering, "There was another case where a guy was found shot, and his wife said he was cleaning a gun and his stomach got in the way. All she collected was a three-to-ten stretch in Tehachapi." Stanwyck replies, "Perhaps it was worth it to her."[4]

When it opened in 1932, Tehachapi was the most progressive women's prison in the nation. Started by the Woman's Christian Temperance Union, the League of Women Voters, and the California Federation of Women's Clubs, the prison was independent and separate from the state's men's correctional division; its board of trustees, which decided when inmates would get paroled, was a five-person committee, four of whom were women. Under its indefatigable superintendent, Alma Holzschuh, Tehachapi was designed to resemble an out-of-the-way bucolic college more than a penitentiary. The inmate newspaper, *The Clarion*, seldom referred to Tehachapi as anything but "the campus." Along with coaching convicts on how to become good mothers, the goal inside was to train women for a profession.[5] During World War II, inmates made twenty thousand pillowcases and fifteen thousand mosquito nets for the Navy,[6] and when Inez was an inmate, prison jobs included sewing, gardening,

One of the buildings at the California Institution for Women in Tehachapi in its opening year in 1932.

food preparation, cleaning, and laundering. Prisoners didn't wear uniforms; instead, they were issued cotton-print dresses sewn by inmates. The women lived in two-story cottages with red-shingle roofs. Each had a kitchen, dining room, and common area. A *Christian Science Monitor* article at the time extolled Tehachapi as "more like a country club than prison," and gushed that inmate "kitchens would be the delight of the most meticulous housewife. Equipment is complete even down to electric refrigeration, electric mixers, and aluminum kitchenware."[7] There were no bars on the windows; inmates could roam pretty much wherever they wanted, playing tennis, badminton, bowling on the green, croquet, horseshoes, softball (the prison team was known as the Bomb-A-Dears), or volleyball. Movie night was Saturday. Grazing cattle and tracts of vegetables, as well as peach and pear orchards, surrounded the prison. Inmates were said to take enormous pride in the penitentiary's plentiful rose gardens, where they cultivated Cecile Brunners, Crimson Glories, Triumphs, and polyanthuses.[8]

But Tehachapi was still a prison no matter how many amenities it afforded. The food was terrible. Fights among prisoners were common. Lights-out was at nine sharp. As at every prison, clocks ticked loudly. No one wanted to be there. Two hundred eighty-eight inmates were incarcerated at Tehachapi when Inez arrived in a prison designed to accommodate fewer than two hundred. The largest group was made up of seventy women in for first- or second-degree murder or manslaughter;[9] the second biggest cohort was fifty-three women in for writing bad checks. Almost everyone at Tehachapi was younger than Inez (the average age was thirty-two), and three quarters of the inmates had some kind of alcohol dependency.[10] Inez, Musette, Mabel, and Myrtle were led across a redbrick path into a stately prison building, where they showered and matrons checked their bodies for lice. Their urine was tested, they were given Pap smears for cervical cancer, and Wassermann tests for syphilis. Inez was then shown to Hodder Cottage.[11]

By this point in Inez's life, arthritis had begun to settle in her joints; she alternated massaging the fingers on one hand with the fingers of her other hand. A prison nurse noted that Inez had a persistent, hacking cough. She also noted that Inez displayed bouts of depression, or melancholia as it was called then.

Excluding Inez and her codefendants, only four other inmates at Tehachapi were doing time for performing abortions.[12] That was telling. It meant that the mandate for incarcerating women abortionists in 1948 still wasn't high and that there was little political groundswell to put such female offenders behind bars. As Pat

Brown and Tom Lynch had also learned, getting a guilty verdict in any abortion case was difficult, whether the abortionists were men or women. Brown and Lynch, it turned out, were among the state's vanguard when it came to sending women to prison for providing the illegal service. Prosecutors in most other California counties continued to look the other way, unwilling to upset the status quo. But few of these district attorneys were simultaneously running for statewide office.

Viewed from a wholly other perspective, Inez might well have landed in prison years earlier, if she had ever been charged and convicted of murdering husband, Billy Brown. Not just a few in her family suspected that Inez had poisoned Billy, a kind of familial secret that caused eyes to dart whenever someone was dense enough to bring it up. Neither Pat Brown nor Tom Lynch likely had any inkling that Inez might have killed Billy Brown, and even if they did, by now, there was no way to prove it.

Prison isn't a microcosm of the outside world. It's a select community of persons who chose not to play by the same rules as everyone else and got caught breaking one or more of those rules. In that sense, Inez had something in common with the other inmates at Tehachapi. She was an unrepentant lawbreaker, even though she vigorously believed any law prohibiting a woman's right to abortion was unjust, created by men to control the other half of the population. Inez was never one to suffer fools, and in any prison, there are inmates smart and obtuse, stable and erratic. In her line of work, Inez had had a surfeit of experience with young women of all persuasions to avoid contact with any prisoner who telegraphed trouble. One Tehachapi inmate she met kept two parakeets, Curly and Lady Helene, as constant companions; Inez gave all three a wide berth.[13] Several prisoners considered themselves men and dressed accordingly. As in all prisons, homosexual liaisons were common at Tehachapi, but this was not an activity that interested Inez. At sixty-two, she wasn't about to start.

When word circulated that Inez was an abortionist, several newly arrived inmates anxiously asked her whether she'd perform abortions on them. It was an offer that Inez appreciated but turned down. Always the businesswoman, Inez advised, "See me when you get out," which became an insider joke around the prison.

Inez associated with Musette, Mabel, and Myrtle, the four forming a sort of clique among sister outcasts, with Inez retaining the role as the queen bee who called the shots. In the evenings, they would play pinochle, pitch, California Pedro, bridge, or canasta, a new game that was all the rage in 1948. Inez tried to sneak in poker, but the matrons wouldn't allow it because poker was told to lead to gambling, which of course was prohibited. Musette was a talented pianist and played when she could, although

A medical facility room at the California Institution for Women in Tehachapi, 1933.

two resident cats, Boots and Andy, tried her patience with their habit of parking themselves on the keys, according to *The Clarion*, the prison newspaper.[14] To pass the time, Inez considered taking up knitting and crocheting, but she didn't have the patience, and besides, the activity exacerbated her arthritis. She also looked at it as a hobby for old ladies. She tried her hand at writing short stories and love poems, but that proved to be an enervating activity that gave her headaches. Best not to dwell on what was.

Every six weeks or so, Joe took the train south to visit Inez, each time bringing bars of pink Camay soap, natural-bristle hairbrushes with ivory handles, Dura-Gloss nail polish, and a box of See's assorted chocolates. On his third visit, Joe surprised Inez with a gift, *The Magic of Oz*, which he had found at Argonaut's Books on Kearny Street. While Inez appreciated the thought, she didn't crack open the Baum tome. It was too much a reminder of her past life, and as a prisoner, she had little desire to revisit those years.

Even though she had instructed her family not to visit, several times Inez's granddaughter Caroline and her parents, Carline[15] and William, drove to Tehachapi, as did Inez's son Bob and wife June. "Grandma Iney was usually a nervous wreck, always agitated whenever we visited. I felt sorry for her," Caroline Brown Carlisle, who was fourteen at the time, recalled.[16]

Prison is supposed to be a place of self-appraisal, a time to consider the sins that got you there, and to reform from committing them once you get out. Inez didn't believe in God or the hypocrisy, as she called it, that went hand in hand with religion, but Tehachapi did turn into a kind of reflective, nonsectarian sanctuary for her. On certain evenings, after dinner and before canasta, Inez often stared at the desert landscape from her room in Hodder, listening to the winds that rushed through the Tehachapi Pass, contemplating exactly *why* she had landed in prison. Pat Brown's voracious political appetite, not to mention Tom Lynch's and Judge Murphy's own lofty ambitions, had turned her into a sacrificial lamb to feed the careers of three men, likely more. Each knew the way to do that was to gauge public opinion and ride its back. That's as good a definition of politics as it gets.

But Inez knew she had broken the same law for thirty years, and for all that time she'd been respected, even revered, by tens of thousands of women. There had always been assorted men, for their own particular reasons, who had wanted to take her down, and astute Inez had always been able to outmaneuver them. There had always been a way, mostly with money placed in the right hands. What, she often mused, had changed over the course of three decades?

Women inmates employed in sewing at California Correctional Institution's industrial program in Tehachapi, 1948.

Inez came to realize that it was *how* she was viewed by the average San Franciscan that had changed, particularly after World War II. Pat Brown and Tom Lynch hadn't created that shift in sentiment, but they surely reflected it. Of all women, Inez understood that the average Joe or Jane had a schizophrenic view of sex and lust. Inez's job had simply been to take care of consequences that resulted from both. Women would always need Inez's services. That was a given. The difference now seemed that Inez and other abortionists needed to become invisible. They needed to step into the closet. As though they didn't exist. Those in charge wouldn't allow it any other way. Sex and lust were dirty and indecent these days. When Inez had started out with Dr. West, sex and lust might have been naughty, but they were facts of life that everyone acknowledged with a bemused shrug of the shoulders. Abortion wasn't the fierce crime it had become. The newspapers used to run entire pages of ads for abortionists every day, and while never stated explicitly, everyone knew exactly what these providers offered. All that had changed.

What got Inez the angriest was *who* got to make and enforce the rules—the Pat Browns, Tom Lynches, and Edward Murphies of the world. All men. Of course. Surely, if women were in charge, abortion wouldn't be illegal at all. Hell, the way Inez saw it, abortion would be readily available and sanctioned. No woman should ever be forced to bear a child she neither wanted nor could afford. Inez knew that, as did almost every woman. More often than not, women had been forced into sex by their husbands or boyfriends in the first place, with or without contraception, with or without pleasure, mostly without. The women hadn't been willing, equal partners. Not by a long shot. And the casualty of that one-sided, occasionally violent act often was a pregnancy that the woman would have to pay for the rest of her life.

That Inez had performed tens of thousands of abortions underscored how essential her services had been. In a legal sense, yes, absolutely she had violated the law, and Pat Brown, Tom Lynch, Judge Murphy, and all the others had seen to it that she pay for her so-called crimes. But in a larger sense, what had she really done to be sent away and punished?

They had sought me out.

Inez asked each and every one of her patients, "Are you certain about what you're about to do?" Inez's clients knew the consequences and still they chose to undergo the risks, which were minimal at Inez's practiced hands. Her patients knew that, as did all the doctors, nurses, attorneys, and pharmacists who referred them her way. That's why she'd been so busy for so long. That's why she'd become a millionaire five times over.

If one of the goals of incarceration is to convince prisoners to admit remorse, then prison for Inez proved a failure. She shared no sense of wrongdoing because she knew she had done nothing wrong, except that it was illegal.

Abortion had also provided her with a life of abundance. What would Inez have been without all the excesses—the multitude of hats, gowns, furs, the wild Wednesday night parties, opening night at the opera, the raucous parties at the ranch, the wads of cash, her gorgeous estates scattered everywhere?

During the first week in August 1948, two federal Treasury agents made a trip to Tehachapi to interview Inez about abortion rings that had sprung up in the wake of her trials and incarceration.[17] The latest move authorities were employing to get rid of abortionists was through the back door, prosecuting them in federal court for tax evasion. That way, prosecutors wouldn't have to depend on testimony from patients. Abortionists would be busted on their unreported income, a federal, not a state violation.

Hoping to shorten her time at Tehachapi, the usually tight-lipped Inez traded several morsels of information to one of the federal agents, a Hollywood-handsome man named William Burkett. In addition to Alta Anderson's mother-daughter-run clinic, another ring Inez knew about was run by Dr. Malcolm E. Hoffman, Frances Zoffel, and her son, Raymond Brandt. Zoffel used to work for abortionist Dr. Clayton E. May, who, while practicing medicine in Minneapolis, had performed plastic surgery on John Dillinger to disguise the bank robber's face. The events inspired the Humphrey Bogart film *Dark Passage* in 1947. After serving a two-year stint in federal prison at Leavenworth, Kansas, Dr. May had surfaced in San Francisco, where he became an abortion provider.[18]

There were plenty others, Inez told Burkett. One was a ring that required women to rent hotel rooms, where they'd be met by an abortionist who went by the aliases Paul De Gaston, Dr. Reed, Dr. C. J. Morris,[19] Dr. Scott, and Dr. Leslie Audrain.[20] Other rings included those headed by Chris Dale on Sacramento Street and Sydney Duskin on Gough Street in San Francisco.[21]

When it came to Los Angeles, Inez told agents that no abortionist was able to operate without first paying off Dr. Eric Wilson, the Southland's point man, his going rate of one thousand dollars a month. The payoff was to guarantee protection at city, county, and state levels.[22]

Inez was by no means singular and she knew it. Although she was among the most well-known abortionists in the nation, almost every region in the United States had a flourishing underground network that led women to providers, some highly skilled, others thoroughly incompetent. These were just a few: In Portland, Ruth Barnett performed some forty thousand abortions from 1918 to 1968[23]; in Chicago, there was Ada Martin[24] and Dr. Nathaniel Schaffer[25]; in New York, Alice Mary Heinrich Chairman,[26] Drs. Nathaniel Collins,[27] Emory Klein, Louis G. Small, William J. Haller,[28] Louis I. Duke,[29] and Aloysius Mulholland[30]; in Baltimore and Washington, DC, Dr. George Lotrell Timanus; and in Detroit, abortions were performed by Dr. Edgar Keemer; Dr. Robert Spencer performed forty thousand abortions in coal-mining regions in rural Pennsylvania.[485] Frank Sinatra's mother, Dolly, was an abortionist in Hoboken, New Jersey, where she earned the horrific sobriquet "Hatpin Dolly."[31] In Akron, Ohio, the go-to abortionist was Dr. Roy Odell Knapp.[32] Even in the tiny, north-central Iowa town of Osage, a physician by the name of William R. Owen routinely performed abortions for years.[33]

Two months after she opened up to Burkett, on October twenty-sixth, seven months into her sentence at Tehachapi, Inez and her three other codefendants got word that the US Supreme Court had declined to review their case, ending all hopes of a pardon. Inez had never expected much, but the news sent her into a tailspin, and she spent the next two weeks in the Tehachapi infirmary, complaining that her arthritis had become debilitating.

As more and more prisoners kept pouring into the facility, conditions at Tehachapi worsened. In May 1950, seven inmates lifted knives, overpowered a matron, and tried to bargain for their release. By November, construction had begun on a new, larger women's prison, at Corona, one hundred forty miles south.[34]

During that fall, Inez appeared before the prison parole board. She had fully cooperated with the federal agents, and she'd been a model prisoner. Urging parole board members to release his mother, Inez's son Bob Merritt wrote an impassioned plea:

I am writing this letter on behalf of a wonderful mother who gave all her love and affection to her children and whose words of love, encouragement, and consolation in times of stress have made her most dear to our hearts. We love our mother more than anything in the world. We fully realize her debt to society, but we now feel that the time has come that we should plea before you to grant her a chance to become a good citizen.

At the present time Mrs. Burns has ten grandchildren who would like to see her. Our excuse to them for her long absence is that she is not well and is in a sanitarium. This seems to be the best explanation for her absence, but I feel as time passes I am aware they are forgetting. I do not want this to happen if I can be of any help in making you realize how much sunshine you can bring to these children if you would give favorable consideration for early parole.

In closing I would like to say that your favorable consideration of her early release would bring much happiness to her children. I have never asked a favor as I have felt she did owe a debt to society, but I now feel she should be helped at this time by her children.

I pray that you will help us to have her home again with her family. This letter comes from the heart.[35]

Whether Bob's letter helped is unknown, but the board recommended Inez's release, and on November 9, 1950, after serving a total of twenty-nine months, Inez was set free with twenty dollars and a new inmate-sewn cotton-print dress, the same send-off every Tehachapi inmate got.

"I'll take the money, you keep the dress," Inez told the matron in charge. That was the Inez correctional officers and inmates had grown accustomed to at Tehachapi—smart, tart, and sharp-witted.

Mabel, Musette, and Myrtle were released from Tehachapi shortly thereafter. From San Quentin, Joe Hoff was released, too, at the same time.

Joe had driven from San Francisco to Atherton, picked up granddaughter Caroline, and the two drove all the way to Tehachapi together in a big black Cadillac. When Caroline saw Inez, she was speechless. Inez had lost thirty pounds and looked as though she'd aged a decade. Joe and Caroline knew they'd be asking for trouble if they mentioned anything about her physical appearance, so neither of them said a word.

It was time to collect the money Inez had asked Bob and Nelly to hold for her. Driving north of San Jose, along the Old Bayshore Highway, Joe pulled off at Marsh Road, to Austin Avenue, and into the long driveway of Bob and June Merritt's mansion on Tuscaloosa Avenue, the house Inez had bought for them and still owned.

Inez told Joe and Caroline that she wanted to go in alone. She got out of the Cadillac and marched to the front door. Caroline remembers seeing her grandmother and Bob in the large portico, first hugging, then talking, then arguing. "Don't mind your grandma Iney, Caroline," Joe said, patting her on the knee. "She and Uncle Bobby have some business they need to discuss."

Caroline looked from the car, saw Bob shake his head, shrugging, then turning the palms of his hands up, as though to say there's nothing left for me to do, or perhaps just there's nothing left. Bob retreated into the house and came back with a tinted glass jar with a label on it and gave it to Inez.

After fifteen minutes of back and forth, Inez returned to the car, ashen-faced.

"Bobby said June wouldn't allow him to give me back my money. He said she's already spent it," Inez said, looking straight ahead. Caroline recalls that her grandmother sounded as remorseful as she'd ever heard anyone sound.

"Spent it? Spent all of it?" Joe asked, his anger building. "Spent all of it on *what*? How does someone spend a half million dollars?"

"Our little June didn't seem to have a problem," Inez replied, still looking straight ahead.

"And you're going to let her get away with it?"

"There's nothing I can do, Joe."

"But five hundred thousand dollars! A half a million dollars!"

Inez could hardly believe it herself. "Bobby said he had to abide by his wife's wishes. And he says there's nothing left. My own son and daughter-in-law just robbed me blind."

Inez was in a daze.

"I oughta go in there and knock some sense into that Bobby."

"Kiss that money goodbye, Joe. It's gone."

Inez was too exhausted to argue. "Nelly will have the money I gave her. She won't disappoint. I'm sure of that."[36]

TWENTY-FIVE

ALWAYS FIGHT WITH A FIST

Back at the Guerrero Street house, inside the large tinted bottle that Bob had given Inez were sleeping pills, Nembutals, and she took two, washed down with cognac Joe had poured for her into a Baccarat snifter. Inez didn't get out of her big Hollywood bed for three straight nights and days, the accumulation of twenty-nine months at Tehachapi during which she hadn't been able to catch more than two hours of sleep at a stretch. Too much was looping through her mind. Word had already circulated that Inez was back in town, and her phone was already ringing off the hook.

So much for prison rehabilitation. No way was Inez giving up her business. It was what she did. Pat Brown and Tom Lynch be damned. As long as her arthritis didn't stop her, Inez would continue. Performing abortions was how she defined herself. She wouldn't be able to accommodate in her home anywhere near the number of women she used to see in the clinic. She also was a convicted felon now. That meant if Inez were arrested again, she wouldn't be allowed to post bail during any subsequent trial. She'd be considered a repeat offender. This time around, Inez would have to be selective. She couldn't take chances, at least not too many. She'd have to be cautious. She'd have to be sure of each woman and whoever sent her. Still, to Inez it was worth the risk.

Inez's finances were among her most pressing problems now. She had anticipated getting back the half million dollars that Bob and June had supposedly spent, and she needed to figure out what reserves she actually still had. As Inez had anticipated, Nelly returned the fifty thousand dollars Inez had entrusted her with. Good ole Nelly hadn't even opened the padded envelope. Inez should have let Nelly hold on to the half

327

million dollars. That was more money down the drain than Inez cared to think about. It was gone and it made Inez sick. With the cash back from Nelly at least she could pay off the remainder of what she owed Walter McGovern (who, as promised, returned the furs he had safeguarded), and she'd have some spending money left over. She also knew she'd have to unload some of her real estate before the Feds did it for her.

Inez's first meeting was with her accountant, Bud Felix, who warned her that selling off any of her property would be imprudent. The noose that Pat Brown had placed around her neck was getting tighter. Any sell-off would trigger questions of where the funds had originated and whether Inez had declared that revenue, as well as any profits derived from sales of her holdings. With Inez's criminal conviction and prison term a notch in Pat's belt, her next adversary would likely be the US attorney's office, pressured to go after Inez for more back taxes. The feds would want more than just to recoup taxes on the banner years of profits from the clinic; there'd be fines and liens. Felix warned that it was possible the feds might impose a prison sentence on Inez, even though she was now sixty-four.

But she still needed cash, and to raise it, she'd have to sell some of the stocks she owned: Pacific Gas & Electric, American Telephone & Telegraph, Regal Amber Brewing, and a host of other equities.[1] With some of that money, for a bit of risk, Inez invested in a little-known Reno-based company called Mountain City Consolidated Copper Company. Mabel Malotte had put money into the mining company and had told Inez it'd be a smart investment that would pay off in dividends— monetary and otherwise. Mabel said the right people owned the company.[2]

Bob and June Merritt had already been deposed by agents from the Bureau of Internal Revenue, just one month into Inez's sentence at Tehachapi, and the feds had asked the couple a litany of questions about Inez's cash reserves, savings bonds, safe-deposit boxes, furs, home furnishings, jewelry, and real estate.[3] No doubt the bureau was mounting a case against Inez, and Felix warned her to brace for it.

Inez never trusted Joe with anything financial. Actually, she didn't trust Joe with much. When Inez returned from Tehachapi, she found the Guerrero Street house a mess. Joe hadn't kept on any of the cleaning women Inez had trained, and there was a thick coat of dust everywhere. Her Persian rugs needed vacuuming, and the bank of bay windows facing Guerrero Street were streaked with grime so thick she could hardly see out of them. Piles of dishes teetered in the sink. Joe was helpless. Never short of suspicion, Inez had her own ideas of what Joe had been up to while she'd been doing time.

On top of straightening out her finances, home, and common-law husband, Inez's fourteen-year-old granddaughter, Caroline, began living with Joe and her. Caroline was the only daughter of Inez's third son, William E. Brown, and his wife, Carline, who at age thirty-seven had been diagnosed with ovarian cancer. No way could William, who lived in one of the Atherton homes Inez had bought to shelter her income, juggle his wife's illness and the couple's high-spirited daughter. William, who worked for the plumbing-supply company P. E. O'Hair, didn't have the time or patience to raise a teenaged girl. So Caroline left Sacred Heart, the ritzy all-girls' finishing school in Menlo Park, and started attending Mission High, the public school four blocks away from Inez and Joe's home. Pretty, smart Caroline would receive much of her education from Inez. Caroline reminded Inez of herself as a budding young woman.

Inez's time at Tehachapi would have been rough for any woman, but for Inez, long accustomed to the comforts and status money brings, the prison term had sent her into a tailspin. Even though she had served her time in the state's "country club prison," the two and a half years had taken a toll on her physically and mentally.

Caroline remembers sitting on a stool in the upstairs bathroom, watching her grandmother stare at herself in a large magnifying mirror for what seemed like hours. To Caroline, Inez was peering in at her soul. She'd watch as Inez dabbed and rubbed a multitude of creams and potions on her face. It was the Brazilian Beleza redux, although Caroline had no knowledge of that episode of her grandmother's life so long ago. With both hands, Inez would push and pull the skin on either side of her cheekbones, tightening the hollows in what were becoming jowls. Pat Brown had tried to take away her livelihood and punish her for it. Now gravity and age were doing the same with her beauty.

"Do I look old?" Inez would ask Caroline so often that it became a routine between the two.

"Do you see this wrinkle here?" Inez would ask, pointing to a line under one of her eyes. "Was it there yesterday?"

"You're still beautiful, Grandma," Caroline would answer dutifully. "And you have a great figure for someone in her sixties. You really do."

"Don't mention my age. *Ever!*"

"You're still the most beautiful woman in San Francisco, Grandma." Caroline was parroting what Inez had regaled her about how men used to describe her.

Someone must have told Inez that smiling exacerbated facial wrinkles because her newest war against aging was to refrain from smiling. Whenever her spirits lifted and Inez caught herself smiling, she'd stop herself, which resulted in a stony face that began to match her constant gloomy disposition.

Caroline turned into a kind of personal valet, drawing water for chamomile-and-milk baths, scrubbing Inez's back with sea sponges, laying out her sleep clothes, bringing her rose-hips tea to calm her frayed nerves. Even with the Nembutal, Caroline and Inez would lie in bed together at night as Inez would launch into yet another jag. When Caroline's eyelids would droop and she'd nod off to sleep, Inez would still be gabbing. By the time Inez would look over and find round-faced Caroline sleeping angelically, it'd be two or three in the morning, and there was no one left to talk to. Joe was no help. He'd be asleep down the hall, raising the roof, snoring.

"Get up!" Inez would greet Caroline every morning at seven. "You can't laze around. You have things to do! Hurry, hurry up!"

Coddling was the last thing Caroline was going to get from her grandmother. Inez needed to be strict with her. Inez knew what could happen to a young woman in a city as fast and loose as San Francisco. Men would take advantage of her if she let them. Inez didn't want Caroline to make the same mistakes she'd made. She didn't want to see her granddaughter as a patient, either.

After three months' home, Inez decided it was high time to do something about the multitude of wrinkles and crow's-feet creeping around her eyes. Inez liquidated several of her stocks and, with the profits, in January of 1951, visited a plastic surgeon, most likely Dr. Albert D. Davis, whose offices were next to Shreve & Co. on Post Street. Dr. Davis was the most respected plastic surgeon in San Francisco, likely in California, at the time. Inez had had experience with cosmetic surgery years earlier when she'd undergone the twin operations to excise her pinky toes and the small bones from her rib cage. While plastic surgery was still an operation only the wealthy could afford, plenty of well-heeled women Inez's age were choosing to go under the knife for vanity's sake. The women at the opera got face-lifts, so why shouldn't she?

The operation was performed at San Francisco's Saint Francis Hospital, and after three days of recovery, Inez was moved to the twelfth floor of the Sir Francis Drake Hotel, where a nurse attended to her around the clock. The surgeon had made symmetrical incisions behind both of Inez's ears, which ran four inches from earlobe to hairline; he also made a horizontal incision under her chin to tighten the flaccid skin of her neck.

Following the surgery, Inez's head was bandaged like a mummy. During the recovery, Caroline was sent back home to Atherton. But on a trip to San Francisco with two girlfriends, Caroline recalls running into Inez near the cable car turn-around on Powell and Market Streets. Inez's face was covered with a scarf and the white surgical bandages. But Caroline was certain it was her grandmother. When Inez spotted Caroline, Inez was so embarrassed that all she could do was nod and hurriedly walk past her wide-eyed granddaughter without even saying hello.[4]

The surgery had remade the contours of Inez's face with particular attention to her eyes, chin, jaw, and cheeks.[5] She still had wrinkles, but they seemed finer and less deep. The results were to Inez's liking; she believed the surgery had shaved ten years off her physical appearance. She felt revived and, once again, confident. She allowed herself to smile, just a bit.

Back from the surgery, Inez returned to Guerrero Street with renewed vigor. She became even more exacting than she had been around the house before she'd been sent to Tehachapi. As she did at the clinic, Inez demanded the house be white-glove spotless, with a revolving door of cleaning women trooping in and out, never able to please their fastidious boss. An Italian maid by the name of Anna used to get down on her hands and knees, scouring with a toothbrush crevices between the oak floorboards, then onto the kitchen countertops, cupboards, and cabinets, and crown moldings, all under Inez's watchful eye. She quit after ten days. Anna was followed by a black maid, Irma Skipworth, who after a week told Inez, "They done freed the slaves!" and out she marched. When Caroline's teenage brother, Bill, would come up from Atherton to stay at the house, Inez wasn't hesitant about putting him to work too. "She'd have him dangling on a ledge, cleaning the windows on the second floor. Inez had a thing about streaks on glass," Caroline recalled.

Bill graduated from high school in 1951 and immediately enlisted in the Air Force, so he avoided living with Inez, but he recalls, "She was a real nut about having everything clean. Nothing could be clean enough." Bill also remembers Inez as "not a very loving person. She never told us she loved us. She was cold and at times cruel."[6]

Inez had transformed into her own mother. "You listen to me, Caroline," she'd lecture. "I was constantly reminded how grateful I should be that Inez had allowed me the privilege of living with her." Caroline learned to make coffee just the way Inez wanted it, and when it didn't meet Inez's standards, Inez ordered her to brew a new pot. If Inez thought Caroline had eaten too much, Caroline would be put on the same diet as Inez: six raw eggs, a pinch of wheat germ, and nothing else for the day. "Men don't like fat women," Inez told her.

Soon, Inez began looking at blossoming Caroline as either a protégée or a rival, depending on the day and on Inez's mood. As Inez dressed every morning, she still wore fine French lingerie, and she never failed to tuck into her undergarments a silk "lacy lover's knot," as she called it, then winking and telling Caroline, "You never know what the day will bring." Caroline wasn't sure what the knot was for and was too scared to ask.[7]

As Caroline started dating, Inez demanded to meet every boy who dared ask Caroline out. Inez was an overbearing surrogate mother—with a twist. With her new taut, chiseled face, Inez would often vie for the boys' attention, and sometimes for more.

On one of Caroline's first dates, after interrogating her granddaughter's gentleman caller, Inez announced, "Forget Caroline. I want you for myself!" It was a bald assertion that embarrassed Caroline, causing her cheeks to turn crimson. But even Caroline didn't think that Inez could possibly be serious.

The young man never called on Caroline again. Weeks later, Caroline bumped into him coming out of the Guerrero Street house after he had visited Inez, presumably for a "lesson." An incredulous Caroline stomped into the parlor to blast Inez—who would only laugh at her teenage granddaughter. The suitor wouldn't be the last man Inez would shamelessly poach from Caroline.

An aging libertine, Inez took pleasure in embarrassing Caroline, pushing beyond the pale. "One afternoon, Inez sent a mailman as black as the ace of spades up to my bedroom for what she called a session of 'fun in the sun.' She thought I'd enjoy myself! He knocked on the door, poked his head inside, and said he was all ready to go. I screamed bloody murder."

Back from prison and energized by her new appearance, Inez entertained multiple paramours outside her sputtering relationship with Joe. "One time, she had an old man from Sweden in bed with her. He must have been ninety. I opened the bedroom door and saw the two of them together. It was horrible," Caroline recalled. "If they were good-looking and if she felt like sleeping with them, she would. If she wanted something, she took it. She wanted to be a young woman all over again. And there was nothing to stop her."

Through it all, Inez gave Caroline life lessons of sorts. Caroline should never go out with a man unless he showered her with gifts. And the presents mustn't be trinkets. "She told me that you could tell how much a man loves you by what he gives you," Caroline remembered. One of Inez's callers at the time brought her a diamond ring, but she threw it back at him because it was too small.

"I remember Grandma telling me, 'Never slap with an open hand. Always fight with a fist and go first for the stomach, then hit 'em in the chin.'" It was a replay from Inez's own life as a child, living South of the Slot with her rough-and-tumble mother and her alcoholic father. Inez's knock-down, drag-out arguments with Joe became legendary among friends and neighbors. For drama (or comedy), Inez would chase Joe around the house with a frying pan.

"You fucking bitch!" he'd shout.

"If there's any fucking going on here, I wanna be in on it!" Inez would scream back. "You wore yourself out on Tenderloin whores and now you can't perform. Didja hear that, Caroline?" who'd barricade herself upstairs, her head buried under a stack of pillows.

Inez hadn't been this way as a mother, but that was because she was always busy attending to her patients. She had also relied on governesses to raise her children. Now she seemed on edge constantly. Blame it on her age, the three trials, incarceration, and health issues (her arthritis and depression had gotten worse). All of it had taken a toll.

On more than one occasion, Inez complained to Caroline that Joe was such a drain on her that she wouldn't mind if he were to disappear. On more than several occasions, Inez suggested ways to hasten Joe's death. "She told me she was going to kick Joe down the stairs, and I was to go downstairs to the basement, check his pulse, and call the police when he was dead," recalled Caroline, who didn't know that Inez had experience killing a husband who had grown out of favor. Caroline was never sure whether Inez was just talking or meant what she was said.

Inez was calmest when she was working, and fortunately for everyone around her, she began attending in earnest to pregnant women once again at the house. These were patients who'd been referred through physicians she trusted, usually Drs. Long, Rogers, or Eliaser. Inez resumed her friendship with Dolf Berger, the former city autopsy physician, who also sent pregnant women her way. Dr. Berger spent more and more time at the house, and if Inez was busy or her arthritis was acting up, he'd perform an occasional abortion.[8] Caroline always felt strange around Dr. Berger. Either he had a wild crush on her or he just savored being in the presence of young women. When Caroline complained to Inez, she laughed. Dr. Berger had an awful lot of connections, Inez said, his hands in lots of pots, almost all of them illegal.

By 1952, Inez's fees for performing an abortion had increased to two hundred fifty dollars, and occasionally higher. The amount was dependent on how much Inez assessed that the patient could afford. Such was the case when Caroline remembers the Nordic skater and Hollywood actress Sonja Henie showing up at the Guerrero

Street house. Henie was thirty-eight at the time and, while working for Twenti-
eth Century Fox mogul Darryl Zanuck, had become among the wealthiest stars in
Hollywood. A manager for Henie called Inez and asked whether she'd see the star.
Inez instructed him to get Henie to the house that same evening.

Henie had recently married her second husband, Winthrop Gardiner Jr.,
a wealthy society scion, but the marriage was on the rocks. Henie had had well-
publicized affairs with matinee heartthrob Tyrone Power, heavyweight boxer Joe
Louis, and the blond, blue-eyed actor Van Johnson. Perhaps to camouflage Liberace's
sexual orientation, Henie was also said to have been intimately involved with the
pianist-entertainer. She became a frequent guest of William Randolph Hearst and
Marion Davies at Hearst's castle in San Simeon. Known alternately as the Ice Queen
of Norway, Golden Girl, White Swan, and Little Miss Moneybags, "she was always
in bed with somebody," said Susan Strong David, a skater who worked with Henie.[9]

Henie swept into Inez's house, wearing a hat with a triad of pheasant feathers, a
white mink, and towering high heels. Dangling from her ears was a pair of diamond
drops that seemed to Caroline the size of robin's eggs. Caroline recalls Henie as tiny,
no more than five feet tall and no more than a hundred pounds. Inez profusely greeted
the star and whisked her upstairs. Two hours later, Inez and Henie walked down the
stairs together. Henie was greeted by a man in a heavy overcoat, who escorted her out
of the house, back to her favorite San Francisco hotel, the Huntington on Nob Hill.[10]

As Inez was bit by bit reclaiming her life, Pat Brown continued to plot his
political destiny. In 1947, Pat had been a shoo-in for reelection as district attorney,
and this time he got endorsements from nearly everyone, including the *San Francisco
Examiner*, his onetime archnemesis. In a guide for campaign workers that year, Pat
wrote a kind of manifesto in which he cautioned his lieutenants not to go overboard
on his record of shutting down vice operations, including abortionists.

"You may run into criticism from people on prostitution, gambling, and abortion. Don't try to argue the morality phase; just say that we have taken an oath of
office and any criticism should be directed to the legislature." The memo instructed
campaign workers, "Don't subject yourself to questioning. Close up the talk by
thanking them and start walking off the platform.

"NEVER APOLOGIZE."[11]

Pat overwhelmed his opponent, assistant US Attorney George Curtis, by a
three-to-one margin for a second term as district attorney. With headlines of Inez's
conviction and imprisonment, along with several other high-profile cases Brown's
deputies had handled, Pat had dramatically raised his statewide profile. As Walter

McGovern had predicted, Pat always seemed to be positioning himself in the wings, waiting for a bigger and better role.

By the fall of 1950, Pat's former opponent for attorney general, Fred Howser, had had a disastrous first term in Sacramento. Howser was mixed up with known gangsters, and his staff was said to be extorting protection money from crooks.[12] Governor Earl Warren distrusted Howser so much that he created a Special Crime Study Commission on Organized Crime, whose purpose was to circumvent Howser, the state's chief law enforcement officer. In the Republican primary for attorney general, incumbent Howser ran a lackluster campaign and lost to California GOP chair Ed Shattuck. On the Democratic side, Pat snared the nomination without any serious opposition. Governor Warren stayed out of endorsing his own party's candidate, which was a de facto backing of Pat, who went on to handily beat Shattuck, becoming the only Democrat that year to win statewide office.

Sonja Henie (center right) speaking with Virgina Field (left), Tyrone Power (center left), and Darryl F. Zannuck (right), 1945.

Pat Brown with his wife Bernice at a campaign stop in Los Angeles, 1958.

Finally.

Pat was poised for the political career he had always imagined for himself.

It had been worth the wait, and the wait hadn't been that long—seven years from San Francisco district attorney to California attorney general. As the top-ranking Democrat in California now, Pat was positioning himself to run for governor in four years.

To fill out the rest of Brown's term as DA, San Francisco mayor Elmer E. Robinson, a former superior court judge, chose none other than Pat's first assistant, Tom Lynch. When informed of the mayor's choice by a reporter, Pat's response was "Splendid!" As though it had been a surprise.[13] Lynch would run for DA the next year and win.

In Governor Warren's crime commission report, issued in November 1950, investigators criticized federal authorities for not vigorously pursuing income-tax evasion charges against Inez and fellow abortionist Dr. Charles B. Caldwell. The report noted that Inez and Dr. Caldwell had amassed more than six hundred thousand dollars of undeclared revenue (in reality, it was more). "Both of these cases are several years old, yet there has been no prosecution for income tax evasion and no imposition of a serious civil penalty. In the Burns case the statute of limitations has already run out on the years when the fraud was the largest.[14]

Warren's commission report was embarrassing, and it led to a federal grand jury being convened in San Francisco in early 1951, which promptly indicted Inez for income-tax evasion, stemming from just one year, 1944, during which investigators said she had performed five thousand abortions.

The indictment was a replay of what had happened in 1940, when Inez had pled guilty to tax evasion for 1935 and 1936, was fined ten thousand dollars, and received a three-year suspended sentence. If that's all the feds wanted this go-round, that'd be fine with Inez.

But the US attorney's office wasn't about to let Inez off so lightly this time. The dawning of the 1950s was a wholly different era with a raft of gung-ho crime busters taking office. No prison time would give a green light to any tax evader who thought he (or she) could stiff Uncle Sam. Inez was a convicted felon; for years, she had paid a pittance in taxes compared with what she had been earning, and Inez was way too public for the feds to cut a quiet deal with her. Home from Tehachapi for just three months, she was facing a federal prison sentence this time. Federal District Judge George B. Harris issued an arrest warrant for Inez, and bail was set at twenty-five hundred dollars. Her accountant, Bud Felix, had been right.

Inez in Federal Court Building,
February 1951.

The federal indictment assessed Inez's income for 1944 at $243,519, but Inez had reported only $31,104 and paid taxes of $14,419. The government countered that Inez owed $188,021 in taxes.[15] Federal prosecutors put penalties at four hundred thousand dollars, including a fifty percent fine on unreported income, plus compounded interest on the taxes due. When all her suspected income was tallied, from 1934 to 1945, her tax bill came to $946,772, compared with what she had paid, $148,954. This left Inez owing the government eight hundred thousand dollars.

This time around Walter McGovern didn't take Inez's case, but another local attorney, Frank I. Ford, did. He charged that Inez was being hounded by authorities.[16] When subpoenaed to appear before the federal grand jury, Ford turned to Inez's physician son, Bob Merritt, who wrote an affidavit attesting to his mother's "long-standing heart ailment," as well as "progressively incapacitating arthritis of the degenerative type," that "has been greatly aggravated since her incarceration at Tehachapi." Dr. Merritt reserved most of his concern for his Inez's mental health. "My feeling is that she is suffering from a profound depression or true melancholia which has become progressively worse. . . . Previous to this confinement, she exhibited psychic depression alternating with periods of elated moods, but of late she exhibits a continuous depression or agitated depression in which there apparently appears to be no recovery."[17]

"I hate to see Mrs. Burns separated from her children, with next Sunday Mother's Day," Ford pleaded to the court. Ford's cocounsel, George Hippili, said that Inez's incarceration in Tehachapi had "aged her greatly." He added, "Since her release last November, Mrs. Burns has lost weight and has fallen victim to numerous physical and psychological ailments—among them arteriosclerosis, arthritis, dizzy spells and melancholia, and she now lives the life of a recluse. Such a life sears the soul of some people."[18] None of it swayed Judge Harris in the least. Physicians appointed by the court examined Inez and found that her heart and mental state were fine.

Actually, Inez didn't stand a chance, even before the case was heard. The fix was in for her. In 1941, when then-governor Culbert Olson had nominated George Harris to the municipal court bench, the master of ceremonies at his swearing in at City Hall had been Superior Court Judge Edward P. Murphy. The vacancy that Judge Harris filled on the municipal bench had been created by Judge Murphy, also nominated by Governor Olson, to fill a spot on the Superior Court.[19] Five years later, Judge Harris was nominated by President Truman to fill a newly created fifth seat on the Northern District federal bench of California; and in 1950, President

Truman nominated Judge Murphy to the same bench. Like Pat Brown and Tom Lynch, Harris and Murphy had long been active in Democratic politics, and their rapid trajectory through judicial ranks demonstrated that.[20]

Inez was given little choice but to plead guilty to the tax-fraud charges. This time, though, a prison sentence would accompany the fines. Calling her an "incorrigible evader of income taxes," Judge Harris sentenced Inez to one year and one day in federal prison, fined her ten thousand dollars, and placed a lien on her assets for $1.2 million.[21] Inez was to be sent to the Federal Prison Camp, in Alderson, West Virginia. With good behavior, she'd be out in nine months. For her sentencing, Inez wore to the federal building a large black hat, black suit, alligator purse, and around her shoulders the fur of an unidentified four-foot-long animal with a head, claws, and a bushy tail. A well-dressed woman was always in fashion, even when she was being sentenced to prison.

Joe and Caroline said goodbye to Inez at the Ferry Building on a typically chilly San Francisco morning of fog and mist on May 22, 1951. Joe gave Inez a hug just as the train whistle blew. Once again, he had tears in his eyes, but a stoic Inez chose not to acknowledge them, particularly in front of Caroline.

When Inez and a federal marshal arrived at the Alderson train depot, nestled in the coal-laden foothills of the Allegheny Mountains, a prison wagon met the pair and four other inmates and their escorts. Like Tehachapi, Alderson was touted as a model rehabilitation institution; it was the nation's first federal prison for women, opened in 1928. Some five hundred women lived in redbrick cottages spread over one hundred acres of the "reservation," as Alderson was called.[22]

After arriving at Katharine B. Davis Hall, Inez was shuttled to Cottage 26, to be fingerprinted, photographed, and ordered to stand naked while a nurse inspected her body cavities. Inez was given an enema, her mouth was checked, and her stomach x-rayed to prevent contraband from being smuggled into the prison. She was issued a rayon nightgown and robe, and shown to a room where she stayed for three days in quarantine. Inez was fumigated and deloused, her hair dusted with DDT. Questionnaires were sent to Joe and her sister, Nettie, so federal prison authorities could ascertain any personality traits that might affect her stay at the prison. One question asked whether Inez was a lesbian, to which Joe and Nettie answered in capital letters, "NO."

While Inez was familiar with prison life from her term at Tehachapi, Alderson was a wholly different experience. Because it was a federal prison, Inez joined an

Billie Holiday and Iva "Tokyo Rose" Toguri, two of Inez's fellow inmates at the Federal Reformatory for Women in West Virgina.

eclectic array of inmates convicted of a variety of federal crimes. Some were in for murder and bank robbery, others for high-profile political crimes, still others for forging checks or making moonshine. There weren't many other tax scofflaws besides Inez at Alderson because few women at the time had enough money of their own to merit a prison term for cheating the feds out of their share of it.

Inez became acquainted with another woman from San Francisco at Alderson, Iva Toguri d'Aquino, better known as Tokyo Rose, who had been found guilty of one count of treason in 1949. Another Alderson inmate was Mildred Gillars, known as Axis Sally, in for spreading anti-American propaganda during World War II. Kathryn Kelly, the accomplice of husband and bank robber Machine Gun Kelly, was there, along with her mother, Cora Shannon. Blues singer Billie Holiday, who'd also been sentenced to one year and one day, had served time for trafficking narcotics across state lines and had been released from Alderson three years earlier.

As at thousands of factory towns across America, a whistle at Alderson blasted at eight a.m., noon, one p.m., and five p.m. every day. Guards informed inmates at Alderson that they had no rights, just privileges that could be taken away at any time.

Embittered once again, Inez became more aggrieved and nettled. She was assigned to her own room, but without a nearby bathroom, she had to keep next to her bed a white enamel "night jar" that she emptied each morning.

All prisons have their own eccentricities and Alderson was no exception. Prison officials had a fixation about how shiny the facility's linoleum floors had to be kept, and inmates were perpetually waxing floors to maintain a mirror luster. Illicitly fermented whiskey was rampant at the prison, but after tasting the rotgut once, Inez was cured of any further interest. As Inez had done at Tehachapi, she went to movie nights and inmate talent shows. As much as she could, though, she stayed by herself. Because of either real or manufactured high blood pressure, Inez spent several weeks on different occasions in the prison hospital. She worked part-time in the kitchen and joined other inmates in complaining about the food. For Thanksgiving, one turkey was allotted per sixty women. A popular saying among Alderson inmates at the time was, "They work us like a horse, feed us like a bird, treat us like a child, dress us like a man—and they expect us to act like a lady."[23]

In the evenings, Inez often gazed out a small window from her room facing east to see the moon rising against a blanket of stars in the clear West Virginia mountain air. Train tracks circumscribed the prison, and Inez would sit in a prison-issue straight-backed chair in her room, looking past the tall hardwood trees, and count the cars rumbling by, brimming with bituminous coal. The trains made a grinding, metallic sound of steel against steel. Once when the moon was high, luminescent, and full, the bright silhouette prompted Inez to reflect on another midnight decades earlier, the time when she had thrown three smooth, flat stones into the black Pacific at San Francisco's Lands End, then dragged her toes in the sand, imagining her past lives as Cleopatra, a gypsy, or a slave master during the reign of Nebuchadnezzar.

As when she had been in Tehachapi, Inez didn't want visitors. Joe sent her boxes of See's assorted chocolates, nail polish, and Camay soap bars every month. When word circulated that Inez was in for tax fraud stemming from a thriving abortion business, several newly arrived inmates, as they had done at Tehachapi, asked her whether she'd consider operating on them, a request she turned down with regret.[24]

Ultimately, Inez served nearly nine months at Alderson, eighty percent of her three-hundred-sixty-six-day sentence. She was released February 26, 1952. Joe had ridden the train all the way from San Francisco to Chicago, then south to Alderson to meet her. He arrived too late in the day for Inez to be released that afternoon, so he checked into the White Sulphur Springs Hotel nearby. Between Charleston and

Alderson, he had opened the box of chocolates and eaten all of them. Maybe it was nerves, maybe he was afraid they'd melt, or maybe he just didn't want to be tempted any longer by a box of chocolates that had been sitting on his lap for twenty-eight hundred miles.

At the Jane Addams Administration Building, Inez was shown the clothes she had worn into the prison, the maroon coat and brown suit, and she eagerly changed into them that morning. Once again, she had lost weight during her incarceration, and now the smart clothes were baggy, hanging shapelessly from her emaciated frame. A matron drove Inez to the prison gate, where Joe was waiting. The two embraced, and this time Inez had tears in her eyes. They took the train back to San Francisco, during which Inez slept most of the way. Upon arrival at the Ferry Building, a waiting reporter asked her about Alderson. "I'll take Tehachapi any day," Inez replied, before she and Joe sped away in a Luxor taxicab.[25]

TWENTY-SIX

THE PLIGHT OF WOMEN
AND THE PLEASURE OF MEN

As soon as Inez and Joe got back to the Guerrero house, as she had done when she had returned from Tehachapi, Inez took two Nembutals, climbed into bed, and tried to sleep, which was impossible. Her mind was reeling at the prospect of being back home in San Francisco.

The next day, son Bob Merritt, worried about her health, gave Inez, now sixty-six, a physical. For her arthritis, he told her to take as much aspirin as her stomach could tolerate. To help her sleep, Bob gave her another bottle filled with Nembutals, but she complained that the pills left her drowsy in the morning, so he prescribed Dexamyl, a popular drug that contained both amphetamines and barbiturates in one pill. The amphetamine component was dextroamphetamine, designed to elevate mood and lessen anxiety; the barbiturate portion was amobarbital, to ease the feeling of euphoria and self-aggrandizement the amphetamine created.[1]

In addition to the Dexamyl, Bob advised his mother not to juggle so much. Try to relax, he advised. Rest. Enjoy your newfound freedom. Go for walks. Visit the city's art museums, the de Young and the Legion of Honor. Easy for Bob to say.

Next to visit Inez was accountant Bud Felix. The two sat in the breakfast nook off the kitchen in the back of the house. The ever-cautious Felix warned Inez that now that she was back from Alderson, her every move would be scrutinized all over again. It was the same story he had told her when she had returned from Tehachapi.

The feds would be looking for her to sell off bits and pieces of her stock and real estate portfolio or for her to execute property-title transfers. The agents' first target, Felix said, would be Burns Ranch. They were likely to confiscate the eight-hundred-acre property.

"Lay low," Felix advised. "You can draw on dividends from what's left of your stocks, but that's about it. We don't want to sell anything. We don't want to arouse suspicion."

Then Felix switched gears. "Have you considered taking up any hobbies?"

That was a good one, and Inez burst out in laughter. She hadn't laughed like that for ages. Inez nearly spit out her breakfast of egg yolks and wheat germ.

Felix laughed too, realizing the absurdity of such a question when it pertained to Inez. She wasn't about to become a law-abiding grandmother, baking, gardening, knitting, or worse—watching that newfangled time waster called television. Inez was all about working, and occasionally partying, hard. Retirement wasn't in her lexicon.

What Inez wanted most was for everyone to know that she had roared back into town, stronger and more powerful than ever. Give up her title as San Francisco's Abortion Queen? Not a chance. Inez needed regretful pregnant women with fistfuls of cash. She needed them as much as they needed her. Home after two stints in prison, Inez could outperform abortionists half her age. Even with her arthritis, she was better and safer than anyone in San Francisco, California, and likely the nation.

And just as had happened when Inez returned from Tehachapi, the phone at the Guerrero Street house started ringing once again. Word got round, as it always did. Inez didn't want to return to prison, but she figured if she stayed under five abortions per week she doubted a woman her age would stir up trouble with the authorities. Other abortionists had jumped into the void Inez had created when she'd been incarcerated, and now they had thriving businesses. Pat Brown was no longer in charge, and Tom Lynch and his lieutenants had bigger fish to reel in. A half-dozen cops still professed loyalty to her, and Inez's physician friends were as pleased as ever to send patients her way. In her line of work, there never was a shingle to hang. Women always seemed to find their way to her front door.

On one rare free morning, Inez found herself walking to Lucca Ravioli Company on Valencia Street, when two young priests barely older than twenty-five, strolling from Mission Dolores, accidently brushed against her on the sidewalk, their cassocks flapping in the brisk San Francisco wind. Inez stopped in her tracks.

"Excuse me!" she said, turning to the pair of priests, continuing past her, heads down, deep in discussion about what Inez might have imagined was either the piety of the church or the infallibility of the Pope.

"You two!" she yelled after them. "YOU!"

They turned back toward Inez. "Yes, ma'am?" asked one.

Inez marched over to the priests and, without much of a provocation, let loose a string of invectives, the likes of which these priests had likely never heard before. Wagging a crooked index finger at them, Inez railed, "The church is the most influential organizations in the whole world. Do you realize how much money the church has, how much property it owns? And you treat half the world's population like cattle. No, worse! Cattle you value, women you look at as . . . manure. Do you realize that? Do you realize what you do to women?"

Inez's eyes were ablaze. "But how *would* you? How would you know anything about women?"

Then, shaking her head, she nearly spat on the pair. "Shame on you, both!"

The priests were dumbfounded. They looked at each other and shrugged. A crazy woman in need of the Lord, no doubt.

"And don't waste any of your bless-yous on me! I'm already damned. Bless someone who believes in your goddamn hypocrisy."

Inez strode forth down the sidewalk as angry and disgusted as she'd ever been.

What sprang forth from Inez's mouth was the accumulation of decades of indignation. She had performed abortions not only on plenty of nuns but also on thousands of Catholic women who'd been taught it was a mortal sin to use any form of birth control, other than the useless rhythm method, which wasn't much of a method in Inez's mind. She had operated on Catholic women who had six or seven children and could barely afford one. This was the church's doing. To add generations of misery all over the world, all for the pleasure of men. To make slaves out of women by giving men unwavering control over their wives', daughters', girlfriends' reproductive systems. Inez's two prison terms had made her surer of what she had always known. Once in business primarily for the money, Inez had become a crusader for women. If anyone knew the plight of women and what the lack of birth control does to them, it was Inez.

In addition to Inez's years of pent-up fury, her outburst might also have had to do with her increasing reliance on the Dexamyl son Bob had given her. The drug's initial rush of euphoria fueled a wicked sense of invincibility, eventually tempered by the soporific effect of the barbiturate. The drug had a pronounced effect on Inez, and her out-of-the-blue blast directed at the priests showed that.

Another reason for the outburst was that Inez had become increasingly aware that she had reached a stage in life when she as a woman had turned virtually invisible. Younger men and women looked through her as though she wasn't there. The priests had hardly noticed her. Such was a painful reality for a woman who used to stop men in their tracks.

Twelve days after Inez had been released from Alderson, on March 10, 1952, Caroline's mother, Carline Warfield Brown, Inez's daughter-in-law, died. Carline was thirty-nine, leaving her husband, William, and two children, Caroline and Bill. The family assembled at Holy Cross Cemetery in Colma, where Carline was buried. Once again, sixteen-year-old Caroline returned to live with Inez and Joe, hopscotching from Alice Granelli Kugler's home (where she had lived when Inez was at Alderson) back to Guerrero Street. Inez, Joe, and Caroline soon were once again together, with Inez reprising the role of Caroline's strict but profligate guardian.

Partially to blot Carline's death from Caroline's mind, Inez soon had the two dressing to the nines nearly every evening. Inez's furs came out of cold storage from H. Liebes's vaults; Inez and Caroline made beelines to Nelly Gaffney's, Ransohoff's, and City of Paris, where they partook in wild Saturday afternoon shopping sprees. Inez, Joe, and Caroline once again made grand entrances at San Francisco's marquee restaurants and nightclubs, always with Inez in the lead, sweeping in as though the trio had breathlessly just arrived from Paris. In a two-week period, Inez, Joe, and Caroline dined at Ernie's, Sam's Grill, Tadich Grill, Swan's, the Rathskellar (Joe liked the sausage, sauerkraut, and polka; Inez and Caroline hated everything about the place), and, of course, the Papagayo Room at the Fairmont with its pandemonium of parrots. Inez and Joe saw nothing wrong with Caroline taking sips from their silver fizzes, and soon Caroline ordered her own. Whenever potatoes came with a dish, Inez told the waiter to remove them from her plate. She didn't eat potatoes for two reasons: They were fattening, yes, but potatoes reminded Inez of the meals she'd been forced to eat as a child, and years later in prison.

Inez and Joe started up their Wednesday evening salons once more. Dr. Long Shot came by and once again played tunes on the piano in the parlor. The Rogers and Hammerstein musical *Carousel* was a runaway hit then, and Dr. Long had taken to playing the song "If I Loved You," serenading teenager Caroline until she got red in the face with embarrassment. Several retired cops stopped by, as did Mabel Malotte

A rooftop sign for City of Paris at Geary and Stockton Streets.

for an early nightcap. Cuban cigars and silver fizzes all around. It was a gay time while it lasted.

When Inez was just six months out of Alderson, county authorities slapped on her and Joe the liens that Bud Felix had predicted, to collect taxes due on Burns Ranch in San Mateo County, which amounted to $1.6 million, plus fines and penalties. This meant more attorneys, more attorney fees, more take-it-or-leave-it non-negotiating with prosecutors who took their cues from ambitious bosses wanting to make names for themselves. Inez chalked it up to the cost of doing business, being successful at it, and having to pay the price. As long as she wouldn't have to return to prison.

However discreet Inez had been this go around while performing abortions, Chief Police Inspector Jim English and District Attorney Tom Lynch had received a tip that Inez was back in business. Inez was an itch they had a hard time not scratching. Lynch, in particular, still carried a pathological hatred for Inez. He was a man obsessed; he had turned into the relentless prosecutor in Victor Hugo's *Les Misérables*, with Inez his Jean Valjean. If she performed just one abortion, Lynch would be there to bust her. And if that happened, Inez would be guilty of violating her parole from Tehachapi, and this time, she'd be at Lynch's mercy.

To corner Inez required stealth and planning. English and Lynch devised an elaborate sting operation that took two months to put into play. A female investigator would feign she was pregnant and seek an abortion from Dr. Berger at his office at 899 Hyde Street, across the street from Saint Francis Hospital. Word around town was that Dr. Berger was a front for Inez, who'd actually perform the abortion. If the sting were successful, English and Lynch would be able to arrest both Inez and Dr. Berger, one for procurement, the other for performing the abortion.

When in play, Dr. Berger told the undercover cop that a trusted female colleague would make a house call at the woman's home in San Francisco's Richmond District to perform the procedure. The agreed-upon fee would be five hundred twenty-five dollars, payable to the abortion provider. Dr. Berger assured the "patient" that he would take care of all the arrangements.

On the evening of Tuesday, October 21, 1952, Carl Warfield, the father-in-law of Inez's son William, delivered a black bag of medical instruments to a two-story

The interior rotunda of City of Paris, 1920.

house in preparation for the procedure scheduled for the next day. That morning at eleven, Inez arrived, met the "pregnant" woman, collected her fee, and began making preparations for the procedure. Inez placed pillows atop a dining-room table, where the operation was to take place, and boiled medical instruments in the kitchen to sterilize them.

Unbeknownst to Inez, Police Inspectors Ralph McDonald, John O'Haire, George Murray, and DA Tom Lynch were upstairs in the house rented for the occasion, recording the conversations between the female cop and Inez, who were downstairs. Just as Inez was about to commence the operation, the four came barreling down the steps.

"Hello again," Lynch said to Inez, unable to suppress a wide gotcha grin.

It was a helluva reunion. This was the first time Lynch and Inez had seen each other since the day she and her four codefendants had been sentenced to Tehachapi in Judge Murphy's courtroom.

Lynch had caught Inez red-handed, holding a medical instrument in her right hand. Reels of tape had captured the crime—from Dr. Berger's arrangement of the abortion, the payment of the fee to Inez, and the very moment when Inez was about to start the procedure. This time, no way would any attorney, Walter McGovern included, be able to wiggle Inez out of the evidence.

When confronted, Inez had no explanation, no story, no excuses. She'd been nailed and she knew it.

Inez broke down and became so agitated that Inspector English described her in "complete shock, almost paralyzed."

"I've lived too long anyway. I wanna go back to Tehachapi and get it over," she told the men who surrounded her.

Compared with how she'd handled herself seven years earlier, when she had offered Police Inspector Frank Ahern the three-hundred-thousand-dollar bribe, Inez was a changed woman. Her response showed how despondent Inez had become after serving two prison terms, but it also reflected the potent drug on which she had come to depend. The increasingly larger doses of Dexamyl had made Inez skid to an all-time low.

That same afternoon, Inspector English arrested Dr. Berger at his office. Berger admitted to acting as a go-between for Inez. His bail was set at twenty-five hundred dollars, which he posted immediately. Inez was denied bond and confined to city jail.[2]

Reveling in his success of the sting, Inspector English crowed to the press, "They weren't easy to trap. They both know too much about the business to fall for a casual cock-and-bull story. We had to resort to some pretty fancy scientific stuff," which included intercepting the female cop's blood work at the laboratory, creating bogus lab findings, and returning positive pregnancy results to Dr. Berger. The undercover officer had paid Inez in marked bills. District Attorney Lynch boasted that no way would Inez be able to free herself this time. He planned to present evidence to the grand jury the following Monday for an immediate indictment.

Lynch's checkmate move had been Dr. Berger, whom police had been following for a variety of suspicions. Lynch had long suspected that the former city autopsy physician was crooked, offering narcotics for cash, medically ministering to underworld figures, and performing at-will abortions. Lynch and English now had Berger in a compromising position; flipping on Inez would save him from a prison term and forfeiture of his medical license.

From jail, Inez hired an attorney, this time Joseph C. Haughey, who promptly proposed a plea deal to Lynch, but the district attorney would have nothing to do with it. There was no room for negotiation, Lynch informed Haughey. Inez had violated the terms of her parole, which called for a mandatory return to prison.[3]

Inez didn't have the sustenance nor the money for a prolonged legal battle. Her health had deteriorated. The Dexamyl had dropped her weight to ninety-four pounds and her blood pressure was through the roof. Inez did not wear a fur coat to court this time, but a charcoal-gray wool suit, a soft silk blouse, and black suede midsize heels, once again from Nelly Gaffney.

Inez stood up; she was shaky this time. She pled guilty. Her attorney told the court it was Inez's "wish and desire is to be put in a place where she can have a little rest, even if it is a penitentiary."[4] Superior Court Judge Eustace Cullinan Jr. sentenced Inez to two-to five years, this time at the newly opened California Institution for Women at Corona.

As for Dr. Berger, Judge Cullinan sentenced him to five months in jail, but the judge allowed Dr. Berger to remain free on bail, pending appeal. When Dr. Berger lost the appeal, the judge stayed the physician's jail term. His license to practice medicine in California was suspended for a year, but that made little difference since Dr. Berger had already accepted a position as a health consultant with a fish-packing firm in Juneau, Alaska.[5]

TWENTY-SEVEN

"NO, I NEVER BRIBED ANYONE"

If there was any silver lining to Inez's third round of incarceration, it was that she'd be one of the first inmates at a new prison, located in Corona, fifty miles southeast of Los Angeles. The California Institution for Women at Tehachapi, where Inez had spent her first prison stint, had grown too small to accommodate the increasing numbers of female felons, so on July 21, 1952, when a 7.7 Richter scale earthquake struck Tehachapi, the new penitentiary was quickly readied to house inmates. If an earthquake was going to roil the region, it couldn't have happened at a better time.

Inez was once again transported by San Francisco sheriff's deputies to prison. By the time she arrived at Corona on the afternoon of December fourth, she was well acquainted with life behind bars. Two massive gates greeted her at the new prison's entrance. The first was known as the sally port, beyond which the outside world ceased to exist. After she proceeded forward and waited for the portal behind her to shut, a second gate opened. Once again, Inez was ordered to shower, matrons checked her head and body for lice, then there were physical tests—weight, height, pulse rate, an eye exam. Inez had to submit again to a body-cavity search for drugs, and was confined to a segregated area for orientation, which lasted a week. As though she needed the tutorial.

At sixty-six, Inez was among the oldest inmates at Corona, and that, along with her two-time ex-con status, gave Inez an instant prison cred. Inez had turned into a gruff, hardened inmate. She was acquainted with many of the prisoners who had been moved from Tehachapi, as well as with Superintendent Alma Holzschuh, who had also transferred to Corona.

A typical "cottage room" at the California Institution for Women. Inmates were allowed to choose the color scheme and fix the room, measuring 9 feet by 11 feet, anyway they liked, July 1954.

Inez asked Miss Holzschuh for a refill of the Dexamyl and Nembutal, as well as a daily regime of aspirin to manage her arthritis. The prison warden bucked the matter to one of two prison doctors, a rail-thin man with a head of Brylcreem-infused hair, who advised Inez that the only drug she'd get would be the aspirin, doled out two pills four times daily. Inez redoubled her request for the Dexamyl and Nembutal to Miss Holzschuh, but to no avail.

It took Inez several unpleasant weeks to wean herself off the narcotics. She

The living room of the honor cottage at the California Institution for Women in Corona where inmates could earn the right to live through good conduct, July 1954.

found herself agitated and depressed, but that was nothing new for her, or for that matter any returning inmate. Going cold turkey exacerbated Inez's lifelong predilection for insomnia. As much an accommodation to status and familiarity as to age, Miss Holzschuh assigned Inez to a private room in one of the low-slung brick cottages. Outside of her job in the kitchen, Inez kept to herself. She was too tired and savvy to join any clique of inmates.

As at Tehachapi and Alderson, when inmates discovered that Inez was an abortionist, some sought her out. Inez was as close to a nurse as many of them wanted to get, and prisoners peppered her with questions about everything gynecological, from yeast infections to venereal diseases. The new prison had a small hospital, where pregnant inmates could undergo labor and delivery. Birth certificates did not bear the prison's name, and infants were kept for ten days before being given up for adoption outside the prison system. Many pregnant inmates resolutely didn't want to give birth, even though they had no other option.[1]

In her first months at Corona, Joe visited several times, and for each visit once again he brought offerings—chocolates, nail polish, and Camay soap. Despite the five-hundred-mile trip and the gifts, Joe and Inez often made spectacles of themselves in the prison visitors' area. They bickered and argued. Out of habit or reason, Inez didn't trust Joe when it came to issues of money, law, or fidelity. For the first two, Joe didn't have a head for financial or legal matters, at least Inez didn't think he did; for the third, in Inez's mind, the sixty-four-year-old Joe was busy squiring women around town in her absence. That or picking from Mabel Malotte's stable of prostitutes. During one of his visits to see Inez, an exasperated Joe had had enough and slammed his hand on the prison-manufactured metal table, instantly stopping all conversation.

"And don't think I'm ever coming back to you!" Inez yelled after Joe, her voice trailing him as he stormed out of the prison visitors' room.

During other times, they seemed to get along fine, although this was when Inez talked and Joe listened.

Going back half a century, Inez had never gotten accustomed to depending on anyone. Sooner or later, people will always disappoint, she had told Caroline on more than one occasion. Joe had been an anchor, yes, but also a reminder of a turn her life had taken when she had thrown over broad-shouldered Charlie Granelli and taken up with the handsome up-and-coming Irish politician who never amounted to much in Inez's eyes.

In prison, Inez's arthritis flared up constantly, sending shooting pains from her shoulders to her fingers, which had become bony and disjointed. The aspirin did only so much. With any luck, she'd be paroled after serving two years, the low end of her sentence. That's what she was hoping for.

Until the first week in September 1954, when Miss Holzschuh called Inez into her office to tell Inez her presence was urgently requested back in San Francisco.

Actually, it was more than a request. It was required by a San Francisco grand jury.

Twenty months into her sentence, the former federal Treasury agent William A. Burkett had told an audience at the Commonwealth Club in San Francisco that when he had questioned Inez in Tehachapi back in 1950, she had told him of at least one high-ranking city official she had bribed. "I reported this, but nothing was done," Burkett told the audience of more than three hundred men (women weren't admitted to the Commonwealth Club until 1971) in an address broadcast statewide. It was a revelation that made some in the audience drop their forks. Burkett had certainly gotten their attention. But Burkett pulled back short of naming names. He said he'd reveal the identities of those on the take at the proper place and time.[2]

What agenda was Burkett pushing, besides his own? A Republican at the time, Burkett was hankering to elevate his public profile, and what better way than to dangle the prospect of exposing a horde of politicians on the take.[3] Burkett had taken a page out of Pat Brown's playbook.

Within days, San Francisco's grand jury foreman Charles Ertola righteously announced, "If there is any truth in the statement, we want to go into it."[4] A dentist whose office was in the heart of North Beach above the bohemian Vesuvio Cafe, Ertola was eager to enter electoral politics, and within months snared a plum appointment, filling a seat on the San Francisco Board of Supervisors.[5]

Anticipating a hot story, the *San Francisco Examiner* sent ace reporter Ed Montgomery to interview Inez in prison about Burkett's curious nondisclosure disclosure, reprising the hype of Inez's trio of high-drama criminal trials. Montgomery came back with an exposé of sorts, writing that Inez "named a number of police officials, past and present, and politicians to whom, she says, she gave protection money in large sums." Following Burkett's lead, Montgomery didn't disclose names, except one provocative alias: "Captain Hill" was code Inez said she used for a series of corrupt police captains and lieutenants. "If the cop on the beat spent too much time on the corner and worried arriving patients, I'd simply tell someone to 'Call Captain Hill and have him get that cop out of here,' and within a few minutes the policeman would get a call to some other part of his beat," Inez told Montgomery.[6]

She also told the newspaperman that she paid one hundred twenty-five dollars every day in protection money "just to open the door" of her Fillmore Street clinic, and another five thousand dollars a week to "the brass downtown" to stay in business. When all of her payoffs were added up, she said, the bribes amounted to "nearly one-half the take" of her considerable profits.[7]

William Burkett, Charles Ertola, and Ed Montgomery were gifts that had just dropped into Inez's lap. Not one to give away anything, Inez was soon angling to trade insider information for an immediate release from prison. If authorities were willing to place that deal on the table, Inez would sing.

This time, Inez hired San Francisco attorney Molly Minudri to do her bidding. Inez and Minudri complemented each other. Flamboyant and animated—her trademark was multiple strands of colorful necklaces—Minudri had clients who ranged from prostitutes and marijuana users to confidence men and transvestites. One of her favorite cases was getting a client charged with feeding pigeons in Union Square acquitted.[8]

Minudri's first order of business was to advise Inez not to testify before the grand jury. Minudri's ostensible reason was that because the statute of limitations had already passed on bribery, no criminal prosecution could arise from her testimony. "Were the jury interested in probing more current events—some matter which could result in an indictment or indictments being voted, and it was shown that Mrs. Burns possessed some knowledge of such matter, the jury would be justified in calling her," Minudri teased. "But I cannot subscribe to the jury's calling an ill and distraught woman simply for an evening's entertainment discussing what did or did not take place nine years ago."[9]

Minudri was tossing out a bargaining chip. Unless Inez was paroled, she wouldn't divulge anything. In addition to an immediate release from prison, Minudri wanted to trade Inez's insider knowledge of corruption to get the feds to exonerate Inez from any tax liabilities and penalties. It was worth a try.

Inez had to ask herself whether any of what she had long known would be worth revealing to shave just three months off the two-year sentence she'd likely serve. If timing was everything in life, then Burkett's revelations had come a little too late for Inez's purposes. There'd also be repercussions and risks if Inez went public with even a small amount of what she knew. Inez was accustomed to keeping secrets. That had been the foundation of her business for forty years. While her personal life might have been anything but discreet, when it came to patients and her operations, Inez had learned to keep her mouth shut. Patients, cops, and city officials demanded anonymity and Inez gave it to them. If she was going to burn anyone, it had better be worth her while. And with so little time left on her prison sentence, would it be worth setting ablaze so many bridges? When she got out, she'd need those friends in high places.

There was also the issue of personal safety. In Inez's line of work, that was essential to consider. She didn't want to end up like Nick DeJohn, garroted and stuffed inside a car trunk.

For the moment, District Attorney Tom Lynch and First Assistant Norman Elkington weren't inclined to offer Inez anything. They flatly refused to negotiate with Minudri. They didn't want Inez to serve one less day in prison than what they believed she deserved. They also didn't trust Inez to give the grand jury forthright and honest testimony. In addition, they were worried about what Inez might reveal and whom she might incriminate. That was a worrisome preoccupation of anyone in City Hall or the Hall of Justice.

The man doing much of the telegraphing between Inez, Minudri, Lynch, and Elkington was *Examiner* reporter Edward Samuel Montgomery. In 1951, Montgomery had won a Pulitzer Prize for exposing a phony Nevada mining company, Mountain City Consolidated Copper Company, a corporation in which Inez and Mabel Malotte had invested. The problem with the company was that rogue agents for the Bureau of Internal Revenue had created it and were benefitting from it. Any investors were told they had nothing to worry about should they ever be investigated.[10]

Montgomery had broken that story, the culmination of months of shoe-leather reporting. With jet-back hair and thick eyeglasses, Montgomery was famously hard of hearing, and carried with him a bulky hearing aid connected by a wire to his ear. It wasn't beyond Montgomery to dangle the hearing aid through a ventilator shaft to eavesdrop on any conversation that might make for a good story. That's what he did to get the tip that led to dummy mining company.[11] Montgomery and the *Examiner* hoped that Inez's confession would be an even greater reprise of the Nevada mining story, pitting Inez against the pillars of San Francisco authority and establishment. It was worth a shot.

The whistleblower Burkett was the first witness to testify before the grand jury on the evening of August 30, 1954, and he spilled the names of at least ten cops and public officials Inez had told him she paid off regularly. The closed-door testimony was more than enough to hook grand jurors. Foreman Ertola instructed District Attorney Lynch to seek an immediate court order compelling Inez to appear before the panel.[12]

But with no deal on the table, Inez wasn't about to divulge anything. Inez would dodge all the questions she wanted to avoid. The negotiation at hand was to get a deal before she'd name names. The last thing Inez was about to do was offer Tom Lynch a freebie.

As a walk-up to whatever testimony Inez was about to give, Montgomery flew to Corona once again, where Inez threw down the gauntlet for Lynch. "I've reached the conclusion that nothing would result from my testimony," Inez said, hoping that would be enough to lure Lynch to proffer her a deal.[13]

On the line was Inez's going public once and for all with a serpentine list of scores of public officials who had taken payoffs from her for years. Her revelations could shake San Francisco to its core.

Sheriff Dan Gallagher sent two deputies to Corona to fetch Inez two days before she was scheduled to testify before the closed-door grand jury. The deputies spirited Inez back to San Francisco on a commercial airplane.

It might not have been the opera, but that didn't make any difference. Inez dressed for the occasion, this time opting for a somber and dignified black dress, a three-quarter-length fur coat, and a brown velvet hat with black trim that Nelly had arranged for delivery to Corona. At nine-thirty Monday evening, Inez was ushered into the ornate grand jury room inside San Francisco City Hall. The suspense was palpable. Every head in the courtroom turned as the thick oak doors swung open and Inez walked through.

For an instant, Inez was transported fifty years earlier. Even though her gait was now labored, she imagined herself gliding down the hallway at the Palace, tossing her long reddish tresses over her shoulder, arching her back, tilting her head just so, all the while floating. Everyone was watching her every move, and she knew it.

Inez took her time getting comfortable on the stand. She crossed her legs, then uncrossed them. She scanned the packed hearing room. She glanced over to the grand jurors and smiled graciously. She touched her index and middle fingers to her temples, as though to ready herself for what was to come next. The courtroom was dead silent.

Then she looked up to her inquisitor—that *other* son of a bitch, Tom Lynch.

Lynch started by asking Inez whether she'd ever bribed a police officer or city official. Inez hesitated. Five, ten, fifteen seconds.

Finally, she shook her head.

"No, I don't *think* so," she started.

Then she amended her statement. "No, I never bribed *anyone*."

It seemed as though Inez was scolding Lynch for asking such an impertinent question.

When Lynch followed up, Inez cited her constitutional grounds of self-incrimination, even though such an explanation before a grand jury had little bearing. Inez then proceeded to dance around all of Lynch's subsequent inquiries.

Inez, after appearing before the Grand Jury, September 13, 1954.

Lynch was hardly surprised, but he drilled Inez nonetheless about what she had teased to Ed Montgomery she knew. At one point, Lynch was reprising his role in the criminal trials with Inez on the stand, and to many in the jury box, he was badgering her. His treatment of her was unbecoming a lady, and if no one was going to stop it, Inez would.

"Why, Mr. Lynch, you know I'm supposed to have paid *you* too!" she suddenly tossed back at him.

The nineteen jurors went bug-eyed. That accusation stunned Lynch for a moment, and the only retort he could come up with was a sputtering "You tell that story to the grand jury right now!"

"Oh," Inez replied, now drawing a smile, "I can't remember all of it now."

It was a nice play on Inez's part and seemed to have evened the odds between the two old antagonists.

Seventy-five minutes later, Inez was excused from the sealed grand jury room, emerging "like a well-entertained guest leaving a party," wrote reporter Dick Hyer.

"My, I've had a wonderful time!" Inez told a gathering of reporters in the hallway.

Inez characterized the grand jurors as "lovely people. They're all Santa Clauses." When asked about the allegations she had raised with Montgomery about bribing legions of cops and officials, Inez wouldn't concede anything. "They asked me if I ever gave money. I said I did not. I never gave money to anyone."

A reporter asked whether Police Inspector Al Corrasa was the notorious "Captain Hill."

"I told them, 'Oh yes, that's a good man.' But then they asked if I ever gave him any money. Can you imagine that! Why, that was awful, and I told them so!"

All in all, Inez's much-anticipated appearance before the grand jury was a "washout," as someone inside the grand jury room told Hyer.

"Inez talked a lot but said nothing," Lynch said in the hallway. "As far as I'm concerned, the Burns's phase of any inquiry is a dead duck."[14]

Turning into a stool pigeon never suited Inez. She never liked to give anything away for free. The last thing Inez was about to do was give sonofabitch Lynch a present. And no way was he going to offer up anything in exchange for her sharing specific allegations about how crooked San Francisco had been for years and years. Inez had an arm's length of names, and Lynch knew it. But without a deal, no way would Inez sing. No deal, no names.

While temporarily back in the city of her birth, Inez was afforded the fine accommodations of the city jail, where she complained of a stomachache. And even though she was only a fifteen-minute ride away from her old Guerrero Street house, Joe didn't bother to see her in jail. They must have been in the middle of one of their nonstop fights. When asked about his no-show, Inez shrugged. "How should I know where he is? I wish someone would tell Joe that it's all right to come back now. Maybe he'll read it in the papers."[15] By Friday, Inez was put on a Pullman back to Corona.

Inez served five more months in prison. She was paroled on January 18, 1955, having served a total of twenty-five months. Joe drove to Corona to pick her up, this time without any chocolates.

It turned out that the feds weren't finished with Inez. On March 26, 1956, Inez and the Internal Revenue Service agreed to a further settlement of $745,325 to cover all unreported income from Inez's heyday years, 1942 to 1945. That amounted to taxes on revenues government officials calculated to be $1.4 million; Inez had reported her income for those years to be just $95,000. The total she conceded was $383,080 in taxes, $154,642 in penalties, along with $207,603 in back taxes assayed to Joe Burns, because the couple had filed jointly for two of the four years under question.

By now, Inez had sold off almost all of her real estate, with the exception of her principal domicile, the Guerrero Street house, and all those proceeds had gone to paying off back-tax bills and her attorneys.

"I haven't a darn cent left," Inez told a reporter at the close of her hearing in federal court, in March 1956.[16]

PART V

CODA

Inez at a family wedding, standing third to left, 1966.

TWENTY-EIGHT

STILL STYLISH AND FEMININE AFTER ALL THESE YEARS

In 1971, Inez was interviewed by Robert Patterson, a veteran reporter for the *San Francisco Examiner*, who used to write a gossip column under the byline Freddie Francisco.[1] Patterson was a man-about-town and raconteur, and in his story about Inez, then eighty-four, he wrote, "Though definitely no chick, the aging and petite (one hundred five pounds) underworld luminary of prewar days is still feminine and stylish. Her reddish hair ('titian,' she calls it) is worn in a fluffy short cut, with bangs coming to the eyebrows. Her colorfully patterned dress was modish. Her dialogue is as quick, bright and humorous as it was a quarter of a century ago when this reporter last talked to her."

Inez confessed to Patterson that she detested the word *bribe*, but she allowed, "I've made many a cop very happy." Reflecting on her freewheeling days about town, Inez sighed in a Mae West kind of way, "You can't hardly find sensible men like that anymore."

Her views about abortion or women's rights hadn't leavened one bit. "Scores of women will [continue] to die," she said,[2] two years before the Supreme Court made abortion legal in the landmark *Roe v. Wade* case, which also set up conditions to allow states to regulate the procedure, but only during the second and third trimesters.

Inez, May 24, 1971.

Inez spoke as an unalloyed feminist. She continued to rail against the church's unwavering antiabortion stance,[3] as well as against grandstanding politicians touting family values—usually slippery code for when men made fundamental life decisions on behalf of women.

Inez and Joe still lived in the Guerrero Street house, the last of the long list of properties that hadn't been sold or confiscated by the IRS. Inez had given up performing abortions, not because she'd lost the touch or inclination, but because the arthritis in her hands made firmly holding medical instruments nearly impossible. She spent most days cooking, reading, and mostly brooding. The raucous Wednesday evening salons had stopped long ago. Caroline remembers whenever she visited her grandmother, Inez would ask her to take a pot of home-cooked soup to a widower who lived down the block. She still flirted with men, continuing to take pleasure in holding a man's attention, either through conversation or coquetry. Someone who saw Inez on a weekly basis was Andy Roach, a bachelor in his fifties who came to the United States from Dublin in 1958, and who used to eat often with Inez and Joe. Inez would call Roach on the phone three or four times a week and talk his ear off. "She'd call at ten in the morning, and I couldn't get off until noon or one in the afternoon. She'd tell me that no one appreciated her. I'd just listen, mostly because I never could get a word in edgewise," Roach told me back in 1992, sipping black coffee in a Mission dive called Kenny's. "Everyone was afraid of her. The look that woman could give—no Hollywood actress could scare you more."

To keep herself busy, Inez clipped recipes from the newspaper and pasted them in a brown scrapbook held together with string.[4] She baked loaves and loaves of bread and gave them away to neighbors. She posted hand-printed signs of folk wisdom throughout the house; for whom, it wasn't clear. It certainly wasn't for Joe; he was beyond reforming, and the number of people who stopped by could be counted on one hand. In the bathroom, a sign read, "You better aim"; in the kitchen, "Men build houses, women build homes"; in the front hallway, "Better to be thought a fool than open your mouth and remove all doubt."

Inez seldom left the house. She spent hours staring out the large bay windows and became increasingly withdrawn. "She'd sit in the front room, looking at the street," said Bob Collen, another friend of Inez's I interviewed. "She seemed angry at the world. You felt sorry for her and Joe, two old people lost in a world of their own." The two still argued, hectoring and needling each other, with Inez decidedly holding the upper hand.

By 1973, Inez and Joe, eighty-seven and eighty-two, respectively, couldn't take care of the Guerrero Street house or each other any longer. Neither could easily climb the stairs, and the rigors of maintaining a finicky fifty-year-old house were beyond them.

They moved to a convalescent home in Moss Beach, a community twenty-two miles south of San Francisco on coastal Highway One. Inez and Joe didn't share a room. Men and women living together was not allowed. Maybe it was for the best.

TWENTY-NINE

DOWN THE HATCH

In parts of the crescentic Northern California shoreline south of San Francisco, the fog hovers sinuously over the terrain like a haze of gray gauze. A vapor covers the alluvial soil for days, often weeks. Inez peeked down the steep hill that traversed Marine Boulevard, across Pearl Avenue and Etheldore Street, beyond the conifers and their sticky cones, the just-sprouted ruched daffodils and the blanket of California poppies, all the way to winding Cabrillo Highway at the base. On the rare days when the fog cleared, if Inez craned her neck and gazed west, she could refract her vision just enough to catch a sliver of the jadeite Pacific. But on this morning, the great maritime expanse was impossible to see. Another day of what anyone from anywhere but coastal California might confuse with smoke. And all Inez wanted on this day was to open a window and inhale the ocean's medicinal breezes.

Inez stared through the casement window from the room she shared with two roommates whose names she had forgotten. The room contained three single beds in a tangle of sheets, three straight-backed chairs, three dressers, and an assortment of wrinkled black-and-white photographs tucked inside a mirror's frame. The roommates were gone, sitting out front, staring at who knew what.

Joe, who had stayed devoted to Inez through thick and thin, had died in his sleep three months earlier. He was eighty-four. He grew tired one day, went to his room, lay down, and never woke up. Although the arguments Joe and Inez used to have were legendary, even in the convalescent home, Inez allowed that she missed him.

Inez dressed every day, but as a concession to her age, she now wore slippers. Bunions plagued her feet that were for years accustomed to high heels. If she ever went barefoot, some of the women made comments about the flaps that once had been her pinky toes. She didn't dwell in front of the mirror. Too painful, too much a reminder of what years do. Especially to a woman.

Take Señor Ortega. He was as good a bellwether as any in the Moss Beach nursing home where there were eight women for every man. A gentleman who used to work for Farmers Insurance in Modesto, he moved to be closer to his only son in nearby Pacifica. Señor Ortega dressed every day in a starched white shirt and silk foulard tie whose Windsor knot sat below a bobbing Adam's apple. Inez liked the way he read the *San Francisco Chronicle* every day, neatly folding it into quadrants, page by page. One day, after she smiled at him between the Sporting Green and the business section, they started a conversation.

In their ensuing discussion, Señor Ortega referred to the nursing home as *El Cielo*, Spanish for "the sky." Inez assumed he called it *El Cielo* because the single-story building was perched high in the hills at the end of a near-vertical road. But after dinner that evening, Inez realized that there was another reason: Señor Ortega fully accepted this home as his final earthly destination. "It is God's will," he said, lowering his chin as he raised a spoonful of rice pudding to a small mouth below a neatly trimmed mustache.

As they walked to the T in the middle of the nursing home, at the vertex in a sort of demilitarized gender-neutral zone, Señor Ortega bowed goodbye to Inez in a courtly manner, a custom she thought reminiscent of his homeland. Ten paces down the corridor, Señor Ortega stopped and turned to Inez. "*Vaya con Dios, Señora*," he said.

Poor Señor Ortega. An abiding belief in the Almighty, an invisible hand guiding his direction and decisions. Inez had never been a believer in anyone else calling the shots. Why give up the power that was yours to do whatever you wanted?

As she returned to the women's side of the convalescent home, Inez was reminded of the curious state of women without men. While few in her surroundings ever possessed Inez's combination of beauty and brains, not to tend to the basics— hair, makeup, skin, how they dressed—even here and now, what excuse could these women possibly have? Shuffling behind those aluminum-gray contraptions— "walkers," they called them—with fuzzy tennis balls for feet. Had they given up?

The ability to think clearly at Inez's age was both good and bad. She wasn't just aware of who she had been, but of who she had become. And of the immense chasm separating the two. Who are we if we lose our ability to recall who we once were? To be in possession of a lifetime of memories is a blessing and a curse, particularly when you find yourself in what euphemistically is referred to as a convalescent home. No one convalesces in these places. Señor Ortega was right in that regard.

Inez's musings were interrupted by muted, muffled sounds coming from outside. She placed her ear against the casement window in her room, eavesdropping on what sounded like a faraway celebration. Faint voices, children singing, teasing each other, playing tag at the beach. Past Cypress Street, down from Frank's Place, the old speakeasy. Distant squeals of delight accompanied by what Inez imagined were soft, scampering soles pressing footprints in the spongy sand. Mothers with soaked pant legs rolled to their knees, cautioning their progeny not to get any closer to the white-capped waves chopping at the shore, creating a brume. The undertow could snatch a child by the foot and pull her into the ocean, never to be seen again. The ocean in these parts was subtle and dangerous.

Some days were drearier than others. Blue days, Inez called them. All the more reason today to catch a glimpse of the Pacific. Even better: to stand on the beach, the foamy water with bubbles rushing over her feet, in between her toes. So cold, it stung.

What was wrong with what I did?

That's what stuck in Inez's craw. Still. Any fool knew there was no way to eliminate abortion. It was an immutable fact of life, like prostitution and infidelity. Each had been around before Biblical times and would be around after humans colonized Mars. If a woman wanted to end her pregnancy, she would and did. Always.

They came to me, lining up at my door every day.

Click-click-click against the shiny linoleum floor. Footsteps.

"Hello, girls. How ya doin'?" A sweet, buoyant voice.

"She up all night long," one of the nurses said, shaking her head. "She don't make no sense, talkin' the way she do. The people she say she know. No lady could've done half what Miss Inez say she do. The stories she tell. She got some imagination, Miss Caroline."

Of the tens of thousands of women who had stepped in and out of Inez's life, Caroline had been there the longest. She'd been her greeter, server, receptionist, friend, confidante. She had served tea and cake to all the women while they recovered. Caroline had been there to see everything.

Inez raised her eyes and allowed Caroline a peck on her right cheek. As Caroline took a seat in one of the straight-backed chairs, they talked about the persistent fog, the miserable dining-room food, the snail's-pace traffic all the way from Nineteenth Avenue.

For Caroline, there was always a moment of apprehension whenever she visited. Would Inez bring up the family lore of murder, the multitudes of men, sex, and infidelity? The wild, crazy times. The movie stars who'd been patients. The code Inez had invented so no one would know what the two of them were talking about. Still. *Ni-dash. Glantham.* Like a dying secret club, Caroline and Inez were the only ones left who still knew the passwords.

"Am I in the joint, Caroline?" Inez asked rather suddenly, as though she had just awakened from a deep sleep.

"No, Grandma. You're in a convalescent home. You know that."

"Who'd ever do that to an old woman, Caroline?"

Caroline wasn't sure whether Inez meant being sentenced to prison or put in a convalescent home. Maybe they were one in the same.

And then, Caroline saw it, if just for a second.

Inez arching her back, tossing back her hair, which used to stretch the length of her back, over her shoulder. It was the look of complete and utter confidence.

"Where are my instruments, Caroline? Do you know?"

Once there had been seventeen: forceps, speculums, dilators, tenaculums, curettes. Stainless steel tools of the trade. Inez had to hide them, especially when Pat Brown, Tom Lynch, and that Frank Ahern were about to close in on her. In the bottom of a kitchen cabinet behind the pots and pans. That's where they were. That's where she used to hide them.

"When I go, Caroline, would you do me a favor, dear?"

Inez's tone was so sweet and pliant, so unlike Inez, that it stopped Caroline in her tracks.

"I want you to put the medical instruments—the ones I got from Dr. West, the first instruments I used, the ones in the canvas carrying case that rolls up, I want you to get them and put them in my casket with me. Would you do that for me, Caroline?"

"That sounds so ghoulish, Grandma. Why would you ever want them?" Caroline asked, not with malice, but out of curiosity.

Inez touched her chin with her right hand and thought for a moment.

"Because I relied on them. Because they belong to me. Because they're mine. That's why.

"Don't just say you will, and then forget about it, Caroline. I want them. Do you understand?"

This was the Inez Caroline knew, demanding and sure of herself.

"I'll try, Grandma. I'll try to find them. But it's been so many years."

"I want them with me when I die."

"But why, Grandma?" Caroline asked as gently as you could. "They're not going to do anyone any good in a casket with you."

"Because they're what got me everywhere in my life. That's why I want them. Promise me."

Caroline said she'd do what she could, but she had no idea where the instruments were. They had disappeared long ago. To find them would be impossible. Thank goodness.

After several seconds, Caroline got up and took from a brown Safeway grocery bag a bottle of peppermint schnapps. Not a silver fizz, she knew, but this would have to do. She reached for two goblets atop Inez's dresser.

Baccarat. Heavy and solid. The last of the glory years, the last of all that Inez had once owned. Caroline flicked the goblet's rim with the red-polished nail of her index finger.

Piiiiiiiiiiiiiiiiiiiiiiiiiiiiiiiinnnnnnnnnnnnnnnng.

Caroline poured the clear, syrupy liquid into the two glasses.

The two women raised the glasses and clinked.

"Down the hatch," Caroline and Inez said softly and in unison.

THIRTY

SHE WAS TOO AUDACIOUS

While all of California was engrossed in another headline-grabbing trial about to begin in San Francisco's Hall of Justice—this one of newspaper heiress Patricia Hearst, charged with robbing a bank after she'd been kidnapped by a terrorist group and then joined it[1]—Inez died on Sunday, January 25, 1976, at the age of eighty-nine of congestive heart failure, six months after Joe died. Fewer than a dozen mourners attended her funeral at Skylawn Memorial Park in San Mateo. The inscription on Inez's tombstone read, "Loving Wife and Mother." No mention was made of her role as daughter, sister, or grandmother. Inez was buried next to Joe in an area of the cemetery reserved for veterans; Joe's footstone read, "Regtl Sup Sgt US Army, World War I," with a cross centered beneath.[2]

Years earlier, Inez's lifelong nemesis Pat Brown had told voters that anything was possible in this great state bounded by ocean and mountains with vibrant cities and fecund lands nestled in between. Pat's world was a land of unlimited resources and dreams. Anything could come true in California. Elected to two terms as attorney general and then governor, Pat epitomized California exceptionalism, which transformed the Golden State into the home of the nation's best public university system and the incubator of some of the world's greatest ideas and innovations. In the process, California became the destination of a nonstop, never-ending surge of wide-eyed transplants, smog-belching automobiles on endless freeways that Pat advocated building, and a red-tape bureaucracy that would nearly strangle the state. Pat did whatever he needed to shove himself and California into the forefront of the nation and the world. Like nearly every American politician, he set out to become president, and as California's favorite son, he had a decent shot at it.

John F. Kennedy considered Pat as his running mate in 1960, but instead chose Texas senator Lyndon B. Johnson. In 1962, Pat beat former Vice President Richard Nixon for the California governorship. If it hadn't been for a handsome B-movie actor by the name of Ronald Wilson Reagan running against him four years later,

Pat Brown with his family at a dinner in the Fairmont Hotel, November 1958.

FIRST CHOICE FOR GOVERNOR ★ 'Pat' ★ BROWN

along with bad timing and a political fumble that would detonate Pat's career, the San Francisco native might well have been elected to a third term as governor and then onto the White House. There was talk of Pat running again for governor in 1970, but by then Pat's son, Jerry, had begun his own high-wire political act, and Pat graciously bowed out of electoral politics for good.

In 1993, I called Pat Brown in his Los Angeles Century City office to ask about Inez. By then, he had retired from his law firm, Ball, Hunt, Hart, Brown and Baerwitz, and busied himself by giving an occasional speech, often to a corporation that paid him handsomely. His secretary told me she'd relay my request to the former governor. "I can't promise you anything, but," she said, lowering her voice, "he *does* like to talk to journalists, so we'll just have to see, won't we?" I took this as a positive sign.

Three days later, Pat called back. It was the first time I had ever talked to him, and he sounded as genial as I'd always imagined. I pictured him in his windshield-size gold-rimmed glasses, leaning back in a big chair in an enormous office lined with scores of signed, framed photographs. As a warm-up, we traded stories about old newspaper reporters we both knew. Pat was animated, chatting me up, trying to sense where this interview would go. I expected nothing less from a consummate lifelong politician, who at eighty-seven was still engaged in shaping his persona to his advantage.

When I broached the subject of Inez, Pat hesitated for several seconds. As I had experienced with Corinne, bringing up Inez always brought a tantalizing pause in any conversation.

"Inez Burns," the governor said tentatively. "Yes, I remember her. The abortionist." Then Pat seemed to check himself.

"How instrumental was Inez Burns in your career, Mr. Governor?" I asked. No sense in beating around the bush.

"When I started, I had the zeal of a new DA. I was looked at as a fighting DA, and the rest of the state thought that was good."

Pat volunteered that Inez had been "a very good abortionist with a good reputation. Everyone thought she was a necessary evil. But when I became DA, her business had become flagrant."

Pat Brown campaigning for governor ca. 1958.

Pat corroborated that the reason he went after Inez wasn't because she was a public-safety nuisance. That never had anything to do with Pat's relentless prosecution of Inez. She did what she did well, Pat allowed, but she was too audacious, too public. To stay in business, she had paid off hundreds of police and city officials, he said.

For a man of so many talents and accomplishments, I sensed that Pat Brown in his remaining years didn't want any discussion of his career to focus on who he considered to be a minor supporting actor who had shared his panoramic stage for a single scene. Inez had been one of numerous conquests Pat had made in a hard-fought career that spanned more than forty years. If it hadn't been Inez who had helped vault ebullient Pat's political career to what it became then it surely would have been someone else. That was Pat's world—getting your name in front of as many voters and donors in whatever way ensures success. Ultimately, Inez had been one of thousands of criminals Pat's office had prosecuted long ago. Inez and her peculiar legacy barely existed for Pat, like the tens of thousands of abortions she had performed.

Pat Brown would die three years after our conversation, and is buried in Holy Cross Cemetery, in Colma, sixteen miles away from Inez's plot. He was accorded all the requisite honor due a wildly popular and accomplished two-term governor.

More recently, I sought to interview Pat's son, California Governor Jerry Brown, who declined my repeated requests. Jerry was nine when his father had been San Francisco district attorney. There was little Jerry could add to Inez's story, his press secretary told me. There also was little chance that he would open up about his father and Inez, even if he knew anything. The progressive left-wing Democrat was an avowed proponent of women's reproductive rights and had nothing to gain by talking about his father's campaign to put Inez out of business and in prison.

Despite abortion being illegal during all the years Inez ran her clinic, women themselves, not the government, determined whether they would become mothers. Ironically, abortions were easier to obtain than they are today, more than four decades after the Supreme Court's *Roe v. Wade* decision. Recorded abortion rates in the United States have reached their lowest numbers for several reasons: the greater availability and acceptance of birth control; sex education among adolescents; the advance of prenatal imaging; the advent of heroic, high-tech medicine; an increased marketplace for adopted babies; strategic national agitation from antiabortion groups; and the lessening of the stigma surrounding unwed couples and single men and women becoming parents. Unlike the decades when Inez plied her trade, today abortion is thought by many to be inherently wrong, if not for religious and political reasons, then because it undermines what die-hard antiabortion advocates have long called "the sanctity of life." In some ways, the strident Our Bodies Ourselves movement among women in the 1960s and '70s is not as fervent as it used to be, particularly among tens of millions of women of childbearing age. Thousands of hospitals and clinics have eliminated abortions from the procedures they offer, and the pool of physicians performing them continues to shrink. Today, eighty-nine percent of all counties in the United States lack a single clinic or hospital where the procedure is performed.[3]

Pat Brown wasn't the only politician whose career was built on Inez's shoulders. Pat's political appointments were a revolving door with Pat playing the doorman, pushing as many cronies as he could through, while Inez served as the unwitting starter. Norman Elkington, the prosecutor who presented the district attorney's case against Inez before two grand juries, was appointed by Pat to the superior court, and later as a justice of the California Courts of Appeal. Prosecutor Thomas Lynch, Pat's trusted deputy, succeeded Pat as San Francisco district attorney, sworn in by none other than then–federal judge Edward P. Murphy. When Pat was elected governor, he appointed Lynch attorney general to succeed him. Lynch ran unsuccessfully for the California Democratic presidential primary in 1968, running behind Robert F. Kennedy and Eugene McCarthy. Police Inspector Frank Ahern, who turned down Inez's bribe of three hundred thousand dollars, became San Francisco's police chief.

Defense Attorney Walter McGovern tried a multitude of criminal cases following Inez's trial, but none generated the same headlines. William A. Burkett, the Treasury agent who spilled to the Commonwealth Club that Inez had bribed cops and city officials, ran for state treasurer in the 1978 primary but lost to incumbent Jesse Unruh. Inez's old friend, Mable Malotte, who ran the high-end house of prostitution on Bay Street, was convicted and served a year's sentence at the California Institution for Women at Corona. Nelly Gaffney flourished as San Francisco's arbiter of fashion for forty years. Inez's sister, Nettie, kept amassing real estate throughout the Bay Area and eventually moved to Redwood City, south of San Francisco.

Today, almost everyone associated with Inez has died. Thomas Lynch died in 1986. Norman Elkington died in 1989. Police Inspector Frank Ahern died of a heart attack in 1958 at Seals Stadium during the fifteenth inning of a baseball game between the Giants and the Dodgers. Walter McGovern died in 1975. Judges William Traverso (the first trial), Herbert Kaufman (the second trial), and Edward Murphy (the third trial) died in 1975, 1963, and 1958, respectively. Pat Brown's two early political opponents died: District Attorney Matthew Brady in 1952; Attorney General Fred Howser in 1987. Inez's four codefendants died: Musette L. Briggs in 1986, Joseph M. Hoff in 1975, Myrtle Ramsey in 1953, and Mabel Spaulding in 1974. Gloria Davenport Shannon, who wrote the banner-headline exposé of Inez and her clinic, died in 1964. Sonja Henie died in 1969. Newspaper reporter Ed Montgomery died in 1992, Mabel Malotte in 1958, and Nelly Gaffney in 1966. Dr. Claude C. Long, aka Dr. Long Shot, died in 1953. Nettie Ingenthron died in 1955.

When I first became interested in telling Inez's story, I visited 327 Fillmore Street, where her clinic had flourished for two decades. By then, the once-elegant two-story building had been converted into a patchwork of apartments. In the backyard, I discovered the incinerator that Inez had once used to dispose of fetal remains. It had been sealed with concrete and was covered with gnarled, overgrown vines. I also visited the Guerrero Street house where Inez and Joe had lived for five decades. I found banisters with removable caps, hidden wall compartments, and hollowed wall coverings that Inez had used to stash cash. All had been painted shut. A year after her death, US marshals auctioned off the custom-built home for past taxes Inez's estate still owed. An attorney who specialized in sex-offense cases placed a sealed bid for $81,500[4] and came away with the property, which he turned into a nocturnal resort specializing in sadomasochistic parties. The owner put the house on the market for $240,000 in 1980, when it was bought by a physician, who continued the house's peculiar legacy.[5] When that owner died in 1989, he bequeathed the house to a friend, Bruce McGee, who one day, while searching for dish detergent under the kitchen sink, discovered a sliding partition and, behind it, a yellowed canvas carrying case. He had no idea what he had come across.

McGee carefully unwrapped the cloth case and found seventeen stainless steel instruments, ranging in length from eight to eighteen inches. He thought they were tools of some kind but had no idea about their origin or use. He kept them in a cupboard under a stack of pot holders and dish towels. They were a bizarre curio of *something*, but McGee had neither the interest nor the incentive to find out.

When I discovered their existence, I dropped everything. "Do you know what these instruments are?" I asked McGee over the phone, barely able to contain my excitement. "Do you know who used to own them?"

"I've heard something about them," McGee answered in a noncommittal kind of way. "I'll show them to you if you like." We made plans to meet at a bar in the Mission that evening.

I got to our meeting early and took a seat. I felt a little uneasy waiting for a stranger to appear with century-old medical instruments that had been used in thousands of abortions. As I waited, I wasn't quite sure exactly why I was there or what I hoped to accomplish. All I really wanted was to see the instruments, to witness proof that *something* of Inez still existed. If these instruments could talk, what a story they'd tell.

"You here to see the tools?" asked a short, balding man who slid onto the stool next to me. Bruce McGee pulled from a maroon accordion folder a worn canvas carrying case and placed it on the bar.

"Do you mind?" I asked impatiently, reaching to unroll the kit.

I untied the sash, and spread out the apron of instruments on the bar.

There they were, laid out in front of me: stainless steel with no traces of rust, dulled in sheen. Tools of destruction and relief, instruments of guilt and purpose. Tools that had led to freedom and to incarceration.

Then I noticed.

On the inside flap, a barely visible black-ink scrawl of a name:

Inez Brown

The name, Brown, dated the instruments back to before Inez had taken on Joe Burns's name, before the three trials, and before Inez's three prison terms. These may have been the instruments Inez had stolen from Dr. West's office after she had learned she was pregnant just before the Great Earthquake and Fire. These were the instruments she made her own by having her name inked on the carrying case. If that was so, they could have been the instruments used in the abortions Inez performed in the shady grove of pungent eucalyptus trees in Sharon Meadow at Golden Gate Park in 1906. They could have been the instruments Inez used when she attended to labor activist Edith Suter, as well as thousands of other desperate women awaiting her services.

They were all that was left of Inez. Everything else had disappeared.

I picked up several of the instruments to take a closer look, holding them, feeling them, imagining.

"Hey," McGee said suddenly. "I gotta go. You wanna buy them?"

I thought for several seconds, going back and forth, and finally I said no. They belonged to Inez.

McGee rolled up the canvas carrying case, put it back inside the accordion folder, and walked out of the bar. That was the last I ever saw of him or the instruments.

ACKNOWLEDGMENTS

Inez never kept a diary (at least none that I could find), and she wasn't really a public figure until 1938, when the *San Francisco News* sent two undercover reporters to her Fillmore Street clinic and published a blockbuster account of what went on inside. While Inez was widely known as a safe and reliable abortion provider for decades, little had appeared in print about her before then. When Inez was pursued by San Francisco District Attorney Pat Brown in 1945, local newspapers published a spate of articles about her, but none covered anything more than her upcoming legal tribulations. By then, Inez was close to sixty years old.

This posed a challenge to any biographer who sought to capture the full story of larger-than-life Inez. I was fortunate to interview the few people still alive who knew her, as well as rely on a trove of historical documents, government records, genealogical materials, and family correspondence. By necessity, I recreated certain private conversations and encounters. Every line in *The Audacity of Inez Burns* carries forth what I believe is the essence of a woman who has captivated me for more than a quarter of a century.

While there is only one author of this book, any work that culls so many disparate facts, observations, theories, and conclusions is possible only because of the labor of hundreds of unsung contributors.

First, my deepest thanks go to the anonymous newspaper reporters whose day-to-day coverage allowed me to put into context Inez Burns's impact on San Francisco, California, and the nation. Much of the narrative of *The Audacity of Inez Burns* is based on the in-depth reporting that appeared in the four competitive newspapers of Pat and Inez's era. All court proceedings were taken from the newspaper reporters who covered them; no transcripts remain of the trials. All trial exhibits have been destroyed. While few of the thousands of articles I read carried the modern-day journalistic credit known as a byline, the reporters listed below helped me reconstruct many of the accounts of the events of the day. To these exemplars of the profession that has defined me for decades go my gratitude and admiration: Carolyn Anspacher, Earl C. "Squire" Behrens, Jerry Burns, Herb Caen, Arthur Caylor, Jane Eshleman Conant, George Draper, William Flynn, Alfred Frankenstein, Dick Friendlich, Willie Green, Lisa Hobbs, William Hogan, Alvin D. Hyman, R. W. Jimerson, William H. Jordan, Mary Ellen Leary, Ernest Lenn, Nancy Barr Mavity, June Morrall, Ninon, Al Ostrow, Le Pacini, Blanche Partington, Robert Patterson, Dick Pearce, Katherine Pinkham, Laura Bride Powers, Leon Racht, Charles Raudebaugh, Peter Robertson, Joseph B. Sheridan, Harry B. Smith, Peter Trimble, Bucky Walter, and Dwight Whitney. These journalists were terrific reporters, but special mention goes to two whose work was particularly stellar: Richard V. Hyer and Ed Montgomery.

There are many terrific books that detail the rich history of San Francisco, and I want to acknowledge those that stand out, which I relied on. *This Is San Francisco: A Classic Portrait of the City,* by Robert O'Brien, a collection of columns that first appeared in the *San Francisco Chronicle,* was published in 1948, then republished in 1994, and is the singular compendium of San Francisco's array of rich characters prior to 1906. Kevin Starr's *Golden Dreams: California in the Age of Abundance* is an exemplar of in-depth and compelling writing. Both are premier chronologies of San Francisco's contribution to the nation's history. For insight into San Francisco's bawdy past, there is no better book than Herbert Asbury's *The Barbary Coast,* published in 1933. To get a glimpse of walking down the midway at both of San Francisco's two grand world's fairs, in 1915 and 1939, I relied on Laura A. Ackley's magnificent tome, *San Francisco's Jewel City: The Panama-Pacific International Exposition of 1915,* and Richard Reinhardt's folksy *Treasure Island: San Francisco's Exposition Years.* To help understand San Francisco's central involvement in launching tens of thousands of GIs into the Pacific, I scanned scores of historic photos from *San Francisco in World War II,* by John Garvey and the California Center for Military History. I've loved Herb Caen ever since I wrote a profile on him for the college student newspaper, the *Daily Californian,* when I was a student at the University of California, Berkeley, and he promptly wrote back a thank-you note. All of his books are wonderful, but my favorites are the classics *Don't Call It Frisco* and *Baghdad by the Bay.* Jerry Flamm's books *Good Life in Hard Times: San Francisco's '20s & '30s* and

Hometown San Francisco: Sunny Jim, Phat Willie, and Dave are fabulous reads. One of the premier historians of San Francisco was the inestimable Oscar Lewis, and I relied on two of his books: *San Francisco: Mission to Metropolis* and *Bonanza Inn: America's First Luxury Hotel* (cowritten with Carroll D. Hall). To understand the historic gastronomic contours of San Francisco, I turned to Clarence E. Edwords's *Bohemian San Francisco: Its Restaurants and Their Most Famous Recipes*. Other books essential to learning about the era when Inez lived included John Wesley Noble and Bernard Averbuch's *Never Plead Guilty: The Story of Jake Ehrlich*, George Dorsey's *Christopher of San Francisco*, Don Herron's *The Dashiell Hammett Tour*, Fred Lyon's *San Francisco: Portrait of a City 1940–1960*, and Ben Procter's *William Randolph Hearst: The Later Years*. Another book by Kevin Starr, *Golden Gate: The Life and Times of America's Greatest Bridge*, helped put into context the transition of San Francisco from Pacific city to world metropolis.

To re-create the aftermath of the Great San Francisco Earthquake and Fire, I relied on a host of books, including *Denial of Disaster: The Untold Story and Photographs of the San Francisco of 1906*, by Gladys Hansen and Emmet Condon; *Three Fearful Days: San Francisco Memoirs of the 1906 Earthquake & Fire*, by Malcolm E. Baker; Simon Winchester's *A Crack in the Edge of the World: America and the Great California Earthquake of 1906*; and Dennis Smith's *San Francisco Is Burning: The Untold Story of the 1906 Earthquake and Fires*.

Valerie Steel's tome *The Corset: A Cultural History* gave me an understanding of Inez's commitment to the standard of beauty during the era in which she lived, as well as an appreciation for the quandary of whether or not Inez underwent surgery to have her smallest ribs removed.

Librarians and archivists helped me immeasurably, particularly at the Bancroft Library of the University of California, Berkeley, and San Francisco Public Library's San Francisco History Center. San Francisco archivist Susan Goldstein, former city archivist Gladys Hansen, San Francisco History Center's special collections librarian Andrea V. Grimes, photo curator Christina Moretta, and the center's director Tom Carey opened their archives, as well as their wisdom, to me. Amelia R. Fry's groundbreaking research, as part of the Earl Warren Oral History Project at the Bancroft Library, includes lengthy recollections of Edmund G. Brown Sr., Norman Elkington, and Thomas C. Lynch, and was invaluable.

Dana Dorman and Suzanne Johnston, independent researchers affiliated with the Historical Society of Pennsylvania in Philadelphia and the Senator John Heinz

History Center in Pittsburgh, respectively, helped me piece together Inez's years in Pittsburgh. Scott Merritt provided genealogy help, as did Charles Lee. Tim Gregory, known as the "building biographer," assisted me in searching Los Angeles County records for the addresses of properties Inez owned in the area. Del Troy, an indefatigable historical researcher in Tehachapi, California, provided me with a treasure trove of information about the town and prison.

Matt Conens, a public-information officer for the California Department of Public Health, was ready and willing to access for me century-old death certificates, as well as birth statistics. Ethan Rarick, director of the Robert T. Matsui Center for Politics & Public Service at University of California, Berkeley, was forthcoming about a grand politician who has long captivated both of us. His book *California Rising: The Life and Times of Edmund G. (Pat) Brown* is the most complete compendium on everything Pat Brown.

To help decipher William F. Brown's 1921 death certificate and how the diagnosis of pernicious anemia could masquerade as the result of lethal arsenic poisoning, I turned to Dr. Sheldon Zane, a friend and physician, who died before seeing this book reflect his wisdom. Dr. Morey Filler, a gifted obstetrician-gynecologist in San Francisco, lent his knowledge to the sections of the manuscript that dealt with the medical aspects of abortion. Anne Lahey provided her expertise of antiques to assess Inez's parlor rooms at the Fillmore Street clinic.

Lou Cannon's *Ronnie and Jessie: A Political Odyssey*; Bill Boyarsky's *Big Daddy: Jesse Unruh and the Art of Power Politics;* Roger Rapoport's *California Dreaming: The Political Odyssey of Pat & Jerry Brown*; Orville Schell's *Brown*; and Robert Pack's *Jerry Brown: The Philosopher Prince* gave me insights into the younger Brown's persona and where it comes from.

Katie Townsend, an attorney for the Reporters Committee for Freedom of the Press, and Tom Burke, an attorney in private practice in San Francisco, spent hours strategizing with me about how to wrest vital documents so the public would be allowed to benefit from heretofore secret California state government files, sealed at the Bancroft Library. When the Bancroft Library relented under pressure, Vickie Baranetsky, an attorney for the Reporters Committee for Freedom of the Press, was there to open six cartons that contained reams of historically significant classified documents. The boxes were investigative records personally kept by Warren Olney III, the former counsel to California Governor Earl Warren's Special Study Commission on Organized Crime, and had been kept under lock and key since they were given to Bancroft in 1975. Without the will and resources of the Reporters Committee for Freedom of the Press, these papers would have arbitrarily stayed classified until 2028.

In assessing Inez's historic contributions, there were many who graciously shared their wisdom with me. These include Laura X of the Laura X Institute and the founder of the Women's History Library in Berkeley; documentary filmmaker Dorothy Fadiman of Concentric Media and producer of *When Abortion Was Illegal*; Rebecca Griffin of NARAL Pro-Choice California; Joe Spiedel, Claire D. Brindis, and Carole Joffe of the Bixby Center for Global Reproductive Health at the University of California, San Francisco. Books that helped me place into context Inez's pivotal role included James C. Mohr's *Abortion in America: The Origins and Evolution of National Policy*, Leslie J. Reagan's *When Abortion Was a Crime*, Marvin Olasky's *Abortion Rites: A Social History of Abortion in America*, Horatio R. Stoner's *Criminal Abortion: Its Nature, Its Evidence, and Its Law*, and Janet Farrell Brodie's *Contraception and Abortion in Nineteenth-Century America*.

Colleagues at the School of Journalism & Mass Communication at the University of Iowa gave me generous support, particularly David Dowling and Mike Hendrickson. My literary agent, Bridget Wagner Matzie of Aevitas Creative Management, supplied me with never-ending encouragement from idea to execution to publication. Bridget's exhortation—write an "unputdownable" book—became an entry in my family's lexicon and guided me through the writing of *The Audacity of Inez Burns*. Regan Arts Executive Editor Alexis Gargagliano loved the story from the start and her editorial comments steered me through the manuscript. Regan Arts Associate Publisher Lynne Ciccaglione was patient, gracious, and prescient throughout all stages of putting together *The Audacity of Inez Burns*. I leaned on Lynne way too often to tweak sentences and paragraphs when I had assured her I was done. For that and more, I thank her. Framed on Publisher Judith Regan's office wall is a line from San Francisco beat poet Kenneth Rexroth's 1957 essay, "Disengagement: The Art of the Beat Generation": "Against the ruin of the world, there is only one defense—the creative act." It's a credo we both wholeheartedly share.

The woman whom I called Corinne Patchen started me on my exploration of Inez more than twenty-five years ago. It was Corinne who propelled me into Inez's story when she answered a question I posed to her one afternoon in 1992: "Does the name Inez Burns ring a bell?" Corinne died at age ninety-one in the winter of 2017.

Inez's granddaughter, Caroline Brown Carlisle, whom I first interviewed in

1992 and then again on more than ten occasions in 2016, proved to be invaluable in recalling life with Inez. Inez was a singular influence on Caroline, and her unfailing memory of her grandmother made Inez into a real person, warts and all. Caroline was proud that *The Audacity of Inez Burns* was being published so that Inez would finally get her just deserts. Alas, Caroline would never live to see the book. She died ten days after her eighty-first birthday on February 4, 2017.

My deepest appreciation, of course, goes to Inez for inspiring me to undertake *The Audacity of Inez Burns*. Her colossal life was a prism through which to understand not just San Francisco but America and the turbulent times during which Inez lived. Sadly, what Inez stood for—abortion on demand—is once again under attack, more than one hundred years after Inez performed her first illegal procedure in Dr. Eugene West's medical office.

ENDNOTES

AUTHOR'S NOTE

1 Jeffrey L. Carrier, *Tallulah Bankhead: A Bio-Bibliography* (New York: Greenwood, 1991), 185.

PROLOGUE

1 Pinky Lee (whose real name was Pincus Leff) did make frequent trips to Burns Ranch, where he entertained Inez and her entourage. Unfortunately, there is no record of the songs Lee sang while there, and as such, the lyrics to these two particular ditties are the author's creation, based on a review of the entertainer's acts and routines.

ONE: MISFORTUNE IN THE PROMISED LAND

1 See www.wellsfargohistory.com/faqs.

2 See Gary Kaiya's stories, "Twain Found His Calling in San Francisco Stories," in *The New York Times*, November 13, 2010, A29, www.nytimes.com/2010/11/14/us/14bctwain. html and "How Mark Twain Got Fired in San Francisco," in the *San Francisco Chronicle*, October 9, 2015, www.sfchronicle.com/bayarea/article/How-Mark-Twain-got-fired-in-San-Francisco-6562309.php. Additional writers—some natives, others transplants—also made their names in San Francisco in the wake of Twain. They include Ambrose Bierce, Bret Harte, Charles Warren Stoddard, Joaquin Miller, Henry George, and Jack London.

3 Herbert Asbury, *The Barbary Coast: An Informal History of the San Francisco Underworld* (New York: Alfred A. Knopf, 1933), 32.

4 James R. Smith *San Francisco's Landmark* (Sanger, CA: Word Dancer Press, 2006), 176.

5 Robert O'Brien's wonderful Riptides columns have been collected by another former *San Francisco Chronicle* columnist, Adair Lara, and published as *This Is San Francisco: A Classic Portrait of the City* (San Francisco: Chronicle Books, 1994). This quote comes from a column about the famous San Francisco restaurant, the Poodle Dog.

6 By far, the most detailed description of the area is *Rincon Hill and South Park: San Francisco's Early Fashionable Neighborhood* by Albert Shumate (Sausalito, CA: Windgate Press, 1988). See also the comprehensive *Streets of San Francisco: The Origins of Street & Place Names* (San Francisco: Lexikos, 1984).

7 Details of the trip on the *Hemisphere* were obtained from the ship's manifest, at the online registry http://germanroots.com/onlinelists.html.

8 See Kathy Gosz's fascinating research on German immigrants headed to America from Le Havre at http://19thcenturyrhinelandlive.blogspot.com/2011/10/look-at-le-havre-less-known-port-for.html. For more information on America's first immigration station, go to www.castlegarden.org, where there is an interactive index of all families who immigrated through Castle Garden.

9 The lineage of the Ingenthron family was obtained by searches through a number of genealogy sites, principally Ancestry.com, Mocavo.com, and familysearch.org.

10 *Chicago Daily Tribune*, "The City," June 3, 1885, 8; *Chicago Daily Tribune*, "Dedicating a Monument," July 4, 1887, 8; *Chicago Daily Tribune*, "War on Franchise Grabbers," May 21, 1898; *The Inter Ocean*, "Claim He Is Not Insane," September 7, 1898, 3; *Chicago Daily Tribune*, "Deplores Khartum Victory," September 18, 1898, 2; the *New York Times*, "Anti-Imperialists Declare for Bryan," August 17, 1900, 3.

11 See Shumate's *Rincon Hill and South Park*, 48.

12 Statistics on cigar making, as well as the ethnicity of who rolled and assembled stogies, were obtained from *Appendix to the Journals of the State and Assembly of the Twenty-Seventh Session of the Legislature of the State of California, Vol. VII* (Sacramento, CA: State Office, 1887), 438–39.

13 A terrific account of the battle for control of the San Francisco cigar industry can be found at http://cigarhistory.info/Cigar_History/Whitelabor.html, from which much of this account comes.

14 Selected portions of the later part of Frederick's life in San Francisco come from an unpublished, handwritten manuscript given to the author by its author, Inez Burns's granddaughter Caroline Brown Carlisle, based on conversations with Inez Ingenthron Brown Granelli Burns.

15 For historical descriptions of Bernal Heights, see *San Francisco Chronicle*, November 14, 2015, "House reflects telling changes in S.F." by Carl Nolte, www.sfchronicle.com/bayarea/article/House-reflects-telling-changes-in-S-F-6632720.php, and *San Francisco's Bernal Heights*, with foreword by Carl Nolte (Charleston: Arcadia, 2007), 7–8.

16 *San Francisco Chronicle*, "Names of Some of the Fortunate," June 8, 1889, 8.

17 Such characterizations are from Inez Burns's granddaughter Caroline Brown Carlisle, whom the author interviewed on numerous occasions, both in 1993 and in 2016.

18 In the 1894 *San Francisco Directory*, Edwin Conhem Hawkins lists his profession as stenographer, but a year later, it had changed to artist.

19 *San Francisco Call*, July 20, 1894, cited in www.sfgenealogy.com/sf/sfcall1894.htm; *Los Angeles Herald*, "Wedding Presents: What a San Francisco Woman Wants Besides a Divorce," April 11, 1895, 1; *San Francisco Call*, "Too Much Mother-in-Law," April 27, 1895, 16; *San Francisco Call*, under "Divorce Proceedings," November 22, 1895, 13. The location of Judge Hall's courtroom is listed in the 1896 city directory.

20 *San Francisco Call*, December 21, 1898, "Scots at the Festal Board," 7.

21 *San Francisco Call*, February 12, 1899 (no title), 26.

22 See O'Brien's *This Is San Francisco: A Classic Portrait of the City*, 99, and Don B. Wilmeth's *The Cambridge Guide to the American Theatre* (New York: Cambridge University Press, 2007), 141.

23 Oscar Lewis and Carroll D. Hall, *Bonanza Inn: American's First Luxury Hotel* (New York: Alfred A. Knopf, 1939), 11. Ralston, by the way, never lived to see his magnificent hotel open to the public. Five weeks before the Palace debuted, Ralston drowned while swimming in the San Francisco Bay. In a dedication to the hotel, the new owner, Nevada senator William Sharon, called the Palace a "glorious temple of hospitality." The *Daily Alta California* trumpeted the hotel simply as "the greatest inn in the world."

TWO: THE WONDERFUL WIZARDESS OF THE PALACE HOTEL

1 Take a look at any of these paintings by Titian and you'll see what Inez's smitten client may have been talking about: *Danaë, Venus of Urbino, Venus Anadyomene, Vanity, Flora,* or *Woman With a Mirror.* Studying these paintings, it seems likely that the client wasn't referring to the Venetian painter's rendition of his models' hair, but of their provocative figures.

2 Descriptions of some of the rich and famous, including Emma Nevada, who stayed at the Palace, come from Lewis and Hall's *Bonanza Inn* and O'Brien's *This Is San Francisco.*

3 Details about White Hat McCarty come from O'Brien's *This Is San Francisco: A Classic Portrait of the City; San Francisco Chronicle,* "Eccentricities of Dress of Prominent San Franciscans," August 12, 1900, 26; *San Francisco Chronicle,* "Schoolmate to Run in Special," February 24, 1905, 8; *San Francisco Chronicle,* "Petrolia Wins for White Hat," April 1, 1904, 8; *Thoroughbred Racing,* "Looking back: The lost tracks of the San Francisco Bay Area," by Paul Roberts, Isabelle Taylor, and Laurence Weatherly, February 15, 2015; *San Francisco Call,* "Man Who Won a Fortune on One Chicago Derby," by Willie Green, June 8, 1913, 6. The *Chronicle* reporter wrote that McCarty's hat was a "peculiar and wooly piece of freakish headgear."

4 For an informative tour of this fashion during the period, see Valerie Steele's *The Corset: A Cultural History* (New Haven, CT: Yale University Press, 2001).

THREE: WAYWARD GIRLS AND LECHEROUS ROGUES

1 Much of this section about culinary San Francisco comes from Clarence E. Edwords's *Bohemian San Francisco: Its Restaurants and Their Most Famous Recipes* (Washington, DC: Westphalia Press, 2014).

2 Information about Dr. Bazan is from the *San Francisco Chronicle,* "A Hot Time in a Hamman," September 12, 1898, 10, and the *Daily Alta California,* June 30, 1884, under "Weddings," 7. Multiple advertisements for his bathhouse appear in the city directories from 1885 to 1905.

3 For more on the medical eclectics, see *Medical Protestants: The Eclectics in American Medicine, 1825–1939,* by John S. Haller Jr. (Carbondale: Southern Illinois University Press, 2013).

4 From *Directory of Deceased American Physicians, 1804–1929.*

5 Coverage of the sensational Addie Gilmour case comes from the *San Francisco Chronicle,* "Is It Foul Play?," September 20, 1893, 10; *San Francisco Call,* "Woman's Head," September 20, 1893, 10; *San Francisco Call,* "Her Sad Fate," September 21, 1893, 3; *San Francisco Chronicle,* "Plymire Talks," September 23, 1893, 8; *San Francisco Call,* "Light Dawns,"

September 23, 1893, 3; *San Francisco Call*, "Is Now His Wife," September 27, 1893, 3; "Piece by Piece," September 28, 1893, 7; *San Francisco Call*, "Held for Murder," October 5, 1893, 8; *San Francisco Call*, "Is It Addie's?," October 20, 1893, 8; *San Francisco Call*, "Dr. West Ill," December 7, 1893, 10; *San Francisco Call*, "A Further Delay," February 8, 1894, 10; *San Francisco Call*, "Hope for Dr. West," February 13, 1894, 12; *San Francisco Call*, "Dr. West's New Trial," March 9, 1894, 10; *San Francisco Call*, "Mrs. West on the Stand," December 19, 1895, 5; *San Francisco Call*, "West Is Acquitted," December 27, 1895, 5; the *Los Angeles Herald*, "Dr. West Acquitted," December 27, 1895, 1; *San Francisco Chronicle*, "Dr. West Accuses and Is Acquitted," December 27, 1895, 14.

6　*San Francisco Chronicle* classified advertisement, December 5, 1907, 10.

7　*San Francisco Call*, "Agnes Smith's Death," July 18, 1893, 7.

8　See Marvin Olasky's *Abortion Rites: A Social History of Abortion in America* (Wheaton, IL: Crossway Books, 1992), 90, and Kristin Luker's *Abortion & the Politics of Motherhood* (Berkeley: University of California Press, 1984), 67–68. The one exception of this in most states was for "therapeutic reasons," that is, if the health of the woman could be demonstrably shown to be at risk should she give birth. This, of course, left wiggle room if a physician performed the abortion and was used as an ostensible reason for physicians to justify performing an abortion, particularly on wealthy white women who could afford higher fees for the procedure. It was a gray area that seldom affected working-class women who found themselves pregnant. Often these women went to midwives who charged less and had no formal training in medicine.

9　Dr. Funke's Clinic, as well as other facilities, attracted young pregnant women through word of mouth, as well as daily advertisements in the classified sections of local newspapers, including one under the category "Adoption": *San Francisco Call*, May 28, 1909, 13.

10　See virtually any classified section of any big-city newspaper of the time for hundreds of such in-code advertisements for abortion providers.

11　See several excellent examinations of abortion in the United States at the time, including Carole Joffee's *Doctors of Conscience: The Struggle to Provide Abortion Before and After Roe V Wade* (Boston: Beacon, 1996); Leslie J. Reagan's *When Abortion Was a Crime: Women, Medicine and Law in the United States, 1867–1973* (Berkeley, CA: University of California Press, 1997); James C. Mohr's *Abortion in America: The Origins and Evolution of National Policy, 1800–1900* (New York: Oxford University Press, 1993); Janet Farrell Brodie's *Abortion and Contraception in Nineteenth-Century America* (Ithaca, NY: Cornell University Press, 1994).

12　See California Penal Code No. 274 for a fuller description of the law.

FOUR: MEN WITH RESOURCES

1　There is an abundance of evidence to corroborate physicians at the time prescribing cocaine to their patients, as well as using the drug themselves. See Jill Jones's "The Rise of the Modern Addict," in the *American Journal of Public Health* 85, no. 8 (August 1995), 1157–62; Stephen R. Kandall's *Substance and Shadow: A History of Women and Addiction in the United States—1850 to the Present* (Cambridge: Harvard University Press, 1996).

Lisa J. Merlo and Mark S. Gold's "Prescription Opioid Abuse and Dependence Among Physicians: Hypotheses and Treatment," in the *Harvard Review of Psychiatry* 16, no. 3 (May-June 2008), 182; and Howard Markel's *An Anatomy of Addiction: Sigmund Freud, William Halsted, and the Miracle Drug, Cocaine* (New York: Vintage, 2012) For a general historical assessment, see Richard Ashley's *Cocaine: Its History, Uses and Effects* (New York: Warner Books, 1982).

2 Selected portions of Inez's tutelage under Dr. West come from an unpublished handwritten manuscript given to the author by its author, Inez's granddaughter Caroline Brown Carlisle.

3 Addresses and other pertinent information are taken from the 1900 census.

4 Legal notice of the divorce of Mary Gertrude Merritt and George W. Merritt on the grounds of desertion, from the *San Francisco Call*, August 5, 1905, 7.

5 George W. Merritt's literary claims seemed farfetched, but he did eventually copyright with the Library of Congress a four-act play he wrote under the name George Washington Lee, called *Miss Julie and Mass Henry*. The copyright is dated April 16, 1928. The time period of the play is in the 1880s.

FIVE: MONEY SOAP, ITALIAN POTION NO. 12, AND THE BRAZILIAN BELEZA

1 *San Francisco Call*, legal notices, Friday, August 5, 1904, 7; 1900 federal census data.

2 *San Francisco Call*, "Hotel Nymphia Objectors Are Ready to Fight," June 26, 1899, 8; Herbert Asbury, *The Barbary Coast: An Informal History of the San Francisco Underworld* (New York: Alfred A. Knopf, 1933), 262–6.

3 For more on contraceptives of the era, see Janet Farrell Brodie's fascinating *Contraception and Abortion in 19th-Century America* (Ithaca, NY: Cornell University Press, 1994), 207–24.

4 In the US census and other federal government documents, George W. Merritt listed his profession as "manufacturer." What products he manufactured were never specified.

SIX: THE EARTH MOVES

1 "Elaborate Gowns Mark Second Night," in *San Francisco Chronicle*, April 18, 1906, 5, and "Fashionable Society Comes Out Radiantly on the Second Night," by Laura Bride Powers, in *San Francisco Call*, April 18, 1906, 5.

2 From a letter in *The Sketch*, published in London, reprinted in *The Theatre* magazine, July 1906, reposted by the Virtual Museum of San Francisco, http://www.sfmuseum.net/1906/ew19.html.

3 "Caruso Superb in the Role of Don Jose," by Peter Robertson, in *San Francisco Chronicle*, April 18, 1906, 5.

4 "Caruso Makes Don Jose the Leading Role: 'Carmen,' by Olive Fremstad, Is Overshadowed by the Splendid Interpretation of His Part," by Blanche Partington, in *San Francisco Call*, April 18, 1906, 5.

5 "Fashionable Society Comes Out Radiantly on the Second Night," by Laura Bride Powers, in *San Francisco Call*, April 18, 1906, 5.

6 Gladys Hansen and Emmet Condon's epic and important reevaluation of the quake,

Denial of Disaster: The Untold Story and Photographs of the San Francisco Earthquake and Fire of 1906 (San Francisco: Cameron and Company, 1989), 8.

7 Both statistics are from Dennis Smith's authoritative *San Francisco Is Burning: The Untold Story of the 1906 Earthquake and Fire* (New York: Viking, 2005), 4.

8 Recollections of residents roaming San Francisco streets in the wake of the earthquake come from a number of sources, including Barker's *Three Fearful Days: San Francisco Memoirs of the 1906 Earthquake & Fire*; NPR's "Remembering the 1906 San Francisco Earthquake," by Renee Montagne, April 11, 2006, www.npr.org/templates/story/story .php?storyId=533441; and assorted letters maintained by the California Historical Society.

9 Cited in both Malcolm E. Barker's *Three Fearful Days: San Francisco Memoirs of the 1906 Earthquake & Fire* (San Francisco: Londonborn Publications, 1998), and Hansen and Condon's *Denial of Disaster.*

10 Hansen and Condon, *Denial of Disaster,* 40.

11 See the shoot-to-kill proclamation signed by Mayor Schmitz through the Virtual Museum of the City of San Francisco, at http://www.sfmuseum.org/1906.2/killproc.html.

12 There are many renditions of Caruso's exit from the Palace and San Francisco; this one from Oscar Lewis and Carroll D. Hall's *Bonanza Inn* seems among the most plausible.

13 See the San Francisco 1906 Earthquake Marriage Project, which details a number of marriages that stemmed from the ruins of a city, as part of SanFranciscoGenealogy.com, www.sfgenealogy.com/1906/06slinkey.htm.

SEVEN: PICKLED IN PITTSBURGH

1 Hansen and Condon, *Denial of Disaster,* 80.

2 Classified advertisement in the *Pittsburgh Press,* April 7, 1907, 27.

3 The birth certificate for George W. Merritt Jr. is available through Ancestry.com.

4 From a fascinating remembrance of George W. Merritt Jr., Charles Lee's recollection of his colorful grandfather posted on Ancestry.com.

5 The H. J. Heinz Company Collection of photographs, maintained by the Senator John Heinz History Center's Library & Archives. Photos and descriptions graphically detail the workplace environment. See http://digital.library.pitt.edu/images/pittsburgh/heinz .html.

6 History of the H. J. Heinz Company (Pittsburgh, 1869–1995), created by the Historic Pittsburgh Project, the University of Pittsburgh, and Historical Society of Western Pennsylvania.

7 See Mrs. John Van Vorst and Marie Van Vorst's *The Woman Who Toils: Being the Experiences of Two Gentlewomen as Factory Girls* (New York: Doubleday, Page & Company, 1903), 7–58, for a diary of the work environment at the H. J. Heinz Pickle Factory; Peter R. Shergold, *Working-Class Life: The "American Standard" in Comparative Perspective 1899–1913* (Pittsburgh: University of Pittsburgh Press, 1982), 69; and Elizabeth Beardsley Butler, *Women and the Trades: Pittsburgh, 1907–1908* (New York: Russell Sage Foundation, 1909), 35, 38.

8 This specific anecdote comes from Inez through her granddaughter Caroline Brown

Carlisle, who vividly recalls Inez describing how she packed pickles during the frigid Pittsburgh winters.

9 Classified advertisements in the *Pittsburgh Press*, July 24, 1904, 30; August 23, 1904, 13.

10 The birth certificate for Robert Edward Lee Merritt is available through Ancestry.com.

11 Legal notice in the *Pittsburgh Post-Gazette*, May 8, 1909, 13; the incorporation papers list as Merritt's partners as Pittsburgh-area residents Charles T. Marsh, Charles A. Glaser, Albert C. Rohland, and William H. Winterhalter.

12 Commonwealth of Pennsylvania incorporation papers, enrolled in Charter Book No. 110, page 154, signed by Robert McAfee, Secretary of the Commonwealth, recorded June 11, 1909.

13 *Avalon, Pennsylvania, 1875–1975 Centennial Book*, 88.

14 See wording of the classified advertisement "couple leaving city," in the *Pittsburgh Press*, July 26, 1909, 12; 1910 US Federal Census, 35 Assembly District, part of Precinct 2, Sheet 4B; 1920 US Federal Census, 23 District Assembly, San Francisco, California, Sheet 2B.

EIGHT: DREAMLAND, THE PLEASURE PALACE, AND A PAIR OF DEAD BODIES

1 1910 US Federal Census, 35 Assembly District, part of Precinct 2, Sheet 4B.

2 *San Francisco Call*, real estate transactions, January 10, 1909, 47.

3 *San Francisco Call*, real estate transactions, February 22, 1912, 13.

4 *San Francisco Call*, "Tighten Dragnet Around Dr. West," October 24, 1909, 38; and *San Francisco Chronicle*, "Girl's Death Leads to Doctor's Arrest," October 23, 1909, 1.

5 *San Francisco Call*, "West Case Continued," October 29, 1911, 41; *San Francisco Examiner*, "Doctor Arrested Upon Dying Girl's Statement," October 11, 1911.

6 *San Francisco Chronicle*, "Body of Babe Creates Suspicion," November 5, 1911, 45.

7 *San Francisco Chronicle*, classified ad for Dr. West, January 15, 1915, 8.

8 *Directory of Deceased American Physicians, 1804–1929*.

9 Joseph de Maistre, Albert Blanc (ed.) *Correspondance diplomatique*, tome 2 (Paris: Michel Lévy frères libraires éditeurs, 1860), 196.

10 The best and fullest analysis of the 1915 world's fair can be found in Laura A. Ackley's absorbing *San Francisco's Jewel City: The Panama-Pacific International Exposition of 1915* (Berkeley, CA: Heyday, 2015).

11 I know this because when I was the press secretary to former Mayor Frank Jordan in 1993, a narrow closet in my office next to the mayor's chambers had a sealed back partition that led to a rickety spiral stairway, which old-timers at City Hall swore to me was used long ago to squire Miss Page in and out of the building without detection. At least, that was the lore that went for fact. Elements of Miss Page's career are from *The New York Times*, "Anita Page Silent Film Siren, Dies at 98," by Robert Berkvist, September 8, 2008, A21.

12 Much of the description of James Rolph's tenure as mayor comes from Jerry Flamm's terrific *Good Life in Hard Times: San Francisco's '20s & '30s* (San Francisco: Chronicle Books, 1999) and *Hometown San Francisco: Sunny Jim, Phat Willie & Dave* (San Fran-

cisco: Scottwall, 1994), as well as Oscar Lewis's *San Francisco: Mission to Metropolis,* Kevin Starr's outstanding *Golden Dreams: California in the Age of Abundance* (New York: Oxford University Press, 2008), and Tony Quarrington's "An Englishman's Love Affair With San Francisco: Great San Franciscan Characters #9, Sunny Jim Rolph," at https://tonyquarrington.wordpress.com/2011/03/03/great-san-franciscan-characters-9-sunny-jim-rolph.

13 See Valerie Steele's *The Corset: A Cultural History* (New Haven, CT: Yale University Press, 2001) for a provocative discussion of the fashion accoutrement, as well as the era's instances of rib removal to accentuate the female figure.

14 *San Francisco Chronicle,* Marriage Licenses, December 20, 1915, 17.

15 *Crocker-Langley San Francisco Directory,* 1913, 1914, 1917, 1918, 1919, 1920.

16 *San Francisco Chronicle,* "Armed Woman Halts Work on Monroe School," June 11, 1919, 1; *Oakland Tribune,* "Woman's Will, Plus Shotgun Halts School," June 11, 1919, 12.

17 *Marin Journal,* "Union Label League to Form Tonight," April 1, 1915, 8. *Oregon Daily Journal,* "Labor Representative Reports to Central Body on Conference," September 18, 1915, 7. *San Francisco Chronicle,* "Labor News," March 9, 1916, 56; June 27, 1917, 4; November 27, 1917, 11; *Garment Worker,* October 11, 1918, vol. XVII, no. 52, 1.

18 *San Francisco Chronicle* obituary notice, May 27, 1920, 6.

19 *San Francisco Chronicle,* "Mystery Veils Death of Union Labor Woman," May 25, 1920, 1.

20 *San Francisco Chronicle,* "Edith Suter's Death Laid to Malpractice," May 26, 1920, 5.

21 *San Francisco Chronicle,* "Illegal Operation," June 3, 1920, 12; "Experts Will Pass on Physician's Diagnosis," May 27, 1920, 17.

22 This account is taken primarily from David Yallop's authoritative account of the incident, *The Day the Laughter Stopped* (New York: St. Martin's Press, 1976).

23 Deborah Blum, *The Poisoner's Handbook: Murder and the Birth of Forensic Medicine in Jazz Age* (New York: Penguin, 2011), 1.

24 Author interview with Caroline Carlisle, March 3, 2016.

25 San Francisco Area, California, Funeral Home Records, 1850–1931, vol. 10, pages 8301–8593, 1921.

26 William F. Brown's certificate of death, August 5, 1921, State Index No. 1194, Local Registered No. 1475.

27 Ibid.

28 Peter M. Selzer and Marilyn A. Ancel, "Chronic Arsenic Poisoning Masquerading as Pernicious Anemia," *Western Journal of Medicine,* August 1983, 139: 219–20.

NINE: LUXURY HEELS

1 *San Francisco Chronicle,* August 6, 1921, 42.

2 William F. Brown's certificate of death, August 5, 1921, State Index No. 1194, Local Registered No. 1475.

3 Author interview with Caroline Carlisle, March 22, 2016. Some cultural historians of the female body, such as Valerie Steele, say flatly that rib removal is a myth and never took place. Today, although not endorsed by American plastic surgeons, the procedure

is performed, if not in the United States, then overseas. Considering the evidence for or against whether Inez ever underwent the procedure, it seems, short of an exhumation, there is no definitive answer.

4 Author interview with Caroline Brown Carlisle, March 3, 2016.

5 Author interview with Bill Brown, Inez's grandson, who vividly recalled both rooms, May 23, 2017.

6 See Jerry Flamm's *Good Life in Hard Times: San Francisco's '20s & '30s* (San Francisco: Chronicle Books, 1990), pages 72–83.

7 Genealogical information on Charles Granelli was obtained from US census data, the National Archives and Records Administration, Ancestry.com, New York passenger arrival lists (Ellis Island), 1892–1924, FamilySearch.org, and New York City marriage records, 1829–1940.

8 *Crocker-Langley San Francisco Directory*, 1918.

9 *San Francisco Chronicle*, "Burns Sued for $150,000 for Granelli, Rich S.F. Man," November 4, 1927, 1.

10 *San Francisco Chronicle*, April 26, 1925, 12.

11 1930 US census data.

12 *San Francisco Chronicle*, "Death Charged to Policemen," May 13, 1932; "Police Beating Charge Awaits Trial Result," September 21, 1931.

13 *San Francisco Examiner*, "Candidate in Political Row," August 23, 1928.

14 *Oakland Tribune*, "Mullins, Davis Chosen Supervisor Nominees, Koford and Carter Win," August 29, 1928, 1.

15 *San Francisco Examiner*, "Hubby Gets Cash to Let Wife Flirt," December 10, 1927; *San Francisco Chronicle*, November 4, 1927, 14.

16 *San Francisco Chronicle*, "Connivance Laid by Wife to Granelli," December 10, 1927, 14.

17 *San Francisco Examiner*, "S.F. Assemblyman Sued for $150,000 as Love 'Pirate,'" November 4, 1927.

18 No record of a marriage license seems to exist for Inez and Joe, so presumably they never formally married. Some family members suggest they were married in 1932, but the author has no proof of any formal union between the two. In the 1940 census, Inez lists her relationship to Burns as "wife," but she also lists her name as Ida.

19 *Ogden Standard-Examiner*, December 10, 1927, 1.

20 *San Antonio Light*, January 8, 1928, 40.

21 From Burns's World War I draft registration Card, 1917, obtained through the National Archives and Records Administration.

22 Descriptions of the interior at 327 Fillmore are taken from photographs obtained from the Bancroft Library, from the *San Francisco Examiner* collection housed there, as well as from the *Examiner* article, "Mrs. Warren Shannon Exposes Inez Burns's House of Horrors," January 20, 1946, 1.

23 Author interview with Caroline Brown Carlisle, March 22, 2016, as well as the author's visit to the former Fillmore Street clinic in the spring of 1993, where the then-covered concrete incinerator was examined.

24 Even today, such a comprehensive, accessible registry of real estate holdings is difficult to

access. Banks, dummy corporations, and legal entities, as well as trusts, can easily obfuscate property ownership.

25 These recollections come from four interviews with Caroline Brown Carlisle during the winter of 2016.

TEN: ALL AND EVERYTHING THAT FASHION GIVES

1 Such personal recollections come from interviews with Caroline Brown Carlisle on March 10 and 21, 2016.

2 *San Francisco Chronicle*, "Runaway Auto Injures Woman," April 7, 1929, 8.

3 Author interview with Caroline Brown Carlisle, September 19, 2016.

4 Documents obtained from the Recorders Office of the County of San Francisco.

5 *Daily Racing Form*, "Silas B. Mason Passes On," April 16, 1936, 22; *Brooklyn Daily Eagle*, "Silas B. Mason, Dam Builder, Dies," April 15, 1936, 15; *Keeneland* magazine, "Paradise Maintained," Winter 2013, 30–7. Suzanne Burnett Mason died when she choked on a piece of meat in Palm Beach, Florida, in April 1960.

6 *Hayward Daily Review*, "Gold Armor Is Winner of Agua Caliente Race," July 24, 1944, 4; *San Mateo Times*, "Turntable Wins Again at Tijuana," March 19, 1945, 9.

7 From an internal IRS memorandum and deposition anonymously obtained by the author, dated April 29, 1948.

8 For a florid description of opening night, look at Carolyn Anspacher's front-page story in the *San Francisco Chronicle*, "Opera Opens in Brilliant S.F. Fashion," November 2, 1935.

9 *San Francisco Chronicle*, "Sparkling, Gilded Pageant of Beauty and Fashion Parades to Drama," by Ninon, November 2, 1935, C.

10 *San Francisco Chronicle*, "Milady Wears Rare Jewels, Lavish Gowns," November 2, 1935, A.

11 *San Francisco Chronicle*, "Opera on Tonight," by Alfred Frankenstein, November 1, 1935, 13.

12 *San Francisco Chronicle*, "Ring Operas Beautifully Staged, Sung, Says Critic," by Alfred Frankenstein, November 11, 1935, 6.

13 *San Francisco News*, "Inez Brown in U.S. Tax Fight," May 10, 1938.

14 *San Francisco News*, "Abortions Admitted by Girl Patients," May 4, 1938.

15 Here is the entire story, as it appeared in the *San Francisco News*, May 4, 1938. Miss X was Mary Ellen Leary, the identity of the other reporter is unknown. The story carried the byline "By a Staff Writer":

> Arranging for an abortion today at 327 Fillmore Street was so simple and casual that we came out feeling like we had been cheated. We expected an exciting experience, Miss X of the news staff and I—a feeling of self-conscious shame, or nervous fear. It was about as exciting as making a date with a dentist. And about as businesslike.
>
> All it required was a wedding ring and a normal amount of cheek.
>
> Inez runs the place. Her card says, "Inez L. Brown." She sometimes uses other last names, but seems fond of the Inez part. Police know her well. Two years ago they seized $2,000 worth of her hospital equipment. But that didn't bother Inez. She didn't even trouble to change addresses.
>
> It is the upper flat. We walked up a flight of stairs and rang a doorbell. Someone upstairs rang a buzzer that opened the door for us.

Over the banister leaned a pleasant-faced middle-aged woman in a nurse's uniform. "Have you an appointment," she smiled. We didn't. But that did not matter.

"Just come in here and wait," she said, leading us into an airy living room that looked down on Fillmore Street.

We saw two other waiting rooms to the left and right of us. In the one on the left, alone, was a motherly woman of about 38, sitting quietly and holding her hands. The one on the right appeared to be empty.

Across from us in the living room was a plain woman of about 35 who appeared agitated. While we waited she picked up and laid down a magazine several times, stared out the window, stared at us and stared at the floor.

After five minutes a second nurse entered. She was younger than the other, with red hair and blue eyes and a sharp face. Her uniform was white and stiff with starch. She approached the nervous woman.

"Your sister is all right and doing fine," she said. "I suggest you call us in about an hour." She handed the woman a card. Then she turned to Miss X.

"All right, you just come with me," she smiled. "Your husband must remain behind."

Here Miss X takes up the story:

We went into a room to the right of the living room and the nurse sat down at a desk.

"Who sent you?" she asked.

I made up a name.

"Was she a patient of ours?"

"Yes, about four years ago."

She made no effort to verify this.

We discussed the length of "my pregnancy," which was established at two months.

"It is best for you to come in within just a very few days," said the nurse. "Then it will be $55—$50 for the operation, and $5 for the anaesthetic.

"If you wait longer than two months, it will be $75 for the operation and $5 for the anaesthetic. That's the way we handle it—the charge increases the longer you wait."

Friday morning was suggested.

"That would be fine," said the nurse. "Friday is a good day—much better than Saturday because on Saturday we have so many business girls. We try to hold that day free for them. You don't work, do you? Well, then, it's better to come Friday. Besides, we like to get away as early Saturday afternoon as we possibly can.

"You don't need to worry about it. It's very easy, and you can be sure it will be taken care of. We examine you that morning, and if everything isn't perfectly all right, we won't do it.

"We have done thousands—yes, thousands and thousands—of these operations.

"It won't be any different for you than for any of the other girls. No reason why it shouldn't be very easy. If it isn't going to be all right, we can tell beforehand and we won't do it. So don't worry.

"In the morning we take your blood pressure and examine your heart. Don't eat any breakfast before you come—that's because of the gas we will give you. It is more likely to make you sick if you have eaten."

"I'm a little frightened," I confessed. "Can you tell me something about it—I've never done this before. I—I just wondered what it will be like."

"My dear," she smiled, "even if I told you, you wouldn't understand."

"Do I come right here? Do you do it right here?" I persisted.

"Yes, you come right here—let's say 9:30 Friday morning. And we take you up upstairs."

"Do I have to stay overnight?"

She laughed with a note of professional sympathy in her voice.

"No, indeed. Won't take you more than two or three hours. . . ."

She asked my name, but made no written record, only giving me her card as I left. That concluded the interview with Miss X. While she and the nurse were talking it over, I looked around.

The living room where I waited was neatly furnished, but lacking all those little things which, scattered around a room, mark it as the place where someone lives.

I heard a rustle of sound from the adjoining room and moved to a divan where I could look in. There, seated in a corner, was a good-looking blonde reading a magazine. She looked up once, her face blank, and returned to her magazine.

I was sorry I had moved where I could see her. I felt like an intruder.

Once the doorbell rang and someone was admitted, but she was not brought into the living room.

Then Miss X returned and the nurse smiled us out.

16 The reporter was Mary Ellen Leary.

17 *San Francisco News*, "Abortions Admitted by Girl Patients," May 4, 1938; *San Francisco Examiner*, "Police Raid Flat as Abortion Hospital," May 5, 1938.

18 *San Francisco Chronicle*, "Abortion Laid to Two Women Seized in Raid," May 5, 1938, 3.

19 *San Francisco Chronicle*, "Women on the Bench," by Blake Green, September 25, 1981, 15. Judge Meikle was also the first female assistant district attorney and first female superior court judge in San Francisco.

20 *San Francisco Chronicle*, "Abortion Mill Case Dismissed," June 1, 1938, 7; *San Francisco Examiner*, "Inez Brown Wins Freedom," June 1, 1938.

21 *San Francisco Chronicle*, This World section, "Richest Racket," July 21, 1946, 2–3.

22 *San Francisco Examiner*, "Inez Brown's Husband: J. F. Burns Married to Suspect," May 6, 1938.

23 Author interview with Caroline Brown Carlisle, March 10, 2016.

ELEVEN: MEAN LITTLE BASTARD AND PROUD OF IT

1 Herb Caen, *Only in San Francisco* (Garden City, NY: Doubleday, 1960), 238.

2 Ethan Rarick, *California Rising: The Life and Times of Pat Brown* (Berkeley, CA: University of California Press, 2005), 20.

3 *San Francisco Chronicle*, "Local Voters Renominate All but One for Assembly," August 29, 1928, 1.

4 Edmund G. Brown Papers, 1907–1996, the Bancroft Library, University of California, Berkeley, BANC MASS 68/90 c.

5 "Edmund G. Brown Sr.: The Governor's Lawyer," in an interview conducted by Amelia Fry, as part of the Earl Warren Oral History Project, March 20, 1975, 45.

6 "Thomas Lynch: A Career in Politics and the Attorney General's Office," in an interview with Amelia Fry, as part of the Regional Oral History Office of the Bancroft Library, University of California, Berkeley, April 21, 1978, 75.

7 Federal Bureau of Investigation, Freedom of Information Act request on Matthew F. Brady, from memoranda to the director, J. Edgar Hoover, September 5 and 10, 1935, written by FBI Special Agent in Charge Jay C. Newman.

8 Rarick, *California Rising*, 27.

9 "Thomas Lynch: A Career in Politics and the Attorney General's Office," 26.

10 *San Francisco Examiner*, "Attempt to 'Use' Grand Jury Bared," November 8, 1939.

11 *San Francisco Chronicle*, "Suits Endanger Absentee Ballots; Registrar Stymied, Await Decisions," by Earl C. Behrens, October 15, 1939, 6.

12 *San Francisco Chronicle*, "Reisner Wins Ruling," October 17, 1939, 8.

13 *San Francisco Chronicle*, "Final Count in S.F.," November 9, 1939, 12.

14 *San Francisco Examiner*, "Jury Criticizes City Officials," December 12, 1939.

TWELVE: NO PIECE OF CAKE

1 Perhaps the best description of the Great Depression's effect on abortion rates is Leslie J. Reagan's masterful *When Abortion Was a Crime: Women, Medicine and Law in the United States, 1867–1973* (Berkeley, CA: University of California Press, 1997), 132–81.

2 *San Francisco News*, "Solves Thousands of Death Mysteries; Now Turns to Life," by Arthur Caylor, December 3, 1932.

3 From *San Francisco Examiner*'s clipping file's completed "Biographical Material on You," form in the San Francisco History Center.

4 Eugene Aureguy was caught in an undercover sting, trying to bribe *San Francisco Examiner* reporter Robert Patterson (aka Freddie Francisco) to "lay off" a client of his. See *San Francisco Examiner*, "Reporters Tell Detective of Attempted Bribery," by Edward Montgomery, April 24, 1948.

5 *San Francisco News*, "'I Did It for a Kid Who Deserved a Break,' Says Hard-Boiled

6 See the San Francisco Recreation & Parks Department's website on Coit Tower, at http://sfrecpark.org/destination/telegraph-hill-pioneer-park/coit-tower/.

7 A discussion with Jon Christensen, John King, and Anthea Hartig on the occasion of the bridge's seventy-fifth anniversary provides a terrific retrospective of the Golden Gate Bridge, in the *Atlantic* magazine, "The Color, Romance, and Impact of the Golden Gate at 75," May 23, 2012, http://www.theatlantic.com/technology/archive/2012/05/the-color-romance-and-impact-of-the-golden-gate-at-75/257721/.

8 Kevin Starr, *Golden Gate: The Life and Times of America's Greatest Bridge* (New York: Bloomsbury Press), 4.

9 Ibid, 15.

10 Bay Area Census, Population by County, 1860–2000, http://www.bayareacensus.ca.gov/historical/copop18602000.htm.

11 *The New York Times*, "Golden Gate Fair Pictured by Rossi," by Angelo J. Rossi, July 5, 1937, 8.

12 Richard Reinhardt, *Treasure Island: San Francisco's Exposition Years* (San Francisco: Scrimshaw Press, 1973), 50.

13 *The Union*, "Nevada County Nightingale: Emma Nevada," by Gary Noy, January 17, 2005.

14 Specifics of the great baseball drop come from a multitude of sources: Reinhardt's *Treasure Island*, page 106; *San Francisco Chronicle*, Herb Caen column, December 13, 1973, page 33, and Glenn Dickey's column, September, 20, 1977, page 50; and Le Pacini's "Lord of the High Flies," in *California Living*, the Sunday magazine of the *San Francisco Examiner*, May 8, 1977, pages 40, 44. For tips on tracking a baseball in "high sky," I relied on Jim Bain's excellent primer, "How to Play a High Sky," from http://ezinearticles .com/?How-To-Play-A-High-Sky&id=6008033.

THIRTEEN: OFF HER BACK

1 Before being appointed to the federal bench, Harold Louderback had been the San Francisco Superior Court judge who presided over the first murder trial in 1921 of Roscoe "Fatty" Arbuckle, which resulted in a hung jury.

2 *San Francisco News*, "Inez Brown in U.S. Tax Fight," May 10, 1938; *San Francisco Examiner*, "Abortion Case Figure Indicted on Tax Charge," October 12, 1939; "'Inez Brown' Admits U.S. Tax Cheating," February 14, 1940; "10,000 Tax Fine Paid U.S. by Inez Burns," March 17, 1940. *San Francisco Chronicle*, "Mrs. Inez Burns Pleads Guilty," February 14, 1940, 5; *Oakland Tribune*, "Woman Pleads Guilty of U.S. Tax Evasion," February 14, 1940, 13.

3 *San Francisco Call-Bulletin*, "Mailliard Quits Over Quinn Ouster," February 15, 1940, 1.

4 *San Francisco Chronicle*, "Changing of the Guard," February 18, 1940, 6–7.

5 *Oakland Tribune*, "S.F. Police Chief Ousted in Shake-Up," February 15, 1940, 1.

6 *Images of America: San Francisco in World War II*, by John Garvey and the California Center for Military History (Charleston, SC: Arcadia Publishing), 2007, 7, 8.

7 "Don't Come to San Francisco Now" advertisement, reprinted in *Images of America: San Francisco in World War II*, 57.

8 *National League for Women's Service Magazine*, Women's City Club, published monthly at the state headquarters, 465 Post Street, San Francisco, from "Two Years Old" by Marion Leale, March 1943, 9, 17.

9 Federal Bureau of Investigation, Freedom of Information Act request of Edmund G. (Pat) Brown, internal memorandum to the director, July 20, 1944, signed by "Pieper."

10 March 16, 1942, letter to the U.S. War Department; March 23, 1942, letter to Federal Reserve Bank of San Francisco, December 12, 1942, Pat Brown to Governor Culbert L. Olson to consider him for an appointment to be a municipal court judge. All letters are contained in the Edmund G. Brown Papers, 1907–1996, the Bancroft Library, University of California, Berkeley, BANC MASS 68/90 c.

11 *San Francisco Chronicle*, "The Outlaw—A Lavish Western," February 8, 1943, 8.

12 *San Francisco Examiner*, "Warrants Due on Actress' Poster Post," February 20, 1943.

13 *San Francisco Chronicle*, "E. G. Brown Will Run for District Attorney," September 8, 1943.

14 *San Francisco Chronicle* advertisement titled, "Who Is for Edmund G. Brown for District Attorney," November 1, 1943, 12.

15 "Edmund G. Brown Sr.: The Governor's Lawyer," in an interview conducted by Amelia Fry, as part of the Earl Warren Oral History Project, March 20, 1975, 43.

16 *Hollywood Rajah: The Life and Times of Louis B. Mayer* (New York: Holt, Rinehart and Winston, 1960), 298; Edmund G. Brown Papers, 1907–1996, the Bancroft Library, University of California, Berkeley, BANC MASS 68/90 c., letter dated December 27, 1943.

17 *San Francisco Examiner*, "Acted for Notorious Joints," October 31, 1943.

18 *San Francisco Examiner*, "Brady's Splendid Record," September 25, 1943.

19 *San Francisco Examiner*, Editorial, November 1, 1943.

20 *San Francisco Chronicle*, "Brown for District Attorney," October 21, 1943.

21 San Francisco Examiner, "Brady Blasts Opponent's Record," October 29, 1943.

22 Rice, Richard B., et al., *The Elusive Eden: A New History of California* (New York: McGraw-Hill, 2012).

23 *San Francisco Examiner*, "Why Outstanding Citizens Endorse Brady," October 29, 1943.

24 *San Francisco Examiner*, "Brady Says Opponent Backed by Underworld," November 1, 1943.

25 From a February 23, 1999, interview with Bernice Brown, as cited in Ethan Rarick's *California Rising: The Life and Times of Pat Brown* (Berkeley, CA: University of California Press, 2005), 38.

26 *San Francisco Chronicle*, "Complete Returns," November 4, 1943, 6.

27 Ibid.

28 *San Francisco Chronicle*, "Brown's Speech: 'I Will Act on Behalf of All–Not a Few,'" January 9, 1944, 6.

29 *San Francisco Examiner*, "Brown to Fill 39 Posts," November 4, 1943; *San Francisco Examiner*, "New District Attorney Adds Five Deputies," December 10, 1943.

30 *San Francisco Chronicle*, "Dullea Services Warning to Bookies Open Shop Again," by Earl C. Behrens, March 4, 1944, 7.

31 *San Francisco Examiner*, "Four Bookies Face First Felony Charges Today," May 5, 1944.

32 District Attorney's Office, "Report of the Crime Prevention Department for 1944," accessed through Edmund G. (Pat) Brown's FOIA files from the FBI, page 10, stamped 31017.

33 *San Francisco Examiner*, "New Drive on Vice Pledged," October 4, 1944.

34 *San Francisco Chronicle*, "23 Bottles of 'Cut' Liquor Seized in Bar," June 20, 1944, 8.

35 *San Francisco Examiner*, "Police Sue to Padlock Hotel," June 23, 1945.

36 *San Francisco Chronicle*, This World section, advertisement for "Your District Attorney in Action," March 26, 1944, 22; John Dunning, *On the Air: The Encyclopedia of Old-Time Radio* (New York: Oxford University Press, 1998), 464–65.

37 From *Mr. District Attorney: The Case of the Unknown Source*, https://www.youtube.com/watch?v=GKswwjo1Jmg. The show was based on real-life cases of New York district attorney Thomas Dewey.

38 Bill Boyarsky, *Big Daddy: Jesse Unruh and the Art of Power Politics* (Berkeley, CA: University of California Press, 2007), 112.

39 "Edmund G. Brown Sr.: The Governor's Lawyer," in an interview conducted by Amelia Fry, as part of the Earl Warren Oral History Project, March 20, 1975, 20.

40 Edmund G. (Pat) Brown's FOIA files from the FBI, March 5, 1946.
41 Ibid, March 13, 1946.
42 "Edmund G. Brown Sr.: The Governor's Lawyer," in an interview conducted by Amelia Fry, as part of the Earl Warren Oral History Project, March 20, 1975, 46.
43 Ibid.
44 "Norman Elkington: From Adversary to Appointee: Fifty Years of Friendship with Pat Brown," Regional Oral History Office, the Bancroft Library, University of California, Berkeley, December 13, 1978, 17.
45 "Thomas Lynch: A Career in Politics and the Attorney General's Office," in an interview with Amelia Fry, as part of the Governmental History Documentation Project, Goodwin Knight/Edmund Brown Sr. Era., Bancroft Library, University of California, Berkeley, 57, 58.

FOURTEEN: THE NATURE OF THE BEAST

1 Highlights from Pat Brown's leather-bound 1946 agenda, for instance, a list: Herb Caen — Mel Belli (January 17); Chinese Sportsman Club's annual dinner (January 19); Warehouse Union — Local 6 convention (January 25); Stag Banquet Marin Rod & Gun Club (January 26); Commonwealth luncheon at the Palace (February 8); St. Boniface Church speech (February 10); St. Thomas Moore Society at the Palace (February 14); cocktails, Fairmont Hotel; 1945 grand jury (February 14); Demonstration for Palestine at War Memorial Opera House (February 17); Talk at luncheon, Negro Business Men of Fillmore District (February 19); Installation Dinner, 26th Assembly District Demo. Club, Veneto Restaurant (February 23); Herb Caen —- Mel Belli (February 22); lunch with Mel Belli at the St. Francis (February 28); Homecoming Dance at National Guard Armory (March 2); Dentist Thomas Ryan Flinn (March 6 and 7); Mel Belli (March 7); St. Patrick's Day address (March 13); 7th Annual Retreatants' Mass (April 7); [*San Francisco Examiner* Publisher] George Hearst lunch, Palace Hotel (April 8); "Call Judge Murphy" (April 16); Dinner for [US Vice President] Henry A. Wallace at Palace (April 22); Judge Murphy's Chambers (April 26); Democratic Candidates Lunch, Palm Court, Palace (May 4); Barbecue — H & H Ranch, San Mateo County Democratic Committee (May 5); Vets Anniversary Ball at War Memorial Building, Meet Earl Warren (May 17); "Meet Chief Dullea outside bldg." (June 17); "Call Mel Belli & ask him to send $250 check over" (June 21); Executive Board, National Lawyers Guild, Judge Murphy's Chambers (June 24); Chief Dullea (July 2); Filipino Community Banquet, Fairmont Hotel (July 6); "Cancel Judge Murphy lunch" (July 9); "Call Judge Murphy" (July 10); "Call Herb Caen" (July 19); "Call Walter Jones, Sacto Bee" (July 28); Mary Ellen Leary (August 1); State Convention, American Legion (August 18–21); Grand Jury Room 457 City Hall (Newman Wood Products Matter) (August 19); National Convention, American Legion (September 30–October 3); Jake Ehrlich and Newsom (November 13); Judge Murphy (November 20); Herb Caen (December 2); Grand Jury Mtg @ Olympic Club (December 5); Dentist 8 a.m. (December 5); Hebrew Donor Dinner, St. Francis Hotel (December 8); Dentist (December 17); Buy box of cigars, Eyman (December 18).
2 George A. Engelhardt letter, dated November 4, 1943, from the Edmund G. Brown Papers, the Bancroft Library.

3 A.H. Jacobs letter, dated November 4, 1943, from the Edmund G. Brown Papers, the Bancroft Library.

4 Here's a letter written to Pat Brown on behalf of budding San Francisco Attorney Melvin Belli. It shows the extent of Belli's desire to initiate Pat into a particular men's club of the era. Not only did Belli's 1946 invitation reflect the extent that men of a certain age insulated themselves from the world of women, but it shows how men talked when they were out of earshot of women.

"Dear Pat:

The great Dr. Belli is on his way home and the advance guard informs me that the doctor is anxious for a reunion with his friends.

By order of his royal decree, I herewith tender to each of you the doctor's compliments and his invitation to join him for a Tuolumne County Fishing weekend, October 1 and 2. Provisionally, the arrangements are that we shall leave here sometime on Friday, September 30, and return late Sunday, October 2. This is strictly for men and virile entertainment is assured.

Now, don't send us any fancy acceptances, just call this office and give my secretary the following information:

1. The amount of Scotch you feel capable of consuming over one weekend.

2. If you are a two or three steak man.

3. Whether your wardrobe contains warm wool sox.

4. How you intend to get away with this. Will you tell your wife about it?

5. Have you heard any good stories lately?"

5 All letters from the Edmund G. Brown Papers, the Bancroft Library.

6 Letter from Tertius Chandler, dated January 21, 1946, and response from Pat Brown, from the Edmund G. Brown Papers, the Bancroft Library.

FIFTEEN: PILLARS OF MONEY, FOUNTAINS OF PAYOFFS

1 *Los Angeles Times*, "Fred Howser, Fiery, Controversial Ex-Prosecutor, Dies," by Burt A. Folkart, April 29, 1987.

2 Arthur H. Samish and Bob Thomas, *The Secret Boss of California: The Life and High Times of Art Samish* (New York: Crown Publishers, 1971), 125.

3 Estes Kefauver, *Crime in America* (Garden City, NY: Doubleday, 1951), 238–39.

4 See Kevin Starr's outstanding chronicle of this period in the state, *Embattled Dreams: California in War and Peace, 1940–1950 (New York: Oxford University Press, 2003)*, 265.

5 *San Francisco Examiner*, "Cop Neighbor of Inez Talks," December 22, 1945.

6 *San Francisco Chronicle*, "Doctor Jailed in Operation Death Case," May 23, 1937, 1–3.

7 *San Francisco Chronicle*, "Macabre Tales of Death Told at Long's Trial," August 5, 1937, 3.

8 *San Francisco Chronicle*, "Doctor Long Guilty; Wife, Nurse Freed," August 8, 1937, 1.

9   *San Francisco Chronicle*, "Dr. Long Must Go to Prison," January 21, 1941, 10.

10 Author interview with Caroline Brown Carlisle, March 22, 2016.

11 Information about Bud Felix was obtained from interviews with Caroline Brown Carlisle, March 3, 10, 21, 22, and November 17, 2016, as well as from the *San Francisco Chronicle*, and searches conducted through Ancestry.com.

12 *San Francisco Chronicle*, "He Faces an Operation," November 21, 1939, 6.

13 *San Francisco Chronicle*, "City Hall Veteran Without an Enemy," by Jerry Burns, February 18, 1975, 6.

14 *San Francisco Examiner*, "Supervisor Shannon to Wed," August 5, 1942.

15 For a fuller discussion of Americans traveling to Mexico for abortions, see Leslie J. Reagan's "Crossing the Border for Abortion: California Activists, Mexican Clinics, and the Creation of a Feminist Health Agency in the 1960s," in *Feminist Studies* 26, no. 1, 323–48.

16 Author interview with Caroline Brown Carlisle, March 1992.

17 *San Francisco Examiner*, Gloria Davenport Shannon, "Mrs. Shannon Tells Horror House Visit," January 21, 1946, 1.

18 *San Francisco Examiner*, "Grand Jurors Defend Stand in Burns Case," by Richard V. Hyer, December 29, 1945.

19 *San Francisco Examiner*, "Mrs. Warren Shannon Exposes Inez Burns' House of Horrors," by Gloria Davenport Shannon, January 20, 1946, 13.

20 *Santa Rosa Press Democrat*, "Santa Rosa's Connection to the Mob," by Gaye LeBaron, October 5, 2013; *San Mateo Times*, "The Mysterious Murder of Nick DeJohn," by June Morrall, May 10, 2002, 1, in "Other Times."

21 *San Francisco Chronicle*, "5 of DeJohn's Pals Slain," July 24, 1947.

22 From San Francisco police chief Thomas J. Cahill: "A Life in Review," available from the Police Department's website. http://sanfranciscopolice.org/chief-thomas-jcahill-life-review.

23 *San Francisco Examiner*, "Oliva and Woman Termed Key Links in DeJohn and Surgery Extortion Cases," November 25, 1948; *San Mateo Times*, "Killing of Mobster Nick DeJohn a Man of Mystery in 1947," by June Morrall, April 26, 2002, 1, in "Other Times"; *San Mateo Times*, "Daughter to Take Stand," March 13, 1956, 2.

24 From a real estate prospectus of the property, dated 1939, and author interview with Caroline Brown Carlisle, March 3, 2016.

25 *San Francisco Chronicle*, "Notebook from Inez Burns' Home Lists Daily 'Payoff,'" March 6, 1946, 6.

26 From an internal IRS memorandum and deposition anonymously obtained by the author, dated April 29, 1948.

27 The Virtual Museum of the City of San Francisco, http://www.sfmuseum.net/war/garay .html.

28 Real estate information comes from a search of Los Angeles County Recorder records.

SIXTEEN: UNAPOLOGETIC

1   "Thomas Lynch: A Career in Politics and the Attorney General's Office," in an interview with Amelia Fry, as part of the Governmental History Documentation Project,

Goodwin Knight/Edmund Brown Sr. Era., Bancroft Library, University of California, Berkeley, 57, 58.

2 According to the State of California Public Health Report, in 1945 in San Francisco there were 16,118 births.

3 *San Francisco Examiner*, "No Indictments Voted; Report to Be Asked," November 19, 1946.

4 The two trapdoors were noted in a Herb Caen column in the *San Francisco Chronicle*, May 14, 1949, 11.

5 *San Francisco Examiner*, "Garage Man Testifies at Burns Hearing," January 31, 1946.

6 *San Francisco Examiner*, "Records Vanish as Police Sift Crime Surgery," September 28, 1945.

7 *San Francisco Examiner*, "Woman Jailed in Operations, $300,000 Found," September 27, 1945.

8 *San Francisco Examiner*, "Raid Tip-Off Probed," December 7, 1945; "Grand Jury to Get Shannon Case Evidence," by Richard V. Hyer, December 14, 1945; "Full Jury Quiz in Burns Tipoff Report Slated," January 25, 1946.

9 *San Francisco Examiner*, "Surgery Mill Case Goes on Minus Indictment," October 4, 1945.

10 *San Francisco Examiner*, "Records Vanish as Police Sift Crime Surgery," September 28, 1945.

11 *San Francisco Examiner*, "Jury to Probe Fillmore St. Surgery Mill," September 29, 1945; "New Arrest in Surgery Mill," October 30, 1945.

12 *San Francisco Examiner*, "Surgery Mill Case Goes on Minus Indictment," October 4, 1945.

13 *San Francisco Examiner*, "Many Prominent S.F. Women May Be Involved," November 8, 1945; "Surgical Mill Hearing Due to Start Today," November 26, 1945.

14 *San Francisco Chronicle*, "The Case of Inez Burns," November 8, 1945, 1, 8.

SEVENTEEN: TRAITORS!

1 John Wesley Noble and Bernard Averbach, *Never Plead Guilty: The Story of Jake Ehrlich* (New York: Farrar, Straus and Cudahy, 1955), pt. 3, ch. 1, 144, 157; *San Francisco Chronicle*, "Attorney Will Tell 'All' in Krupa Case," July 21, 1943, 7; *San Francisco Chronicle*, "Judge Neubarth Dies in Courtroom," by Caroline Anspacher, June 24, 1969, 1.

2 *San Francisco Chronicle*, "The Abortion Mill Case," December 5, 1945, 1; *San Francisco Examiner*, "Burns Couple Won't Testify," January 28, 1946.

3 *San Francisco Chronicle*, "Abortion Case," November 27, 1945, 1; *San Francisco Examiner*, "Wife Describes Surgery Mill at Burns Trial," November 27, 1945.

4 *San Francisco Chronicle*, "The Burns' 'Abortion Mill' Trial," November 29, 1945, 10.

5 *San Francisco Examiner*, "Woman Reports Threat on Life," November 29, 1945.

6 *San Francisco Chronicle*, "Shannons Sought," December 1, 1945, 1; *San Francisco Examiner*, "Abortion Mill Lawyer Hits at Shannon," November 30, 1945.

7 *San Francisco Examiner*, "Abortion Mill Lawyer Hits at Shannon," November 30, 1945.

8 *San Francisco Examiner*, "Cartoonist Homer Davenport Is Dead, Dies of Pneumonia in

New York," May 3, 1912. Homer Davenport and Teddy Roosevelt had been friends, and the two had ridden Arabian horses on Davenport's three-hundred-acre New Jersey ranch.

9 *San Francisco Examiner,* "Subpoenas Await Arrival of Shannons," December 28, 1945.

10 See Nellie Bly, *Ten Days in a Mad-House* (A Nellie Bly Book, 2012), and Upton Sinclair, *The Jungle* (New York: Penguin, 2006).

11 *San Francisco Examiner,* "Shannon Called Author of Surgery Mill Book," by Richard V. Hyer, December 10, 1945.

12 Descriptions of the Shannons from the *San Francisco Chronicle,* "Shannons Sought," December 1, 1945, 1.

13 *San Francisco Examiner,* "New Abortion Expose Hinted," December 21, 1945.

14 Ibid.

15 *San Francisco Examiner,* "Sadism Laid to Owners," by Richard V. Hyer, December 21, 1945.

16 *San Francisco Examiner,* "New Abortion Expose Hinted," December 21, 1945.

17 *San Francisco Examiner,* "New Disclosures Made in Surgery Mill Payoff Probe," by Richard V. Hyer, December 8, 1945.

18 *San Francisco Examiner,* "Jury to Probe Abortion Mill Raid Tipoff," by Richard V. Hyer, December 13, 1945.

19 *San Francisco Chronicle,* "The Abortion Trial–And Crime Prevention," December 2, 1945, 1; *San Francisco Examiner,* "To Quiz Him on Story," December 1, 1945; "Pair Found in Bakersfield," December 2, 1945.

20 *San Francisco Examiner,* "Claim Book Will 'Lift Lid' on Abortion 'Racket,'" December 18, 1945.

21 *San Francisco Examiner,* "Mrs. Shannon Writes from Hideout; Says She Will Be Star Witness," December 18, 1945.

22 *San Francisco Chronicle,* "Abortion Case," December 20, 1945, 1.

23 *San Francisco Examiner,* "D.A. Quizzes Shannons," December 20, 1945.

24 *San Francisco Chronicle,* "The Abortion Case," December 4, 1945, 1.

25 *San Francisco Chronicle,* "The Abortion Case," December 4, 1945, 1; *San Francisco Examiner,* "Officer Bares Bribe Offer at Burns Hearing," December 4, 1945.

26 "Abortion Trial Order for Inez Burns, 4 Others," December 6, 1945, 1; *San Francisco Examiner,* "2 Defendants Freed for Lack of Evidence," December 6, 1945.

27 *San Francisco Examiner,* "Rift Reported Among Burns Defendants," by Richard V. Hyer, December 13, 1945.

28 *San Francisco Examiner,* "New Action in Burns Case Set for Next Week," December 15, 1945; "Brennan Quits as Burns 'Abortion Mill' Counsel, December 16, 1945.

29 *San Francisco Chronicle,* "Irene Mansfeldt Takes Stand, Tells Background of Slaying," by Carolyn Anspacher, December 4, 1945, 1.

30 See *Never Plead Guilty,* pages 205–17; *San Francisco Chronicle,* "Missing Women," by Stanton Delaplane, December 13, 1945, 1. Ehrlich described Cline as "the most fantastic client I have ever run into and read about. His is the strangest criminal mind I have ever encountered."

31 *San Francisco News,* "McGovern Will Pass Up Criminal Cases While Service on Police Commission," November 15, 1938.

32 *San Francisco Chronicle*, "Services for Walter McGovern," October 1, 1975.

33 *San Francisco Chronicle*, Herb Caen column, October 5, 1975.

34 *San Francisco Examiner*, "Police Handed Surgery Mill Tipoff Clew," December 8, 1945.

35 *San Francisco Examiner*, "Vet Sought $20,000," by Richard V. Hyer, December 9, 1945.

36 *San Francisco Examiner*, "Abortion Mill Aide Who Fled State Named," by Richard V. Hyer, December 31, 1945.

37 *San Francisco Chronicle*, "Pair Deny Threatening the Shannons," January 13, 1946, 10.

38 *Oakland Tribune*, "S.F. Police Knew of Alleged 'Mill,' Charges Shannon," December 30, 1945, page 3.

39 *San Francisco Examiner*, "D.A. to Sift Burns Loan," by Richard V. Hyer, January 1, 1946.

40 *San Francisco Examiner*, "Conferences Explained," by Richard V. Hyer, January 13, 1946.

EIGHTEEN: THE OTHER SHOE

1 Elenore Meherin, *Chickie* (New York, Grosset & Dunlap, 1925).

2 *San Francisco Examiner*, "Mrs. Warren Shannon Exposes Inez Burns' House of Horrors," by Gloria Davenport Shannon, January 20, 1946, 1.

3 *San Francisco Chronicle*, "Mrs. Burns Replies," January 21, 1946.

4 *Newsweek*, "To San Simeon's Taste," February 4, 1946, 86.

5 Biographical material completed by Maginn maintained by the *San Francisco Examiner* library, now in possession of the San Francisco History Center.

6 *San Francisco Chronicle*, Herb Caen column, January 19, 1946, 7.

7 *San Francisco Examiner*, "Shannons Ask Church Aid in Fight on Abortion Mills," January 12, 1946.

8 *San Francisco Examiner*, "Burns Couple Won't Testify," January 28, 1946.

9 *San Francisco Chronicle*, "Abortion Tipoff," January 26, 1946, 5.

10 *Oakland Tribune*, "Operation Mill Trials to Open," February 18, 1946, 11.

11 *San Francisco Chronicle*, "Mrs. Burns Returns; Trial Slated Today," February 18, 1946, 7.

NINETEEN: BUSTER BROWN TO THE RESCUE

1 *San Francisco News*, "McGovern to Pass Up Criminal Cases While Serving on Police Commission," November 15, 1938; *San Francisco Call*, "Compliments of the Week to Senator Walter McGovern," December 3, 1938; *San Francisco Examiner*, "All Political Races Shunned by M'Govern," March 23, 1938; *San Francisco Chronicle*, Herb Caen column, October 5, 1975; "Thomas Lynch: A Career in Politics and the Attorney General's Office," an oral history conducted by Amelia Fry in 1978, Oral History Office, the Bancroft Library, University of California, Berkeley, 71.

2 Ethan Rarick, *California Rising: The Life and Times of Pat Brown* (Berkeley, CA: University of California Press, 2005), 40; *San Francisco Examiner*, "Official: Atty. Gen. Tom Lynch," August 17, 1964, 1; *San Francisco Examiner*, "No Smiler, He Can Grin," by Lisa Hobbs, August 17, 1964, 10; *San Francisco News Call-Bulletin*, by Joseph B. Sheridan, August 17, 1964, 5; "Thomas Lynch: A Career in Politics and the Attorney General's Office," an oral history conducted by Amelia Fry in 1978, Oral History Office, the Bancroft Library, University of California, Berkeley.

3   *San Francisco Chronicle*, "Judge Traverso Dies of Injuries," January 23, 1975, 32; "Traverso to Retire from Bench," March 9, 1965, 2; *Golden Gate Speranza Lodge No. 30 F & A.M. History From 1852 to 2005*, 18; Ancestry.com, http://person.ancestry.com/tree/66168287/person/44147389723/story.

4   *San Francisco Call Bulletin*, "Inez Trial on; Delay Refused," February 18, 1946, 1.

5   *San Francisco Chronicle*, "Shannon Relative Found on Jury," February 21, 1946, 7.

6   *San Francisco Examiner*, "Trial Begins for Inez Burns, Four Others," February 19, 1946.

7   *San Francisco Call Bulletin*, "State Hints at Calling Inez Aide," February 19, 1946, 1; *San Francisco Examiner*, "Burns Defense Hits 'Politics' in Picking Jury," February 20, 1946, 3.

8   *San Francisco Chronicle*, "The Abortion Trial," February 22, 1946, 9.

9   The jurors were Fred A. Vogel Jr., 2216 Larkin Street, auditor at American-Hawaiian Sugar Refinery; Vivian G. Murdoch, 891 Post Street, stenographer for General Petroleum Corporation; Jean Hibbitts, 1418 Alemany Boulevard, housewife; Thomas Cahalan, 525 Turk Street, retired; Marie Rowe, 756 Twelfth Avenue, housewife; John G. Den Besten, 1479 Thomas Avenue, Bank of America clerk; Leland J. Badaracco, 2158 Thirty-fourth Avenue, employee at Metropolitan Life Insurance; Jacob Abrams, 2945 Twenty-first Avenue, retired; Anna M. Linder, 3314 Broderick Street, housewife; Rose Williams, 111 Meadowbrook Drive, housewife; Dalton K. Stern, 2330 Sixteenth Avenue, auditor at Wells Fargo Bank; and William P. Gillespie, 101 San Ramon Way, cashier at Bank of America.

10   *San Francisco Examiner*, "Two Surprise Witnesses Hit at Mrs. Burns," February 27, 1946, 3.

11   *San Francisco Call Bulletin*, "Woman Collapses at Trial of Inez," February 26, 1946.

12   *San Francisco Call Bulletin*, "Woman Witness Called Back in Burns Trial," February 27, 1946.

13   See "Thomas Lynch: A Career in Politics and the Attorney General's Office," an oral history conducted by Amelia Fry in 1978, Oral History Office, the Bancroft Library, University of California, Berkeley, 69; and "Whatever Happened to Buster Brown Shoes?" from "The Straight Dope," http://www.straightdope.com/columns/read/2839/whatever-happened-to-buster-brown-shoes.

14   *San Francisco Chronicle*, "New Turn in Burns' Case," February 28, 1946, 1.

15   *San Francisco Examiner*, "Girl Accuses Inez Burns at Plot Trial," February 28, 1946, 13.

16   *Oakland Tribune*, "Oakland Branch of 'Mill' Hinted," February 28, 1946, 1.

17   *San Francisco Call Bulletin*, "Burns' Patient Testifies," February 28, 1946, 1.

18   *Oakland Tribune*, "Records Show 'Mill' Prospered," by Nancy Barr Mavity, March 1, 1946, 3.

19   *San Francisco Chronicle*, "Burns Abortion Trial," March 1, 1946, 10.

20   *San Francisco Chronicle*, "New Turn in Burns' Case," February 28, 1946, 1.

21   *San Francisco Examiner*, "Lawyers in Clash," February 28, 1946.

22   Normally court records are open to the public, but when the author sought to retrieve records of the 1946 trial from the superior court of San Francisco, he was told that all records had been destroyed.

23   *San Francisco Examiner*, "New Witnesses Back Charge in Burns Trial," March 2, 1946; *Oakland Tribune*, "Records Show 'Mill' Prospered," by Nancy Barr Mavity, March 1, 1946, 3.

24 *San Francisco Chronicle*, Herb Caen column, March 1, 1946, 13.
25 *San Bernardino Sun*, "First San Francisco Patrolman Ever Jumped to Police Chief Has the City's Full Attention," an Associated Press article, by Katherine Pinkham, January 29, 1956, 12.
26 *Oakland Tribune*, "'Little Brown Books' Spark Burns Trial," by Nancy Barr Mavity, March 5, 1946, 1.
27 The physicians' names and locations were Dr. Winston, Oakland; Dr. George Hall and Dr. Jackson, Sacramento; Dr. Hedy, Manteca; Dr. Snodly, Vallejo; Dr. Stuck, Oakland; Dr. Banks, Dr. Van Meter, Dr. Frazier, San Francisco.
28 *San Francisco Examiner*, "Payoff Notebooks Shown to Burns Jury," March 6, 1946; *San Francisco Call-Bulletin*, "Inez Card Introduced," March 6, 1946.
29 *San Francisco Examiner*, "Final Arguments Begin in Burns Conspiracy Case," March 7 1946.
30 *San Francisco Chronicle*, "Burns Defense Rests—With No Testimony," March 7, 1946, 1.
31 Ibid.
32 *San Francisco Examiner*, "Evidence Ends in Burns Case; Pleas Begin," March 7, 1946.

TWENTY: AMBITION FEEDS ON STRANGE FOODS

1 See Clare Brandt's *The Man in the Mirror: A Life of Benedict Arnold* (New York: Random House, 1994).
2 See Patrick Geoghegan's *Robert Emmet: A Life* (Dublin: McGill-Queen's University Press, 2002), 202.
3 See Joseph Stevenson's *Documents Illustrative of Sir William Wallace: His Life and Times* (Maitland Club, 1841), 189. Wallace's life was portrayed in the popular 1995 film *Braveheart*.
4 *San Francisco Chronicle*, "A Plea for Mrs. Burns," March 8, 1946, 1. All of Walter McGovern's appeals to the jury come from this article.
5 The scripture in full reads, "Judge not, that ye not be judged. For with what judgment ye judge, ye shall be judged; and with what measure ye mete, it shall be measured to you again."
6 *San Francisco Chronicle*, "A Plea for Mrs. Burns," March 8, 1946, 1.
7 *San Francisco Examiner*, "Retrial of Burns Case Expected in June; New Charges Threatened," March 10, 1946.
8 *San Francisco Examiner*, "Arsonist Sets 2 Blazes in Inez Burns Building," March 11, 1946.
9 *Oakland Tribune*, "S.F. to Probe Burns Mistrial," March 11, 1946.
10 *San Francisco Chronicle*, "Brown Starts Work on New Burns Trial," March 11, 1946, 1; *San Francisco Examiner*, "Arsonist Sets 2 Blazes in Inez Burns Building," March 11, 1946.
11 *San Francisco Examiner*, "Arsonist Sets 2 Blazes in Inez Burns Building," March 11, 1946.
12 *San Francisco Chronicle*, "Brown Starts Work on New Burns Trial," March 11, 1946, 1.
13 *San Francisco Chronicle*, "Brown Asks for More Funds," March 12, 1946, 8. Dr. Caldwell,

who had been on trial for performing an abortion that resulted in the death of a patient, was eventually acquitted in July 1946, shortly after Inez's second hung jury.

TWENTY-ONE: DISTRUST

1   *San Francisco Chronicle*, "Burns Witness Says She Was Not Threatened," March 18, 1946, 12. Homicide Inspector Edward Penaat, quoted in the article, said she tried to commit suicide.

2   Susan A. Newfield, Mittie D. Hinz, Donna Scott-Tilley, Kathryn L. Sridaromont, and Patricia J. Maramba, *Cox's Clinical Applications of Nursing Diagnosis* (Philadelphia: F. A. Davis, 2007), 65.

3   The pseudonymous Corinne Patchen died while I was finishing writing this book.

4   *San Francisco Chronicle*, Herb Caen column, March 13, 1946.

5   See Ethan Rarick's *California Rising: The Life and Times of Pat Brown* (Berkeley, CA: University of California Press, 2005), 47–48.

6   *San Francisco Examiner*, "Retrial Today for Inez Burns," May 13, 1946, 6.

7   *San Francisco Chronicle*, "Kaufman Slogan: 'Justice Delayed Is Justice Denied,'" April 12, 1944, 13.

8   Biographical material, dated February 21 1947, from the *San Francisco Examiner*'s library, in the San Francisco History Center.

9   *San Francisco Chronicle*, "Prospective Jurors Stubborn; Defense Seems to Be Stalling," by Richard V. Hyer, May 16, 1946, 8; "Burns Abortion Trial," May 17, 1946, 13.

10 The jurors were Hazel Mayo, 975 Bush Street, wife of a ship engineer; Mina Tait, 13 Alhambra Street, another marine engineer's wife; Nora Roth, 1350 Eighth Avenue, wife of a musician; Rita Abrams, 1850 Gough Street, widow of a real estate broker; Mary Weaver, 940 Powell Street, a United Airlines employee; Louise Jenkins, 470 Third Avenue, a Southern Pacific employee; Attilio Celillo, 2806 Golden Gate Avenue, produce company clerk; John O. Wagner, 1801 Larkin Street, grain company manager; Elizabeth W. French, 2250 Green Street, widow; John Parker, 380 Eddy Street, retired Southern Pacific operator; Fern Erre, 2815 Van Ness Avenue, wife of an auto dealer; and Oscar W. Nelson, 2488 San Bruno Avenue, motor parts supplier employee.

11 *San Francisco Examiner*, "Boast Linked to Inez Burns," May 22, 1946, 8; *San Francisco Chronicle*, "The Burns Abortion Case," by Richard V. Hyer, May 22, 1946, 13.

12 *San Francisco Chronicle*, "Burns Defense Loses Motion for Acquittal," May 25, 1946, 9.

13 Portia says in Act IV, Scene 1 in *The Merchant of Venice*: "That, in the course of justice, none of us should see salvation: we do pray for mercy; And that same prayer doth teach us all to render the deeds of mercy." Leopold and Loeb were two University of Chicago students who in 1924 kidnapped and killed a fourteen-year-old boy; Darrow's twelve-hour close suggested, "If I should succeed, my greatest reward and my greatest hope will be that for the countless unfortunates who must tread the same road in blind childhood that these poor boys have trod—that I have done something to help human understanding, to temper justice with mercy, to overcome hate with love." Leopold and Loeb were sentenced to life in prison.

14 *San Francisco Call-Bulletin*, "3rd Burns Trial Held Possible," May 28, 1946, 1.

15 *San Francisco Call-Bulletin*, "Brown to Try Inez Again; 2nd Jury Fails," May 29, 1946, 1.

TWENTY-TWO: THE BRIDGE OF SIGHS

1 *San Francisco Examiner,* "Doubleday Forbidden to Print 'Memoirs of Hecate County,'" by Leon Racht, November 28, 1946.

2 See *San Francisco Chronicle,* Herb Caen column, October 7, 1946, 13; *San Francisco Chronicle,* "California," in "This World" section, December 15, 1946, 2; *San Francisco Examiner,* "Judge to Let Jury Rule in Salacious Book Trial," September 19, 1946.

3 After eight minutes of deliberation, a jury declared the novel not obscene, and therefore bookseller Stuart Cunningham was not guilty. "We decided that the book was no more immoral than many other books considered classics, which are available to anyone," said jury foreman Everett Porterfield.

4 *Los Angeles Times,* "Brown Seems Democratic Winner Over Howser," June 8, 1946, 3.

5 *San Francisco Chronicle,* This World section, July 21, 1946, 2.

6 *San Francisco Chronicle,* "Brown Tells Situation in Burns Case," by Richard V. Hyer, September 19, 1946, 15.

7 *San Francisco Examiner,* "Judge Quits Burns Trial," September 11, 1946, 1.

8 *San Francisco Chronicle,* "U.S. Judge Edward P. Murphy Dies," December 14, 1958, 1,4.

9 *San Francisco Chronicle,* "Brown Tells Situation in Burns Case," by Richard V. Hyer, September 19, 1946, 15.

10 *San Francisco Examiner,* "Judge Warns Burns Jurors," September 18, 1946, 10; *San Francisco Chronicle,* "Third Burns Trial," September 18, 1946, 3.

11 The jurors were Vera G. Adams, 151 West Clay Park, wife of an army major; Gus P. Hernthal, 601 Masonic Avenue, accountant; Bertha G. Larsen, 101 Twenty-seventh Street, shipfitter's wife; Fred Newman, 30 Miramar Avenue, bank teller; Elizabeth A. Moses, 1432 Lake Street, physician's wife; Frances E. Smith, 735 Miramar Avenue, housewife; Alice McGuire, 1603A Church Street, housewife; Sverre C. Kloster, 1783 Tenth Avenue, oil company accountant; Frank L. Rush, 1218 Third Avenue, steamship company employee; Margaret Crane, 3065 Clay Street, jewelry saleswoman; Lawrence A. Bailey, 2290 Sixteenth Avenue, department-store employee; and Genevieve Peacock, 288 Faxon Avenue, piano teacher.

12 *San Francisco Chronicle,* "Judge Locks Up Burns Jurors," by Richard V. Hyer, September 20, 1946, 1.

13 *Inez L. Burns, Mabel Spaulding, Myrtle Ramsey, et. Cal., Petitioners, v the People of the State of California,* 335 U.S. 844 (1948). PETITION: File Date: 8/12/1948. 76 pp. Term Year: 1948. *U.S. Supreme Court Records and Briefs, 1832–1978.*

14 *San Francisco Chronicle,* "Burns Jury Locked Up," by Richard V. Hyer, September 20, 1946, 1.

15 During a parade heralding the United States' entry into World War I, a suitcase bomb exploded on Steuart Street, just south of Market, killing ten and wounding forty bystanders, including a young girl whose legs were blown off. It still is the worst terrorist attack in San Francisco history. Two labor leaders, Thomas Mooney and Warren K. Billings, were convicted in separate trials by the sequestered jurors, and sentenced to death

by hanging. Subsequent findings showed witnesses offered perjured testimony; Mooney and Billings's lives were spared, and thirty-three years after their convictions, the men were pardoned by California Governor Culbert Olson.

16 *San Francisco Examiner*, "Judge Locks Up Burns Jurors," September 20, 1946, 1.

17 *San Francisco Chronicle*, "Hospital Equipment Is on Display at the Burns Trial," September 24, 1946, 3.

18 Ibid.

19 Ibid.

20 *San Francisco Chronicle*, "Burns Trial Sensation," September 25, 1946, 1.

21 Ibid.

22 *San Francisco Examiner*, "Witness Found in Burns Case," September 25, 1946, 5.

23 *San Francisco Call-Bulletin*, "Inez Case May Go to Jury Today," September 26, 1946, 5; *San Francisco Chronicle*, "The Burns Case," September 26, 1946, 3.

24 Ibid; *San Francisco Call-Bulletin*, "Inez Case May Go to Jury Today," September 26, 1946, 5.

25 *San Francisco Chronicle*, "Inez Burns Convicted," September 27, 1946, 1.

26 Ibid.

27 *San Francisco Chronicle*, "Inez Burns Convicted," September 27, 1946, 1; *San Francisco Call-Bulletin*, "Inez Burns, Found Guilty, Weeps as She Goes to Jail," September 27, 1946, 1.

28 *San Francisco Chronicle*, "Brown Plans Wider Inquiry on Abortions," September 28, 1946, 3.

29 *Inez L. Burns, Mabel Spaulding, Myrtle Ramsey, et al., Petitioners, v. the People of the State of California, Petition / WALTER MCGOVERN / 1948 / 219 / 335 U.S. 844 / 69 S. Ct. 66 / 93 L. Ed. 394 / 8-12-1948.*

30 *San Francisco Chronicle*, "Burns Case Sentences," by Richard V. Hyer, October 1, 1946, 1.

TWENTY-THREE: HYPOCRITES!

1 *San Francisco Chronicle*, "Brown Plans Wider Inquiry on Abortions," September 28, 1946, 3.

2 *San Francisco Chronicle*, "Will Inez Burns 'Sing' If She Gets the Book Thrown at Her?" September 29, 1946, 12.

3 *Los Angeles Times*, "San Franciscan Hits at Howser on Lux Case," October 4, 1946, 4.

4 *San Francisco Examiner*, "Inez Burns to Appeal Case," September 28, 1946.

5 *San Francisco Chronicle*, Herb Caen column, December 14, 1946, 9. Whether the reported "Emily" story is true, conjecture, or perhaps fed to Caen by antagonists of Inez is unknown. Caen's longtime refrain at the *Chronicle*—"Check 'em and lose 'em"—referring to his protocol of reporting unsubstantiated rumors without substantiating their veracity may or may not have come into play with this allegation.

6 Edmund G. Brown Papers, 1907–1996, the Bancroft Library, University of California, Berkeley, BANC MASS 68/90c.

7 *San Francisco Chronicle*, "Police Shifts Put Captains in New Posts," March 17, 1938, 1.

8 *San Francisco Chronicle*, "The Payoffs on Payoffs?" by Richard V. Hyer, October 17, 1946, 1.

9   Both Levina Blanchette Queen's petition for naturalization and her signed citizenship certificate are available online through Ancestry.com.

10 *San Francisco Chronicle*, "Husband of Burns' Helper Fined $1000," December 19, 1946, 7.

11 *San Francisco Chronicle*, "Burns Trial Sensation," September 25, 1946, 1; *San Francisco Chronicle*, Burns Jury Locked Up," by Richard V. Hyer, September 20, 1946, 1.

12 *San Francisco Examiner*, "Jury to Probe Abortion Mill Raid Tipoff," by Richard V. Hyer, December 13, 1945.

13 *San Francisco Chronicle*, "The Tipoff Blowup," by Richard V. Hyer, October 19, 1946, 1.

14 *San Francisco Examiner*, "Grand Jury Maps Action," October 15, 1946.

15 *San Francisco Chronicle*, "Jury to Treat Tip-offs in Its Yearly Report," November 26, 1946, 2.

16 *San Francisco Chronicle*, "Grand Jury Split Quashed Tipoff Inquiry," January 11, 1947, 9.

17 *San Francisco Chronicle*, "Police Board Says 'There Was a Tipoff,'" November 27, 1946, 3.

18 *San Francisco Chronicle*, "Jury to Treat Tip-offs in Its Yearly Report," November 26, 1946, 2.

19 *San Francisco Chronicle*, "Heat," in "This World" section, October 27, 1946, 2.

20 During part of his fourteen-year tenure as district attorney of Alameda County, from 1932 to 1934, Warren had been chair of the California Republican Party.

21 For a description of Cornero and his gambling ships, see "The Wild Reign of Captain Tony and His Floating Casinos," by Jeer Witter in *Los Angeles* magazine, March 1965.

22 *Los Angeles Times*, "San Franciscan Hits at Howser on Lux Case," October 4, 1946, 4.

23 *Los Angeles Times*, "Howser Accused Brown of 'Smear Campaign,'" October 9, 1946, 6.

24 *San Francisco Chronicle*, "Brown's Forces Split," by Earl C. Behrens, October 10, 1946, 1.

25 *San Francisco Chronicle*, "Ex-Campaign Chief Assails 'Pat' Brown," October 24, 1946, 10.

26 *Los Angeles Times*, "California's Next Attorney General," August 31, 1946, 2, editorial section; Ethan Rarick, *California Rising: The Life and Times of Pat Brown* (Berkeley, CA: University of California Press, 2005), 51.

27 *The Southern Cross*, the official newspaper for the Diocese of San Diego, the editorial "Catching the Brass Ring," contained in the Edmund G. Brown Papers, 1907–1996, the Bancroft Library, University of California, Berkeley, BANC MASS 68/90 c.

28 *San Francisco Chronicle*, "Great Victory for State GOP Indicated," by Earl C. Behrens, November 2, 1946, 1, 3.

29 *San Francisco Chronicle*, "State GOP's Power Rises in Congress," by Earl C. Behrens, November 9, 1946, 2.

30 *San Francisco Chronicle*, "Elks to Hold Annual Memorial Exercises," December 1, 1946, 26; and "Donors' Dinner for Hebrew Nursing Home," December 8, 1946, 46.

31 *San Francisco Chronicle*, "Brown to Receive Evidence on Fake Medical Diplomas," January 31, 1947, 2; "Red Light Law Invoked for First Time Since 1941," January 29, 1947, 10; "S.F. Is 'It' in the Traffic Tag Game," January 17, 1947, 1; "Cigarette Suit Injunction Denied," January 16, 1947, 8.

32 *San Francisco Chronicle*, Herb Caen column, February 3, 1947, 15, and May 21, 1947, 15; *Polk's Crocker-Langley San Francisco Directory*, 1951, 53.

33 *San Francisco Chronicle*, advertisement, "New Science of Healing," April 9, 1944, 60; "Defense Attacks State's Star Witness in Nutritionist Trial," October 6, 1948, 16.

34 *San Mateo Times*, "Abortion Raid at Colma Laid to Newton Tip," January 3, 1947, 1.

35 *San Francisco Chronicle*, "Abortions Charged," January 3, 1947, 1.

36 Ibid.

37 Details about Nick DeJohn come from the *San Francisco Chronicle*, "DeJohn Inquest" and "DeJohn Story Told Before the Grand Jury," June 5, 1947, 24; *San Francisco Examiner*, "DeJohn Killing Laid to Chicago Gang Leaders," July 29, 1947; *San Francisco Examiner*, "Accused Trio to Be Freed," by Dick Pearce, March 10, 1949; *San Mateo Times*, "Killing of Mobster Nick DeJohn a Mystery in 1947," by June Morrall, April 26, 2002, page 1 in "Other Times"; *San Mateo Times*, "The Mysterious Murder of Nick DeJohn," in "Other Times," by June Morrall, May 10, 2002, 1.

38 *San Francisco Chronicle*, Herb Caen column, May 21, 1947, 15.

39 *San Francisco Chronicle*, "High Court Appeal by Inez Denied," March 26, 1948, 12; *Inez L. Burns, Mabel Spaulding, Myrtle Ramsey, et al., Petitioners, v. the People of the State of California, Petition / WALTER MCGOVERN / 1948 / 219 / 335 U.S. 844 / 69 S. Ct. 66 / 93 L. Ed. 394 / 8-12-1948.*

40 *San Francisco Examiner*, "Inez Burns, 4 Aides on Way to Prison; New Stay Refused," March 30, 1948.

TWENTY-FOUR: STIFF UPPER LIP

1 *San Francisco Examiner*, "Inez Burns and 3 Aides Leave for Tehachapi Today," March 31, 1948.

2 From the city of Tehachapi's website: www.tehachapilife.com.

3 Jon Anthony Dosa, *Reel Life 101: Classic Movie Lines that Teach Us about Life, Death, Love, Marriage, Anger and Humor* (Bloomington, IN: AuthorHouse, 2006), 207.

4 Billy Wilder, *Double Indemnity* (Berkeley, CA: University of California Press, 2000), 34.

5 Richard Morales, "History of the California Institution for Women, 1927–1960: A Women's Regime," Ph.D. dissertation, University of California, Riverside, 1980, 349.

6 *Final Report of the Senate Standing Committee on Institutions*, Senate of the State of California, Goodwin Knight, president of the Senate (Sacramento, 1949), 62.

7 *Christian Science Monitor*, "California Helps Women Get Back on Straight Road," November 28, 1933.

8 *The Clarion*, California Institution for Women, vol. 11, nos. 7, 8, July/August 1948, 2–3.

9 Those serving time for murder during the same time as Inez's incarceration included Shirleen Michel Kunin, a Beverly Hills mother in for the beating death of her two-year-old daughter; Rebecca McEnespy, from Martinez, doing time for killing her seventeen-month-old niece; Helen Wigney, twenty-five, from Bellflower, convicted of shooting her landlord six times after he made passes at her (Wigney's attorney said she was under a hypnotic spell placed by her husband); Isa Lang, a Los Angeles boarder who killed her landlady; and Agnes Garnier, a fifty-four-year-old woman from West Riverside who shot her millionaire boss during a quarrel.

10 *Final Report of the Senate Standing Committee on Institutions*, Senate of the State of California, Goodwin Knight, president of the Senate (Sacramento, 1949), 61.

11 Much detail is taken from three excellent appraisals of the prison: Kathleen A. Cairns's *Hard Time at Tehachapi: California's First Women's Prison* (Albuquerque, NM: University of New Mexico Press, 2009); Leonie van Zesch's *Leonie: A Woman Ahead of Her Time* (Beverly Hills, CA: Lime Orchard Publications, 2011), Chapter 22, "Prisoners for Patients," 299–310 (for many years, Dr. van Zesch was the prison dentist at Tehachapi); and John R. Van Westen's unpublished account, "The California Institution for Women." Van Westen was an employee of California Department of Corrections from 1947 to 1973.

12 Ibid, 33.

13 *The Clarion*, California Institution for Women, April 1950, 3.

14 *The Clarion*, California Institution for Women, August/September 1949, 10.

15 Carline Brown's legal name was Caroline Brown, but she was always referred to as Carline.

16 Author interview with Caroline Brown Carlisle, March 10, 2016.

17 *San Francisco Chronicle*, "Agents Check Inez Burns' Earnings," August 24, 1948, 13.

18 *San Francisco Chronicle*, "Pair Accused of Dillinger Aid," April 19, 1934, 28; "Dillinger's Doctor Seized," April 15, 1938, 3; "Murder Laid to Dr. May by Jury," April 27, 1938, 5; "Dillinger Doctor Held in Murder," May 7, 1938, 13.

19 Dr. C. J. Morris had been listed in the Black Dahlia murder victim Elizabeth Short's address book in 1947; Short's bisected nude body was found in a Los Angeles park and remains an unsolved murder. See *Los Angeles Times*, "Doctor's Story Faces Check-Up," October 13, 1936, 40; Don Wolfe's *The Black Dahlia's Files: The Mob, the Mogul, and the Murder That Transfixed Los Angeles* (New York: William Morrow, 2006), 257, 269, 272.

20 *Los Angeles Times*, "Doctor's Story Faces Check-Up," October 13, 1936, 40; Wolfe, *The Black Dahlia's Files*, 257, 269, 272.

21 *San Francisco Chronicle*, "Abortion Ring Indictments Are Voted," October 12, 1948, 15.

22 From the University of California's Bancroft Library's "Special Crime Commission on Organized Crime," 80/4, carton 9, folder 14-2.

23 See Rickie Solinger's *The Abortionist: A Woman against the Law* (Berkeley, CA: University of California, 1996).

24 *Chicago Daily Tribune*, "Ada Martin, 52, Dies; Accused in Abortion Deals," December 8, 1946, 41.

25 *Salute*, "Menace of Abortion Racket," September 1947.

26 *Time*, "Abortionist Convicted," March 6, 1944.

27 *Time*, "Sin No More!" July 28, 1941.

28 *Brooklyn Eagle*, "Hogan Hits Court on Doctor's Bail," April 30, 1942, 8.

29 *Brooklyn Eagle*, "Madden Quits Active Duty as Geoghan Aide," April 24, 1939, 1.

30 *The New York Times*, "Doctor Gets Prison Term," January 29, 1944, 7.

31 Drs. George Lotrell Timanus, Edgar Keemer, and Robert Spencer are described in Leslie J. Reagan's *When Abortion Was a Crime: Women, Medicine, and Law in the United States, 1867–1973* (Berkeley, CA: University of California, 1997); see also *Time*, "Abortion in the U.S.," June 2, 1958.

32 James Kaplan's *Frank: The Voice* (New York: Anchor, 2011), 6.

33 *Time*, "One Doctor's Choice," March 12, 1956.

34 From a conversation with Iowa physician Maurice Champion, M.D., January 17, 2017.

35 Morales dissertation, "History of the California Institution for Women," 337–38.

36 Private correspondence, dated April 26, 1951.

37 Author interview with Caroline Brown Carlisle, March 21, 2016.

TWENTY-FIVE: ALWAYS FIGHT WITH A FIST

1 *San Francisco Examiner*, "Police, State Officials, Inez Burns Tells of Half-Million Cash Payoffs to Officials in Surgery Mill," by Ed Montgomery, August 30, 1954, 1.

2 Heinz-Dietrich Fischer, *The Pulitzer Archive: Local Reporting 1947–1987* (New York: K-G-Saur, 1989), 29–32.

3 Private correspondence, dated April 29, 1948, given to the author by Scott Merritt, Inez Burns's great-grandson.

4 Author interview with Caroline Brown Carlisle, November 17, 2016.

5 The description of Inez's face-lift comes from a medical essay entitled, "History of Cosmetic Surgery," by Melvin Shiffman, in *Cosmetic Surgery: Art and Technique* (New York: Springer, 2013), 9. In November 1951, Dr. Albert D. Davis was elected national president of the American Society of Plastic and Reconstructive Surgeons.

6 Author interview with William Brown, May 23, 2017.

7 Neither was the author ever able to find out.

8 Author interview with Caroline Brown Carlisle, November 17, 2016.

9 Details about Sonja Henie come from Raymond Strait and Leif Henie's *Queen of Ice, Queen of Shadows: The Unsuspected Life of Sonja Henie* (New York: Stein and Day, 1985), 205–30; Richard Bak's *Joe Louis: The Great Black Hope* (New York: Da Capo Press, 1998), 190; *Vanity Fair*, "Sonja Henie's Ice Age," by Laura Jacobs, February 2014, www.vanityfair.com/hollywood/2014/02/sonja-henie-ice-skating-queen.

10 All of Caroline Brown Carlisle's recollections are from author interviews with Ms. Carlisle, conducted in 1992 and in 2016.

11 Edmund G. Brown Papers, 1907–1996, the Bancroft Library, University of California, Berkeley, BANC MASS 694:23.

12 Ethan Rarick, *California Rising: The Life and Times of Pat Brown* (Berkeley, University of California Press, 2005), 60.

13 *San Francisco Chronicle*, "Tom Lynch to Be D.A.," November 11, 1950, 1.

14 *Final Report of the Special Crime Study Commission on Organized Crime* (Sacramento: State of California, November 15, 1950), 54.

15 *San Francisco Call*, "U.S. Indicts Inez Burns on Taxes," February 14, 1951.

16 *San Francisco News*, "Inez Burns Indicted on U.S. Tax Charges," by Al Ostrow, February 15, 1951.

17 Private correspondence, dated April 26, 1951, supplied to the author by Scott Merritt, Inez Burns's great-grandson.

18 *San Francisco Chronicle*, "Prison for Inez Burns," May 9, 1951.

19 *San Francisco Chronicle*, "George Harris Inducted as City Judge," July 18, 1941, 13.

20 *San Francisco Chronicle*, "Democratic Donnybrook," by Earl C. Behrens, September 6, 1949, 8.

21 *San Francisco Examiner*, March 2, 1952; *San Francisco Chronicle*, Herb Caen column, April 25, 1952.

22 From "Social Factors Related to the Violation of the May Act as Revealed in the Se-lected Case Records of Women Committed to a Federal Reformatory," master's thesis by Gladys V. Bowman, department of sociology, University of Southern California, June 1947; *Chicago Daily Tribune*, "Prison Without Bars," by Norma Lee Browning, January 11 and 18, 1950; and Billie Holiday with William Dufty, *Lady Sings the Blues* (New York: Penguin, 1956), 131–143.

23 Ibid, page 159.

24 A Freedom of Information Act (FOIA) request submitted to the US Department of Justice, Federal Bureau of Prisons, revealed little of Inez's incarceration at Alderson, ex-cept to provide a single intake card with her name on it. Her activities at Alderson were construed from other inmate reminiscences of the same time period, including Bow-man's thesis, Brown's newspaper articles, and Lucas's and Holiday's books cited above, along with inferences drawn from Inez Burns's more widely reported prison term at the California Institution for Women at Tehachapi.

25 *San Francisco Examiner*, "Inez Burns Returns After Serving Tax Sentence," March 2, 1952.

TWENTY-SIX: THE PLIGHT WOMEN AND THE PLEASURE OF MEN

1 See Edward Shorter's *Before Prozac: The Troubled History of Mood Disorders in Psychiatry* (New York: Oxford University Press, 2008), 33, 236. Interview with Caroline Brown Carlisle, June 18, 2016.

2 Details about the police sting and the arrest of Inez Burns and Dr. A. A. Berger come from the *San Francisco Chronicle*, Herb Caen column, October 24, 1952; "Inez, Doctor Arrested in New Abortion Case," October 23, 1952; "Police Used Fancy Science to Trap Inez," October 24, 1952; *San Francisco Examiner*, "Inez Burns and Doctor Held in Surgery Plot," October 23, 1952; "Inez Burns Confesses," October 24, 1952; "Inez Burns Reported Seeking Deal With D.A. to Minimize Sentence in Surgery Case," November 21, 1952.

3 *San Francisco Chronicle*, "Sports Mirror," by Harry B. Smith, January 20, 1939, 2; "Hospi-tal Equipment Is on Display at the Burns Trial," September 24, 1946, 3.

4 *San Francisco Examiner*, "2 to 5 Years for Inez Burns on Guilty Plea," November 22, 1952; *San Francisco News*, "Inez Burns Gets Wish to Go Back to Prison," November 22, 1952.

5 *San Francisco Examiner*, "Convicted S.F. Doctor Suspended," July 2, 1955; "Berger Freed to Take Job," August 6, 1955.

TWENTY-SEVEN: "NO, I NEVER BRIBED ANYONE"

1 The intake protocol for prisoners at the California Institution for Women comes from Edna Walker Candler's *Women in Prison* (Indianapolis, IN: Bobbs-Merrill, 1973). A fur-ther description of inmate life at California Institution for Women, although much of it is sanitized, comes from an article in *Cosmopolitan* magazine by Harriet LeBarre, "Model Prisons: The California Institution for Women," October 1957, 52–7.

2 *San Francisco Examiner,* "Inez Burns' Charge," August 25, 1954.

3 Many years down the road, in 1977, when Burkett was sixty-four, the former state superintendent of banks and now a wealthy banker himself, announced his intention to run against Pat Brown's son, Jerry, for governor, in the Democratic primary. He pulled out of the governor's race and ran unsuccessfully in the race for state treasurer against veteran Jesse M. Unruh, Pat Brown's longtime nemesis.

4 *San Francisco Chronicle,* "Jury Asks Burkett to Repeat Payoff Charges," August 25, 1954, 1.

5 *San Francisco Chronicle,* "It's News to Me," Dick Friendlich column, December 13, 1954, 29; "Supervisor Charles Ertola Dies," May 21, 1964, 1.

6 *San Francisco Examiner,* "Politicians Accused," by Ed Montgomery, August 29, 1954, 1.

7 *San Francisco Examiner,* "Police, State Officials, Inez Burns Tells of Half-Million Cash Payoffs to Officials in Surgery Mill," by Ed Montgomery, August 30, 1954, 1.

8 *San Francisco Chronicle,* Molly H. Minudri obituary, October 27, 1982, 43.

9 *San Francisco Examiner,* "Inez Fights Return Here for Jury Quiz," by Ed Montgomery, September 3, 1954, 1.

10 *The Kefauver Committee Report on Organized Crime* (New York: Didier, 1952), 80.

11 *The Palm of Alpha Tau Omega,* "Tau Reporter Gets Top Honor for Newspaper Story," by Larry Coffin, September, 1951, 6, 28.

12 *San Francisco Call-Bulletin,* "Hint Jury Quiz for S.F. Cops," by Dick Hyer, August 31, 1954, 1; *San Francisco Chronicle,* "Burkett Tells Jury of 'Police Payoffs,'" August 31, 1954, 1.

13 *San Francisco Examiner,* "Inez Burns to Be Silent at Jury Quiz," by Ed Montgomery, September 2, 1954.

14 *San Francisco Examiner,* "Prosecutor Will Drop Inez Burns Payoff Quiz," by Ed Montgomery, September 15, 1954, 1.

15 Inez's grand jury testimony comes from *San Francisco Call-Bulletin,* "Inez Quiz Flops," by Dick Hyer, September 14, 1954; *San Francisco Examiner,* "Knew Cops, She Said," by Ed Montgomery, September 14, 1954, 1; *San Francisco Chronicle,* "Inez Burns Denies She Paid Off Cops," September 14, 1954, 1.

16 *San Francisco Chronicle,* "Inez Burns Tax Pact—3/4 Million," by Charles Raudebaugh, March 27, 1956, 1.

TWENTY-EIGHT: STILL STYLISH AND FEMININE AFTER ALL THESE YEARS

1 Patterson once set up Inez's private investigator, Eugene Aureguy, in a sting operation in which Aureguy paid Patterson not to write about a client. The transaction was recorded and a subsequent story appeared in the *San Francisco Examiner.*

2 *San Francisco Examiner,* "Inez Burns Raps Abortion Law," by Robert Patterson, May 25, 1971, 3.

3 http://caselaw.findlaw.com/us-supreme-court/410/113.html

4 The recipe scrapbook is in the possession of Caroline Brown Carlisle and was viewed by the author on March 10, 2016. Among the entries: Spicy Marble Coffeecake, Mother's Pot Roast, Swedish Ginger Cookies, Meringue, Chocolate Cream Pie, Coconut

Cream Pie, Best Lemon Pie, Cheesecake, Fruit Sundae Cream Pie, Toasted French Cheese Bread, Boston Brown Bread, Buttermilk Butter, Cocoa Drop Cookies, Peach Cobbler Pie, Black Midnight Cake, Cherry Winks, Southern Pecan Bars, Walnut Ginger Drops, Seafood Newburg, Chafing Dish King Crab Newburg, Beef Scaloppine, Lemon Heaven Pie, Abalone from Bardelli's, Bacardi Party Punch, and Swedish Meatballs.

THIRTY: SHE WAS TOO AUDACIOUS

1 Similar to Inez's first trial in February 1946, the *San Francisco Examiner* called the Patricia Hearst trial "the Trial of the Century"; "Patty, Tania and 'the Trial of the Century,'" by Stephen Cook, January 25, 1976, 8.

2 Regtl Sup Sgt is a reference to Regimental Supply Sergeant, Joe Burns's rank when he served in the Army during World War I.

3 R.K. Jones and J. Jerman, "Abortion incidence and service availability in the United States, 2011," *Perspectives on Sexual and Reproductive Health* 46 (2014): 3–14, doi:10.1363/46e0414; Guttmacher Institute, September 2016; Planned Parenthood, "Roe v. Wade: Its History and Impact," plannedparenthood.org.

4 *San Francisco Chronicle*, "Abortionist's Home Sold–$80,150," April 29, 1976, 24.

5 The *San Francisco Chronicle* classified ad for the house read, "Spacious: 274 Guerrero. 10 Rm. Mansion. 3 car garage. By Owner," October 7, 1980, 49.

IMAGE CREDITS

Library of Congress, LC-DIG-ppmsca-07823, endpapers; Library of Congress, LC-USZ62-107985, ii–iii; Courtesy of Caroline Carlisle, iv; iStock.com/joecicak, xii; Bettmann / Getty Images, xv; Library of Congress, LC-USZ62-77079, xx–1; Library of Congress, LC-G403-BN-0265-C, 2; Library of Congress, HABS CAL,38-SANFRA,89--1, 4–5; Collection of San Francisco Bay Area Theater Images and Memorabilia, Museum of Performance + Design, 8; Courtesy of the California History Room, California State Library, Sacramento, California, 11, 42, 298; Library of Congress, LC-USZ62-3207, 14; Library of Congress, LC-DIG-ppmsca-50069, 15 (top); Courtesy of California State Archives, 15 (bottom); Library of Congress, LC-G403-0097-A, 16–17; Courtesy of Scott Merritt, 19, 60, 108, 132, 368; Library of Congress, LC-USZ62-77078, 20; Library of Congress, LC-USZ62-70342, 21; Library of Congress, LC-USZ62-70341, 22; Library of Congress, LC-USZ62-37495, 23; California Heritage Collection, BAN PIC 1996.003:Volume 8:33c--fALB, Courtesy of The Bancroft Library, University of California, Berkeley, 26; Library of Congress, LC-USZ62-22031, 32; California Heritage Collection, BAN PIC 1905.02623--A, Courtesy of The Bancroft Library, University of California, Berkeley, 34; Library of Congress, LC-USZ62-62962, 36–37; California Digital Newspaper Collection, Center for Bibliographic Studies and Research, University of California, Riverside, http://cdnc.ucr.edu, 48; Library of Congress, LC-DIG-hec-03951, 50; Library of Congress, LC-USZ62-137812, 62–63; Library of Congress, LC-USZ62-53992, 69; Library of Congress, LC-USZ62-44926, 72–73; Library of Congress, LC-DIG-ppmsca-09830, 74–75; Library of Congress, LC-DIG-det-4a13255, 76–77; Library of Congress, LC-DIG-det-4a25729, 78; Library of Congress, LC-USZ62-113371, 80–81; Library of Congress, LC-USZ62-133043, 82–83; Library of Congress, LC-DIG-anrc-04175, 84; Library of Congress, LC-USZ62-138705, 84–85; Library of Congress, LC-USZ62-100975, 86; Courtesy California Historical Society, FN-35426, 97; Library of Congress, LC-DIG-ppmsca-26057, 98; Library of Congress, LC-DIG-ppmsca-26107, 102–103; San Francisco History Center, San Francisco Public Library, 104, 124, 125, 142, 160–161, 211, 214–215, 216, 228–229, 244, 248–249, 272, 282, 379; Library of Congress, LC-DIG-pga-04324, 107; Library of Congress, LC-USZ62-131704, 108–109; Library of Congress, LC-DIG-ggbain-33071, 113; Library of Congress, LC-USZ62-136851, 114; Fang Family San Francisco Examiner photograph archive negative files, BANC PIC 2006.029:127676.04.04:NEG, The Regents of the University of California, The Bancroft Library, University of California, Berkeley, 127; Library of Congress, LC-DIG-hec-29041, 140; Courtesy the Sonoma County Library, 146–147; Library of Congress, LC-DIG-fsa-8b32862, 148; Photographs from the Edmund G. Brown papers, BANC PIC 1968.011--PIC, Courtesy of The Bancroft Library, University of California, Berkeley, 154, 380; Fang Family San Francisco Examiner photograph archive negative files, BANC PIC 2.006.029:131354.06.02--NEG, The Regents of the University of California, The Bancroft Library, University of California, Berkeley, 157; Library of Congress, LC-USZ62-127223, 159; Library of Congress, LC-USZ62-100678, 162; Library of Congress, LC-USZC2-1771, 163 (top left); Library of Congress, LC-USZC2-5540,

163 (top right); Library of Congress, LC-USZC2-5734, 163 (bottom left); Library of Congress, LC-USZC2-5735, 163 (bottom right); Library of Congress, LC-USF34-081814-E, 170; Library of Congress, LC-USE6-D-009783, 171; Library of Congress, LC-USZ62-34565, 172; Library of Congress, LC-USZ6-1025, 173 (top); Library of Congress, LC-USZ62-133825, 173 (bottom); Library of Congress, LC-USZ62-23602, 174–175; California State University, Chico, Meriam Library Special Collections, 177; San Francisco Chronicle / Polaris, 181, 246, 339; Bill Young / San Francisco Chronicle / Polaris, 194; Library of Congress, LC-DIG-ggbain-03840, 219; Fang Family San Francisco Examiner photograph archive negative files, BANC PIC 2006.029:12761.6A.01.01--NEG, The Regents of the University of California, The Bancroft Library, University of California, Berkeley, 221; Courtesy of Brad Hall, 224–225; Courtesy San Francisco Examiner, 233; Fang Family San Francisco Examiner photograph archive negative files, BANC PIC 2006.029:12761.6.05.03--NEG, The Regents of the University of California, The Bancroft Library, University of California, Berkeley, 237; Library of Congress, LC-USZ62-68683, 240; Duke Downey / San Francisco Chronicle / Polaris, 242, 302–303; Fang Family San Francisco Examiner photograph archive negative files, BANC PIC 210,6.029:127616G.05.01--NEG, The Regents of the University of California, The Bancroft Library, University of California, Berkeley, 256; Fang Family San Francisco Examiner photograph archive negative files, BANC PIC 2006.029:141669.01.11-NEG, The Regents of the University of California, The Bancroft Library, University of California, Berkeley, 266; Library of Congress, LC-USF34-019532-C, 306–307; Fang Family San Francisco Examiner photograph archive negative files, BANC PIC 2A06.029:12761,6K.04.02--NEG, The Regents of the University of California, The Bancroft Library, University of California, Berkeley, 308; Fang Family San Francisco Examiner photograph archive negative files, BANC PIC 2006.029:127616K.05.03.01--NEG, The Regents of the University of California, The Bancroft Library, University of California, Berkeley, 311; Los Angeles Times Photographic Archives (Collection 1429), UCLA Library Special Collections, Charles E. Young Research Library, UCLA, 314–315, 318, 336–337; Los Angeles Daily News Negatives (Collection 1387), UCLA Library Special Collections, Charles E. Young Research Library, UCLA, 320–321, 342 (left); Herald-Examiner Collection / Los Angeles Public Library, 335, 355, 356–357; By David Shapinsky from Washington, D.C., United States (Public Domain: WWII: "Tokyo Rose" (NARA)) [CC BY-SA 2.0 (http://creativecommons.org/licenses/by-sa/2.0)], via Wikimedia Commons, 342 (right); Library of Congress, HABS CAL,38-SANFRA,135—24, 349; Library of Congress, HABS CAL,38-SANFRA,135—78, 350; Fang Family San Francisco Examiner photograph archive negative files, BANC PIC 2@6.029:131354.09.02--NEG, The Regents of the University of California, The Bancroft Library, University of California, Berkeley, 363; Library of Congress, HAER CAL,38-SAN-FRA,140--20, 366–367; Fang Family San Francisco Examiner photograph archive negative files, BANC PIC 2.006.029:141669.01.11--NEG, The Regents of the University of California, The Bancroft Library, University of California, Berkeley, 370; Library of Congress, LC-USF346-016148, 386; Library of Congress, HAER CAL,38-SANFRA,141--325, 426.